Lessing Yearbook / Jahrbuch LI
2024

Lessing Yearbook / Jahrbuch LI, 2024

Founded by Gottfried F. Merkel and Guy Stern
at the University of Cincinnati in 1966
continued by Richard Schade, Herbert Rowland, and Monika Fick

Monika Fick, *senior editor*
Carl Niekerk, *managing editor*
University of Illinois, Urbana-Champaign
Thomas Martinec, *associate and book review editor*
Universität Regensburg

Editorial Board

Wolfgang Albrecht, *Klassik-Stiftung Weimar*
Barbara Becker-Cantarino, *Ohio State University – Emerita*
Wolfgang F. Bender, *Universität Münster – Emeritus*
Helmut Berthold, *Lessing-Akademie, Wolfenbüttel*
Mary Helen Dupree, *Georgetown University*
Sarah V. Eldridge, *University of Tennessee, Knoxville*
Matt Erlin, *Washington University*
Monika Fick, *RWTH Aachen University – Emerita*
Daniel Fulda, *Martin-Luther-Universität Halle-Wittenberg*
Peter Gilgen, *Cornell University*
Sander L. Gilman, *Emory University, Atlanta – Emeritus*
Willi Goetschel, *University of Toronto*
Alexander Košenina, *Leibniz-Universität Hannover*
Avi Lifschitz, *University of Oxford*
Barbara Mahlmann-Bauer, *Universität Bern*
Thomas Martinec, *Universität Regensburg*
Monika Nenon, *University of Memphis*
David Price, *Vanderbilt University*
Nicholas Rennie, *Rutgers University*
Heidi Schlipphacke, *University of Illinois at Chicago*
Ann C. Schmiesing, *University of Colorado, Boulder*
Birka Siwczyk, *Arbeitsstelle für Lessingrezeption – Lessing-Museum Kamenz*
Stefanie Stockhorst, *Universität Potsdam*
Liliane Weissberg, *University of Pennsylvania, Philadelphia*
W. Daniel Wilson, *University of London – Emeritus*
Carsten Zelle, *Ruhr-Universität Bochum – Emeritus*

Lessing Yearbook/Jahrbuch
LI
2024

Edited for the Lessing Society by
Carl Niekerk (University of Illinois at Urbana-Champaign)

Book Reviews edited by
Thomas Martinec (Universität Regensburg)

WALLSTEIN VERLAG

Gedruckt mit freundlicher Unterstützung des College of Liberal Arts and Sciences der University of Illinois at Urbana-Champaign.

Englische Artikel sollten den Regeln des MLA Handbook, deutsche denen des Wallstein Verlags folgen.

Anschrift:

c/o Prof. Dr. Carl Niekerk, Department of Germanic Languages and Literatures, University of Illinois, Urbana-Champaign, IL 61801-3676;
E-Mail: niekerk@illinois.edu
c/o Prof. Dr. Thomas Martinec, Institut für Germanistik, Universität Regensburg, Universitätsstraße 31, D-93053 Regensburg;
E-Mail: thomas.martinec@ur.de

Wallstein Verlag, Geiststraße 11, D-37073 Göttingen. Web Site: www.wallstein-verlag.de

Der Umschlag zeigt das von Johann Friedrich Bause nach einem Ölgemälde von Anton Graff gestochene Porträt Lessings (Leipzig 1772: Herzog August Bibliothek Wolfenbüttel, Signatur A 12373).

© 2024 Wallstein Verlag, Göttingen
www.wallstein-verlag.de
Druck und Verarbeitung: bookSolutions Vertriebs GmbH, Göttingen
ISBN 978-3-8353-5750-1
ISSN 0075-8833

Inhalt

KARL PIOSECKA
Philosophie und Politik in Lessings Dramenentwürfen
Alcibiades und *Alcibiades in Persien* 9

BAIYU LU
Das Politikum des apolitischen Odoardo
in Lessings *Emilia Galotti* 29

ELLWOOD WIGGINS
Sophocles's *Philoctetes* and the Hidden Structure
of Lessing's *Laokoon*: The Moral Aesthetic of the Scream 51

FORUM
Reading Forster, Reading Race: Philosophy, Politics,
and Natural History in the German Enlightenment
edited by Jennifer Mensch and Michael Olson

JENNIFER MENSCH • MICHAEL OLSON
Reading Forster, Reading Race: Philosophy, Politics, and Natural
History in the German Enlightenment 75

JENNIFER MENSCH
Georg Forster and the Politics of Natural History:
A Case Study for Students of Kant 79

MADHUVANTI KARYEKAR
Classical Quotations in Georg Forster's Anthropological Essays:
»Pausing on the Threshold« 91

ANTJE KÜHNAST
Reflections on Translating Georg Forster's »O'Taheiti« (1779/1789),
or: (What Is) Getting Lost in a Translation? 103

HEATHER MORRISON
Proximity and (Dis)Comfort with Georg Forster's »O-Taheiti« . . 111

JOSEPH D. O'NEIL
Aufklärung as Vocation in Georg Forster's »Cook, der Entdecker«:
Reality, Mirror, or Rorschach Test? 121

JEFFREY JARZOMB
Kant's Reviews of Herder:
»Es mag ihn wohl ein *böser* Mann gesagt haben« 131

PETER GILGEN
Kant contra Herder: Persius and Tahiti 139

DANIEL PURDY
Vieh, or Humans as Domestic Animals:
On a Dispute between Herder and Kant 149

SALLY HATCH GRAY
Forster's Critique of Slavery in Meiners's Natural History:
On Objectivity and Cultural Creativity 157

MICHAEL OLSON
Slavery and Enthusiasm in the German Enlightenment:
The Case of Christoph Meiners 169

Reviews / Rezensionen,
edited by / herausgegeben von Thomas Martinec

LESSING, GOTTHOLD EPHRAIM, *Nathan der Weise*, hg. von
  Bodo Plachta (Kai Bremer) 177
NIEFANGER, DIRK, *Lessing divers – Soziale Milieus,
  Genderformationen, Ethnien und Religionen* (Heidi Schlipphacke) . 180
TRAVANTI, ELEONORA, *Lessings exoterische Verteidigung der
  Orthodoxie. Die Wolfenbütteler Beiträge gegen die
  Aufklärungstheologie (1770-1774)* (Robert Vellusig) 182
VELLUSIG, ROBERT, *Lessing und die Folgen* (Ritchie Robertson) . . . 185
ZIMMERMANN, DANIEL, *Göttliche Zufälligkeiten. G. E. Lessings
  Vernunftkritik als Theodizee der Religionen* (Christoph Bultmann) . 187
ADLER, HANS / ESSEN, GESA VON / FRICK, WERNER (eds.),
  *Der ›andere Klassiker‹. Johann Gottfried Herder und die
  Weimarer Konstellation um 1800* (Johannes Schmidt) 191
ADLER, JEREMY, *Goethe. Die Erfindung der Moderne.
  Eine Biographie* (Astrida Orle Tantillo) 195

BOHNENGEL, JULIA / KOŠENINA, ALEXANDER (Hg.), *Joseph Marius von Babo (1756-1822). Dramatiker in Mannheim und München. Mit einem Lexikon der Theaterstücke* (Till Kinzel) 197
BOHNENGEL, JULIA / WORTMANN, THOMAS (Hg.), *»Die deutsche Freiheit erdolcht«. Neue Studien zu Leben, Werk und Rezeption August von Kotzebues* (Klaus Gerlach) 199
KOTZEBUE, AUGUST VON, *Ich, eine Geschichte in Fragmenten.* hg. von Max Graff (Hamilton Beck) 201
LA ROCHE, SOPHIE VON, *Erscheinungen am See Oneida.* Hg. von Claudia Nitschke und Ivonne Pietsch und
LA ROCHE, SOPHIE VON, *Mein Schreibetisch.* Hg. von Bodo Plachta (Monika Nenon) 204
LEE, DAVID E. / OSBORNE, JOHN C. (Hg.), *»mein lieber deutscher Horaz«. Der Briefwechsel zwischen Johann Wilhelm Ludwig Gleim und Karl Wilhelm Ramler* (Claudia Brandt) 206
POTT, UTE (Hg.), *Plötzlich Poetin!? Anna Louisa Karsch – Leben und Werk* (Joanna Raisbeck) 208
REEMTSMA, JAN PHILIPP, *Christoph Martin Wieland. Die Erfindung der modernen deutschen Literatur.* In Zusammenarbeit mit Fanny Esterházy (Nils Gelker) 210
BACHLEITNER, NORBERT with Chapters by PÍŠA, PETR / SYROVY, DANIEL / WÖGERBAUER, MICHAEL, *Censorship of Literature in Austria 1751-1848* (Florian Gassner) 212
ERB, ANDREAS, *Die Deutschen Gesellschaften des 18. Jahrhunderts. Ein Gruppenbild* (Maximilian Görmar) 215
GRUBNER, BERNADETTE / WITTEMANN, PETER (Hg.), *Aufklärung und Exzess. Epistemologie und Ästhetik des Übermäßigen im 18. Jahrhundert* (Peter Philipp Riedl) 218
SCHEIN, XENIA, *Die Öffentlichkeit im Privaten. Identität und Realität im bürgerlichen Drama von Autorinnen des achtzehnten und beginnenden neunzehnten Jahrhunderts* (Mary Helen Dupree) . . . 220
SCHLIPPHACKE, HEIDI, *The Aesthetics of Kinship: Form and Family in the Long Eighteenth Century* (Patricia Anne Simpson) 223
SCHNEIDER, MARTIN, *Agonalität und Menschenliebe: Gefühlspolitik im Drama des 18. Jahrhunderts* (Edward Potter) 225
SCHWARZ, OLGA KATHARINA, *Rationalistische Sinnlichkeit. Zur philosophischen Grundierung der Kunsttheorie. 1700 bis 1760. Leibniz – Wolff – Gottsched – Baumgarten* (J. Colin McQuillan) . . 227
SIEG, CHRISTIAN, *Die Scham der Aufklärung. Zur sozialethischen Produktivkraft einer Emotion in der literarischen Kultur des 18. Jahrhunderts* (Franziska Solana Higuera) 229

STANITZEK, GEORG (Hg.), *Semantik und Praktiken der Freundschaft im 18. Jahrhundert* (Cord-Friedrich Berghahn) 231
WOLF, NORBERT CHRISTIAN, *Glanz und Elend der Aufklärung in Wien. Voraussetzungen – Institutionen – Texte* (Matthias Mansky) 235
WURST, KARIN A., *Imaginaries of Domesticity and Women's Work in Germany around 1800* (Patricia Milewski) 238

Philosophie und Politik in Lessings Dramenentwürfen *Alcibiades* und *Alcibiades in Persien*

Karl Piosecka

Die Entstehungsgeschichte der Fragment gebliebenen Dramen *Alcibiades* und *Alcibiades in Persien* lässt sich kaum rekonstruieren. Anzunehmen ist, dass beide Entwürfe während Lessings Anstellung als Gouvernements-Sekretär des preußischen Generalleutnants Friedrich Bogislav von Tauentzien zur Zeit des Siebenjährigen Kriegs in Breslau entstanden sind. Dies verdeutlichen die Aufzeichnungen des Breslauer Lehrers Samuel Benjamin Klose, der mit Lessing während seiner Anstellung in regem Austausch stand. Kloses Aufzeichnungen zufolge entstanden die Stücke im Zeitraum der ersten Jahre in Breslau, jedoch noch vor dem Frieden von Hubertusburg im Jahre 1763.[1]

Wilfried Barner hat in der einzigen umfassenderen und damit grundlegenden Studie zu den beiden Entwürfen auf die enge biographische Verbindung zwischen der (historischen) Figur des Alcibiades (5. Jhd. v. u. Z.) und Lessing aufmerksam gemacht, wobei Barner sowohl auf die Flucht-, ›Exil-‹ und Kriegserfahrung als auch auf »den existentiellen Normenkonflikt des selbsterlebten Zwischen-den-Fronten-Stehens« hinsichtlich der Auseinandersetzung Lessings mit dem Patriotismus seiner Freunde in den 1750er Jahren hinweist.[2]

Sowohl Barner als auch Monika Fick sehen nachvollziehbare Ähnlichkeiten zu anderen, ebenfalls unvollendeten Dramenentwürfen dieser Lebensphase Lessings, zum Beispiel die in einem Brief an Mendelssohn mitgeteilten Überlegungen zum *Codrus*, die Entwürfe *Kleonnis* und *Der Horoscop* sowie das 1759 anonym veröffentlichte Trauerspiel *Philotas*. Alle Stücke teilen das ambivalente Verhältnis zu Patriotismus und Krieg. Der sowohl im *Codrus*- als auch im *Horoscop*-Fragment essenzielle Orakelspruch klingt in *Alcibiades* nur noch in der Aussage Timons an (»denn deine Größe ist das Verderben des Volks«), die von der Figur Timandra als prophetisch charakterisiert wird.[3] Auch die im Kern stehenden Bruder-, Vater- oder Kindsmorde (*Kleonnis*, *Horoscop*) spielen keine zentrale Rolle mehr: Lediglich der ›Sturz‹ des Susamithres in das Schwert seines Vaters Pharnabaz weist eine Parallele zum Suizid des *Philotas* auf und deutet auf den väterlichen Femizid in *Emilia Galotti* voraus.[4]

Laut Monika Fick seien der *Alcibiades*-Komplex sowie die übrigen, Fragment gebliebenen, tragischen Sujets unter anderem durch ihre »psychische[n] Extremsituationen« und ihre »politische Akzentuierung« gekennzeichnet.[5]

Die *Alcibiades*-Entwürfe, in denen die titelgebende, historische Figur des aus Athen stammenden Politikers und Strategen die Kriegsparteien Athen und Sparta gegeneinander ausgespielt und beide Städte zeitweise als politisches Exil genutzt hatte, bevor er endgültig Asyl in Persien suchte,[6] lassen sich, dem Aspekt der politischen Akzentuierung Ficks folgend, als Dramen der »politische[n] Aufklärung« deuten, wie Gisbert Ter-Nedden dies beispielsweise für das Trauerspiel *Philotas* vorschlägt.[7] Die Nähe zur griechischen Tragödie, mit der sich Lessing in diesem Zeitraum auseinandersetzte, ist dementsprechend sowohl formal als auch inhaltlich naheliegend,[8] scheint mir jedoch die Entwürfe interpretatorisch nicht zu erschöpfen. Die von Fick konstatierte »Nemesis-Struktur« der beiden Entwürfe respektive die »Modernisierung [...] der göttlichen Nemesis« schlägt hier natürlich die Brücke zum griechischen Trauerspiel, verleiht den beiden Entwürfen jedoch einen merkwürdig metaphysischen, transzendenten Unterton und lässt eine Interpretation in einem simplen Tun-Ergehen-Zusammenhang münden.[9] Es geht in den *Alcibiades*-Entwürfen weder um Schicksal und Verdammnis noch um Erlösung oder Vergebung (im transzendenten Sinne), sondern stattdessen um einen immanenten, menschlichen Konflikt.

Barners Lesart, die starke Parallelen zwischen Lessing und Alcibiades sieht beziehungsweise zieht, mündet in einer durchaus positiven Beurteilung der Figur; die Ideen von Individualität und Autonomie legen diese Parallelen auch durchaus nahe.[10] Doch scheint mir Lessings Auseinandersetzung mit den Ereignissen und Auswirkungen des Siebenjährigen Kriegs sowie seine letztliche Behauptung des Kosmopolitismus gegenüber dem Patriotismus wenig mit den egoistischen und machtpolitischen Ambitionen des (historischen wie literarischen) Alcibiades vereinbar. In den *Alcibiades*-Entwürfen begleitet das Kriegsszenario die Politik wie ein Schatten, spielt jedoch, verglichen mit *Kleonnis* oder *Philotas*, nur noch eine untergeordnete Rolle; sie sind weder ›Kriegs-‹ noch ›Schicksalsdramen‹. Die Entwürfe weisen stattdessen eine reflektierte Distanziertheit zu diesen Themenkomplexen auf, die paradoxerweise diametral zur biographischen ›Frontnähe‹ verläuft.

Ich habe andernorts diese Entwicklungslinie vom frühen *Henzi*-Fragment bis zum *Philotas* nachgezeichnet und Lessings Auseinandersetzung mit dem Patriotismus seiner Zeit unter verschiedenen strategischen Gesichtspunkten analysiert. Vergleicht man die *Alcibiades*-Entwürfe in diesem Sinne mit den anderen unvollendeten Entwürfen wie *Codrus*, *Der Horoscop* und *Kleonnis*, wird nicht nur die ›realistischere‹ Folie der *Alcibiades*-Fragmente deutlich, sondern auch die Metaebene. Die beiden Texte arbeiten sich – im Vergleich zu den unmittelbaren Vorgängern – meiner Auslegung nach weniger an dem sich immer stärker offenbarenden menschenverachtenden Charakter des Patriotismus zur Zeit des Siebenjährigen Kriegs ab.[11] Beide Dramentexte spiegeln dieses Abstraktions- und Reflexionsniveau in dem Maße wider, als sie die Themen Krieg, Patriotismus und Schicksal durch Philosophie und Politik ersetzen und damit das Verhältnis des Individuums zu diesen als Spannungsverhältnis ausgeben, das maßgeblich durch die Figur Alcibiades verkörpert wird.

Diese sich diametral gegenüberstehenden Aspekte sind weder in den Forschungsbeiträgen zur Aufklärung im Allgemeinen noch zu Lessing neu.[12] Reinhart Koselleck stellt in seiner wirkmächtigen Studie *Kritik und Krise* die Genese des Bürgertums im achtzehnten Jahrhundert maßgeblich anhand der strikten Spaltung von Moral und Politik durch den absolutistischen Staat in Folge des Dreißigjährigen Kriegs dar. Dem politisch ›ohnmächtigen‹ Bürgertum sei die »der Vernunft zugeordnete Kritik und die der Moral zugeordnete Zensur [...] für das bürgerliche Selbstbewußtsein zur gleichen, und zwar sich selbst begründenden Tätigkeit« geworden.[13] Durch diese dialektische Betrachtungsweise sei die bürgerliche Moral zur indirekten und vor allen Dingen unter einem ›Deckmantel‹ operierenden Gewalt geworden, die sich staatlich-absolutistischer Macht- und Gesetzausübung entziehe und widersetze.[14] Als Paradebeispiel für diese »Institutionalisierung im Hintergrund« sieht Koselleck die sich überall in Europa formierenden Freimaurerlogen an, deren vielgehütetes Arkanum gerade das Wissen um die politische Kraft der scheinbar unpolitischen Moral und die damit zusammenhängende Kritik von Staat und Politik verbergen sollte.[15] Lessing habe diese ›Verschleierungstaktik‹ der »politische[n] Konsequenz der moralischen Pläne« erkannt und in dem berühmten Freimaurergespräch *Ernst und Falk* verhandelt.[16] Kosellecks These gibt den Blick frei auf jenes Spannungsverhältnis, das ich anhand der Begriffe Philosophie und Politik untersuche. Im Gegensatz zu Koselleck teile ich jedoch nicht die Konsequenz, die Moral sei ein verborgenes, gegen den absolutistischen Staat operierendes Politikum, das mithilfe der Konstruktion einer geschichtsphilosophischen Utopie und Legitimation zum Untergang eben jenes politischen Gebildes geführt hätte, die Koselleck aus seiner Analyse zieht.[17] Gerade die Begriffsverschiebung von Moral zu Philosophie mit Hinblick auf eine Interpretation der *Alcibiades*-Entwürfe verdeutlicht, wie sehr diese Auseinandersetzung zwischen Philosophie und Politik im Licht der lediglich kurzen Texte geführt wird und nicht in ihren Schatten. Die Entwürfe gewinnen das Gewicht ihrer politischen Aufklärung dementsprechend aus dem Konfliktpotenzial und den Konsequenzen, die sich das Individuum angesichts der Herausforderungen durch Philosophie und Politik sowie den Grenzen und Wechselwirkungen der beiden zu stellen habe.

Neben einer genauen Analyse der beiden Entwürfe werde ich Lessings Quellenverweisen folgen: Wiederholt finden sich im *Alcibiades*-Entwurf Referenzen auf Plutarchs *Alcibiades*-Biographie, die genutzt werden können, um inhaltliche Leerstellen interpretatorisch zu füllen und die Figur Alcibiades weiter auszuleuchten. Hierzu werde ich auf vielfältige Forschungsliteratur zurückgreifen, die sich unter anderem mit Alcibiades' Auftritt in Platons *Symposion* beschäftigen, mit dem Lessing zweifellos vertraut war. Das Spannungsverhältnis zwischen Philosophie und Politik wird auch in diesen Forschungsbeiträgen thematisiert, sodass diese eine Brücke zu der Figur des Alcibiades aus Lessings Entwürfen und meiner Interpretation schlagen.

Soweit ich dies überblicken kann, liegt eine grundlegende Problematik hinsichtlich einer Deutung in der Wahrnehmung und Beurteilung der Figur Alcibiades, die schon Erich Schmidt in seinen kurzen Ausführungen Ende des 19. Jahrhunderts durchweg positiv deutete:

> Nicht umsonst hat er einst zu den Füßen des Sokrates gesessen, und alle Keime des Schönen-Guten, welche dieser Erzieher gehegt, sollen sich nun endlich ungestört entfalten. Der alternde Sokratesschüler will in ruhiger Abgeschiedenheit den kurzen, kalten Lebensrest der Weisheit weihen [...]. Und seine Weisheit soll sich als eine gesellige Philosophie katechetisch leitend und entwickelnd an einen lieben Partner [gemeint ist Susamithres beziehungsweise Zaris; K. P.] wenden: [...] Eine stille sokratische Gemeinde, angesiedelt in einer fernen Au des Morgenlandes, ist das Ideal des Alcibiades.[18]

Diese sehr zukunftsbezogene Deutung Schmidts von Lessings *Alcibiades* ist schwierig aufrechtzuerhalten, da beide Entwürfe weniger die Zukunft als Alcibiades' problematische Vergangenheit beleuchten; bildlich gesprochen, hält diese die Figur fest im Griff.[19]

Bereits die Notizen zum ersten Auftritt des ersten Aufzugs, der nahezu idyllisch »[i]n der Ebene von Persepolis, (Elymais) an dem Fluße Araxes« spielt, zeugen von einer später (wohl eher: verspäteten) (Selbst-)Erkenntnis des Alcibiades (*WB* 5/1: 385). Es scheint, als habe den Schüler des Sokrates zunächst wenig mit der sokratischen Philosophie verbunden, da Alcibiades von Ehrgeiz und Stolz regiert wurde: »Und wessen ist ein Ehrgeiziger nicht fähig; wie der größten Tugenden, so der schändlichsten Laster, mit dem Unterscheide nur, daß diese Laster ganz unfehlbare Laster, und jene Tugenden sehr zweifelhafte Tugenden sind« (*WB* 5/1: 385). Die Einsicht, dass dies so ist, führt überraschenderweise nicht zu einer Art von Reue, habe er selbst doch »vierzig Jahr der Wollust und dem Ehrgeize, der ganzen schrecklichen Schar der Laster, gefront« (*WB* 5/1: 386). Es geht offensichtlich wenig um irgendeine Form von Vergangenheits*bewältigung*; stattdessen offenbart sich das Wahl-Exil Persien als Ruhestätte für den politisch verfolgten Staatsmann, der nun sich selbst, den »wahre[n] Alcibiades leben« will (*WB* 5/1: 386). Dies sei seit jeher das Ziel seines Lehrers Sokrates für ihn gewesen, die Kenntnis seiner selbst, doch habe er es aus Stolz nicht erkennen können (vgl. WB 5/1: 385).

Selbsterkenntnis stellt hierbei das zentrale Schlagwort dar, doch mutet die Willensbekundung, »als ich selbst, und mir selbst leben« (*WB* 5/1: 386), egozentrisch an und paart sich mit einer naiven Vergangenheits*verdrossenheit*, die Alcibiades' Rückzug in die Einöde von vornherein als zum Scheitern verurteilt entlarvt: Ellwood Wiggins' Reflexionen über den bekannten, griechischen Aufruf *gnothi seauton* beschäftigen sich unter anderem mit Platons *Alcibiades* und liefern wertvolle Hinweise für die Interpretation der Entwürfe:

> Coming to know oneself is a change that never ceases and occurs through the constant shuffling of interpersonal display. [...] As long as knowing oneself depends on the perceived perceptions of others, it can never rest but exists through endlessly varied iteration. [...] Knowing oneself is a function of others' repeated acknowledgment of the roles one plays in the back-and-forth of the performance of recognition.[20]

Lessings Alcibiades charakterisiert sich selbst als einen Meister des Rollenspiels, der sich »leicht in alle Gestalten umgeschaffen« und diese »spielen« konnte (*WB* 5/1: 386). Beide Entwürfe konfrontieren Alcibiades immer wieder mit anderen Figuren, die ihn auf eine bestimmte, vermeintlich abgestreifte Rolle ansprechen beziehungsweise die Titelfigur in ebendieser Rolle wahrnehmen: Philosoph, Politiker, Heerführer, Liebhaber, Freund, Exilant, Athener, Spartaner etc. Die Selbsterkenntnis, die dem Selbstleben vorausgehen muss, würde zwischen dem wie auch immer zu verstehenden ›wahren‹ Alcibiades und seiner Außenwahrnehmung durch andere Personen vermitteln; aufgrund dieser Außenwahrnehmung durch andere würde Alcibiades einsehen, dass Selbsterkenntnis prozessual und von sozialer Interdependenz abhängig ist.

Die Notizen für die erste Szene in *Alcibiades in Persien* beginnen dementsprechend mit einer subjektiven Zentriertheit, die die politischen Umstände des Exils (zum Beispiel aufgrund von Bestechungsvorwürfen und militärischen Niederlagen)[21] völlig unterschlagen und das Exil als Folge einer autonomen und anmaßend genialen Entscheidung deklarieren. Wenn es zur Selbsterkenntnis immer eines anderen bedarf, wie Ellwood Wiggins konstatiert, mutet es ironisch an, wenn Alcibiades zunächst von sich in der dritten Person spricht, bevor er in die erste Person wechselt: »O wie glücklich hat den Alcibiades sein freiwilliges Elend gemacht! Es war der göttlichste Gedanke, den ich jemals gehabt, mich nach Persien zu verbannen!« (*WB* 5/1: 393) Der philosophische Wunsch des Selbstlebens wird zur Selbsttäuschung, weil Unredlichkeit und Egozentrik die eigentlichen Motive überblenden. Der egozentrische Charakter der Titelfigur spiegelt sich nicht nur darin wider, dass Alcibiades das ›Gravitationszentrum‹ bildet, das die Nebenfiguren räumlich anzieht, sondern auch darin, dass Vergangenes im Punkt der Gegenwart wieder eingeholt und durch die Reden der Nebenfiguren aktualisiert wird und somit als zeitlicher Stillstand verstanden werden kann.

Alcibiades flieht also nicht nur vor politischer Verfolgung durch die Griechen, sondern auch vor dem Hof des Königs Artaxerxes. Besonders Letzteres weist eine interessante Parallele zu den Dramen *Emilia Galotti* und *Nathan der Weise* auf.[22] Zentral ist, dass der Wunsch des Selbstlebens nicht ohne die Frage nach der Sphäre des Politischen gestellt werden kann, wobei die Figuren in ihren Handlungen jedoch der Täuschung unterliegen, es handle sich um eine zu verwirklichende apolitische Absicht.[23] So ist Odoardo Galotti entzückt über den Wunsch des Grafen Appiani, »in seinen väterlichen Tälern sich selbst zu leben« (*WB* 7: 312), der auch Odoardos zurückgezogener Lebensweise auf dem Landgut der Familie entspricht. Bereits Wilfried Wilms hat diese Täler als »apolitischen Nicht-Ort«[24] charakterisiert, wobei er in seiner Studie argumentiert, dass der gesamte Konflikt in *Emilia Galotti* um das Eindringen des Öffentlichen und Politischen in den vermeintlich privaten, familiären und apolitischen Raum kreise, wodurch die Konfliktfähigkeit der Familie fokussiert sowie deren Souveränität infrage gestellt werde.[25]

In *Nathan der Weise* ist es der Derwisch Al-Hafi, der sich vom Hof des Sultans Saladin zurückzieht, um nicht als »Werkzeug« (*WB* 9: 540), sondern am Ganges als Mensch unter Menschen zu leben. Auf die Frage, ob Nathan ihn begleiten wolle, reagiert die Titelfigur zögerlich, woraufhin Al-Hafi zu bedenken gibt: »Wer überlegt, der sucht / Bewegungsgründe, nicht zu dürfen. Wer / Sich Knall und Fall, ihm selbst zu leben, nicht / Entschließen kann, der lebet andrer Sklav / Auf immer« (*WB* 9: 540). Al-Hafi lässt die Sphäre des Politischen hinter sich; es stellt sich dabei jedoch die Frage, ob ›der Ganges‹ nicht ebenfalls in Anlehnung an Wilfried Wilms als apolitische Utopie (eben: Nicht-Ort) zu verstehen ist. Nathans Weg führt dementsprechend jenseits des utopischen Ideals in die reale, politisch-religiöse Konfliktsituation. Für den Weisen scheint sich die Herausforderung durch diese Konfliktsituation so ernsthaft und unausweichlich zu stellen, dass sie nicht ignoriert werden kann und darf. Das Projekt des sich selbst Lebens muss sich in diesem politischen und sozialen Raum behaupten, wenn die Aufgabe des Weisen (oder des Aufklärers) auch dementsprechend verstanden wird: Schranken und Hindernisse im Hier und Jetzt zu überwinden.[26]

In den ersten Szenen der Entwürfe wird uns Alcibiades mit seinem empfindsamen Freund Susamithres (beziehungsweise Zaris) räsonierend in der Einöde präsentiert, nur um unmittelbar darauf von Timandra, das ist die griechische Geliebte der Titelfigur, überrascht und verspottet zu werden, während sich von Ferne bereits der persische König Artaxerxes ankündigt. Der dritte Auftritt vermerkt hierzu lakonisch: »Weil Alcibiades den Artaxerxes nicht sucht, so muß Artaxerxes den Alcibiades suchen« (*WB* 5/1: 386). Dieser »doppelten Flucht«[27] (vor den Griechen und Persern) wird im Entwurf sofort eine doppelte ›Heimsuchung‹ anbei gestellt (durch die Griechen und Perser). In diesem ›heimsuchenden‹ Sinne bedauert Timandra die verlorenen Zeiten, nämlich »die glücklichen Zeiten, da, statt altvätrischer Sinnbilder, ein kleiner Liebesgott, den Blitz in der Rechte, von deinen goldnen Schilden schreckte? Da der lange Purpur nachlässig hinter dir her floß. [...] da dich die Aristophons in dem Schoße der zärtlichen Nemea malten etc. [...], und der drängende Pöbel das Gemälde voll Wohlgefallens angaffte« (*WB* 5/1: 386). Im Zusammenhang dieses Zitats verweist Lessing auf Plutarch als Quelle. Timandra nennt hier drei entscheidende Merkmale des Alcibiades, die durch die Quelle weiter erhellt werden: So schreibt Plutarch, bevor er auf den Mantel zusprechen kommt, dass sich Alcibiades zwar durch politisches und rhetorisches Geschick auszeichne, doch ebenso »viel Schwelgerey in seiner Lebensart, und viel Unartigkeit im Trinken und in Liebeshändeln« zeige.[28] Der Purpurmantel symbolisiert hier Eitelkeit, Prunksucht und Stolz.[29]

Der kleine Liebesgott, Eros, mit Zeus' Blitz in der Hand verdrängte also die sonst üblichen altväterlichen Sinnbilder, die in diesem Zusammenhang für Sitte und Gesetz stehen.[30] Alcibiades trug diesen Schild unmittelbar vor der katastrophalen Sizilien-Expedition; Eros verweist hier nicht nur auf den Eros der Philosophen, sondern auf eine ungebändigte, nahezu narzisstische Leidenschaft, also auf das genaue Gegenteil der Sokratischen Mäßigung, die man als tyrannische Neigung interpretieren könnte.[31] William Arrowsmith spricht passenderweise von »erotic politics of Alcibiades«: »Eros, specifically and indeed commonly, was applied, from Aeschylus to Plato and Aristotle, to activities and traits which we would normally classify as political: ambition, the love of glory, envy, lust for power, partisan zeal, greed for money or conquest«.[32] Dieser Befund wird noch einmal durch Plutarchs Aussagen über das Gemälde unterstützt: »Ingleichen wurden die ältern Männer unwillig, und hielten es für unerlaubt, und nur einem Tyrannen anständig«, dass sich Alcibiades so abbilden ließ.[33]

Natürlich kann nur gemutmaßt werden, ob Lessing diese Passage noch weiter ausgeführt hätte, doch scheinen die beiden Plutarch-Notizen plausibel darauf hinzuweisen; zumindest kann konstatiert werden, dass er die Ambivalenz der Schilderung kannte. Die politische Größe Alcibiades' und seine verführerische, manipulative Macht über das Volk, das ihm allerlei Fehler und Schwächen deswegen vergab,[34] manifestiert sich im Gemälde und wird zugleich konterkariert durch den vorgebrachten Argwohn der

Tyrannei. Timandras Spott über Alcibiades' Idee des sich Selbstlebens wird darauffolgend noch erweitert, da sie ihn als einen zweiten, aber lächerlicheren Timon betitelt, der Alcibiades »das Verderben des Volks« vorausgesagt hatte (WB 5/1: 387). Alcibiades Antwort berührt seine eigene politische Motivation, nachdem er zunächst einmal einsichtig äußert, Timon habe die Wahrheit gesagt:

> Ich Elender – War ich es nicht, der aus Ehrgeiz die Athenienser zu dem törichten Unternehmen, Sicilien zu erobern brachte? [...] Nicht um die Athenienser mächtiger zu wissen, nein um meine eigne Größe auf das überwundne Sicilien zu gründen. Der ich alle Nächte im Traume Karthago einnahm, Afrika unter das Joch brachte, von da nach Italien überging, als der Sieger des ganzen Peloponnes zurückkam, ich wollte aus Sicilien nichts als einen bequemen Waffenplatz für mich machen. (WB 5/1: 387)

Deutlich klingt ein imperialistischer Größenwahn an,[35] der allein auf egoistischen Motiven gegründet ist und ein deutliches Moment der Selbstüberschätzung offenbart.[36] Die Schwierigkeiten, vor denen Lessing unzweifelhaft gestanden haben muss, diesen ›Sinneswandel‹ vom egoistischen, rücksichtslosen, und tyrannischen Politiker und Strategen zum zurückgezogenen Weisen psychologisch plausibel zu gestalten, sind augenscheinlich.

Verstehen wir Politik im ursprünglichen Sinne, als auf das Gemeinwesen bezogene Handlungen, offenbart sich ein weiterer Widerspruch, da Alcibiades' Motivation ganz offensichtlich nichts mit der Vorrangstellung des Stadtstaats zu tun hatte, sondern mit einer pervertierten Form des politischen Eros – symbolisiert durch den kleinen Liebesgott auf dem goldenen Schild:

> [A] politics that refuses all the old modalities and that, deliberately and passionately, coolly and erotically, risks everything it has in the hope of winning more. In short, the politics of insatiable greed – of *pleonexia* – in a world where world-conquest, or something like it, lay within shooting distance. But the hunger for world conquest conceals a galactic, and ultimately, a universal hunger. It has, as Thucydides' Alcibiades effectively says, no terminus; it must always expand. If the horizon always recedes, the hope of overreaching it never dies. This is what I mean by a politics of Eros.[37]

Lessing scheint sich dieses Spannungsverhältnisses zwischen Philosophie und Politik im Lebenslauf des Alcibiades durchaus bewusst gewesen zu sein. So finden sich im Entwurf, der lediglich mit *Alcibiades* überschrieben ist, mehrere Szenen, die dieses Spannungsverhältnis exemplarisch vor Augen führen und die ich im Folgenden besprechen werde. Diesen Auftritten ist gemein, dass in ihnen Alcibiades' Entscheidung für das kontemplative sich Selbstleben grundlegend durch politische Inanspruchnahmen durch verschiedene Parteien herausgefordert wird.

Im geplanten zweiten und dritten Aufzug, also dem Zentrum des Stücks, ernennt König Artaxerxes Alcibiades zum Heerführer der persischen Truppen, um gegen die Griechen ins Feld zu ziehen, sodass dieser die Stelle des eifersüchtigen Pharnabaz einnimmt, der sich deshalb »mit den griechischen Abgesandten zum Verderben des Alcibiades [verbindet]« (*WB* 5/1: 388). Während Susamithres es kaum erwarten kann, an der Seite seines Freundes zu kämpfen, versichert ihm Alcibiades, dass er aufgrund seiner »Liebe zum Vaterlande« nicht kämpfen werde (*WB* 5/1: 389). Dieser »Punkt tiefer Ambiguität«[38] verdient eine besondere Aufmerksamkeit. Lessings ambivalentes Verhältnis zum Vaterland und (insbesondere) zum (preußischen) Patriotismus seiner Zeit ist bereits hinlänglich untersucht worden; seine Abneigung manifestierte sich in jenen kritischen Briefen an Johann Wilhelm Ludwig Gleim, den er für seine chauvinistischen Ausbrüche rügte.[39]

Die Liebe zum Vaterland kann im *Alcibiades*-Entwurf auch im Sinne des bereits angesprochenen politischen Eros verstanden werden. Die Keimzelle des destruktiven Imperialismus ist demnach ein pervertierter Patriotismus, der sich seiner gemeinnützigen Tugendhaftigkeit – »eine Betonung der Rechtschaffenheit, der redlichen Absicht und des Interesses an der allgemeinen Wohlfahrt« – entledigt, das Moment der selbstlosen Staatsräson durch Eigeninteresse ersetzt und sich aus machtpolitischen Gründen der philosophisch-moralischen Reflexion verwehrt.[40] Aus dieser Liebe zum Vaterland erwächst als machtpolitische Manifestation eines unverstandenen philosophischen Kosmopolitismus Alcibiades' Imperialismus als Ausdruck eines Subjekts, das nur Extrema kennt.[41] Mary Nichols widmet sich in ihrer Studie *Philosophy and Empire* anhand von Alcibiades' Auftritt in Platons *Symposion* genau diesem Problemkomplex: »If Alcibiades' vision of world empire is a political version of a cosmopolitan and transcendent philosophy, divorced from the limits of mortal, human life, it is not one that can be properly traced to Plato's Socrates«.[42] Nichols argumentiert weiter, dass Alcibiades' Vorstellungen der zwei Pole Philosophie und Politik eine grundlegende Reziprozität fehlt und er dadurch den mediatorischen Charakter der Philosophie, den Sokrates für ein gelingendes, gutes politisches und menschliches Leben voraussetze, verfehlt. Eine vernünftige politische Philosophie versuche, die eigenen Bedürfnisse und Möglichkeiten mit denen der anderen auszubalancieren.[43]

Alcibiades' Motivation für die Expansionsunternehmungen ist in Lessings Entwürfen allein ichbezogen; seine Motivation, nun nicht gegen die

Griechen zu ziehen, offenbart weniger eine pazifistische Einsicht und eine Absage an kriegerische Handlungen im Allgemeinen, sondern stattdessen eine nicht abgelegte politische Identifikation. Dass die Absage die Forderung des Asylgewährenden zurückweist, scheint für ihn nicht ausschlaggebend zu sein. In seiner Analyse des *Henzi*-Fragments konstatiert Robert Jamison: »Patriotism is [...] the antithesis of self-interest«.[44] Die Vaterlandsliebe des Alcibiades ist, Jamisons Aussage wörtlich nehmend und auf die Entwürfe übertragend, zugleich sein Untergang, die ›Selbstauflösung‹ durch die Hand der Kompatrioten. Den kosmopolitischen Absprung, den die Flucht des Alcibiades impliziert und auch notwendig werden lässt, sich selbst und seine damit verbundenen philosophischen Ambitionen auszuleben, hat Alcibiades nicht vollzogen. Es bleibt die Frage offen, inwiefern die Entwürfe Alcibiades als eine doppelt scheiternde Figur vorstellen wollten – sowohl in der Sphäre der Philosophie als auch in der Sphäre des Politischen. Damit würde das Stück auch an die Darstellung des Alcibiades im *Symposion* anknüpfen, wie Michael Gagarin diese deutet:

> Now Alcibiades also fails as a political figure, and although the reasons for this failure are more complex, it too is in part traceable to Socrates. In his own analysis [...] Alcibiades sees himself torn between the attraction of Socrates' intellectual and moral advice and the force of popular glory. [...] His reasons for rejecting a life of philosophy are not made clear until the seduction episode, [...] which reveals the true nature of his relation with Socrates, nameley that he was frustrated in his past attempt to acquire beauty, wisdom, and virtue from Socrates.[45]

Im ersten Auftritt des vierten Aufzugs kommt es dann zum Gespräch zwischen der griechischen Gesandtschaft, die Alcibiades überreden will (und darin auch erfolgreich ist), nach Griechenland zurückzukehren. Der Athener Critias verweist in seiner Ansprache auf den politischen Eros des Alcibiades mit seinen imperialistischen Implikationen: »Durch dich schwört noch jetzt die athenienische Jugend in dem Agraulischen Hayne, so oft die kriegrische Trompete sie ruft, ihres Vaterlands Grenzen nicht enger als jenseit aller bewohnten und bebauten Erdstriche zu setzen« (*WB* 5/1: 390).[46] Der Entwurf legt hier eine Parallele zwischen Sokrates und seinen Schülern (darunter ja auch die Titelfigur) sowie zwischen Alcibiades und jungen athenischen Soldaten hinsichtlich des Einflusses der beiden Persönlichkeiten auf die Jugend nahe. Der Ruf der kriegerischen Trompete sucht (um im Bilde zu bleiben) noch jetzt den Alcibiades heim und spornt militärische Expansionen an. Man könnte geneigt sein, im Ruf der Trompete jenen Vorwurf der Korruption der Jugend zu vernehmen, der auch Sokrates den Tod brachte.[47]

Alcibiades wird schließlich überredet. Bereits Barner betont die (tragische) Ironie dieser ganzen Szene, indem er auf den zehnten Literaturbrief Lessings verweist.[48] Dort schreibt Lessing, wie Alcibiades sich Sokrates' Kunst der Überredung als Mittel zum politischen Zweck, »die Kunst zu überreden, und die Gemüter der Zuhörer zu lenken«, angeeignet habe und nicht, »um Weisheit und Tugend von ihm zu lernen« (*WB* 4: 476). Lessing nimmt dabei eine sorgfältige Trennung zwischen der esoterischen, »der wahren« (*WB* 4: 476), und der exoterischen Philosophie vor, wobei erstere die auf eine geheime Weise vermittelte Lehre über bestimmte Wahrheiten für eine bestimmte elitäre, philosophische Gruppe ist, während letztere eine an die Allgemeinheit adressierte, öffentliche und zugänglichere Doktrin bezeichnet, die mitunter bewusst gegensätzlich zur esoterischen Lehre ausfallen kann.[49] Alcibiades war also in höchstem Maße ein Schüler der exoterischen Lehre des Sokrates, um Politiker und nicht Philosoph zu werden (vgl. *WB* 4: 476).[50] Wird Alcibiades' ganzes Streben, nun sein restliches Leben der Sokratischen Weisheit zu widmen – er hatte »dem Schutzgeiste des Socrates« sogar einen Altar aufgerichtet (*WB* 5/1: 389) – nicht in ein völlig anderes Licht gerückt? Es stellt sich die Frage, ob die klare Trennung zwischen dem vergangenen politischen Leben und dem philosophischen Leben im persischen Exil, die die Entwürfe uns ganz eindeutig präsentieren (zum Beispiel im Rückzug vom Hof des Artaxerxes) und die beide negative, destruktive Folgen nach sich ziehen, nicht genau den wunden Punkt des Alcibiades-Komplexes berühren. In *Alcibiades in Persien* betont die Titelfigur gegenüber dem Freund Zaris (Susamithres), dass er sich nun der Ruhe und den Betrachtungen widmen will. Dass die politische Vergangenheit durch das Wort ›Geschäfte‹ charakterisiert wird, in die sich Alcibiades hat *ver*-wickeln lassen und er seinen Anteil daran also höchst passiv beurteilt (vgl. *WB* 5/1: 393), unterstreicht, wie wenig sich Alcibiades *ent*-wickelt hat, da man Geschäfte sonst einfach *ab*-wickelt, sie also (im Idealfall) abgearbeitet werden und ohne Konsequenzen bleiben.

Das politische Leben im Rampenlicht erwies sich jedoch nicht nur als instabil und unkontrollierbar, sondern auch unentrinnbar. War das Volk zunächst zu seinem Gemälde geströmt, um es zu begaffen, wendete sich diese Gunst zügig, wie Lessings Alcibiades gegenüber Critias beklagt:

> Ich sollte dem Volk trauen? Ich diesem vielköpfigen Ungeheuer? Heut wird es dich vergöttern, wenn du willst; und morgen dich als den Schaum der Übeltäter verdammen. Ein einziger heimtückischer Verleumder, ein einziger Teucer ist genug es wider dich in Harnisch zu jagen. [...] Da ich mich am festesten in seiner Gunst glaubte, ward ich als der verfluchte Verstümmler heiliger Bildsäulen, als der Verräter der Geheimnisse der Ceres angeklagt und verdammt. (*WB* 5/1: 391)

Die Kunst der Überredung, die ihn nun im persischen Exil verdammt, verurteilte ihn schon damals, als er als Entweiher der athenischen Hermen und Mysterien von Eleusis unmittelbar vor der Sizilienexpedition angeklagt worden war. Sein persischer Gegenspieler, Pharnabaz, überredet Artaxerxes, das Gespräch zwischen Alcibiades und der griechischen Gesandtschaft »im verborgenen zu hören« (WB 5/1: 390). Ähnlich wie damals Teucer klagt auch Pharnabaz Alcibiades beim König der ›Häresie‹ an, als würden sich jene Vorwürfe Teucers wiederholen.[51] Eine doppelte ›Heimsuchung‹ auch hier:

> Siehe wie jeder dieser Ungläubigen sich einen eignen Gott schafft! Anstatt den einigen Gott im Feuer auf seinem ewigen, sichtbaren Throne der Sonne, anzubeten, betet jeder sein eigenes Hirngespinst, oder welches noch lächerlicher ist, und du hier siehst, das Hirngespinst eines Freundes an! (WB 5/1: 390)

Die ›Schlagkraft‹ der öffentlichen Meinung beschäftigte dabei nicht nur den fiktiven Alcibiades, sondern auch den historischen in der Schilderung Thukydides'. So sei Alcibiades bestrebt gewesen, seinen ausschweifenden privaten Lebensstil strikt von der Wahrnehmung seiner Person in der Öffentlichkeit und der Ausübung seiner politischen Ämter zu trennen.[52] Als Alcibiades angeklagt worden war, entstand früh das Gerücht, dass es sich hierbei um eine Gruppe von Religionsverächtern gehandelt hätte, die sich gegen die Republik Athens verschworen hätten, und Alcibiades dieser angehören oder sogar vorstehen würde, was sowohl Senat als auch Volk in Aufruhr versetzte.[53] Parallel dazu verunglimpft auch Pharnabaz im Entwurf Alcibiades gegenüber Artaxerxes als Religionsverächter, da er nicht der staatsreligiösen Praxis folge (vgl. WB 5/1: 788), um ihn nicht nur moralisch-sittlich zu diffamieren, sondern vor allen Dingen auch politisch zu delegitimieren. Obwohl es sich hierbei lediglich um eine private Verehrung des philosophischen Lehrers handelt – zumal im kürzeren Entwurf *Alcibiades in Persien* die Öffnung und das Interesse der Titelfigur gegenüber dem Zoroastrismus mehr als deutlich werden (vgl. besonders WB 5/1: 394) –, nutzt Pharnabaz diesen Umstand aus, um ihn als ›öffentliche Angelegenheit‹ zu deklarieren. Die gleiche Strategie verfolgte zuvor die athenische Elite, deren politische Bedenken gegenüber Alcibiades ohne Unterstützung durch die Öffentlichkeit wenig Schlagkraft zu besitzen schienen. Zuerst musste Alcibiades in den Augen der Öffentlichkeit als moralisch unsittlich respektive unfromm diffamiert und die öffentliche Meinung gegen ihn mobilisiert werden. Lessing übernimmt also die historische Ausgangssituation, wie Plutarch sie schildert, und lässt sie in Pharnabaz als den ›persischen Wiedergänger‹ des Teucers kulminieren. Im Entwurf wird in Grundzügen das Spannungsverhältnis zwischen Politik und Religion beziehungsweise die Funktion der Religion für das politische Gemeinwesen sowie die Konsequenz für deviante Praktiken angesprochen.

Da die Bezugslinien zu Lessings Studien in Breslau sowie die Verhältnisse zwischen Philosophie, Politik und Religion sicherlich eines eigenen Aufsatzes bedürften, wird die religionsphilosophische Thematik in meinen Ausführungen bewusst ausgeklammert. In der ersten Szene von *Alcibiades in Persien* gibt es diesbezüglich allerdings einen wichtigen (vermeintlichen) Eingangsmonolog der Hauptfigur: »Es war der göttlichste Gedanke, den ich jemals gehabt, mich nach Persien zu verbannen! Aus dem *weisen* Griechenlande, wo Aberglaube und gesetzlose Frechheit den Pöbel, Ehrgeiz und Ohnegötterei die Großen regiert, in das *barbarische* Persien, wo Wahrheit und Tugend den alten Thron besitzen« (*WB* 5/1: 393). Bereits Barner hat auf diese problematische, ostentative Umkehrung zweier Extrema aufmerksam gemacht.[54] Es stellt sich nur die Frage, ob Alcibiades' Darstellung Persiens als Sitz der Wahrheit und Tugend nicht im Text selbst als subjektive Auffassung der Figur dargestellt und weiterhin dadurch unterlaufen wird, dass Lessing explizit die »heilige Abscheu« der persischen Figuren gegenüber dem Altar des Sokrates thematisiert und Pharnabaz diesen als »Hirngespinst« betitelt (*WB* 5/1: 390). Immerhin befiehlt Artaxerxes, »den Altar des Sokrates zu zerstören, den Ort zu reinigen, und ein Pyreum an die Stelle zu bauen« (*WB* 5/1: 391). Damit scheint mir Barners Darstellung, Lessing sei »sichtlich bestrebt, persische Sittlichkeit und persische Religion als der ›Wahrheit und Tugend‹ *praktisch* dienend hervorzukehren«, zweifelhaft.[55] Auch Ficks Aussage, die Perser seien im Besitz einer natürlichen Religion, die der griechischen überlegen sei,[56] wird durch die Figuren Pharnabaz und Artaxerxes konterkariert.

Vielleicht hätte sich im Text diesbezüglich ein weiterer Konflikt zwischen den ›Philosophen‹ Alcibiades und Susamithres und den ›Politikern‹ auf der anderen Seite hinsichtlich religiöser Vorstellungen entspannen. Zumindest steht zur Disposition, ob Pharnabaz nicht ähnlich wie die Griechen im Stück Religion und Frömmigkeit zur sittlichen Diffamierung seines politischen Gegners benutzt. Somit unterscheiden sich auch Susamithres' und Pharnabaz' Praktiken, die sie aus der gemeinsamen Religion ziehen. So äußert Zaris (das ist Susamithres) beispielsweise seine »wahre Hochachtung« für Sokrates gegenüber Alcibiades (*WB* 5/1: 394).[57] Die »religiös-moralische Antithese«, die Persien gegenüber Griechenland im Text einnehme,[58] wäre dann noch einmal innerhalb der persischen Figuren gespiegelt.

Die manipulierende Rede der griechischen Gesandtschaft bewegt, wie der Entwurf zum Schluss vermerkt, schließlich auch Alcibiades, woraufhin Artaxerxes die Deckung verlässt, »dem Alcibiades die härtesten Vorwürfe« macht und ihn aus seinem Schutz entlässt (*WB* 5/1: 391). In den Notizen zum vorletzten Auftritt des Stücks vermerkt Lessing nüchtern und vorwegnehmend: »Alcibiades kömmt verwundet zurück und stirbt« (WB 5/1: 392). Die Titelfigur wird schließlich nicht, wie von ihr gewünscht, durch die Hand des Freundes, sondern durch den Gegenspieler Pharnabaz ermordet. Am Ende des Stücks ruft Lessing das Bild des triumphierenden Jägers über den ›Löwen‹ Alcibiades auf. Der von Land zu Land geflohene endet schließlich wie ein gehetztes Tier, wenngleich der Löwe hier durchaus als Symbolbild für den einst so mächtigen und dementsprechend gefährlichen Staatsmann gedeutet werden kann (vgl. WB 5/1: 392, 789).

Abschließend bleibt zu fragen, was die Entwürfe im Sinne einer politischen Aufklärung auszeichnet. Philosophie und Politik sind die beiden zentrale Pole, dessen Spannungsverhältnis sich in den Entwürfen niederschlägt. Alcibiades' neuer Lebensentwurf, sich ganz der Philosophie zu widmen, wird durch die Heimsuchung seiner politischen Vergangenheit sowohl auf ideeller Ebene konterkariert, als sich diese zugleich in Form der griechischen Gesandtschaft physisch manifestiert und in Timandras Anwesenheit bereits ihren Vorklang findet. Der durch Alcibiades' Flucht erzwungene Schnitt zwischen dem politischen und dem philosophischen Leben scheint also das maßgebliche tragische Potenzial in sich zu bergen. Doch beide Lebensentwürfe offenbaren sich als grundlegend mangelhaft, da sie beide egoistische Züge aufweisen: Die intrinsische Motivation der politischen Ambitionen war Alcibiades' Ehrgeiz, während seine extrinsische Motivation Ruhm und Anerkennung war; und auch die intrinsische Motivation im Exil speist sich aus dem Wunsch, sich selbst zu leben, während die extrinsische Motivation sich letztendlich aus der Vermeidung und Flucht vor politischen Konsequenzen und den höfischen Geschäften speist.

Die Entwürfe geben keine letzten Antworten, werfen sie doch vielmehr die Fragen auf, wie sich das philosophische Leben zu dem politischen Leben und *vice versa* zu verhalten habe und ob diese Trennung, auf textlicher Ebene durch Vergangenheit und Gegenwart verdeutlicht, nicht generell irreführend ist, da beide aufeinander angewiesen seien. Alcibiades' Lebensentwurf ist blind gegenüber dem Austragungsort seiner philosophischen Ambitionen, die sich nicht durch einen scheinbaren Ausstieg, also außerhalb gesellschaftlicher und politischer Reichweite, verwirklichen lassen. Die Gefahr der politischen Vereinnahmung, sei es nun durch den König Artaxerxes oder durch die griechische Gesandtschaft, besteht trotz des Wunschs nach Abgeschiedenheit; ein Entzug ist nicht möglich. Der von Alcibiades angestrebte philosophische Lebensentwurf, das sich Selbstleben in der Einöde (vgl. WB 5/1: 393), mag sich in der theoretischen Betrachtung von der öffentlichen Meinung, von Normen und Gesetzen befreien können, doch für die praktische und öffentliche Lebensführung bemerkt Mary Nichols: »Transcending the political has political implications«.[59] Die politische Aufklärung der Entwürfe mag darin liegen, das Politische weder als Machtinstrument zu missbrauchen noch als Fessel wahrzunehmen, sondern als eine notwendige Herausforderung aufzufassen, der sich der philosophische Lebensentwurf zu stellen hat. Und auch das politische Leben, in den Entwürfen omnipräsent durch die Vergangenheit der Titelfigur, läuft Gefahr, sich durch die philosophische Befragung seiner Grundsätze zu entledigen und durch rhetorisches Geschick sich an seiner Macht zu berauschen.[60] Schlussendlich erliegt Alcibiades der Täuschung, durch das eine dem anderen zu entkommen; doch politische Aufklärung bedeutet vielmehr »Ent-Täuschung«.[61]

Lessings *Philotas* wurde bekanntlich von den Zeitgenossen verkannt und beispielsweise von Gleim als patriotisches Stück gedeutet und schließlich auch umgedichtet; der mitunter fanatische Patriotismus der Zeitgenossen Lessings erschwerte eine reflektierte und kritische Lektüre des Stücks erheblich.[62] Vorstellungen einer nationalpädagogischen,[63] kulturpatriotischen[64] Literatur, die Lessing zeitweise in Gleims ›Grenadierliedern‹ erkannte, verdeutlichen den schmalen Grat, der zwischen Enttäuschung und Verblendung verläuft.[65] Vielleicht fürchtete Lessing, dass die Intention seiner *Alcibiades*-Texte ähnlich verkannt werden könnte wie die des *Philotas*. Vielleicht waren die beiden Entwürfe zu verkopft, geschichtlich in zu weiter Ferne und ihre Modi als Trauerspiel nicht für Lessings Intention geeignet, weshalb er sie nicht zu Ende brachte. Vielleicht fehlten ihnen die spielerische Herzlichkeit und politische Aktualität der *Minna von Barnhelm*. Und vielleicht waren sich Alcibiades und Lessing, der sich vor dem Hintergrund des Siebenjährigen Kriegs in Breslau ganz den Studien zu widmen gedachte, dann doch zu ähnlich.

Universität Osnabrück

---

1 Vgl. Wolfgang Albrecht, Lessing. Gespräche, Begegnungen, Lebenszeugnisse. Ein kommentiertes Lese- und Studienwerk. Teil 1. 1729 bis 1782, Kamenz 2005, S. 143-144.
2 Wilfried Barner, »Vaterland« und »freiwilliges Elend«. Über Lessings *Alcibiades*, in: »Laut denken mit einem Freunde«. Lessing-Studien, hg. von Kai Bremer, Göttingen 2017, S. 239-251 (Zitat S. 241). Auch Hugh Nisbet betont die autobiographischen Züge der Entwürfe, verweist aber auch auf inhaltliche Parallelen zu *Nathan der Weise* (Lessing. Eine Biographie, München 2008, S. 390-391).
3 Gotthold Ephraim Lessing, Werke und Briefe in zwölf Bänden, hg. von Wilfried Barner u.a., Frankfurt a.M. 1985-2003. Im Folgenden zitiert mit der Sigle *WB* mit Band- und Seitenangabe (Alcibiades, *WB* 5/1: 385-392; *Alcibiades in Persien*, *WB* 5/1: 393-394).

4 Vgl. *WB* 5/1: 392. In *Kleonnis* (vgl. *WB* 4) tötet der König Euphaes unwissentlich seinen Sohn Kleonnis, nachdem dieser zuvor ebenfalls unwissentlich seinen Bruder Demarat im Kampf tötete; der unvollständige Entwurf thematisiert jedoch nur die Vorahnung des Königs, dass seinem Sohn etwas zugestoßen sein könnte (vgl. zur vermutlichen Inhaltsangabe des *Kleonnis* Erich Schmidt, Lessing. Geschichte seines Lebens und seiner Schriften. Bd. 1, Berlin 1884, S. 340-343). Die Parallele zwischen *Alcibiades* und *Emilia* zog bereits Barner, »Vaterland« und »freiwilliges Elend« (Anm. 2), S. 246.
5 Monika Fick, Lessing-Handbuch. Leben – Werk – Wirkung, 4. Aufl., Stuttgart 2016, S. 299.
6 Vgl. zur Biographie: Herbert Heftner, Alkibiades. Staatsmann und Feldherr, Darmstadt 2011; Peter J. Rhodes, Alcibiades. Athenian Playboy, General and Traitor, Barnsley 2011.
7 Gisbert Ter-Nedden, Der fremde Lessing. Eine Revision des dramatischen Werks, hg. von Robert Vellusig, Göttingen 2016, S. 202-203.
8 Vgl. Ter-Nedden (Anm. 7), S. 194-203; Barner, »Vaterland« und »freiwilliges Elend« (Anm. 2), S. 243-244; Fick (Anm. 5), S. 298-302.
9 Fick (Anm. 5), S. 301.
10 Vgl. auch Wilfried Barner, Lessings Fluchten, in: »Laut denken mit einem Freunde«. Lessing-Studien, hg. von Kai Bremer, Göttingen 2017, S. 379-388, besonders S. 387-388.
11 Vgl. bezüglich der anderen Entwürfe aus der Zeit des Siebenjährigen Kriegs: Karl Piosecka, Lessings strategische Selbstpositionierungen im Patriotismusstreit der 1750er Jahre, in: Praktiken der Provokation. Lessings Schreib- und Streitstrategien, hg. von Magdalena Fricke, Hannes Kerber und Eleonora Travanti, Hannover 2024, S. 85-114.
12 Vgl. zum Beispiel Carsten Zelle, Lessings *Philotas* im Siebenjährigen Krieg, in: Lessing Yearbook/Jahrbuch, Bd. 47 (2020), S. 31-51, hier S. 40-41, und auch S. 49-50, Anm. 31.
13 Reinhart Koselleck, Kritik und Krise. Eine Studie zur Pathogenese der bürgerlichen Welt, 14. Aufl., Frankfurt a. M. 2018, S. 45. Eine ähnliche Perspektive nimmt auch die Studie von Wolf Lepenies, Kultur und Politik. Deutsche Geschichten, München, Wien 2006 ein; so urteilt Lepenies (S. 46): »Kultur war in Deutschland lange Zeit ein Ort der Kompensation für vorenthaltene politische Partizipation«.
14 Vgl. Koselleck (Anm. 13), S. 45-46.
15 Vgl. Koselleck (Anm. 13), besonders S. 49-68 (Zitat S. 53).
16 Koselleck (Anm. 13), S. 74.
17 Vgl. Koselleck (Anm. 13), besonders S. 154-157.
18 Schmidt (Anm. 4), S. 356.
19 Vgl. auch Fick (Anm. 5), S. 301.
20 Ellwood Wiggins, Odysseys of Recognition: Performing Intersubjectivity in Homer, Aristotle, Shakespeare, Goethe, and Kleist, Lewisburg, PA 2019, S. 149.
21 Vgl. Rhodes (Anm. 6), S. 99-102.
22 Ähnlich auch schon Barner, »Vaterland« und »freiwilliges Elend« (Anm. 2), S. 244-245.
23 Vgl. zum vermeintlich apolitischen Charakter des sich Selbstlebens in *Emilia*

Galotti und *Nathan der Weise* auch Baiyu Lus Beitrag zu *Emilia Galotti* in diesem Band (Vortrag Lessing Workshop, 25. April 2024).
24 Wilfried Wilms, Im Griff des Politischen – Konfliktfähigkeit und Vaterwerdung in *Emilia Galotti*, in: DVjs, Bd. 76.1 (2002), S. 50-73, hier S. 55.
25 Vgl. Wilms (Anm. 24), S. 50-73.
26 Vgl. dementsprechend die Ausführungen von Hannes Kerber, Die Aufklärung der Aufklärung, Lessing und die Herausforderung des Christentums, Göttingen 2021, S. 220 zur Deutung der Ringparabel auch mit Hinblick auf den vorausgegangenen ›Fragmentenstreit‹. Weiterhin ergibt sich eine interessante Parallele dahingehend, dass Al-Hafi derselben Religion angehört wie die persischen Figuren in den *Alcibiades*-Entwürfen: dem Zoroastrismus (vgl. *WB* 9: 1263).
27 Barner, »Vaterland« und »freiwilliges Elend« (Anm. 2), S. 244.
28 Plutarch, Alcibiades, in: Biographien des Plutarchs. Zweyter Theil, hg. von Gottlob Benedict von Schirach, Prag, Wien 1796, S. 220-281, hier S. 240.
29 Vgl. zum Thema Eitelkeit, Selbstberauschung und Machtmissbrauch auch: Wendy Brown, Nihilistische Zeiten. Denken mit Max Weber, Berlin 2023, S. 64-65.
30 Vgl. hierzu auch Plutarch (Anm. 28), S. 240.
31 Vgl. Mary P. Nichols, Philosophy and Empire: On Socrates and Alcibiades in Plato's *Symposium*, in: Polity, Bd. 39.4 (2007), S. 502-521. Siehe auch Brown (Anm. 29), S. 65: »Wenn ein politischer Akteur zur Sache bzw. zum Anliegen wird, anstatt es auf den Weg zu bringen, verschwinden Reflexivität, Abgeklärtheit, Zurückhaltung und vor allem Verantwortung in der Versenkung und rückt der Machtkitzel in den Mittelpunkt.«
32 William Arrowsmith, Aristophanes' Birds: The Fantasy Politics of Eros, in: Arion. A Journal of Humanities and the Classics. New Series, Bd. 1.1 (1973), S. 119-167, hier S. 133; vgl. auch S. 140-141. Siehe auch Victoria Wohl, The Eros of Alcibiades, in: Classical Antiquity, Bd. 18.2 (1999), S. 349-385, insbesondere S. 376.
33 Plutarch (Anm. 28), S. 241.
34 Vgl. ebd. Vgl. auch Barner, »Vaterland« und »freiwilliges Elend« (Anm. 2), S. 243.
35 Vgl. auch Barner, »Vaterland« und »freiwilliges Elend« (Anm. 2), S. 245; Arrowsmith (Anm. 32), S. 135.
36 Zum Aspekt der Schuld siehe Edmund F. Bloedow, »Not the Son of Achilles, but Achilles Himself«: Alcibiades' Entry on the Political Stage in Athens II, in: Historia, Bd. 39.1 (1990), S. 1-19, hier S. 18-19.
37 Arrowsmith (Anm. 32), S. 130.
38 Barner, »Vaterland« und »freiwilliges Elend« (Anm. 2), S. 245.
39 Vgl. hierzu besonders die Studien von Wilfried Barner: *Res publica litteraria* und das Nationale. Zu Lessings europäischer Orientierung, in: »Laut denken mit einem Freunde«. Lessing-Studien, hg. von Kai Bremer, Göttingen 2017, S. 145-171; ders.: Patriotismus und Kosmopolitismus bei Lessing während des Siebenjährigen Krieges, in: »Laut denken mit einem Freunde«. Lessing-Studien, hg. von Kai Bremer, Göttingen 2017, S. 213-224.
40 Vgl. Rudolf Vierhaus, »Patriotismus« – Begriff und Realität einer moralisch-politischen Haltung, in: Deutschland im 18. Jahrhundert. Politische Verfassung, soziales Gefüge, geistige Bewegungen. Ausgewählte Aufsätze, hg. von dems., Göttingen 1987, S. 96-109 (Zitat S. 97).

41 Lessing sah in seinem eigenen Umfeld, wie leicht ein vermeintlich tugendhafter Patriotismus durch politische Freund-Feind-Schemata pervertiert werden kann. Erschütternd blutrünstig und menschenverachtend ist beispielsweise Gleims Grenadierlied *An die Kriegsmuse nach der Niederlage der Russen bey Zorndorf*. Hier maßt sich der fiktive Grenadier an, er spreche für die Menschheit, wodurch er seine Gewaltfantasien moralisch legitimiert sieht. Siehe Johann Wilhelm Ludwig Gleim, Preussische Kriegslieder von einem Grenadier, hg. von August Sauer, Heilbronn 1882, S. 43: »So lange du, o Vater, vor uns her / Die schreckliche Blutfahne trugst, und nichts / In deiner Arbeit für das Vaterland / Dein Leben achtetest, so lange floß / Für jede Thräne deines Volkes Blut, / So lange schlug das rächerische Schwerd / Nicht deinen sondern aller Menschheit Feind, / Und mähete die ungeheure Brut / Unmenschen weg, aus deines Gottes Welt.« Lessing warf daraufhin Gleim vor, dass dieser über seinen extremen Patriotismus vergessen habe, ein Weltbürger zu sein, woraufhin Gleim schwer getroffen bat, diesen Vorwurf zurückzunehmen. Vgl. hierzu WB 11/1: 305, 308; vgl. zu diesem Thema auch Piosecka (Anm. 11).
42 Nichols (Anm. 31), S. 520.
43 Vgl. Nichols (Anm. 31), S. 504-505, 519-521.
44 Robert L. Jamison, Classical Republicanism in Lessing's *Samuel Henzi*, in: Lessing and the Enlightenment, hg. von Alexej Ugrinsky, New York 1986, S. 105-112, hier S. 107.
45 Michael Gagarin, Socrates' »Hybris« and Alcibiades' Failure, in: Phoenix, Bd. 31.1 (1977), S. 22-37, hier S. 34.
46 Es scheint sich hierbei um eine wörtliche Übernahme (respektive Übersetzung) aus der Plutarch-Quelle zu handeln, da diese bereits im Original mit Anführungszeichen versehen ist, weshalb ich sie in einfache Anführungszeichen umgewandelt habe. Siehe hierzu auch Plutarch (Anm. 28), S. 239.
47 Zum Korruptionsvorwurf und Sokrates' Einfluss auf Alcibiades vgl. Christos C. Evangeliou, Political Ambition and Philosophic Constraint: Alcibiades, Socrates and the Sicilian Expedition, in: Philosopher Kings and Tragic Heroes. Essays on Images and Ideas from Western Greece, hg. von Heather L. Reid und Davide Tanasi, Sioux City, IA 2016, S. 111-126. Vgl. zum Beispiel auch die Ausgangssituation in Platons *Euthyphron*.
48 Vgl. Barner (Anm. 2), S. 243, 246.
49 Vgl. grundlegend Arthur M. Melzer, Philosophy Between the Lines. The Lost History of Esoteric Writing, Chicago, London 2014, S. 1-2; für eine Studie mit explizitem Bezug zu Lessing und jüngst veröffentlicht, siehe: Eleonora Travanti, Lessings exoterische Verteidigung der Orthodoxie. Die Wolfenbütteler Beiträge gegen die Aufklärungstheologie (1770-1774), Berlin/Boston 2023.
50 Lessing nimmt hier explizit auf Alcibiades Bezug.
51 Auch historisch sei Teucer einer der Hauptankläger gegen Alcibiades im Fall des Religionsfrevels gewesen; vgl. Plutarch (Anm. 28), S. 247-248.
52 Zum Verhältnis von Privatsphäre und Öffentlichkeit vgl. Bloedow (Anm. 36), S. 6.
53 Vgl. Plutarch (Anm. 28), S. 244-248.
54 Vgl. Barner, »Vaterland« und »freiwilliges Elend« (Anm. 2), S. 247, 251.
55 Barner, »Vaterland« und »freiwilliges Elend« (Anm. 2), S. 247.

56 Vgl. Fick (Anm. 5), S. 301.
57 Susamithres verteidigt Alcibiades auch gegenüber seinem Vater, indem er sich »auf das persische Gesetz wider die Undankbarkeit [beruft], nach welchem er durchaus strafbar sein würde, wenn er den Alcibiades, in so gefährlichen Umständen verließe« (*WB* 5/1: 392).
58 Vgl. Barner, »Vaterland« und »freiwilliges Elend« (Anm. 2), S. 247.
59 Nichols (Anm. 31), S. 503.
60 Vgl. Nichols (Anm. 31), S. 504-505, 521.
61 Ter-Nedden (Anm. 7), S. 202.
62 Vgl. den Briefwechsel zwischen Lessing und Gleim im Frühjahr und Sommer des Jahres 1759 in *WB* 11/1: 213-219; vgl. weiterhin Friedrich Vollhardt, Gotthold Ephraim Lessing. Epoche und Werk, Göttingen 2018, S. 173.
63 Vgl. Barner, Patriotismus und Kosmopolitismus bei Lessing (Anm. 39), S. 219.
64 Vgl. Vollhardt (Anm. 62), S. 171.
65 Vgl. Vollhardt (Anm. 62), S. 173; vgl. weiterhin Piosecka (Anm. 11), besonders S. 91-107. Dass die philosophisch und politisch höchst anspruchsvollen sowie wachsamen *Alcibiades*-Fragmente sicherlich nicht »der Ambivalenz der Aufklärung, die proportional zu ihrem Prozeß der Entlarvung politisch verblindet«, ausgeliefert sein sollten, ist augenscheinlich (Koselleck [Anm. 13], S. 154); doch feit die Intention nicht vor falscher Rezeption und willkürlicher Auslegung.

Das Politikum des apolitischen Odoardo in Lessings *Emilia Galotti*

BAIYU LU

Schon in den 1750er Jahren war Lessing mit der Geschichte der Virginia aus Livius' *Ab urbe condita* bekannt und beabsichtigte, daraus ein dreiaktiges Stück über »eine bürgerliche Virginia« zu schreiben (*WB* 11/1: 267).[1] Auch nach zwanzig Jahren war Lessing noch immer von der Bearbeitung des Virginia-Stoffes fasziniert, und 1772 ist *Emilia Galotti* entstanden. Ihn interessiere eher das Allgemein-Menschliche, das in der Tötung der eigenen Tochter durch den Vater im Namen der Tugend eher negativ zum Ausdruck gebracht wird, so heißt es in der Forschung, als der politische Heroismus eines traditionellen republikanischen Trauerspiels, in dem der Tod eines unschuldigen Mädchens nur als Anlass zur politischen Revolution dient.[2] Lessing selbst versicherte seinem Bruder, »daß es weiter nichts, als eine modernisierte, von allem Staatsinteresse befreite Virginia sein soll« (*WB* 11/2: 362). Im Gegensatz zur Virginia-Geschichte ist die Herrschaft von Prinz Gonzaga in *Emilia Galotti* nicht gefährdet; der Vater wartet am Ende des Dramas hingegen darauf, dass der Prinz als Richter ihn als Tochtermörder verurteilt. Über den Grund jedoch, warum Odoardo den Dolch nicht auf den Prinzen, sondern auf die unschuldige Tochter richtet, wird viel spekuliert. Dadurch taucht das Thema des Politischen unvermeidlich auf.

Sozialgeschichtlich wird Odoardo dem politisch ohnmächtigen Bürgertum zugeordnet, das keine andere Waffe als die Moral beziehungsweise die moralische Autonomie gegen den despotischen Absolutismus einsetzen kann und schließlich an dessen skrupellosen Machtausübung scheitern muss.[3] Eine andere Richtung in der Forschung geht auf die institutionellen Ursachen des tragischen Ereignisses ein. Es liege nicht an einzelnen moralisch verdorbenen Menschen, die durch Machtmissbrauch eine Katastrophe verursachen, sondern an der unumschränkten politischen Machtausübung im Absolutismus, nämlich sein Machtmonopol. Die Lösung der Aufklärung sei folgerichtig das Prinzip der Gewaltenteilung, das aber besonders in der vom Despotismus bedrängten, absolutistischen Monarchie gefährdet sei.[4] Diese Schlussfolgerung impliziert, dass ein Tyrannenmord sinnlos wäre, wenn er nicht auf eine Veränderung der Staatsverfassung ziele oder diese zur Folge hätte. Mit seinem Stück fordere Lessing nichts weniger als eine systematische politische Reform, wenn nicht Revolution. Die Behauptung der Entpolitisierung des Virginia-Stoffes sei nur ein Deckmantel, um die politische Brisanz des Stücks zu verhüllen.[5] Ter-Nedden schlägt eine andere Deutungsrichtung ein. Sein Ausgangspunkt ist die prinzipielle Vermeidbarkeit der Katastrophe. Der Prinz zeige sich bereit, auf Odoardo und seine moralischen Einstellungen einzugehen. Tyrannenmord oder Tötung der eigenen Tochter seien nicht die einzigen Alternativen. Beide gründen sich auf die unvernünftige Gewaltausübung. Die wirkliche Alternative zur Konfliktbewältigung sei vernünftige Rede und Kommunikation.[6]

Hervorgehoben in der bisherigen Forschung wird vor allem eine Erklärung der Wirkungsabsicht, um begreiflich zu machen, warum im Drama ein Tyrannenmord unterbleibt. Die Frage, warum Odoardo darauf verzichtet, findet wenig Beachtung und ist deshalb noch nicht zufriedenstellend beantwortet. Schließlich ist Odoardo ein Oberst außer Dienst, der dem Prinzen unerschrocken auch mit Gewalt begegnet. Es muss Lessing Schwierigkeiten bereitet haben, Odoardos Verzicht auf einen Tyrannenmord überzeugend darzustellen. Das schlug sich in dem unregelmäßigen Schreibprozess Lessings nieder. Anfang November 1771 beschloss Lessing, *Emilia Galotti* zu Papier zu bringen. In drei Monaten schrieb er die ersten vier Akte. Doch je mehr er sich dem Schluss näherte, desto langsamer kam er voran. Während des gesamten Februars arbeitete er nicht am Text. Wahrscheinlich hatte Lessing Schwierigkeiten bei der Ausarbeitung des fünften Aktes und stellte ihn erst Anfang März fertig (WB 7: 835), wobei die ersten fünf Szenen, mehr als der Hälfte des fünften Aktes, gerade das Ausbleiben eines Tyrannenmords behandeln.

Als Dramaturg fordert Lessing, dass »die Bewegungsgründe zu jedem Entschlusse, zu jeder Änderung der geringsten Gedanken und Meinungen« dem Charakter der Figuren entspringe (WB 6: 192). Wir erwarten von ihm als Dramatiker, dass er das Tun und Lassen seiner Figuren auch mit überzeugenden Motiven ausstattet. Odoardos Verzicht auf den Tyrannenmord erklärt sich tatsächlich aus seiner Persönlichkeit, oder genauer: aus seiner Einstellung gegenüber dem Politischen. Es ist wiederum die Eigengesetzlichkeit des Politischen, durch die ihm die Hände gebunden sind. Schließlich verdient es die folgende Frage Monika Ficks, noch einmal gestellt zu werden: »Warum versäumt es Odoardo, der im Streit um Sabionetta die Zivilcourage hatte, sich dem Prinzen heftig zu widersetzen und dafür von diesem hochgeachtet wird, ihn mit seinem Unrecht zu konfrontieren?«[7]

1. Der apolitische Ungehorsam

Wie sein Gegenstück Virginius hat Odoardo in der Armee gedient und aktiv an den politischen Angelegenheiten des Landes teilgenommen, wie es sein Engagement in der Staatsangelegenheit über Sabionetta an den Tag legt (WB 7: 297). Er hat sich jedoch seitdem aufs Land zurückgezogen, weil er, wie er im Gespräch mit seiner Frau Claudia im vierten Auftritt des zweiten

Aktes deutlich artikuliert, von dem angeblich moralisch korrupten Hof von Gonzaga zutiefst enttäuscht ist.

Was tatsächlich am Hof Gonzaga vor sich geht, ist allerdings nicht so klar, wie es zunächst scheint. Lessing stellt anscheinend absichtlich im ersten Akt einen inkompetenten Monarchen, gar einen Despoten, dar, dessen Fahrlässigkeit in gesetzlichen Angelegenheiten dabei besonders hervorgehoben wird. In der berühmten Eröffnungsszene sieht man einen Prinzen, der zwar das politische Amt als Herrscher fleißig ausübt, diesen Verpflichtungen aber nur widerwillig nachkommt. Er gewährt eine inadäquate Petition, nur weil die Klägerin ebenfalls Emilia heißt. Die Nachlässigkeit gipfelt in der letzten Szene des ersten Aktes, in der Gonzaga im Begriff ist, ein Todesurteil mit einem »recht gern« (*WB* 7: 307) zu unterschreiben, ohne es vorher zu prüfen, damit er die letzte Chance ergreift, seine Liebe zu Emilia zu gestehen.

Es ist wohl kein Zufall, dass Gonzagas Unzulänglichkeiten als Herrscher vor allem die Gesetzlichkeit in Guastalla gefährden. Der entscheidende Unterschied zwischen einer Monarchie und einer Despotie, beides Regierungsformen der Alleinherrschaft, liegt laut Montesquieu darin, ob die Herrschaft nach festen und etablierten Gesetzen oder nach eigener Willkür ausgeübt wird.[8] Die rechtmäßige monarchische Regierung werde institutionell vor allem durch die Stelle eines Hüters der Gesetze garantiert. Dieser Hüter und Richter gewährleistet die Durchsetzung der Gesetze gegen die mögliche Willkür des Fürsten.[9]

Dass Guastalla den Eindruck macht, eine rechtmäßige Monarchie statt einer Despotie zu sein, ist dem Ratsherrn Camillo Rota zu verdanken.[10] Wie in der Gestalt des Titelhelden von J.M. Loëns Staatsroman, *Der redliche Mann am Hofe* (1740), bekundet sich in der Figur Rota das politische Wunschbild der Aufklärung. Er tritt zwar nur in einer Szene kurz auf, spielt jedoch eine entscheidende Rolle, die klar macht, wie der politische Zustand in Guastalla einzuschätzen ist und ob Gonzaga noch als ein legitimer Monarch oder schon als ein Despot regiert.

Bevor Gonzaga zur Kirche eilt, erteilt er Rota die Befugnis, die Petition, die er aus reiner Willkür gewährt, nachzuprüfen und schließlich die Entscheidung auch selbstständig zu fällen: »[D]ie Sache ist keine Kleinigkeit – Lassen Sie die Ausfertigung noch anstehen. – Oder auch nicht anstehen: wie Sie wollen« (*WB* 7: 307). Es ist Gonzaga klar, dass die Bewilligung der Petition nicht gesetzkonform ist; er rechnet auf die Gerechtigkeit und Integrität des »Hüters der Gesetze«, vertraut ihm an, den Fall selbstständig zu entscheiden, und damit schränkt der absolutistische Fürst bewusst seine judikative Macht ein. Mit der Antwort, »Nicht wie ich will« (*WB* 7: 307), impliziert Rota, dass es nach dem Willen des Gesetzes und den Grundsätzen der Gerechtigkeit geschehen soll. Als Rota feststellt, dass Gonzaga aus Gedankenlosigkeit kurz davor ist, das Todesurteil voreilig zu unterzeichnen, kommt er zu dem Schluss, dass der Prinz in diesem Moment nicht in der Lage ist, seine Aufgaben als Richter zu erfüllen, und schiebt die Unterzeichnung des Todesurteils umsichtig auf, um zu verhindern, dass Gonzaga einen Rechtsbruch begeht.[11]

Es stellt sich heraus, dass Gonzaga in diesem kleinen Fürstentum mit absoluter Macht zwar über beträchtliche judikative und exekutive Befugnisse verfügt, diese aber nicht monopolisiert, sondern sein Handeln bewusst einschränken lässt. Die Justiz wurde in Guastalla nicht auf ein Instrument zur Durchsetzung der fürstlichen Willkür reduziert, wie es bei einem Despoten der Fall ist. Der Hüter der Gesetze kontrolliert die Machtausübung des Monarchen und stellt die bedrohte Gerechtigkeit im Staat Guastalla wieder sicher. Die Tatsache, dass Gonzaga Rota zu schätzen weiß und dass Rota, obwohl kritisch über die Fahrlässigkeit des Prinzen, sich immer noch bereit zeigt, weiter am Hof Gonzaga zu dienen, beweist, dass am Hof nicht nur Hofschranzen wie Marinelli dienen, wie Odoardo es sich vorstellt.

Außerdem zeigt Gonzaga im ersten Akt im Gegensatz zu Odoardos Urteil politische Tugenden wie Großzügigkeit und politische Einsicht. Unter der Regie eines Despoten wäre es kaum vorstellbar, dass Odoardo die politische Ambition des Fürsten, nämlich sich Sabionetta anzueignen, vereiteln konnte. Auch wenn Gonzaga mit Odoardo politisch nicht übereinstimmt, weiß er seine Integrität zu schätzen (»Ein alter Degen; stolz und rau; sonst bieder und gut!«; *WB* 7: 297). Die Feindschaft zwischen seinem Günstling Marinelli und dem Grafen Appiani hindert ihn nicht daran, Appiani gebührend zu würdigen, und er äußert den Wunsch, gegenüber Marinelli, Appiani später am Hof einzusetzen.[12]

Lessing vermeidet es in der Tat sorgfältig, Gonzaga als politisch fragwürdig darzustellen.[13] Das Mittel, mit dem Gonzaga die Hochzeit Emilias zu sabotieren versucht, basiert nicht auf politischer Gewalt. Selbst der berüchtigte Ruf, mit dem Gonzaga als Despot gebrandmarkt wird – »Alles, Marinelli, alles was diesen Streich abwenden kann« (*WB* 7: 305) –, bezieht sich eigentlich auf die Verschiebung der Hochzeit Emilias und nicht auf einen Meuchelmord. Die Legitimität und Legalität seiner Herrschaft bleiben de facto bis zum Ende des ersten Aktes unangefochten.

Wie aus der vorangegangenen Analyse hervorgeht, ist Odoardos negative Vorstellung vom Hof Gonzaga von unbegründeten Vorurteilen verdreht. Anstatt den aufrechten Hofbeamten Rota wahrzunehmen, fixiert er seinen Blick auf den Höfling Marinelli. Odoardo kontrastiert das autarke Leben auf dem Land im idyllischen Piemont mit dem korrupten Leben am Hof Gonzaga, indem er jenes mit »befehlen«, dieses mit »dienen« kennzeichnet (*WB* 7: 312). Das Wort »befehlen« bezieht sich weniger auf die Herrschaft über andere, sondern vielmehr auf die Möglichkeit überhaupt, das eigene Leben nach dem eigenen Willen zu gestalten, wie Odoardo es lapidar zusammenfasst: »sich selbst zu leben« (*WB* 7: 312). Sein eigener Herr zu sein, sich selbst Befehle zu erteilen, anstatt auf die Befehle anderer hören und nach dem Willen anderer handeln zu müssen, ist Odoardos Lebensideal. Von diesem Ideal aus wird das Dienen am Hof einer selbst gewählten Sklaverei gleichgesetzt. Die Worte, mit denen Odoardo das Dienen am Hof beschreibt, nämlich »sich bücken, schmeicheln und kriechen« (*WB* 7: 312), legen die knechtische Akzeptanz des Herrschaftsverhältnisses, die Unterwerfung des eigenen Willens unter den fremden Willen und den Zustand der Abhängigkeit nahe. Odoardos selektive Blindheit gegenüber den positiven Facetten des politischen Lebens am Hof ergibt sich aus der radikalen Polarisierung der Gegensätzlichkeit zwischen Moral und Politik[14] und bezeugt eher seine Abneigung gegen *jegliche* Form von Herrschaft als gegen die spezifische Form der Monarchie. Immerhin bedeutet Dienen soviel wie Gehorsam, dem jedes Herrschaftsverhältnis zugrunde liegt,[15] und Gehorsam jeder Form ist für Odoardo eine Beleidigung für den eigenen freien Willen. Zwischen »sich selbst zu leben« und »sich bücken, schmeicheln und kriechen« gibt es keine andere Alternative. Wer freiwillig am Hof bleibt, der muss ein Marinelli sein.

Odoardos Gesinnungsbruder Al-Hafi sieht die zögernde Reaktion seines Freundes Nathan auf seine Einladung, sich mit ihm an den Ganges, ein anderes Piemont, zurückzuziehen, ebenfalls als fragwürdig: »Wer / Sich Knall und Fall, ihm selbst zu leben, nicht / Entschließen kann, der lebt andrer Sklav / Auf immer. [...] – Mein Weg liegt dort; und Eurer da« (*WB* 9: 540). Diesen Entschluss fasst Al-Hafi, als er mit seinem euphorischen Reformprogramm in Jerusalem gescheitert und von der Unverbesserlichkeit der politischen Welt überzeugt ist. Die apolitische Einstellung von Odoardo sowie Al-Hafi ist insofern moralisch motiviert, dass beide die Unmöglichkeit einsehen, ihr moralisch begründetes persönliches Ideal – unabhängig und frei in dieser Welt zu leben – politisch durchzusetzen. Beide sehen in der politischen Ordnung der Welt nur das Gegenteil von ihrem Egalitäts- und Freiheitsideal, nämlich die Despotie. Es ist entsprechend wenig verwunderlich, dass Odoardo in Gonzaga nur einen Despoten sieht. Alle Machthaber werden aus dem Blickwinkel des radikalen Gegensatzes von Moral und Politik unweigerlich zu Despoten. Koselleck stellt die Folgen der radikalen Moralkritik an der Politik auf folgende Weise dar: »Macht ist für den hypokritischen [d. h.: unaufrichtigen, B. L.] Aufklärer immer Mißbrauch der Macht. Daß die Macht den Mächtigen inspiriere, darum weiß er nicht. In der Perspektive des politischen Privatiers verwandelt sich Macht in Gewalt. Daraus ergab sich für den späten Aufklärer von selbst, daß ein guter Monarch schlimmer sei als ein böser, weil er die getretene Kreatur daran hindere, den Unfug des absolutistischen Prinzips zu durchschauen«.[16] Genau deshalb ist es wichtig für Odoardo, darauf zu bestehen, dass Gonzaga nicht nur ein Despot ist, sondern dazu auch vom Anfang an in moralischer Hinsicht unfair handelt.

Ob das moralische Ideal jemals innerhalb einer spezifischen Staatsverfassung zu verwirklichen ist, zum Beispiel in einer Republik, verdient eine kritische Überprüfung. Die Abklärung der Differenz, ob Odoardos Abscheu sich auf ein bestimmtes politisches System richtet, das wegen seiner institutionellen Mängel unvermeidlich zur Korruption führt, oder auf jedes politische System, das notwendig korrupt ist, hilft uns Odoardos Einstellung als eine grundsätzlich apolitische zu verstehen. Ein Vergleich mit dem Titelhelden von Lessings Tragödienfragment *Samuel Henzi* (1749) dient zur Aufklärung dieser Frage.

Odoardos Rückzug und Henzis Verschwörung kennzeichnen die apolitische beziehungsweise politische Variante des zivilen Ungehorsams.[17] Während Odoardo auf seinen Dienst am Hof und seine Teilhabe an dem politischen Leben freiwillig verzichtet, wird Henzi von dem korrupten Großen Rat Berns aus dem Amt entlassen (*WB* 1: 500). Während Odoardo sich mit einer Existenz im privaten Freiraum begnügt, denkt der seiner politischen Funktion beraubte Henzi beharrlich vom Standpunkt eines Staatsbeamten aus: »Wär jedes Amt im Staat mit einem Mann bestellt, / Der dienen kann und will; ich spräch als jener Held« (*WB* 1: 500). Mit »dienen« ist sein ganzes Denken und Handeln auf das Wohl des Vaterlands (*WB* 1: 501, 511) und vor allem die »Freiheit« der Bürger (*WB* 1: 501) *im* politischen Leben, ausgerichtet. Angesichts eines korrupten Staatsoberhaupts (von Henzi wie Odoardo auch »Wütrich« genannt; *WB* 1: 501) reagiert Henzi nicht mit einem Rückzug aufs Land, sondern er sucht engagiert Verbindungen mit seinen Mitbürgern und seinen Freunden, die seine politische Überzeugung teilen. Sein Ungehorsam gegenüber der herrschenden Regierung basiert auf einer politischen Beziehung eines Staatsbürgers zum Staat, die auf die Liebe zur eigenen politischen Gemeinschaft rekurriert.

Odoardos moralische Kritik an der Politik zielt dagegen nicht auf die Verteidigung öffentlicher Tugenden wie der Liebe zum Gemeinwohl und der bürgerlichen Freiheit. Er kümmert sich nur um seine eigene moralische Integrität. Er fokussiert sein Augenmerk einzig und allein darauf, dass das Übel des politischen Lebens nicht seine eigene moralische Integrität gefährdet. Diese Unterscheidung zwischen der öffentlichen und der privaten Tugend bildet den Ausgangspunkt für das Verständnis der Tugend als republikanischer Triebkraft.[18] Montesquieu betont ausdrücklich, dass es sich bei der republikanischen Tugend nicht um die private Moral handelt, sondern um die politische Tugend, nämlich die Liebe zum Vaterland und zur Gleichheit, die auf das Gemeinwohl zielt.[19] Odoardo, nach eigener moralischer Integrität strebend, erweist sich demnach ungeeignet für einen typischen Republikaner. Seine apolitische Haltung lässt sich mit Hannah

Arendt wie folgend zusammenfassen: »Er kommt in diese Welt, in erster Linie nicht um sie zu einem besseren Ort zum Leben zu machen, sondern um in ihr zu leben, sei sie gut oder schlecht«.[20] Daraus erklärt sich auch Odoardos Reaktion, als er von der nicht ganz anständigen Begeisterung des Prinzen für seine Tochter erfährt. Er spielt sofort mit dem Gedanken: »Das gerade wäre der Ort, wo ich am tödlichsten zu verwunden bin!« (*WB* 7: 313) Dies belegt nicht so sehr seinen egozentrischen Fokus auf die eigene Ehre.[21] Vielmehr ergibt sich daraus, dass er nur darauf bedacht ist, dass die moralische Integrität seiner Tochter und somit seine eigene nicht von der Außenwelt befleckt wird. Im Gegensatz zu Henzi liegt Odoardo die öffentliche Welt nicht am Herzen. Dass eine verdorbene und korrupte Regierung die Mitmenschen gefährden könnte, die unter dieser Regierung leben, stellt für Odoardo kein Thema dar.

Die Zivilcourage, die Odoardo gegen Gonzagas Anspruch auf das Nachbarland Sabionetta an den Tag legte, erscheint demnach in einem anderen Licht. Man erfährt, dass sich das Landgut von Odoardo fern von der Hauptstadt Guastallas und in der Nähe von Sabionetta befindet (*WB* 7: 303), dass die ganz privat gehaltene Heirat nur von ein paar Freunden aus Sabionetta besucht werden wird (*WB* 7: 310). Zudem wird kein Freund aus Guastalla bei der Hochzeit zugegen sein. Henzi kann hingegen ohne seine einheimischen Freunde sein politisches Ideal nicht in die Tat umsetzen. Das Leiden des Berner Volkes unter der Tyrannei empfindet er auch. Hätte hingegen Guastalla unter Gonzaga Unrecht erlitten, wäre Odoardo allenfalls aus der Verletzung eigener persönlichen Integrität, nicht jedoch aus der Sorge um das leidende Volk empört gewesen. Sein Widerstand gegen die Annexion Sabionettas durch Guastalla ist höchstwahrscheinlich durch keinen Sinn für politische Gerechtigkeit, sondern durch die private Sorge um seine Freunde im Nachbarland motiviert.

Die zwei zeitgenössischen Virginia-Bearbeitungen, die eine vom Engländer Henry Samuel Crisp (1754) und die andere vom Spanier Agustín Montiano y Luyando (1750), mit denen sich Lessing 1754 beschäftigt, präsentieren einander entgegengesetzte Bilder des Virginius, die dem Gegensatz zwischen Henzi und Odoardo entsprechen. Crisps Virginius ist der Inbegriff des traditionellen republikanischen Helden, ein Mann von öffentlichem Ansehen und Beredsamkeit. Er zeigt seine Verachtung gegenüber dem despotischen Decemvir auch öffentlich (*WB* 7: 856-857), während der Virginius von Montiano Odoardo nahekommt: Dort tritt Virginius in die Armee ein, »aus fester Skepsis, Entsagung und Verachtung für die politische Welt« (*WB* 3: 1092). Während der Hass des englischen Virginius dem despotischen Decemvir gilt, ist es die politische Welt als Ganzes, der der spanische Virginius den Rücken kehrt. Diese »Ehrversessenheit« des spanischen Virginius (*WB* 3: 1092) tritt ebenfalls wie Odoardo mehr für die eigene persönliche Integrität ein als für die Verteidigung des republikanischen Ideals.

Nach Koselleck fungiert im achtzehnten Jahrhundert die aus dem individuellen Gewissen gespeiste moralische Kritik am politischen Leben selbst als politischer Akt, auch wenn ihre Auswirkungen notwendigerweise auf die nicht-politische Sphäre beschränkt bleiben.[22] Diese Schlussfolgerung setzt jedoch voraus, dass der Akt der moralischen Kritik Teil der öffentlichen Meinung sei beziehungsweise den Öffentlichkeitsinstanzen bekannt werden müsse. Nur dann bringe sie den Gruppenwillen der Bürger als Mitglieder der Gesellschaft zum Ausdruck und nehme sie einen gesetzesähnlichen Charakter an, der den vom Souverän auferlegten Gesetzen in der öffentlichen Sphäre entgegenwirke.[23] Gesinnungen, die im eigenen Gewissen fundiert sind, erlangen erst dann politische Bedeutung, »wenn eine Reihe von Menschen in ihrem Gewissen übereinstimmen und [...] sich entschließen, an die Öffentlichkeit zu gehen und sich dort Gehör zu verschaffen«.[24] Aber dann hören sie auf, rein privat nur im Gewissen begründet zu sein. Im politischen Raum werden Gesinnungen zu Meinungen, die sich von anderen Meinungen nicht unterscheiden. Die Kraft der Meinung liegt in ihrer Überzeugungskraft, die durch vernünftige Rede und Kommunikation zu erzielen ist, während im Streit um die Gesinnungsfrage, wie zwischen Odoardo und Marinelli oder, weniger radikal, zwischen Al-Hafi und Nathan, nur die persönliche Entscheidung gilt. Überzeugen lässt sich der eine so wenig wie der andere. Die politische Einstellung, die sich auf das Gewissen beziehungsweise auf die Tugend stützt, stellt sich paradoxerweise als apolitisch dar.

Solange sich Odoardo und Gonzaga in ihrem eigenen privaten und politischen Bereich bewegen, kann Odoardo sein privates idyllisches Glück ungestört pflegen. Die Liebe Gonzagas für Emilia schneidet den apolitischen Odoardo aber von seiner utopischen Idylle ab und zwingt ihn dazu, sich im Wirbel des Politischen einen Ausweg zu erdenken.[25] Am Ende muss Odoardo gestehen, dass er an der Eigengesetzlichkeit des Politischen scheitert, wegen deren er gerade dem Politischen fernbleibt.

2. Keine gewaltsame Entführung

Im ersten Akt beauftragt Gonzaga Marinelli, die bevorstehende Hochzeit von Emilia zu sabotieren, damit sie nicht noch am selben Tag stattfindet. Marinelli rät Gonzaga, »mir [dem Prinzen selbst, BL] [zu] sagen, dass ich nicht vergebens sein wolle, was ich bin – Herr!« (*WB* 7: 305) Dieser Satz bezeugt Marinellis despotisches Verständnis von der politischen Macht, weist zugleich auf das staatliche Gewaltmonopol hin, das Max Weber als die Quintessenz des modernen Staates bezeichnet: »Staat ist diejenige menschliche Gemeinschaft, welche innerhalb eines bestimmten Gebietes [...] das Monopol legitimer physischer Gewaltsamkeit für sich (mit Erfolg) beansprucht. [...] [Der Staat] gilt als alleinige Quelle des ›Rechts‹ auf Gewaltsamkeit«.[26] Das staatliche Gewaltmonopol setzt den Verzicht der Staatsbürger auf die eigene Gewaltausübung voraus. Anstatt seine Rechte und Ansprüche durch die individuelle Ausübung von Zwang durchzusetzen, vertraut das Volk den Schutz seiner Interessen und Ansprüche den Justiz- und Exekutivorganen des Staates an, nämlich den Gerichten und der Regierung. Die Justiz ist verpflichtet, die ihr übertragene Kompetenz zur Gewaltanwendung im Rahmen der Gesetze zu beanspruchen. Nur unter dieser Prämisse ist ihre Gewaltanwendung legitim. Wenn die Gewaltanwendung des Herrschers gegen die Prämisse des legitimen Gewaltmonopols verstößt, begeht er einen Rechtsbruch. Ohne den Legitimität-Grund lässt sich ein Staat von einem Räuberband nicht unterscheiden, denn die geltende Rechtsordnung gründet in dem Staat und den seinem Recht transzendenten Werten,[27] während der Einsatz der Gewalt von Räubern nur ihr eigenes Interesse auf Kosten anderer verfolgt. Es ist in diesem Kontext, dass Odoardo die angebliche Illegalität der Regierung Gonzaga mit einer Räuberbande vergleicht (vgl. *WB* 7: 355, 368).

Gonzaga zeigt sich dieser Unterscheidung bewusst, indem er Marinellis »Verführung« zurückweist: »Schmeicheln Sie mir nicht mit einer Gewalt, von der ich hier keinen Gebrauch absehe« (*WB* 7: 305). Das Wort »hier« bezieht sich auf den politischen Raum, wo eine Gewaltanwendung zur Befriedigung des privaten Interesses nicht als legal gilt. Als Gonzaga erfährt, dass der Plan, Emilias Hochzeit ohne Gewaltanwendung zu sabotieren, gescheitert ist, weigert er sich weiterhin, seine Macht in bloße Gewalt umzuwandeln. In einem spöttischen Ton empfiehlt er Marinelli, dass er seiner Leibwache den Befehl geben soll, dem Mädchen an der Landstraße aufzulauern und öffentlich zu entführen (*WB* 7: 327). Darauf antwortet Marinelli, dass Emilia zwar mit Gewalt entführt wird, jedoch unter dem Vorwand einer Rettungstat (*WB* 7: 327). In dem Kommentar der Barner-Ausgabe wird an dieser Stelle auf die Parallelität mit der Virginia-Fabel hingewiesen (*WB* 7: 946), ohne jedoch auf die Abweichung von ihr einzugehen. Denn von hier an unterscheidet sich die Art und Weise, wie in *Emilia Galotti* ein Mädchen mit Gewalt entführt wird, wesentlich von ihrem Original.

In *Ab urbe condita* vollzieht sich die Entführung in zwei Gerichtsprozessen. Appius stiftet seinen Klienten Claudius dazu an, vor Gericht zu gehen und zu behaupten, Virginia sei das Kind seiner entlaufenen Sklavin und daher sein Eigentum. Appius verkündet im Gericht als Richter, dass er die Rückkehr des Vaters abwarten soll. Während dieser Zeit sollte Virginia jedoch an Claudius übergeben werden. Dieses Urteil verstößt gegen das Gesetz, das Appius selbst erließ. Er begeht folglich den ersten Rechtsbruch und verliert damit seinen legalen Status als Herrscher. In Virginius' Anwesenheit wird der Rechtsfall wieder eröffnet. Appius lässt Claudius nicht ausreden, geschweige denn, dass er Virginius Gelegenheit zur Verteidigung gibt, und er verstößt hierdurch zum zweiten Mal gegen die gesetzlichen Verfahrensregeln. Der Rechtsbruch gipfelt in seinem Rechtsspruch zugunsten der Sklaverei von Virginia. Livius weist ausdrücklich darauf hin, dass Appius' Urteil auf keinerlei Rechtsgrundlage basiert und seine Tat so unglaubhaft erscheint, dass er das Ereignis nur als »nackte Tatsache« feststellen kann.[28] Beide Rechtssprüche sind sowohl dem Schein als auch der Faktenlage nach gesetzwidrig. Appius befiehlt den Liktoren, mit gesetzlicher Gewalt die Rechtsurteile zu vollstrecken. Bei einem tatsächlichen Rechtsbruch durch die Justiz selbst wandelt sich die legitime Gewalt in bloße Gewalt; der fällt auch die Legalität von Appius' Herrschaft zum Opfer. Er darf deshalb tatsächlich als Despot gebrandmarkt werden. Marinelli dagegen führt *privat* eine Räuberbande an, um den Entführungsplan auszuführen. Räuberbanden setzen illegal, ohne staatliche Genehmigung Gewalt innerhalb eines Staates ein. Die Gewalt bei dieser Entführungstat wird nicht in Form von politischer Macht angewendet, obwohl sie sich indirekt auf Marinelli und den Prinzen stützt. Dadurch entlastet Lessing dem Prinzen de facto von der *juristischen* Schuld, Haupttäter zu sein, denn Marinelli (so wie es Lessings Absicht ist!) sorgt dafür, dass bei der Entführung keine Anwendung von der staatlichen Gewalt vorkommt: Man erinnere sich an die im Schloss zurückgebliebene Leibwache von Gonzaga.

Es steht außer Frage, dass Gonzaga indirekt für den Tod von Appiani mitverantwortlich ist. Von dem Zeitpunkt an, als Gonzaga vom Tod Appianis erfährt, ist er zweifellos bereits moralisch mitschuldig. Es ist die moralische Verpflichtung eines Monarchen, das Gemeinwohl seiner Untertanen zu schützen und zu fördern; daraus schöpft sich die Quelle der Legitimität seiner Herrschaft. Gonzaga ist durch die Verwicklung in den Meuchelmord Appianis jedoch selbst der Anlass der Gefährdung seiner persönlichen Sicherheit geworden; damit wird die moralische Legitimität seiner Herrschaft in Frage gestellt.[29] Andererseits müssen die Mittel, mit denen der Herrscher seinen moralischen Verpflichtungen nachkommt, in Form von formaler Rechtmäßigkeit und nicht vom eigenen guten Willen garantiert werden, denn Letzteres führt leicht zur Willkür. Gerade darin unterscheidet sich ein legitimer Monarch von einem Despoten. Die Legalität der Herrschaft eines Monarchen ergibt sich positiv aus der strikten Einhaltung des Gesetzes und, negativ verstanden, aus der Abwesenheit von dessen Verletzung. Das betreffende Gesetz bezieht sich auf das juristische Verfahren anstatt auf das Rechtsgefühl und Sittengesetz. In diesem Sinne ist die Herrschaft Gonzagas nach dem Tode Appianis nicht mehr legitim, allerdings noch immer legal. Es handelt sich dabei um ein sogenanntes legales Unrecht, das Gonzaga als

Herrscher begeht. Daraus erklärt sich der Umstand, dass Odoardo, dem es zwar nicht an Mut zum Tyrannenmord fehlt, am Ende aber den Rat der Gräfin Orsina nicht befolgt, bei der »erste[n], beste[n]« Gelegenheit den Tod Appianis an dem Prinzen zu rächen (WB 7: 355).

In der ersten Szene des fünften Aktes diskutieren Gonzaga und Marinelli darüber, wie sie Odoardo empfangen und ohne jeden Schein der Gewalt dazu zwingen werden, ihnen Emilia zu überlassen. Indessen beobachtet Marinelli, wie Odoardo von seiner anfänglichen Erregung zur Ruhe übergeht: »um ein Großes ruhiger ist er, – oder scheinet er. Für uns gleichviel!« (WB 7: 358) Marinelli deutet zwei Möglichkeiten an: Entweder ist die Ruhe eine aufrichtige – das heißt, Odoardo hat den Tod Appianis als einen Zufall akzeptiert und in Kauf genommen. Oder er hat sie sich selbst abgezwungen – Odoardo wird bewusst, dass die Tat ein als Raubüberfall getarnter Meuchelmord ist, traut sich dabei allerdings nicht zu, Gonzaga mit der Wahrheit zu konfrontieren. Der Schein der Ruhe könnte also auf konträre innere Motive zurückzuführen sein. Marinelli interessiert jedoch vielmehr der Schein als das hinter dem Schein liegende wahre Motiv. Dieses Desinteresse, zwischen beiden möglichen Motiven zu unterscheiden, ergibt sich daraus, dass in der öffentlichen Sphäre nur das sichtbare Handeln und nicht das unsichtbare Motiv zählt. Odoardo kann gegen Gonzaga und Marinelli die härtesten moralischen Urteile fällen, aber solange die Herrschaft Gonzagas noch legal bleibt, also noch die Form und den Schein der Legalität in Anspruch nimmt, ist Odoardo als Untertan dazu verpflichtet, der Autorität des Souveräns einen ihr gebührenden Gehorsam zu erzeigen. In der politischen Sphäre wird nach dem eigentlichen Motiv des Gehorsams nicht gefragt.

Im ersten Monolog von insgesamt drei im fünften Akt legt Odoardo den Grund seiner abgezwungenen Ruhe dar. Vor dem Treffen mit Marinelli hat Odoardo von Orsina erfahren, dass Marinelli Gonzagas Befehl gehorchend Appiani beseitigt hat, damit Gonzaga Emilia für sich allein beanspruchen kann. Odoardo hält es für glaubhaft, dass ein Meuchelmord die Absicht Gonzagas war, zumal dies seinem Bild vom Despoten entspricht: er sei »ein Wollüstling, der bewundert, begehrt« (WB 7: 313), der vor illegalen Mitteln nicht zurückschreckt. Mit dem Dolch, den Orsina ihm in die Hand gedrückt hat, will Odoardo sich an Gonzaga rächen. Es fällt ihm allerdings schwer, Gonzaga und Marinelli als die tatsächlichen Mörder rechtmäßig zu überführen. Denn obwohl die Mord-Absicht klar scheint, kann man sie jedoch aus dem Raubüberfall juristisch nicht nachweisen. Die Täter sind nach dem Überfall sofort über die Staatsgrenze geflohen und befinden sich somit außerhalb der Gerichtsbarkeit von Guastalla. Niemand, selbst Orsina nicht, kann seine Vermutung, so evident sie auch sei, als Beweis vor Gericht darlegen. Der weltliche Richter darf nicht nach der unnachweisbaren Absicht, sondern nur nach dem äußeren nachverfolgbaren Handeln urteilen. Deswegen legt Odoardo es in Gottes Hände, bei dem Mordfall Appianis Gerechtigkeit geschehen zu lassen: »Deine Sache wird ein ganz anderer zu seiner machen!« (WB 7: 359) Die weltliche Rache, die sich Odoardo vorstellen kann, zielt auf die Absicht und damit die Psyche des Mörders. So wie die Schuld Gonzagas eine innere bleibt und sich der strafrechtlichen Gerichtsbarkeit entzieht, so soll die einzig mögliche Strafe psychisch vollgezogen werden. Indem Odoardo Emilia aus der Nähe des Prinzen zu bringen beabsichtigt, versucht er zu verhindern, dass der Prinz seine ursprüngliche Absicht, die den Meuchelmord motivierte, verwirklichen kann: »Dies martere ihn mehr, als das Verbrechen!« (WB 7: 360)

Marinelli sorgt jedoch dafür, dass diese einzig mögliche Strafe auch fehlschlägt. Auf die Besorgnis von Gonzaga, Odoardo werde seine Autorität als Emilias Vater über die Tochter beanspruchen, versichert Marinelli dem Prinzen, dass er bei der Vereitelung von seinem Plan keine Gewalt außerhalb der Grenzen des Gesetzes einsetzen wird (WB 7: 359). Marinelli schlägt Odoardo zunächst vor, dass Gonzaga Emilia zurück in die Stadt begleite, welches Odoardo aufgrund seiner Rechte als Vater schroff zurückweist: »Sie soll mit mir« (WB 7: 360). Das Wort »sollen« hebt nachdrücklich hervor, dass dieser Anspruch sowohl rechtlich als auch moralisch berechtigt und legitim ist. Marinelli hatte die Reaktion des Vaters schon antizipiert und erkennt das absolute Recht des Vaters, über das Schicksal seiner Tochter zu entscheiden, zwar an, fügt jedoch hinzu, dass Odoardo »wohl erlauben müssen« werde, Emilia doch nach Guastalla bringen zu lassen (WB 7: 360). Die Entscheidung treffe nicht ihr Vater, sondern Gonzaga. Das Wort »müssen« impliziert, dass der über seine Tochter verfügende Vater zugleich als Untertan dem »Zwang« des Staates unterworfen ist.

Als Marinelli Odoardo mitteilt, dass Gonzaga über die Freiheit seiner Tochter entscheiden wird, taucht das Motiv des zivilen Ungehorsams auf. Im zweiten Monolog überlegt sich Odoardo, ob sein Widerstand gegen die Befehle des Prinzen legitim wäre:

> Mir vorschreiben, wo sie hin soll? – Mir sie vorenthalten? – Wer will das? Wer darf das? – Der hier alles darf, was er will? Gut, gut; so soll er sehen, wie viel auch ich darf, ob ich es schon nicht dürfte! Kurzsichtiger Wüterich! Mit dir will ich es wohl aufnehmen. Wer kein Gesetz achtet, ist ebenso mächtig, als wer kein Gesetz hat. (WB 7: 361)

Odoardo benutzt wie sein römisches Pendant Virginius den gleichen Rechtsgrund. Der Vater ist davon überzeugt, dass er rechtmäßig den »Vertrag« mit dieser Regierung brechen dürfe, denn mit der Verletzung des Patriarchats begeht Gonzaga offenkundig einen Rechtsbruch und verliert

Das Politikum des apolitischen Odoardo 41

dabei die legale Basis seiner Herrschaft. Ein Monarch, der »alles darf, was er will«, handelt außerhalb des Rahmens des Gesetzes und verwandelt sich in einen Despoten, dessen Willen nicht mehr mit Legitimität sowie Legalität ausgestattet wird. Die Staatsbürger sind folglich nicht mehr zum Gehorsam verpflichtet. Außerhalb der Rechtsordnung bleibt dem Staatsbürger und dem Despoten nur bloße physische Stärke. Beide sind deshalb prinzipiell gleich mächtig. Seine Gegenfigur Virginius bezeichnet den Decemvir Appius als den »einzige[n] außerhalb der Gesetze und außerhalb der bürgerlichen und der menschlichen Gemeinschaft«, weil das Gesetz dem Tyrannen als gewaltsames Mittel zur Befriedigung seiner Begierden zur Verfügung steht, sodass die Bürger um ihr Eigentum, ihr Leben und die Freiheit fürchten müssen, die durch das Gesetz hätten geschützt werden sollen. Derjenige, der eigentlich die Gesetzlichkeit sicherstellen soll, hat sie gerade durch die ihm zugewiesene juristische Kompetenz verletzt.[30]

Wenn Gonzaga, ohne einen legalen Rechtsgrund zu haben, angeordnet hätte, dass dem Vater die Vormundschaft über seine Tochter entzogen werde, handelte er genauso wie der Decemvir Appius. Mit einer gesetzeswidrigen Anordnung ginge der Verlust der Legalität seiner Herrschaft einher. Das wäre die entscheidende Voraussetzung für einen legitimen Tyrannenmord, während die Herrschaft von Gonzaga aus Odoardos Sicht schon längst vor der Entführung Emilias nicht mehr moralisch gerechtfertigt und legitim ist. Weil die fehlende Rechtfertigung als Anlass nicht hinreicht, seine Herrschaft umzustürzen, muss Odoardo warten, bis Gonzaga einen gesetzeswidrigen Befehl erteilt und dabei die Legalität seiner Herrschaft auch verliert, bevor er den Dolch ziehen darf.[31] Marinelli sorgt aber dafür, dass das Moment des Rechtbruchs ausbleibt und die Legalität der Herrschaft Gonzagas intakt bleibt.[32] Diese Intrige in der Form von einer legalen Ermittlung des Mordfalls Appiani zählt zu den originellsten dramatischen Erfindungen Lessings.

3. Der Rechtsfall Appiani

Der fünften Szene des fünften Aktes wird von der Forschung wenig Aufmerksamkeit geschenkt, obwohl sie eigentlich die Schlüsselszene des Stückes ist.[33] Marinelli ersinnt eine Ausrede, die die Entführung Emilias durch Gonzaga legitimiert, so dass Odoardo nicht die notwendigen Voraussetzungen vorfindet, den »Tyrannen« zu töten.

In der einzigen Begegnung mit Odoardo auf der Bühne zeigt Gonzaga gebührenden Respekt vor Odoardos väterlicher Autorität, indem er Odoardo die Erlaubnis erteilt, Emilia mit sich zu nehmen. Damit macht er den Eindruck, ein würdiger Monarch zu sein, der die legitimen Rechte seiner Untertanen zu schätzen weiß. Dann aber schaltet sich Marinelli ein und fordert – nicht in der Rolle eines Günstlings seines Herrschers, sondern als Kläger an den Richter –, den Überfall und die Tötung Appianis als versuchten Meuchelmord zu ermitteln. Lessing ersetzt den Rechtsfall Virginias durch den Appianis. Diese Änderung im Vergleich zur Virginia-Fabel hat nun einen anderen Handlungsablauf zur Folge.

Marinelli tut, als ob er moralisch verpflichtet sei, den Mord seines angeblich vertrautesten Freundes zu rächen. Als seine Freundschaftsbeteuerung von Odoardo in Frage gestellt wird, legt er als Beweis vor, dass der Graf sterbend ihn bestimmt hätte, seinen Tod zu rächen, und als Zeugin nennt er niemand anderen als Claudia. Sie hat Marinelli tatsächlich erzählt, dass sein Name das letzte Wort des Grafen war. Aber das Entscheidende ist nicht der Name selbst, sondern die Art und Weise, mit der Appiani ihn ausspricht: »Ich kann ihn [den Ton] nicht nachahmen, ich kann ihn nicht beschreiben: aber er enthielt alles! alles! [...] Und Marinelli, Marinelli war das letzte Wort des sterbenden Grafen! Mit einem Tone!« (*WB* 7: 338) Claudia versteht aufgrund des Tonfalls, dass Marinelli diesen Überfall inszenierte, absichtlich auf den Tod Appianis zielte und deshalb an seinem Tode schuldig ist. Das Wesen der Intonation besteht darin, dass sie nicht reproduziert werden und den öffentlichen Raum nicht erreichen kann, was Claudia bedauert: »Ha, könnt ich ihn nur vor Gerichte stellen, diesen Ton!« (*WB* 7: 338) Im öffentlichen Raum, vor dem Gericht, wird nicht klar, ob die letzten Worte Appianis Marinelli als seinen Freund anrufen oder ihn eines Mordes beschuldigen. Dort können nur Worte weitergegeben werden, wobei man ihre Bedeutung lediglich aus der eigenen Perspektive auslegen kann, ohne ihre eigentliche Bedeutung mit Gewissheit nachweisen zu können. Selbst Claudia muss lange zögern und abwägen, bis sie schließlich die wahre Bedeutung des Tonfalls für gewiss hält. Von der evidenten Gültigkeit ihrer Schlussfolgerung kann sie aber niemanden mit nachprüfbaren Beweisen überzeugen. Dies nutzt Marinelli aus. Er manipuliert sogar die Aussage Claudias, indem er ihr nachdrücklich wiederholtes »mit einem Ton«, was sie wiederum mit einer Intonation ausspricht, die ihre überraschte Entdeckung der Wahrheit demonstriert und ihre Wut auf den Mörder zum Ausdruckt bringt, eigenmächtig als Beweis für die Freundschaft zwischen ihm und Appiani deutet.

Marinellis Intrige kann deswegen nicht widersprochen werden, weil der einzige Nachweis für seine Schuld, nämlich die Intonation von Appianis Worten, in der öffentlichen Sphäre keine Geltung beanspruchen kann, und auch weil sich das gesamte öffentliche Leben im Bereich des Scheins abspielt. Was in der öffentlichen Sphäre zählt, sind Worte und Handlungen, aus deren Interpretationen keine unumstrittene Evidenz abzugewinnen ist. Die Kraft der Interpretation basiert nicht auf einer evidenten Wahrheit, die wie Werturteile des Gewissens unter Freunden unmittelbar einleuchtend bleibt, sondern sie wirkt vielmehr als eine Meinung, die jeder abhängig

Das Politikum des apolitischen Odoardo

von der eignen Lage bilden kann. Selbst Gonzaga muss sich dieser Eigengesetzlichkeit des öffentlichen Raums unterwerfen, da er fürchten muss, als Verehrer von Emilia dem Verdacht nicht entrinnen zu können, vor der Öffentlichkeit als der Drahtzieher der Ermordung Appianis zu erscheinen, obwohl er den Tod Appianis nicht arrangiert und ursprünglich auch nicht gewollt hat (*WB* 7: 342).

Insofern lässt sich der Rechtsfall Appiani in einen Zusammenhang mit dem apolitischen Lebensideal Odoardos bringen: Aus dem eigenen Gewissen wird die Evidenz des moralischen Urteils abgeleitet. Ob die Schlussfolgerungen, die aufgrund des eigenen Gewissens gezogen werden, für andere auch gelten, hängt ganz davon ab, ob der andere auch aus reinem Gewissen denkt und handelt. Für denjenigen/diejenige, der/die nicht auf gleiche Weise denkt und handelt, ist die Wahrheit weder einleuchtend, noch kann sie den anderen nachgewiesen werden.[34] Aus dieser Eigenschaft des Gewissens lassen sich erhebliche politische Konsequenzen ziehen.

Erstens kann und soll das Gewissen nicht politisiert werden, denn man kann nicht alle gleichermaßen zu Gewissensfragen zwingen, um damit zur gleichen Schlussfolgerung zu kommen. Eines der wesentlichen Elemente des politischen Lebens besteht darin, diejenigen, mit denen man nicht einverstanden ist, durch sprachliche Mittel zu überzeugen und somit zu einem Konsens zu kommen. Eine auf dem Gewissen beruhende Gemeinschaft kann nicht durch rationale Überzeugungen errichtet werden.[35] Deswegen entsteht eine Freundschaft nicht durch Überredung und Argumentation, sondern vor allem durch die unmittelbare Evidenz der Aufrichtigkeit des Gegenübers.[36] Die an Unmöglichkeit grenzende Schwierigkeit, Marinellis Behauptung über seine Freundschaft mit Appiani zu widerlegen, ist ein eindeutiger Beweis dafür. Es ist auch von Bedeutung, dass zwischen Odoardo und Appiani, den beiden Seelenfreunden, kein Wort auf der Bühne gewechselt wird, denn ihre Freundschaft bedarf keiner Beteuerung, weil sie in Gefühlsausdrücken wie Umarmungen mit Händen zu greifen ist. Die Affinität Gonzagas zur bürgerlichen Lebensform lässt sich ebenfalls nicht rational begründen und ist allenfalls auf eine individuelle Neigung zurückzuführen. Diese tugendhafte Gesinnung nämlich, nach seinem Gewissen zu leben, bleibt auf den privaten Bereich beschränkt und kann nicht als Modell für die Öffentlichkeit verallgemeinert werden. Zweitens ist das Leben nach dem eigenen Gewissen, die Gestaltung des Lebens nach dem eigenen Willen, auch Ausdruck einer persönlichen Vision, die Werte und Ideale betrifft, deren Erfüllung auch ohne die Teilnahme am politischen Leben erreicht werden kann. Odoardo ist zwar Staatsbürger des Fürstentums Guastalla, führt jedoch sein Leben ungestört am Rande des Landes. Die Grenze zwischen dem nur »sich selbst leben« wollenden Individuum und dem öffentlichen Leben stellt das Gesetz dar. Erhöbe das moralische

Ideal den Anspruch, Maßstab des weltlichen Gesetzes zu sein, würde dies unweigerlich zum absoluten Krieg der Gerechten gegen alle anderen führen. So wie das Gesetz das Gewissen in die Schranken verweist, hat das Gewissen keinen Grund, einen öffentlichen Angriff gegen die politische Sphäre zu unternehmen, solange diese rechtmäßig bliebe.

Bisher richtet sich der Fokus von Marinellis Intrige scheinbar auf den Tod Appianis. Emilia bleibt als Opfer in diesem Rechtsfall juristisch irrelevant. Allerdings behauptet Marinelli, dass laut Gerüchten Appiani von einem von Emilia begünstigten Nebenbuhler und unter ihrer Komplizenschaft ermordet worden wäre (WB 7: 364-365). Inspiriert wird Marinelli durch die Aussage von Orsina, deren Kundschafter den Annäherungsversuch Gonzagas in der Kirche als ein vertrauliches Liebesgespräch interpretiert hatte (WB 7: 355). Die einseitige Liebeserklärung Gonzagas hätte dazu führen können, dass Orsina als seine verratene Geliebte ein Komplott der beiden vermutet. Unterschiedliche Vermutungen über das Motiv für ein- und dasselbe Ereignis führen wiederum zu konträren Schlussfolgerungen. Marinelli stellt die Komplizenschaft Emilias nur als eine unwahrscheinliche Möglichkeit vor, die jedoch schwerwiegende juristische Konsequenzen nach sich ziehen könnte. Denn dadurch wird Emilia als (aus rein juristischer Sicht) Verdächtige in den Rechtsfall Appiani verwickelt und muss sie vor dem Gericht ihre Unschuld beweisen. Auf diesem indirekten Rechtsweg wird Emilia der Verantwortung des Gerichts unterworfen und mit legalen Mitteln dem Schutz ihres Vaters entrissen.

Marinelli bittet Gonzaga als Richter im Namen der verfahrensrechtlichen »Gerechtigkeit«[37] Emilia von ihren Eltern zu trennen und in die Stadt zu einem Gerichtsprozess einzuliefern. Odoardo meint, jetzt zeige Gonzaga das wahre Gesicht eines Tyrannen, indem er Emilia als Mittäterin schuldig spricht und somit einen Rechtsbruch begeht. Als Gonzaga auf ihn zukommt, greift Odoardo nach seinem Dolch, bereit um ihn in dem Moment des Gesetzesverstoßes zu töten:

> MARINELLI [...] Die Form des Verhörs erfodert diese Vorsichtigkeit schlechterdings. Und es tut mir leid, gnädiger Herr, daß ich mich gezwungen sehe, ausdrücklich darauf anzutragen, wenigstens Emilien in eine besondere Verwahrung zu bringen.
> ODOARDO Besondere Verwahrung? – Prinz! Prinz! – Doch ja; freilich, freilich! Ganz recht: in eine besondere Verwahrung! Nicht, Prinz? nicht? – O wie fein die Gerechtigkeit ist! Vortrefflich! *fährt schnell nach dem Schubsacke, in welchem er den Dolch hat*
> DER PRINZ *schmeichelhaft auf ihn zutretend*: Fassen Sie sich, lieber Galotti – ODOARDO *bei Seite, indem er die Hand leer wieder heraus zieht*: Das sprach sein Engel! (WB 7: 365)

Gonzaga beruhigt Odoardo »schmeichelhaft« und versichert ihm, Emilia anstatt ins Gefängnis zu werfen »in eine besondere Verwahrung zu bringen«, nämlich in das Haus eines unparteiischen Dritten, seines Kanzlers Grimaldi (*WB* 7: 365). Seine Absicht ist jedem Leser erkennbar: Es ist in der Vorstellung des Prinzen der *locus amoenus*, wo er sich in Emilia verliebte. Das Haus Grimaldi steht für die verdorbenen höfischen Werte, die Odoardo und Emilia verabscheuen (obwohl Emilia sich von der sinnlichen Welt zugleich auch angezogen fühlt). Dem Schein nach werden die moralischen Werte der Gesetze durch die Verfahrensgerechtigkeit nicht beschädigt: »Hier ist die Strenge der Gesetze mit der Achtung gegen unbescholtene Tugend leicht zu vereinigen« (*WB* 7: 365), wie es Gonzaga formuliert. Während Appius Virginia dazu verurteilt, Claudius' Sklavin zu werden, und den Liktoren den Befehl gibt, sie mit Gewalt vom Vater wegzuraffen, gewährt Gonzaga Emilia eine anständige Behandlung und Odoardo die größtmögliche bürgerliche Freiheit: »Sie selbst, Galotti, mit sich, können es halten, wie Sie wollen. [...] Es wäre lächerlich, Ihnen vorzuschreiben« (*WB* 7: 366). Emilias rechtlicher Status bleibt bis zu ihrem Tod unentschieden. Gonzaga spricht sie *noch* nicht schuldig. Es ist umgekehrt Odoardo, der darauf besteht, dass Emilia in dem tiefsten Kerker eingesperrt werden soll. Denn nur dadurch wäre ein Mord an Gonzaga berechtigt.

Odoardo muss am Ende feststellen, dass sein »Voraussehen« mit der Realität nicht übereinstimmt (*WB* 7: 364). Er hatte erwartet, dass Gonzaga seine öffentliche Macht missbrauchen würde, aber Gonzaga übt sie dank der Intrige von Marinelli ganz legal aus. Von dem Zeitpunkt der Ermordung Appianis an bis zu dem Zeitpunkt, als Odoardo sich einverstanden erklärt, Emilia Gonzaga zu überlassen, laufen alle Gräueltaten ohne den illegalen Einsatz staatlicher Gewalt und unter Beibehaltung des Scheines der Rechtmäßigkeit ab. Selbst wenn Odoardo den Mord an Appiani strafrechtlich verfolgen lassen sollte und Gonzaga vor ein höheres weltliches Gericht gestellt würde,[38] wäre Gonzaga die von Odoardo gewünschte juristische Sanktion wohl erspart geblieben: Er wäre nur für seine Nachlässigkeit, nicht aber für die strafrechtliche Verantwortlichkeit haftbar gewesen.

Als einzige kompetente richterliche Instanzen, die diesen Rechtsfall mit absoluter Evidenz entscheiden könnten, bleiben nur das eigene Gewissen und Gott übrig. Denn Menschen können nur über äußere Taten richten, Gott allein durchschaut das Innere.[39] Da Odoardo davon überzeugt ist, dass Gonzaga als skrupelloser Despot kein Gewissen besitzt, kann er sich nur auf die Autorität des göttlichen Richters berufen, um dem Tod Emilias und Appianis Gerechtigkeit widerfahren zu lassen (*WB* 7: 359, 371).

* * *

Das apolitische Lebensideal von Odoardo, in einer Gesinnungsgemeinschaft in Übereinstimmung mit dem eigenen moralischen Willen zu leben, in der ohne Herrschaft doch Ordnung herrscht, wie das Bild der Ameisengesellschaft in den *Freimäurergesprächen* es illustriert (*WB* 10: 23), setzt jedoch eine entscheidende Bedingung voraus, nämlich dass jeder »sich selbst zu regieren weiß« (*WB* 10: 23) und jeder seinem eigenen Gewissen gehorcht. Dagegen ist im politischen Raum Ordnung nur auf Kosten der absoluten Freiheit des Gewissens im Herrschaftsverhältnis zu verwirklichen. Das aufklärerische Autonomie-Ideal Odoardos liegt der Negation des Eigenwertes des Politischen zugrunde. Indem Lessing absichtlich vermeidet, Gonzaga als einen Despoten darzustellen, und indem er das Zerrbild Odoardos von ihm als Despoten sichtlich hervorhebt, weist Lessing auf die problematischen Konsequenzen hin, die es gibt, wenn man diese unvermeidlichen moralischen Übel als »unmoralische Willkür« wahrnimmt.[40] Das Bild der legitimen Regierung von Gonzaga vor dem Mordanfall Appianis erklärt Lessings kritische Distanz zur moralischen Vernunftkritik über das Politische.[41] Ein Staatsumsturz bleibt in *Emilia Galotti* aus, Odoardo erdolcht den Prinzen nicht, nicht weil Lessing unpolitisch denkt, sondern weil er die politische Lösung der unvermeidlichen politischen Übel für eine unrealistische Alternative hält.

Indem Lessing eine verwickelte Geschichte über die Ermordung Appianis und die darauffolgende problematische Ermittlung dieser Tat konstruiert, zeigt er seine Skepsis, dass das moralische Übel institutionell zu bewältigen ist. Denn die Unmöglichkeit, die Wahrheit dieses Falls juristisch festzustellen, hängt mit der Eigengesetzlichkeit des Politischen zusammen, nämlich dass in der Öffentlichkeit statt unsichtbarer innerer Motive, sei es aus Gewissen oder Kalkulation, nur sichtbare Taten gelten, was in diesem Fall schließlich zur Trennung zwischen dem, was legal, und dem, was legitim ist, führt. Dies zählt zu den »unvermeidlichen Übeln«, die jeder Form von politischer Verfassung innewohnen, »ohne welche auch der glücklichste Bürger nicht sein kann« (*WB* 10: 37). Sie »gehör[en] zur Struktur der geschichtlichen Realität«.[42] Koselleck zufolge zeigt sich Lessing eben durch diese Einsicht als ein genuin politischer Denker.

Odoardos Tyrannenmord scheitert an der Legalität der »Entführung« Emilias. Ihm bleibt nichts anderes übrig als den Tod der eigenen Tochter zu bewirken, um auf Kosten des Lebens seiner Tochter sein apolitisches Ideal der Autonomie zu bewahren. Das ist der dem Text zugrundeliegende Skandal. Die Absurdität der Logik zeigt die problematische Seite dieses Ideals. Für eine adäquate Vorstellung des Politischen muss man auf *Ernst und Falk* und *Nathan der Weise* warten.

Peking University

1 Alle Hinweise auf Lessings Texte beziehen sich auf die folgende Ausgabe: Gotthold Ephraim Lessing, Werke und Briefe in zwölf Bänden, hg. von Wilfried Barner u. a., Frankfurt a. M. 1985-2003, zitiert mit der Sigle WB und Band- und Seitenangabe.
2 Vgl. dazu Lessings Brief an Nicolai vom 21. Jan. 1758, WB 11/1: 267; die unterschiedlichen Forschungspositionen zur politischen Problematik in *Emilia Galotti* analysiert Monika Fick in: Lessing Handbuch. Leben – Werk – Wirkung, 4. Aufl., Stuttgart 2016, S. 365-366.
3 Vgl. Peter Szondi, Die Theorie des bürgerlichen Trauerspiels im 18. Jahrhundert, Frankfurt a. M. 1973, S. 167; Gert Mattenklott, Drama – Von Gottsched bis Lessing, in: H. A. Glaser (Hg.), Deutsche Literatur. Eine Sozialgeschichte, Bd. 4, Reinbek 1980, S. 130-147 und 295; Simonetta Sanna, Lessings »Emilia Galotti«, Tübingen 1988, S. 87.
4 Vgl. Fick (Anm. 2), S. 365-366.
5 Vgl. Peter André Alt, Tragödie der Aufklärung, Tübingen 1994, S. 265; H. B. Nisbet, Lessing. Eine Biographie, übers. von K. S. Guthke, München 2008, S. 656-657.
6 Vgl. Gisbert Ter-Nedden, Lessings Trauerspiele. Der Ursprung des modernen Dramas aus dem Geist der Kritik, Stuttgart 1986, S. 228-229.
7 Fick (Anm. 2), S. 366.
8 Vgl. Montesquieu, The Spirit of the Laws, übers. und hg. von Anne M. Cohler u. a., Cambridge 1989, Buch 2, Kap. 1, S. 10.
9 Vgl. Montesquieu (Anm. 8), Buch 2, Kap. 4., S. 17-18.
10 Ter-Nedden arbeitet den Sinn des sprechenden Namens »Rota« heraus. Es soll aus »Sacra Romana Rota« stammen, der kreisrunden Richterbank, dem Namen des obersten päpstlichen Gerichts. Rota wiederum ist für die Gesetzlichkeit des Staates zuständig. Vgl. Ter-Nedden, Der fremde Lessing. Eine Revision des dramatischen Werks, hg. von Robert Vellusig, Göttingen 2016, S. 342.
11 Vgl. dazu auch Fick (Anm. 2), S. 366.
12 Nisbet (Anm. 5, S. 655) ist der Meinung, dass der Prinz Marinelli viel nähersteht als Rota, wobei er übersieht, dass Marinelli nur für das private Leben des Prinzen zuständig ist, während Rota sich um das politisch-öffentliche Leben des Staates kümmert.
13 Ter-Nedden (Anm. 6, S. 186-187) ist einer der wenigen, die die Ansicht vertreten, dass Lessing nicht beabsichtigt, Gonzaga als Despoten darzustellen.
14 Vgl. Reinhart Koselleck, Kritik und Krise. Eine Studie zur Pathogenese der bürgerlichen Welt, Frankfurt a. M. 1973, S. 48.
15 Herrschaft bezeichnet »ein auf Dauer angelegtes [...] Über- und Unterordnungsverhältnis zwischen Herrschenden und Beherrschten«. Siehe Martin Hartmann und Claus Offe (Hg.), Politische Theorie und Politische Philosophie. Ein Handbuch, München 2011, S. 219.
16 Koselleck (Anm. 14), S. 99. In einer dazugehörigen Anmerkung zitiert Koselleck die Spätaufklärer Diderot und Rousseau (S. 205, Anmerkung 197) und rechnet beide der Kategorie der hypokritischen Aufklärung zu (vgl. zu Rousseau auch S. 135). Lessing, der einen Monarchen im positiven Licht darstellt, distanziert sich insofern von dieser aufklärerischen Einstellung. Der Begriff Hypokrisie bezieht sich bei Koselleck auf die politische Motivation der von den Aufklärern be-

haupteten neutralen und unpolitischen Kritik (vgl. S. 81-82), die an den wahren Intentionen des Monarchen kein Interesse hat. Odoardo trennt die Moral von der Politik zwar genau so gründlich wie »die hypokritischen Aufklärer«, erstrebt allerdings gerade keine totale Moralisierung des Politischen, wie ich weiter unten zeigen werde.

17 Die Begriffe stammen aus: Hannah Arendt, Civil Disobedience, in: Crises of the Republic, New York 1972, S. 49-102.
18 Vgl. Montesquieu (Anm. 8), Buch III, Kap. 3, S. 22.
19 Vgl. Montesquieu (Anm. 8), Buch III, Kap. 5, Anmerkung, S. 25.
20 Arendt (Anm. 17), S. 60, eigene Übersetzung.
21 Vgl. Ter-Nedden (Anm. 5), S. 199.
22 Vgl. Koselleck (Anm. 14), S. 58 und passim.
23 Koselleck (Anm. 14), S. 45.
24 Arendt (Anm. 17), S. 67-68, meine Übersetzung.
25 Die Einsicht in die Ubiquität des Politischen sieht Wilfried Wilms als etwas fundamental Neues in Lessings politischem Denken, das sich in *Emilia Galotti* manifestiert. Vgl. ders., On the Political Productivity of a Paradox in Lessing's Drama, in: Lessing Yearbook, Bd. 35 (2003), S. 61-78, hier S. 70.
26 Max Weber, Politik als Beruf, 11. Aufl., Berlin 2010, S. 8.
27 Vgl. H. Hofmann, Legalität, Legitimität, in: Joachim Ritter u. a. (Hg.), Historisches Wörterbuch der Philosophie, Bd. 5, Basel 1971-2007, S. 163.
28 Titus Livius, Römische Geschichte. Buch I-III, hg. von Hans Jürgen Hillen, übers. von Josef Feix, 4 Aufl., München 2007, S. 425.
29 Fick (Anm. 2), S. 367.
30 Livius (Anm. 28), S. 449.
31 Ob Odoardos eventueller Mordanschlag auf Gonzaga als ein Tyrannenmord bezeichnet werden darf, ist umstritten. Ein Tyrannenmord ist politisch motiviert und setzt zahlreiche Umstände voraus, wie zum Beispiel, dass der Herrscher das Volk und die Bürger auf Dauer unterdrückt, und der Mord im Namen der Gemeinschaft begangen werden muss. Nach Thomas v. Aquin ist der Tyrannenmord aus persönlicher Initiative nicht erlaubt. Zur Begründung gibt v. Aquin an, solchen Attentätern sei jede Herrschaft, auch die guter Fürsten, lästig, und das Volk könne auf diese Weise auch einen guten Herrn verlieren. Vgl. Rudolf Sieverts u. a. (Hg.), Handwörterbuch der Kriminologie, Bd. 4, Berlin 1979, S. 166-167. Über die Legitimität der Gewaltanwendung siehe auch Carl Niekerk, Enlightened Citizenship in Lessing's Emilia Galotti and Mozart's Lucio Silla, in: Nobert Bachleitner u. a. (Hg.), Taking Stock: Twenty-Five Years of Comparative Literary Research, Leiden / Boston 2020, S. 156-186, hier S. 172-173.
32 Ter-Nedden bemerkt dazu auch, dass »[z]um Tyrannenmord hier nicht der mutige Bürger, sondern der Tyrann und der Ausnamezustand despotischer Gewaltherrschaft« fehlen. Siehe ders. (Anm. 5), S. 166.
33 Vgl. Friedrich Vollhardt, Gotthold Ephraim Lessing. Epoche und Werk, Göttingen 2018, S. 285.
34 Vgl. Arendt (Anm. 17), S. 64.
35 Ilsa Graham redet von »Vision des Geistes«, die in der Wirklichkeit, in der feindlichen Welt nicht verwirklicht werden kann. Handlungsbezogene Bilder wie Hand, Zeitgefühl sind Symbole für das Medium, in dem der reine Geist

verlorengeht. Siehe dies., Geist ohne Medium. Zu Lessings ›Emilia Galotti‹, in: Gerhard und Sibylle Bauer (Hg.), Gotthold Ephraim Lessing, Darmstadt 1986, S. 362-375.
36 Vgl. Baiyu Lu, Lessings Freundschaftsbegriff in seinen dramatischen und dialogischen Werken, Würzburg 2014, S. 38-44.
37 Das Wort »Gerechtigkeit« kommt in der vierten Szene des fünften Akts viermal vor. Gonzaga spricht auch von der »Strenge der Gesetze« (WB 7: 365). Marinelli unterscheidet absichtlich nicht zwischen der formalen und sittlichen Gerechtigkeit, wobei Odoardo dies mit Bitterkeit zwar durchschaut, eine Trennung allerdings auch unmöglich unternehmen kann.
38 Appiani versteht sich selbst nicht als Sklave von Gonzaga, sondern als »der Vasall eines größern Herrn« (WB 7: 324).
39 Vgl. Koselleck (Anm. 14), S. 163. In dieser längeren Fußnote blickt Koselleck auf die Trennung von Innen und Außen in der abendländischen Tradition zurück. Koselleck zufolge erkennt die christliche Tradition die Autonomie der politischen Welt an bis auf die radikalen Puritaner, die das Verhältnis vom Innen und Außen zum reinen Gegensatz simplifizierten, den Gegensatz mit dem des Gewissens und der bösen Welt gleichsetzten und auf die Aufhebung der letzteren zielten. Koselleck sieht zweifellos die Aufklärer mit ihrer Vernunftkritik als Nachfolger dieser puritanischen Strömung.
40 Koselleck (Anm. 14), S. 70.
41 Marion Heinz verteidigt in ihrer kritischen Auseinandersetzung mit Koselleck das aufklärerische Erbe, indem sie der Vernunftkritik die allgemeine Dimension, sowohl im moralischen als auch im politischen Bereich, einräumt und somit die Eigengesetzlichkeit des Politischen, die Koselleck in Anlehnung an Carl Schmitt befürwortet, bestreitet. Aufklärer wollen ihre politischen Gegner als Gesinnungsfeinde ausblenden, anstatt sie als Teilnehmer am Politischen zu akzeptieren. Die transzendente, übergeschichtliche Vernunft solle als Norm der Beurteilung über das Faktische (Politik und Moral) festgesetzt werden. Heinz bezeichnet diesen Prozess gegen die Aufklärung als »unfair« und ihre Prämissen als »unbegründet«. Vgl. Marion Heinz, Reinhart Koselleck, Kritik und Krise. Eine Studie zur Pathogenese der bürgerlichen Welt (1959), in: Aufklärung, Bd. 35 (2024), S. 143-161, hier vor allem S. 155 und 160 (Zitate). Den Hinweis auf den Artikel verdanke ich Prof. Friedrich Vollhardt.
42 Koselleck (Anm. 14), S. 70.

Sophocles's *Philoctetes* and the Hidden Structure of Lessing's *Laokoon*: The Moral Aesthetic of the Scream

Ellwood Wiggins

Gotthold Ephraim Lessing's *Laokoon, oder Über die Grenzen der Malerei und Poesie* (1766) is famous for its incisive distinction between the visual and poetic arts. For generations, students have memorized Lessing's lucid explanation: painting depicts bodies and hence is a matter of extension in space while poetry represents actions and thus must unfold in time, as explained cogently in chapter XVI. Those who venture further into the *Laokoon* soon lose the thread of this clear distinction and find themselves puzzled by obscure tangents, vehement polemics, and indulgent digressions. Scholars such as David Wellbery and Carol Jacobs have long tried to make sense of the bewildering organization of Lessing's work. This essay builds on the work of these and others, but follows a different hermeneutical clue. It traces the appearances of Sophocles's *Philoctetes* in the text, and claims that the performance of this tragedy reveals an organizing dramatic structure to the text as a whole.[1] The drama of *Philoctetes* is reenacted in the serpentine lines of Lessing's argument, which is cut off with a necessary if anti-climactic *deus ex machina*. The theoretical achievement of the *Laokoon* is both amplified and undermined in illuminating ways by the figure of the snakebit archer.

Philoctetes's presence does not merely suggest an underlying structural dynamic to Lessing's treatise. It also makes clear the hidden ethical claim of the text.[2] *Laokoon* has most often been read solely as a contribution to aesthetic, semiotic, or antiquarian debates, but the intertextual drama with Sophocles's tragedy reveals a central moral commitment.[3] It turns out that Lessing's fine distinctions between linguistic and visual representation are inextricably involved in our most important ethical obligations to one another as humans. Lessing seems to derive his »laws« of beauty from purely formal considerations, but these rules rest on a more fundamental, though never explicitly articulated, performative moral linked to Philoctetes's incorporation into the text. The stakes of this argument are not limited to the limits of poetry and art, but rather speak to the most basic responsibilities of human interaction.

This essay argues for the centrality of *Philoctetes* for both the formal structure and the theoretical contentions of Lessing's text. After briefly recalling the dramatic structure of Sophocles's tragedy, it becomes possible to trace the dynamic of Philoctetes's appearances in the initial four chapters of the *Laokoon*. The four patterns documented in these passages on

Philoctetes are mirrored in the construction of the fourth chapter, and then again in the organization of the entire *Laokoon*. In conclusion, though the treatise seems to end with an abrupt impasse, I claim that Sophocles's dance in *Laokoon*'s final footnote is both a coda and a productive if dissonant resolution to the intractable paradoxes Lessing's text has been teasing apart. The author of *Philoctetes* himself appears as a *deus ex machina* to save the *Laokoon* from suffering the fate of its namesake: being torn apart limb from limb by writhing, serpentine contradictions.

Sophocles's Philoctetes

Philoctetes was an archer among the Greek warriors headed for Troy when a snake bit his foot. The wound festered and refused to heal. Philoctetes's cries of anguish were so loud and the stench of his rotting flesh so foul that his disgusted comrades were hindered from the performance of religious rites. The Greeks abandoned Philoctetes on the island of Lemnos and forgot about him. Nine years later, after Hector, Achilles, and Ajax have all died and the war drags on with no end in sight, an oracle prophesied that Troy would only fall with the help of Philoctetes and his bow, which had been a gift from Heracles. All three great Attic tragedians wrote a *Philoctetes* tragedy in which Odysseus must bring the bitter archer back to Troy. In Sophocles's version, the only complete one to survive, Odysseus brings Achilles's son Neoptolemus along and convinces the young hero to trick Philoctetes into giving him the bow. The plan backfires when Neoptolemus is so moved with pity for the suffering Philoctetes that he renounces deception, returns the bow, and determines to be an honest hero. To judge from Lessing's detailed summary of the play, one would assume that the tragedy ends at this point – a detail that will prove decisive to my reading of the *Laokoon* – but Sophocles's drama is far from over. No amount of persuasion or promise of a cure can convince Philoctetes to join the Greeks, and only the *deus ex machina* of Heracles's appearance finally resolves the stand-off.

There are two contradictory ways to read Sophocles's *Philoctetes*. A common interpretation of the play involves a story of Neoptolemus coming to know himself and his true heroic nature of honest straightforwardness by means of his compassion for the noble, suffering Philoctetes. In this reading, Neoptolemus's pity for Philoctetes is instrumental in the moral education of the hero. Humanism triumphs.[4] But another interpretation also suggests itself. The very fact that the play has to end in a *deus ex machina* shows the limits of rational discourse and human sentiment. Unlike Achilles with Priam in the final book of the *Iliad*, Philoctetes refuses to let his anger for his enemy be converted into pity. As soon as he gets the bow back, Philoctetes tries to shoot Odysseus and Neoptolemus is unable to persuade

Philoctetes to rejoin the Greeks. In fact, the old man manages to convince Neoptolemus to accompany him in desertion and betrayal. Without the divine appearance of Heracles, the play would have ended in abject failure: all of Neoptolemus's newfound heroic virtue is no match for Philoctetes's hatred.

One of the great strengths of Sophocles's play is that it allows for both the triumphant humanist reading of the power of pity and the sober reflection on the limits of human agency, virtue, and rational discourse. Lessing, like other influential eighteenth-century interpreters of *Philoctetes* seems to plump for the former reading in which pity is an unalloyed force for virtue and edification. Yet instead of doing so by attempting to erase the limits of rationality, by making language and persuasion work again with no uncomfortable remainder, Lessing emphasizes the limits of rational discourse – by reveling in Philoctetes's screams in which articulation and the entire system of language break down.

The Dramatic Structure of Laokoon *1-4*

The main business of the *Laokoon* according to its subtitle and introduction is to elucidate the limits between the visual and poetic arts. Lessing has two handy exempla to guide this study: the eponymous statuary group of the Trojan priest with his sons, and the narrative description of the same scene from Virgil's *Aeneid*. Why is Virgil's Laocoon allowed to scream and wail while the sculptor's Laocoon can get away with a sigh? Yet throughout the first books of Lessing's *Laokoon*, Philoctetes upstages the title character. One tends to forget that though the essay is launched as a polemic against Winckelmann, Lessing does not in fact disagree with the art critic's claims about the Laocoon statue. Instead, it is an offhand remark about Philoctetes to which he dedicates his very first scathing criticisms. Philoctetes is absolutely crucial not only to the beginning of the text, but he holds together and organizes the treatise as modeled in the first four chapters.

In the first chapter, Philoctetes establishes the naturalness of screaming, the untheatricality of stoicism, and the expressivity necessary for sympathy. This allows the second chapter to deduce beauty as a law of the visual arts – under the unspoken assumption that sympathy is the purpose of all the arts. This second chapter closes with Lessing imagining what a lost ancient sculpture of Philoctetes would have looked like. The third chapter follows up on this by proposing the pregnant moment for visual arts: an artist must choose precisely that frozen time-point to represent that will spur the greatest motion in the imagination of the viewer. The fourth chapter then caps all this off by admitting that dramas share properties of both visual and narrative art and engages in a long analysis of sympathy in Sophocles's

Philoctetes. The lame Greek archer thus motivates all the theoretical inquiries that propel the plot of these four chapters. This trajectory is reflected in the overall structure of the whole book, and it is instructive to examine each turn in detail.

Chapter One: »To Give Suffering Nature her due«

The first chapter takes the logical form of a reductio ad absurdum. Lessing introduces Winckelmann's explanation for the expression on the Laocoon statue's face and then proceeds to show all the ways this assumption would lead to contradictions. The final paragraph then demands »einen andern Grund« (*WB* 5/2: 22)[5] for Laocoon's appearance. *Philoctetes* provides more grounds for Lessing's objections than any other single source. Philoctetes's appearances in this first chapter predetermine the course of the entire text, blur the clear lines of argumentation to come, and speak to issues that Lessing was later criticized for leaving out.

Like all Lessing's great works, the *Laokoon* thrives on polemics. The *Laokoon* opens with an extensive quotation from J. J. Winckelmann's *Gedanken über die Nachahmung der griechischen Werke in der Malerei und Bildhauerkunst* (1755). In this essay, the father of art history had coined the famous motto for a classicizing view of Greek antiquity: »edle Einfalt und stille Grösse.« But Lessing does not take issue with this sweeping judgment.[6] In fact, he follows the long citation with an entire paragraph about all the points of agreement he has with Winckelmann. Everything the art critic says about the Laocoon statue finds Lessing's approval, except that »in dem Grunde, welchen Herr Winckelmann dieser Weisheit giebt […] wage ich es, anderer Meinung zu sein« (*WB* 5/2: 18). Two things bother Lessing: »der mißbilligende Seitenblick« Winckelmann throws at Virgil, and the comparison with Philoctetes: »Von hier [Philoktet] will ich ausgehen, und meine Gedanken in eben der Ordnung niederschreiben, in welcher sie sich bey mir entwickelt« (*WB* 5/2: 18). This sentence divulges the organizing principle and modus operandi at work in the *Laokoon*. Lessing expressly makes Philoctetes the starting point for the entire treatise, which is set up from the beginning as a contest. Since he then claims that he will proceed by recording his thoughts just as they occur, the *agon* of the text is configured as a race course, albeit a meandering one. Though Philoctetes proves to be, quite literally, a stumbling block to the plans of Odysseus in the play, he is the starting block that allows *Laokoon* to take off. In Lessing's conceit of a stream-of-consciousness composition, it would not be fallacious to claim that Philoctetes is the *post hoc ergo propter hoc* organizing principle for the entire book.[7]

After establishing Philoctetes as the motivating inception of the study,

The Moral Aesthetic of the Scream 55

Lessing repeats a line from the Winckelmann quotation: »Laokoon leidet, wie des Sophokles Philoktet,« and then asks: »Wie leidet dieser?« (*WB* 5/2: 18) Lessing answers his own question with a long list of Philoctetes's sufferings: »Die Klagen, das Geschrei, die wilden Verwünschungen, mit welchen sein Schmerz das Lager erfüllte, und alle Opfer, alle heilige Handlungen störte, erschollen nicht minder schrecklich durch das öde Eiland, und sie waren es, die ihn dahin verbannten« (*WB* 5/2: 18). This description is meant to set up the defense of expressive Greek sentimentalism against the barbaric Roman and modern suppression of feeling. Yet although Philoctetes certainly does moan and wail as drastically as Lessing makes out, his claim here also includes grounds for the opposite conclusion. If the Greeks were really as accepting of pathetic displays of voluble suffering as Lessing alleges, they would hardly have marooned poor Philoctetes on the desert island! The actual effect of the screams had been disgust and abandonment.

Lessing quickly suppresses the reaction that Philoctetes's cries evoke in the real world, but he plays up the Greeks' enthusiasm for beholding these screams in the theater. If archaic Greek tolerance for expressive pain is belied by the tragedy's mythic backstory, the representation of this vociferous sufferer will garner applause – and first prize – in Classical Athens. To crown his sensational tally of screams, Lessing continues, »Welche Töne des Unmuts, des Jammers, der Verzweiflung, von welchen auch der Dichter in der Nachahmung das Theater durchhallen ließ« (*WB* 5/2: 18). Not only do Lessing's Greeks refuse to stifle their cries of pain, but they even weave screams into their dramatic art. Two points are important here: First, Lessing's elision of the real-world reactions in favor of theatrical art displaces morality from reality to its aesthetic representation. Lessing's seeming equivalence of the imitation (*Nachahmung*) of shrieks with the real thing appears to be in direct opposition to his later claims forbidding the representation of disgusting things as present (chapters 23-25). Second, even before he formally announces the two art forms, poetic and visual, the limits of which he aims to establish, Lessing is already introducing the limit case (*Grenzfall*) where the two overlap: the theater. It turns out that these two apparent transgressions are related.

A careful parsing of the two sentences reveals a spectrum of differentiation. Philoctetes's awful cries first fill up (*erfüllen*) the Greek camp, then they ring out (*erschallen*) on the unpopulated island, and finally they echo through (*durchhallen*) the theater. In the first place, unwilling auditors leave the wailer all alone. In the final case, an eager audience expressly gathers to listen to Philoctetes wail. Where the shrieking man was present as real, the effect was revulsion and the resulting action was the expulsion of the shrieker. Where an actor shrieked in imitation as part of a theatrical performance, the effects were fear and pity, and the action (as Aristotle and Lessing would hope) may be catharsis in the auditors.[8] With three successive verbs of what sounds can do in space, Lessing bridges the domains of painting (space) and poetry (time). The spectra implied in these early sentences – real and imitation; space and time; disgust and compassion – adumbrate Lessing's main theoretical distinctions in the rest of the *Laokoon*. Put them together and you have the axes of a three-dimensional graph onto which one can plot all the aesthetic claims Lessing will make in the text. The real/imitation axis, moreover, can be cast in today's terms of performativity/theatricality (expressiveness vs. expressiveness with an aesthetic frame), which will turn out to have decisive consequences.[9]

This histrionic account is set off from the rest of the paragraph by dashes – as if imitating the interruption of Philoctetes's cries into the dialogue of the play. It immediately succeeds Lessing's introduction of his divergent reading and is followed by a speculation about the length of the third act of the tragedy. This disquisition on details of Greek theatrical practice may seem like a digression, but it speaks directly to the issue of time implied by the previous succession of verbs. Lessing agrees with other critics[10] that the ancients did not take pains to keep the acts of their plays similar in length. In the case of *Philoctetes*, however, he imagines that the performance time of the »third act« could well have equaled that of the other acts due to how long an actor would need to perform all the onomatopoeiac expressions of pain. To make the shorter text equal the other acts in duration, Lessing seems to think there will be a great deal of hamming it up with melodramatic interludes of moaning and writhing in pain. As evidence, he points to »die ganzen Zeilen voller, παπα, παπα, aus welchen dieser Aufzug bestehet« (*WB* 5/2: 19).

In fact, Lessing is wrong about the technical point he wants to make here: Greek tragedies were not divided into Acts and Scenes, which were entirely the imposition of modern editors. But the details of Lessing's remarks nevertheless provide a solution to both the moral and aesthetic conundrums introduced in the first half of the paragraph. The adjectives and nouns with which Lessing names Philoctetes's cries – »abgebrochen«; »Dehnungen und Absetzungen« (*WB* 5/2: 19) – accurately describe the prosody of Greek tragic verse. The cries of pain are metrically inflected with the same scansion as the dialogue in which they are embedded. Scholars have little idea about the details of performative practice on the Attic stage, but it is clear that the sounds alternately match or syncopate with the iambic trimeter of the surrounding stichomythia.[11] Even if the actor slows the tempo of his declamation or improvises additional utterances of pain at the places marked by »ἄ ἄ ἄ ἄ,« the textual representation of the cries of pain indicates that they bear the same time signature as the spoken words.[12]

Hence it becomes clear why Athenian audiences do not turn away from the wailing Philoctetes with the same disgust as their archaic ancestors: on stage, the actor sings his cries.

This metrical understanding of Philoctetes's cries problematizes the claim with which Lessing begins the very next paragraph: »Schreien ist der natürliche Ausdruck körperlichen Schmerzes« (*WB* 5/2: 19). The Greek actor portraying Philoctetes can hardly be ›natural‹ in his technically practiced and metrically inflected cries. Instead, this first paragraph of critical analysis in the book already sets up a parallel to what Lessing will later deduce as the reason for Laocoon's peaceful expression in the statuary group. Just as Laocoon must turn his distorted grimace to a sigh in sculpture, Philoctetes must intone his disturbing cries as music on the stage. As the law of beauty tempers screams in the visual arts (*WB* 5/2: 24), so must meter inflect wailing in the theater. The only way that Philoctetes can win sympathy for his injured foot is by expressing his pain in metrical feet.[13] His lacerated limb causes repulsion in the real world, but when it dances to the rhythms of iambic feet, disgust turns to delight. The performativity of Philoctetes's screams must be given a theatrical frame to have any salient effect on onlookers.

Herder criticized *Laokoon* for failing to account for music in its division of the arts,[14] but this early paragraph already provides material for all the conclusions the later critic will make. Like visual images and in contrast to words in language, Philoctetes's cries are natural, not arbitrary signs (cf. *WB* 5/2: 123).[15] Yet like language, in opposition to art, they unfold in time. Unlike linguistic signs, screams are inarticulate. Yet importantly, the meter articulates the sounds into discrete and recognizable rhythmic patterns. ›The articulation of inarticulate sound‹ would be a perfect definition of music according to Herder's critique, and this formula is deducible directly from Lessing's claims here about the performance time of the »third act« of *Philoctetes*.

This first chapter ends with speculation about Sophocles's lost tragedy, *Laocoon*. Just as Lessing's comparison of the plastic and epic representations of the Trojan priest were determined by recourse to Philoctetes, the imagined dramatic representation is also upstaged by the wounded archer: »So viel bin ich versichert, daß er den Laokoon nicht stoischer als den Philoktet [...] wird geschildert haben« (*WB* 5/2: 21). Perhaps not, but Sophocles most certainly would not have allowed Laocoon to be attacked by sea snakes in the stage action. All such violence took place offstage in Greek theater. The moment of highest fright and suffering would have been narrated in a teichoscopia or a messenger's report, much as Theseus learns of Hippolytus's similar fate after the raging bull emerges from the sea.[16] The cries of Laocoon and his sons may well have been reported in this account, but they would never have »resounded in the theater.« Although Lessing spends so much of this first chapter in the theater rather than with the sculpture or the epic, the theatrical production he imagines here would have lacked the very cries he wants us to hear.

It is appropriate that Lessing's major claim following this imagined drama is negative: »Alles Stoische ist untheatralisch« (WB 5/2: 21). The rhetorical force of this passage is to defend the expressivity of pain against its macho detractors, but the phrase itself speaks to the impossibility of enacting the scene of Laocoon's demise on stage: it is literally untheatrical. Lessing continues: »unser Mitleiden ist allezeit dem Leiden gleichmäßig, welches der interessierende Gegenstand äußert« (WB 5/2: 21). This claim of equivalence between the pity of the viewer and the voluble pain of the visible sufferer is mathematical in its force, but it will be rendered unlawful by Lessing's own legislation in the very next chapter.

Chapters Two and Three: From »Law of Beauty« to »Free Play of Imagination«

The mystery left by the reductio conclusion of chapter one does not last long. Lessing quickly deduces the law of beauty to explain the sculpture's silencing of the narrated screams. Yet this law, which applies only to the visual arts, is itself derivative. Ostensibly, the »Endzweck der Künste […] ist Vergnügen« (WB 5/2: 25). An even more fundamental basis for this pleasure is revealed a few pages later when Lessing comes to test it in a dramatic thought experiment. The decisive contrast of the *Laokoon*, I claim, is between compassion and disgust. In this core distinction, for which Philoctetes has prepared the way, an ethical criterion ultimately determines aesthetic categories.

Lessing applies the law of beauty for visual art to explain why the sculptor's Laocoon cannot wail like Virgil's. The artist had to turn screams into sighs, namely, »nicht weil das Schreien eine unedle Seele verrät, sondern weil es das Gesicht auf eine ekelhafte Weise verstellet« (WB 5/2: 29). *Ekel*, disgust, is what art must avoid. And now Lessing begins his thought experiment:

> Denn man reiße dem Laokoon in Gedanken nur den Mund auf und urteile. Man lasse ihn schreien und sehe. Es war eine Bildung, die Mitleid einflößte, weil sie Schönheit und Schmerz zugleich zeigte; nun ist es eine häßliche, eine abscheuliche Bildung geworden, von der man gern sein Gesicht verwendet, weil der Anblick des Schmerzes Unlust erregt, ohne daß die Schönheit des leidenden Gegenstande diese Unlust in das süße Gefühl des Mitleids verwandeln kann. (WB 5/2: 29)

This passage distills the effect of art into two fundamental, opposing movements: looking away and turning towards. It has been annoying to scholars that Lessing, for whom *Mitleid* (sympathy) was so important, never gave a precise definition of the term. Much has been written about whether Lessing's *Mitleid* means compassion or empathy in his theoretical works about art and the theater,[17] but this moment in the *Laokoon* provides as clear an explanation as we ever get. Importantly, it is a purely phenomenological account of the subject's pivoting relation to the other: *Mitleid* makes you turn toward the other. Its opposite is *Ekel*, which makes you turn away.

This explanation is in accord with the social and political work of all of Lessing's theater, and also offers a grand-unifying theory of the arts here in the *Laokoon*. Martha Nussbaum has identified compassion and disgust as doing opposing work in fostering or hampering morality in civil society. Compassion can help form the eudaimonistic judgment that transforms emotion into political virtue. Disgust at other people's and culture's differences, in contrast, is an objectifying emotion that undermines that goal.[18] The »law of beauty« is in the service of making people want to look toward others rather than turning them away. Hence the artist's mitigation of wrath into seriousness, anguish into sadness (*WB* 5/2: 27) and screams into sighs (*WB* 5/2: 29). The intensity of the former emotions would distort the face and make people look away. Their softening (*Milderung*) into the latter expressions invites an almost eroticizing fascination with pain meant to turn heads and fix gazes on the sufferer.

This sensual attraction to typically repulsive objects can also be heard in Philoctetes's echoes in this chapter. In an early digression, Lessing gets caught up in a fantasy of expectant mothers having erotic dreams about snakes. Not only, as Jacobs pointed out, are the Laocoon figures bound together by the lines of writhing sea serpents,[19] but it was also a snake that caused Philoctetes's incurable injury. »Die Schlange war ein Zeichen der Gottheit,« Lessing insists as he claims to ›save the dream‹ from its dismissive detractors (*WB* 5/2: 25). The slithering reptiles, so often represented as disgusting or even evil in Western art, are here transformed into voluptuous, phallic gods. Lessing's final justification for his deification of the snakes is uncharacteristically, but hilariously, lame: »eine Ursache mußte es wohl haben, warum die ehebrecherische Phantasie nur immer eine Schlange war« (*WB* 5/2: 26). It is as if the gratuitousness of this obsession with serpentine titillation is announcing itself. Somehow these repellant snakes have slipped past the seemingly secure barrier of the ›law of beauty‹ to germinate the fertile imagination's ›free play.‹

Another law-breaking breach against beauty occurs at the exact transition between chapters two and three, and again Philoctetes is the cause of the infraction. While chapter one closes with speculation about a lost drama of *Laokoon*, chapter two concludes with the invention of a lost sculpture of Philoctetes. The statue is cited as the final example in the chapter's long list of affects that must be toned down in their artistic representation. In the suffering Heracles by an unknown master, his »wild« screams become »finster« (*WB* 5/2: 30). As if on cue, Philoctetes follows his hero onto the stage: »Der Philoktet des Pythagoras Leontinus schien dem Betrachter seinen Schmerz mitzuteilen, welche Wirkung der geringste gräßliche Zug verhindert hätte« (*WB* 5/2: 30). Not only has the sculpture in question here not survived, but Lessing's source does not even identify the statue as representing Philoctetes. With zero philological or archeological evidence, Lessing has ›emended‹ the Latin text of Pliny's *Natural History* to include the Greek hero. Lessing brags about this rather brazen textual intervention in the last two sentences of the chapter: »Man dürfte fragen, woher ich wisse, daß dieser Meister eine Bildsäule des Philoktet gemacht habe? Aus einer Stelle des Plinius, die meine Verbesserung nicht erwartet haben sollte, so offenbar verfälscht oder verstümmelt ist sie« (*WB* 5/2: 30). In the footnote, Lessing quotes the passage from Pliny: »While in Syracuse [he made] a lame man, the spectators of whom even feel the pain of his ulcer when they see it« (*WB* 5/2: 31n).[20] Lessing replaces the accusative object of the first clause, *claudicantem* (limping man), with *Philoctetem*. He does not offer any scholarly justification for this move other than the rhetorical exclamation, »Niemand hatte mehr Recht, wegen solchen Geschwieres bekannter zu sein als Philoktet« (*WB* 5/2: 31n). No modern editors follow Lessing's correction; in fact, the critical apparati of current editions do not even note the word as problematic.[21]

But the cocky announcement of this dubious textual improvement draws attention away from the trouble that the example causes. The audacity of introducing Philoctetes to Pliny's description hides another detail: the sculpture's avoidance of ›gräßliche‹ (disgusting) features. Pliny offers no description of the statue's appearance. Instead, he only writes about the effect that the figure has on spectators. In both counts of how the example has to function for Lessing's argument, therefore, he has cheated a bit: that the sculpture depicts the wounded Philoctetes and that it does so by softening the extreme expression of his suffering. What remains – the only detail that Lessing legitimately extracts from Pliny – works in radical opposition to Lessing's purported aim. The statue's beholders appear to feel the pain of its ulcers in their own limbs: the sculpture »schien dem Betrachter seinen Schmerz mitzuteilen« (*WB* 5/2: 30). The direct transference of agony between bodies is very different from »das süße Gefühl des Mitleids« (*WB* 5/2: 29) which great art is intended to elicit. The distinction is crucial to Lessing's phenomenological ethics of art. This contrast is precisely the one between what psychologists today call ›empathy‹ (feeling with another's feelings, whether positive or negative) and ›compassion‹ (feeling for another's undeserved misfortune).[22] In pointedly displacing compassion with empathy in this manufactured sculpture of Philoctetes, Lessing's text demonstrates the ultimate instability between the two phenomena, which his own argument requires to be separate.

At stake is the etiology of Lessing's gestural aesthetics: turning away in disgust vs. turning toward in compassion. The textual performance of Lessing's examples, real and imagined, keeps violating that basic principle. The disgusting proves to have a powerful allure. Despite his expostulation to the contrary, Lessing has a hard time turning away from what is vile and repugnant. At every turn, Philoctetes's wound and the snake that inflicted it are putting pressure on the sore spots in Lessing's prescriptive theories.

Chapter Four: »Wholly Nature«

The fourth chapter of *Laokoon* features a long and involved interpretation of Sophocles's *Philoctetes*. The structure of this chapter is analogous to that of the *Laokoon* so far. Chapter four begins by explicitly bringing to center stage the major issues that had been determining the first three chapters from behind the scenes. Lessing briefly summarizes poetry's differences from the strictures of the visual arts with the example of Virgil's *Aeneid*: if the artist was correct to stifle Laocoon's screams, the poet Virgil was equally right to make him »raise up horrible cries to the heavens«[23] (cf. *WB* 5/2: 35). This comparison of boundaries brings Lessing quickly to the tricky question of drama, the art that straddles sculpture and poetry as it unfolds in both time and space: »Aber Virgil ist hier bloß ein erzehlender Dichter. Wird in seiner Rechtfertigung auch der dramatische Dichter mit begriffen sein? Einen andern Eindruck macht die Erzehlung von jemands Geschrei; einen andern dieses Gechrei selbst« (*WB* 5/2: 36). This question makes explicit what was implied in Lessing's very first move in chapter one to begin his investigation by describing Philoctetes's theatrical cries. It is as if he is rebooting the entire treatise again, this time spelling out everything hinted at in the first three chapters. In the following sentences, he admits that »je näher der Schauspieler der Natur kömmt,« in enacting the screams, »desto empfindlicher müssen unsere Augen und Ohren beleidigt werden« (*WB* 5/2: 36). Nature here, far from a Rousseauian Eden, is tantamount to repulsiveness, which would not only destroy the desired effect of compassion but drive people away in disgust.

The rest of the chapter consists of four extensive ›Anmerkungen‹ about how Sophocles manages to get out of this quandary. Despite the elements of repugnance in the material, his »Genie« converts it into »eines von den Meisterstücken der Bühne« (*WB* 5/2: 37). Strikingly, each of Lessing's four numbered sections reprises the themes of the first four chapters in new contexts that provide commentary on – while moving forward the dramatic development of – the treatise. Revolting nature is performative; to be pitied, Philoctetes must become theatrical.

The first point (*WB* 5/2: 37-38) stresses the importance of the externality of Philoctetes's wound. Chapter one insisted that people should express their pain rather than keeping it stoically bottled up inside, while this passage praises the visible and physical limp over an ›interior sickness,‹ no matter how debilitating. In chapter one, stoicism was ›untheatrical‹; here, internal maladies are ›less theatrical‹ than the wound. But the paradoxical problems of theatricality discussed above are compounded here: to be believable, the wound must be supernatural. Modern French versions of *Philoctetes* that dispense with the occult snakebite are »weit unwahrscheinlicher« than »das fabelhafte Wunderbare« of Sophocles's myth.

The second point (*WB* 5/2: 38-42) enumerates the many other evils with which Sophocles strategically furnishes Philoctetes. At the climax of chapter two, Lessing rips open Laocoon's mouth to imagine the effects; here he sets up a similar thought experiment. Imagine someone marooned on a desert island like Philoctetes, but »man gebe ihm aber Gesundheit, und Kräfte, und Industrie, und es ist ein Robinson Crusoe« (*WB* 5/2: 39). Both experiments result in a failure of compassion: the screaming Laocoon evokes disgust, the opposite of pity in Lessing's gestural geometry; while the resourceful Crusoe wins our admiration, which is the opposite of pity along a very different axis.[24] If sympathy makes us look toward and disgust away from the other, admiration causes us to look up to her. Whereas chapter two codified the law of beauty and then violated it with an invented ancient statue of Philoctetes, this section also problematizes the neat graph of otherness. Heap all the ills together on one figure, Lessing claims, and the wretch will arouse »Schaudern und Entsetzen.« Fear, the inseparable partner of pity in Aristotle's *Poetics* had previously not made much of an appearance. Then Lessing introduces despair: »kein Mitleid ist stärker, keines zerschmelzt mehr die ganze Seele, als das, welches sich mit Vorstellungen der Verzweiflung mischet. Von dieser Art ist das Mitleid, welches wir für den Philoktet empfinden« (*WB* 5/2: 42). By now the spectators are looking down at the other. This new direction invites a critique of what is an invariable good for Lessing: there are elements of contemptuous condescension in pity. Moreover, though all the vectors of the gestural ethics are now complete (toward / away; up/down), viewers have been rendered impotent, with their useless molten souls, to offer any help.

The clear geometry of the second point, like the simple law of the second chapter, gets muddled and confused again in the following sections. The third note about *Philoctetes* (*WB* 5/2: 42-45) quotes a long passage from

Adam Smith's *Theory of Moral Sentiments* that seems to be in accord with much of what Lessing himself has been saying so far, only to respond with caustic reproach: »Nichts ist betrüglicher als allgemeine Gesetze für unsere Empfindungen« (*WB* 5/2: 43). That is, of course, unless Lessing is the legislator.

The explicit naming of Smith in a polemic against him is surprising because, as Katherine Harloe has persuasively shown, Lessing's *Mitleid* shares many salient features with Smith's sympathy.[25] In the fourth part of chapter four (*WB* 5/2: 46-48), Lessing makes the most fundamental aspect of Smithian sympathy, its performative dynamic, the crowning point of his praise for *Philoctetes*. Smith constructs an anthropological account of human behavior that boils down to a theory of mutual performativity based on the desire to maximize the sympathy one wins from others. It is not just a matter of performing and interpreting performance, but a reflexive »habit […] of considering how everything that concerns himself will appear to others.«[26] This mechanism fosters the development of an »ideal spectator« through a kind of second-order sympathy:

> In the sentiment of approbation there are two things to be taken notice of; first, the sympathetic passion of the spectator; and, secondly, the emotion which arises from his observing the perfect coincidence between this sympathetic passion in himself, and the original passion in the person principally concerned. This last emotion, in which the sentiment of approbation properly consists, is always agreeable and delightful.[27]

Hume characterizes this feature as »the Hinge of [Smith's] System.«[28] This doubling, second-order sympathy is a powerful new explanatory model for human behavior, perfectibility, and social harmony.

Though Lessing never explicitly cites this element of Smith's theory, it is clearly the theoretical lynchpin to his reading of *Philoctetes* in this last part of chapter four. Facing the wounded archer directly, spectators are made uncomfortable and put at a loss for how to behave: »Wie sollen sich also diejenigen verhalten, die mit dem schreienden Philoktet zu tun haben?« (*WB* 5/2: 46) This display would bring about the »widrigste Dissonanz« (*WB* 5/2: 46). Sophocles's solution to this problem is to put other spectators on the stage.[29] The audience beholds not only the expressive suffering of Philoctetes, but also the scene of sympathy performed between him and Neoptolemus: »der Zuschauer [giebt Acht] auf die Veränderung […], die in den Gesinnungen und Anschlägen durch das Mitleid […] entstehet, oder entstehen sollte« (*WB* 5/2: 46). In result, the audience is invited to a third-order reflection: not only do they see Neoptolemus feel compassion with Philoctetes's pain, but they also behold him reflecting on the effect this sympathy has on himself. The young man describes this reaction as one of aporetic confusion: »a strange, terrible pity [οἶκτος δεινὸς] has fallen upon me!« (line 965). According to Smith, then, the external audience will sympathize with Neoptolemus's second-order sympathy both as a match of its distressful confusion and with an approving judgment of the harmony of this match. At this remove, the audience feeling with a character's feelings for another character's feelings, the compound compassion of *Philoctetes* is a dramatic laboratory in the psychology of sympathy.

Hence the rubric of performativity itself, so central to Smith's moral theory, has swooped in to provide the crowning tribute in Lessing's interpretation of Sophocles. The tragedy puts a purely performative scene (in the reality of the fictional world) on stage in a theatrical frame. But as in every previous point, he includes a flourish that invites a skeptical second look. In a moving passage, Lessing articulates this scene of sympathy in terms of nature and pretense: »Philoktet, seiner Schmerzen Meister, würde den Neoptolem bei seiner Verstellung erhalten haben. Philoktet, den sein Schmerz aller Verstellung unfähig macht, [...] Philoktet, der ganz Natur ist, bringt auch den Neoptolem zu seiner Natur wieder zurück« (*WB* 5/2: 45-46). After implicitly making use of Smith's system for his analysis of the play's effect, Lessing now violates the tenets of that system. As Lessing displayed in the opening pages of chapter one, Philoctetes's screams when overpowered by pain are in fact a tour-de-force of *Verstellung*. Not only are they performed with highly skilled histrionic art and inflected by metrical control, but they quite literally distort (*ver-stellen*) the natural features of the face. Neoptolemus's ›nature‹ too is never a simple opposite of ›pretense.‹ Both Odysseus's rhetoric in persuading him to depart from his nature to trick Philoctetes, and the old man's success in convincing him otherwise depend on making Neoptolemus think about how he will appear to others (cf. lns 119; 1310-1314). The contraries of nature and dissimulation are entirely at odds with the performative calculus of Smith's sympathy: it is natural for humans to pretend. But in this passage, Philoctetes becomes ›wholly nature‹ when the pain is so great that he blacks out and lies comatose. Lessing implies that only in the face of unconsciousness, beyond performance, can sympathy do its ethical, life-changing work.

In this vignette, the main point of the fourth part of the fourth chapter and of the entire treatise so far converge: this text that claims to be all about drawing clear boundaries is actually preoccupied with interesting, messy border zones: the theatrical stage where poetry becomes plastic art, nature meets artifice, compassion dances with disgust, and theatricality collapses into performativity.

The Dramatic Structure of the Laokoon

By repeating the general progression of the first four chapters in the four sections of the fourth, the text establishes a pattern:

1. Scream/Wound: A forceful and dense opening with all the future themes packed in hidden layers;
2. Clarity: a simple, over-determining formula that makes crystal clear sense (but ending with a hint of the formula's failure); clarified by compassion;
3. Complexities (*Verwicklungen*): lost clarity; ›prägnanter Augenblick‹ leading toward or away from climax or catastrophe; fertile through disgust;
4. Theatrical Resolution: an embrace of the unsublimatable differences in a performative frame; second-order observation.

This pattern is marked in *Laokoon* by the textual traces of *Philoctetes*, and it matches up with the dynamic of Sophocles's tragedy:

1. Scream/Wound: Neoptolemus is thrust into his deceptive role by Odysseus and then confronts the wounded Philoctetes (lines 1-826);
2. Clarity: The experience of compassion brings Neoptolemus to the moral choice to tell the truth and return the bow (lines 827-1262);
3. Complexities: Philoctetes's trauma prevents him from complying with Neoptolemus's ›reasonable‹ urging to rejoin the Greeks; an excess of pity leads toward betrayal and disaster (lines 1263-1408);
4. Theatrical Resolution: Only a theatrical device, the *deus ex machina* of Heracles's appearance, can force a peaceful ending that still does not erase the underlying trauma (lines 1409-1471).

With the comparison of the structural framework of *Laokoon* 1-4 alongside that of *Philoctetes*, a glaring question comes to light: in Lessing's extensive reading of the tragedy, why does he never address the ending? Lessing's analysis of the play ends at Neoptolemus's decision to return the bow, which brings him only to the second part of the rubric above. What about Neoptolemus's subsequent persuasion by Philoctetes to abandon and betray the Greeks? What about the god in the machine without whom the tragedy would have a much more ›tragic‹ ending?

In fact, although Lessing never explicitly alludes to the remainder of the tragedy, he weaves it into the structure of the treatise as a whole. The first four chapters together, with their dense evocation of all the important issues to be worried over in the book, correspond to the first ›Scream/Wound‹ opening episode. ›Clarity‹ is achieved in the ›dry chain of conclusions‹ (*WB* 5/2: 117) of the famous chapter sixteen. Directly afterwards, however, ›Complexities‹ again begin to cloud the clear view from the deductive height of reasoning, as Lessing involves himself in ever more arcane and obscure debates. They reach their most opaque in a run of three chapters dealing with the niceties of disgust (XXIII-XXV). In the final footnote and

hence the very last page of the entire volume, however, Sophocles makes an appearance that brings all the disparate threads of the book's many concerns together in one dynamic image of ›Theatrical Resolution‹ (XXIX). These last two movements are marked by the reappearance of *Philoctetes* and its author.
1. Scream / Wound: Chapters I-IV
2. Clarity: Chapter XVI
3. Complexities: Chapter XXV
4. Theatrical Resolution: Chapter XXIX

By chapter twenty-five, readers have been slogging their way through many pages of fine distinctions about, and examples of, the ugly and the disgusting. For all Lessing's praise of the ancients for their adherence to the ›law of beauty‹ and admonition of the modern taste for the grotesque, he seems strikingly obsessed with the hideous himself. Scholars have made much of this apparent contradiction, and proposed various solutions to or deconstructions of it.[30] Here I would like to suggest a dramatic trajectory, modeled on Neoptolemus's path, as a way of thinking about the *Ekelsucht*. After his pity for Philoctetes leads to a moment of moral clarity in returning the bow, Neoptolemus tries to convince the older man to rejoin the Greeks and receive the cure for his wound at the Trojan camp. Instead, it is Neoptolemus who is slowly persuaded to betray his countrymen and flee away with Philoctetes. The salutary effect of sympathy devolves, from a conventional Greek point of view at least, into desertion and dereliction of duty. Similarly Lessing's text, after the brief clear vista of sharp distinctions in chapter 16, has lost its way in compulsive and combative digressions. The moral foundation of these aesthetic conclusions, as shown above, was an affective register of turning toward/away. The imperative for other-directed compassion, which justified the »law of beauty« has now been overstepped into its opposite; but instead of driving away Lessing's glance, the ugliness now compels it.

Shortly before this move toward the repulsive reaches its climax, Lessing quotes for the last time from *Philoctetes*. It is an early scene of teichoscopia when Neoptolemus is describing the sight of Philoctetes's cave dwelling: »Wie vollendet der Dichter dieses traurige fürchterliche Gemälde? Mit einem Zusatz von Ekel. ›Ha!‹ fährt Neoptolem auf einmal zusammen, ›hier trockenen zerrissene Lappen, voll Blut und Eiter!‹« (*WB* 5/2: 177) The play makes a reappearance here to mark a ›fruitful moment‹ on the upward curve of revulsion. Lessing even tags the quoted scene as a *Gemälde*, for which he himself had specifically legislated the fruitful moment in chapter 3. It certainly serves to give ›free play‹ to Lessing's imagination, as he continues to follow it up with more and more disgusting examples, culminating in a gratuitously long citation from another play about castaways on a desert island who trade raunchy jokes about cannibalism (*WB* 5/2: 180-182). Although this picture gleefully breaks the ›law of beauty‹ and wallows in its opposite, far from being repelled, Lessing cannot take his eyes away.

Even the elaborately staged return of Winckelmann in chapter twenty-six does not dispel the digressive disorientation. After the initial excitement, Lessing changes tack to relatively trivial questions of comparative dating that trail off in the final pages to a petty list of corrections of Winckelmann's tome. Winckelmann was the initial sparring partner whose offhand remark about *Philoctetes* got the whole ball of Lessing's text rolling, but he is not the god who can set things straight again. For that we have to wait for the very last entry of mistakes Lessing identifies.

The long footnote that extends beyond the end of the entire treatise also begins unpromisingly as another detailed commentary on an error in Winckelmann's dating of *Antigone*, but then Lessing is reminded of another inaccuracy in Winckelmann's first essay that had set the textual thought process of the entire *Laokoon* in motion (*WB* 5/2: 205). There, Winckelmann attested that Sophocles as a youth had danced nude on the stage. Lessing demurs: Sophocles was never naked in the theater, but he did dance around the trophies on the island of Salamis after Athens's naval victory there in 480 BCE (whether nude or clothed, he admits, is contested; *WB* 5/2: 206). Then Lessing goes on to add one last detail:

> Sophokles war nemlich unter den Knaben, die man nach Salamis in Sicherheit gebracht hatte; und hier auf dieser Insul war es, wo es damals der tragischen Muse, alle ihre drei Lieblinge, in einer vorbildenden Gradation zu versammeln beliebte. Der kühne Aeschylus half siegen; der blühende Sophokles tanzte um die Tropäen, und Euripides ward an eben dem Tage des Sieges, auf eben der glücklichen Insel geboren. (*WB* 5/2: 206)

In this remarkable triptych, the divine muse ties together the myriad theoretical strands of *Laokoon* into one suggestive image. The goddess has descended from the stage machinery in the last sentences of the last footnote on the last page of the last chapter. Taking the place of Heracles, the *deus ex machina* of this treatise is the muse of tragedy, *Melpomenē*, literally »the singing one,« who was originally the muse of the chorus. The divinity of the *Laokoon* hence brings together in one figure music, dance, and theater. Significantly, the presiding divinity of this text about distinction is not one of either painting or of epic poetry, but rather theater, the artform where the visual meets the narrative in an inextricable blend.

The three scenes that the muse gathers – of war, dance, and birth – represent the cycles of human life and are moreover reminiscent of the depictions on the Shield of Achilles, which itself features prominently in the *Laokoon* as a locus for drawing divisions between art and poetry. Lessing spends a lot of time and energy comparing the ekphrastic descriptions of Achilles's shield in Homer and of Aeneas's in Virgil to assign the proper province of poetry to the representation of actions rather than of objects (XVIII-XIX). By reprising this comparison with the tableau of the three tragedians in one image at three symbolically important stages of life, the goddess of the text further conflates the domains that the treatise purports to distinguish. Hence, like the divine intervention at the end of *Philoctetes*, the final gesture of the *Laokoon* presents an interpretive equivocation. In the tragedy, Heracles's intercession preserves mythic necessity from the consequences of incurable trauma; in the treatise, the muse's final sentence secures a productive realm of indeterminacy (*apeiron*) threatened by strict prescriptive divisions.

Melpomenē's *deus ex machina* showcases very clearly, however, the vital but complex role that aesthetics plays in human morality. Neither the face-distorting pains of a mother's labor nor the gore and horrors of naval battle were permissible on ancient or neo-classical stages; the moral geometry implicit in the law of beauty would make spectators turn away in disgust at these sights rather than reach out toward the suffering other. Center-stage between life's limits of natality and mortality, however, the youth's dance mediates between birth and death, and draws onlookers' eyes with its beautiful movements. Performative dance becomes a medium of ethical concern. Just as music can be understood as the articulation of inarticulate sound, dance is an arrangement of corporeal motion in rhythmic steps with no destination. The grace of dancing bodies attracts where birth pangs and battle deaths repel: the law of beauty has a basis in morality.

Yet the question of Sophocles's nudity, which motivates Lessing's invocation of the goddess here in the first place, and which Lessing slyly leaves veiled in unanswerable obscurity, amplifies the pointed historicity – and hence ultimate lawlessness – of beauty. The adolescent's naked form (Sophocles would have been sixteen in 480 BCE) was the pinnacle of aesthetic perfection in Attic culture, a sight that attracted spectators daily to the gymnasia of Athens. But in the post-Christian Europe for whom Lessing invites the muse to devise this triptych of birth, battle, and boogie, the spectacle of a nude boy is scandalous, even illegal. Yet Lessing shares Winckelmann's fascination with the image of Sophocles's naked gyrations; the aestheticizing motions of the youth's dance compel prurient, shameful gazes. Disgust and beauty are not the pure opposites they seem in chapter II's clear articulation of the moral aesthetic (*WB* 5/2: 29).

* * *

Reading *Laokoon* alongside *Philoctetes* hence opens up surprising perspectives on some of the most pressing questions of eighteenth-century ethics. The phenomenological distinction between sympathy and disgust provides an ethical geometry that points to performance as the medium of morality. Philoctetes is key to recognizing how Lessing's treatise on the limits of poetry and visual art really takes its impetus from a subterranean division between performativity and theatricality, an ongoing debate among today's performance scholars to which Lessing suggestively contributes.

In four movements from the wound to the god, with clarity and confusion in between, Sophocles's *Philoctetes* helps discern order in Lessing's *Laokoon*. This evidence of the inner coherence and careful architecture, however, does not make Lessing a liar when he declares its rambling method. The best imitation of natural thought must be artificial to the highest degree. Beautiful correspondences and striking organizing principles can sometimes be discovered in close attention to one's interior dialogue with the passing landscapes during a perambulation. And Lessing is never alone in the *Laokoon*. His text is designed not as a solitary walk but a wandering scrimmage or relay race with a series of sparring partners. The hidden structures behind the conversational flow of debate make this text similar to a Platonic dialogue. As in the *Phaedo*, for instance, the *Laokoon* features flawed arguments that spur productive lines of thought for readers; both texts are also studded with moments of revelatory clarity that get lost almost immediately in forgetful confusion. They thus mimic the lived experience of conversation and thinking, and perform the necessity of perplexity in the ongoing process of knowledge.

University of Washington, Seattle

---

1 Two recent contributions pay attention to the importance of Philoctetes in *Laocoon*: Uta Korzeniewski, »Sophokles! Die Alten! Philoktet!« Lessing und die antiken Dramatiker, Konstanz 2003; Katherine Harloe, Sympathy, Tragedy, and the Morality of Sentiment in Lessing's *Laocoon*, in: Rethinking Lessing's *Laocoon*, Oxford 2017, pp. 157-176. Korzeniewski includes a thorough if conventional summary of Lessing's interpretation of *Philoctetes* (pp. 506-539). Harloe draws out the importance of this interpretation for Lessing's theory of tragedy and thinking on sympathy. Neither explores the structural role of the drama for *Laokoon* as a whole nor looks to the intertextual engagement with Philoctetes beyond the fourth chapter of the text.
2 Frederick Beiser, in contrast, identifies the »hidden agenda« of the *Laokoon* as a defense of poetry against the primacy of art: Diotima's Children: German Aesthetic Rationalism from Leibniz to Lessing, Oxford 2009, pp. 277-282.
3 David Wellbery and Katherine Harloe are exceptions to this general trend. Both have recently made claims for the ethical implications of *Laokoon*. Wellbery

began to rethink the semiotic and structuralist emphasis of his influential 1984 monograph in the 1990s: The Pathos of Theory: *Laocoon* Revisited, in: Intertextuality: German Literature and Visual Art from the Renaissance to the Twentieth Century, Columbia, SC 1993, pp. 47-63. In his most recent contribution, Wellbery even claims that formal aesthetic issues may be »secondary« to the more fundamental issues of critical judgment: *Laocoon* Today: On the Conceptual Infrastructure, in: Rethinking Lessing's *Laocoon*, Oxford 2017, pp. 59-86. In the same volume, Katherine Harloe explicitly links Lessing's use of *Philoctetes* to his moral concerns: Harloe (note 1), p. 159. Neither of these »ethical turns« in *Laokoon* scholarship, however, argues for a performative phenomenology of morality, as this essay does.

4 For a modern version of this positive reading of compassion, see Martha Nussbaum, The ›Morality of Pity‹: Sophocles's *Philoctetes,* in: Rethinking Tragedy, ed. by Rita Felski, Baltimore 2008, pp. 148-169.

5 All quotations are taken Lessing, Werke und Briefe in zwölf Bänden, ed. by Wilfried Barner, Frankfurt 1990, cited as *WB*, followed by volume and page numbers

6 For a deconstruction of Winckelmann's idealization of Greek art, see Richard Block, The Spell of Italy: Vacation, Magic, and the Attraction of Goethe, Detroit 2006, pp. 17-48.

7 Lessing's ostensible claims about his writing practice are demonstrably disingenuous. That does not mean they are necessarily false, however, as claims about the performance of the text. See Carol Jacobs, The Critical Performance of Lessing's *Laocoon,* in: MLN, vol. 102.3 (1987), pp. 483-521, here p. 488.

8 For Lessing's interpretation of Aristotelian catharsis, see: Hamburgische Dramaturgie, Ein und achtzigstes Stück (*WB* 6: 585-590).

9 »Performativity« and »theatricality« were certainly not terms deployed in the eighteenth century. The concepts behind them, however, were very much in play. In this article, I follow Fischer-Lichte's usage: Performance is the broader term: any activity done *for* or *before* others. Theatricality is the subset of performances undertaken in the context of an aesthetic frame (which will vary from culture to culture). See Erika Fischer-Lichte, Semiotics of Theater, trans. Jeremy Gaines and Doris L. Jones, Bloomington 1992, pp. 139-140, and: The Routledge Introduction to Theatre and Performance Studies, trans. Minou Armojand, New York 2014, pp. 99-110.

10 Namely Pierre Brumoy, the first translator of *Philoctetes* into a modern language (*WB* 5/2: 18).

11 Philoctetes's cries of pain scan differently at different points. The »ἀτταταῖ« and »ἀπαππαπαῖ, παπαππαπαππαπαππαπαῖ« (lns 743, 746; see also 754, 786) match the surrounding iambic trimeter perfectly. The »ἄ ἄ ἄ ἄ« (lns 733, 739, 782, 785, 790, 795) are shorter interjections between complete lines, technically extra metrum exclamations, but they can also scan as feet in iambic trimeter.

12 For current scholarship on the meter of this section (lines 730-826: the second episode, or »act three« according to Brumoy), see the commentary in Sophocles, Philoctetes, ed. by Seth Schein, Cambridge 2013, pp. 236-246.

13 The prosody of Attic tragedy has its roots in the choral dance. The reason we refer to metrical units as »feet« is that they were measured out by the dancers'

slapping of bare feet on stones. See A. David, The Dance of the Muses: Choral Theory and Ancient Greek Poetics, Oxford 2006.
14 Johan Gottfried Herder, Kritische Wälder. Erstes Wäldchen, in: Werke in zehn Bänden, vol. 2, ed. by Gunter E. Grimm, Frankfurt 1993, pp. 57-245.
15 Yet even here the division is not completely distinct, as »arbitrary signs« insinuate themselves into these supposedly most »natural« of signs. The sounds that Philoctetes screams (ἀπαππαπαῖ, etc.) echo words for »daddy« (παππας) and »child« (παῖς). See Schein's commentary, Philoctetes, p. 238.
16 See Euripides, Hippolytus, lns 1153-1254.
17 E. g., Thomas Martinec, The Boundaries of *Mitleidsdramaturgie*: Some Clarifications Concerning Lessing's Concept of ›Mitleid,‹ in: Modern Language Review, vol. 101.3 (2009), pp. 743-758.
18 See Martha Nussbaum, Upheavals of Thought: The Intelligence of Emotion, Cambridge 2001, pp. 320-321.
19 Jacobs (note 7), p. 483.
20 Cf. C. Plinius Secundus, Naturalis historia, ed. by L. Ian and C. Mayhoff, Stuttgart 1967, book 34, line 25.
21 Plinius (note 20), p. 183.
22 For a helpful discussion of the terminology of sympathy, see Nussbaum (note 18), pp. 301-304. For Lessing's *Mitleid*, see Hans-Jürgen Schings, Der mitleidigste Mensch ist der beste Mensch. Poetik des Mitleids von Lessing bis Büchner, München 1980. Thomas Martinec (note 17, pp. 746-747) makes a valiant and erudite attempt to determine when precisely *Mitleid* means empathy and when it means pity in Lessing's work, but I find his distinctions rather neat and rigid for Lessing's actual usage, even in the examples Martinec cites.
23 Virgil, *Aeneid*, II.222, ed. by H. Fairclough, Cambridge, MA 1916, p. 330.
24 These were the two major terms in Lessing and Mendelssohn's *Briefwechsel über das Trauerspiel* (1756-1757).
25 She does not, however, mention Lessing's unattributed importation of Smith's performative dynamics of sympathy, which I emphasize here. Harloe (note 1), pp. 169-170.
26 Adam Smith, The Theory of Moral Sentiments, Indianapolis 1982, p. 43. This is the anthropological motivation for mitigating the expression of suffering (e. g., screams to sighs) that Harloe correctly attributes to Smith.
27 Smith (note 26), p. 46n.
28 David Hume, Letter 36 to Adam Smith, 28 July 1759, quoted in Smith (note 26), p. 46n.
29 Neoptolemus was not a character in the earlier *Philoctetes* tragedies of Aeschylus and Euripides.
30 See Winfried Menninghaus, Ekel. Theorie und Geschichte einer starken Empfindung, Frankfurt 1999, and Dorothea von Mücke, The Powers of Horror and the Magic of Euphemism in Lessing's *Laokoon* and How the Ancients Represented Death, in: Body and Text in the Eighteenth Century, Stanford 1994, pp. 163-180.

FORUM
Reading Forster, Reading Race: Philosophy, Politics, and Natural History in the German Enlightenment

edited by
Jennifer Mensch and Michael Olson

Reading Forster, Reading Race: Philosophy, Politics, and Natural History in the German Enlightenment

JENNIFER MENSCH • MICHAEL OLSON

Georg Forster (1754-1794) was one of the very few men in the eighteenth century who could credibly claim to have been a *Weltumsegler*. At the age of eleven, in 1765, he accompanied his father, the clergyman and naturalist Johann Reinhold Forster, on a Russian-financed expedition to inspect new German immigrant settlements along the Volga, travelling some 2300 kilometers from Nassenhuben, Pommerania, to Saratov across fields and dusty steppes. Georg's father had brought him along to aid his scientific observations, to keep records, and to draw up accounts of the hundreds of natural specimens the two collected on their trip. This early experience was formative, and when Georg moved to London with his father the following year, he worked alongside him in the antiquarian networks interested in the fossils and other items the two had brought with them. In an early sign of what would become an enduring economic lifeline for the Forster family, Georg published at age thirteen a translation of Russian history into English, followed in short course by his English translation of the travelogue prepared by the French explorer Bougainville. By then JR Forster had begun to lecture at the progressive Warrington Dissenter's Academy in northern England, allowing Georg to be enrolled as a student while continuing his natural history pursuits. In 1772 Georg published his first independent work, a short text on the Polynesian breadfruit. This was enough to convince the British admiralty to allow the seventeen-year-old to accompany his father, newly appointed as the ship's naturalist aboard Captain Cook's HMS Resolution as it set out to explore the South Pacific between 1772 and 1775. Georg Forster's subsequent account of the voyage, published in English (1777) and then in a German translation in two volumes (1778 and 1780), secured his fame as one of the foremost naturalists of his day, and led to his appointment to academic positions in Kassel (1778-1783) and Vilnius (1784-1788), and ultimately as a specialist librarian at the University of Mainz (1788-1793). Forster stayed in Mainz until his support for the revolutionary Mainz Republic saw him banished from the Holy Roman Empire; he died in Paris some six months later at the age of thirty-nine.[1]

Georg Forster brought the insights won over the course of his eventful life to bear on a wide range of intellectual interests and emerging academic disciplines. His *Voyage Round the World* became an instant classic of Enlightenment travel literature, impacting ethnographic studies on the peoples of the South Pacific, especially Tahiti. Forster brought his experiences to bear more generally on debates about the nature and implications of human racial difference, debates which otherwise relied almost exclusively on second- and third-hand information from returning voyagers. His three studies of the breadfruit tree offered, moreover, crucial examples of the way botany was entangled with European colonial expansion. Georg Forster's largest impact, however, might well have come from the work he was least interested in, but nonetheless financially dependent upon: translation. Aided by assistants, and later his wife, Forster worked tirelessly as a conduit of maritime reporting, travelogues, and colonial narratives gathered from across Britain's wide territories. In addition to South Seas literature, Forster was especially interested in accounts from India, producing twenty-eight separate reviews of literature devoted to the subject. Forster published the first German rendering of the ancient Sanskrit drama *Sakontala* from William Jones's English translation,[2] a work which set off a period of ›Indomania,‹ with burgeoning interest in Indian languages and culture from such notable figures as Herder, Goethe, Schlegel, and Wilhelm von Humboldt.

While the life and writings of Georg Forster have been of perennial interest,[3] scholarly work on Forster was significantly enhanced by the preparation of a critical edition of his works started by the Akademie Verlag in East Germany beginning in 1958, thereby transforming discussions of not just Forster, but of the most celebrated authors, themes, and legacies of the German Enlightenment. For example, a great deal of attention has been paid in recent years to Immanuel Kant's (1724-1804) writings on race, work which Forster himself targeted for public criticism in 1786, but which can now also be traced across his letter exchanges at the time.[4] Another target of Forster's criticism, the Göttingen philosopher and historian Christoph Meiners (1747-1810), has been the subject of renewed scholarly interest in the context of eighteenth-century German anthropology and race theory.[5] Other scholars have turned their attention to Herder, whose appreciation for cultural diversity – like Forster's – contrasts favorably with the judgmental eurocentrism of Kant and Meiners.[6] Finally, Forster's robustly international life supports historical studies of the German Enlightenment aiming to show just how engaged Germans were with intellectual and political currents across Europe, Britain, and their colonial possessions in both the Atlantic and the Pacific.[7]

Befitting its focus on Forster, the present forum is a product of a string of international, interdisciplinary collaborations. With support from the Goethe Society of North America, Michael Saman has since 2020 organized an online reading group dedicated to the discussion of literary, anthropological, philosophical, and historical writings touching on the topics of race and imperialism in the German context. For us as historians of philosophy, these discussions have allowed the insights and expertise of our colleagues trained as Germanists, cultural historians, literary critics, and historians of science to broaden our own view of the intellectual dynamics of the German Enlightenment.[8] Inspired by these fruitful interdisciplinary discussions, we organized a seminar on the topic of the German philosophical reception of travel literature from the South Pacific at the 2023 meeting of the German Studies Association in Montréal. The papers that follow grew out of the three mornings of conversations last year in Montréal (and many more since then).

Western Sydney University, Australia, and
Marquette University, Milwaukee, USA

1 Forster's eventful life has been the subject of several recent biographies. See Ludwig Uhlig, Georg Forster. Lebensabenteuer eines gelehrten Weltbürgers (1754-1794), Göttingen 2004; Jürgen Goldenstein, Georg Forster. Zwischen Freiheit und Naturgewalt, Berlin 2015 (translated into English by Anne Janusch as: Georg Forster: Voyager, Naturalist, Revolutionary, Chicago 2019); and Todd Kontje, Georg Forster: German Cosmopolitan, University Park, PA 2024.
2 Sakontala oder der entscheidende Ring, translated by Georg Forster, Mainz and Leipzig 1791; Georg Forsters Werke. Sämtliche Schriften, Tagebücher, Briefe (in the following cited as GFW), vol. 7, Berlin 1958, pp. 277-436.
3 The best history of Forster's reception, both of his person and his works, remains Helmut Peitsch, Georg Forster: A History of his Critical Reception, Frankfurt a. M. 2001.
4 Georg Forster, Noch etwas über die Menschenrassen. An Herrn Dr. Biester, Der Teutsche Merkur, part 4 (1786), pp. 56-86, 150-166; GFW 8: 130-156. Some examples of recent discussions of Kant and race include: David Baumeister, Kant on the Human Animal: Anthropology, Ethics, Race, Evanston, IL 2022; Manfred Geier, Philosophie der Rassen. Der Fall Immanuel Kant, Berlin 2022; and Huaping Lu-Adler, Kant, Race, and Racism: Views from Somewhere, Oxford 2023.
5 See, for example, Stefan Klingner and Gideon Stiening (eds.), Christoph Meiners (1747-1810). Anthropologie und Geschichtsphilosophie in der Spätaufklärung, Berlin 2023. For a broader analysis of anthropology and race in the period, see Carl Niekerk, Enlightenment Anthropology: Defining Humanity in an Era of Colonialism, University Park, PA 2024, especially chapter 4, Race – An Enlightenment Problem (pp. 109-142).
6 See, for example, Gerhard Sauder (ed.), Johann Gottfried Herder (1744-1803). Einheit und nationale Vielfalt, Hamburg 1987; John H. Zammito, Kant, Herder, and the Birth of Anthropology, Chicago 2001; Sonia Sikka, Herder on Humanity and Cultural Difference: Enlightened Relativism, Cambridge 2011; and Nigel DeSouza (ed.), Herder and Naturalism: Philosophy, History, Language, Religion, Berlin 2025.

7 See, for example, Michael Maurer, Aufklärung und Anglophilie in Deutschland, Göttingen 1987; Helmut Peitsch, Georg Forster. Deutsche ›Antheilname‹ an der europäische Expansion über die Welt, Berlin 2017; and Brandan Simms and Torsten Riotte (eds.), The Hanoverian Dimension in British History, 1714-1837, Cambridge 2017.

8 For another product of this collaboration, see the contributions to Michael Saman (ed.), Forum: Race and Imperialism in the Goethe Era, in: Goethe Yearbook, vol. 31 (2024), pp. 84-157.

Georg Forster and the Politics of Natural History: A Case Study for Students of Kant

Jennifer Mensch

Anglophone attention to issues of race and racism, with particular attention to Kant and other members of the German Enlightenment, has long been hampered by a lack of critical editions in English. While this is no longer significantly true for Kant studies, it continues to be the case for many of the most relevant works by Georg Forster and Christoph Meiners. This is a problem for philosophers working exclusively in English, and it is one that is only exacerbated by the field's general lack of interest in not just the intellectual history of philosophy and its figures, but in analyses published in languages other than English today. Ahistorical, monolinguistic approaches become especially problematic, however, when it comes to the philosophical analysis of race and racism, given the need to approach such topics from multiple angles at once – historical, political, cultural, economic, and legal – a fact that is no less true for scholarship on the figures of the eighteenth century than it is for the study of the present one.[1]

My aim in what follows therefore is to fill in a bit of the bigger picture, the specific context within which a writer like Georg Forster and his cohort were working, in order to better frame the kinds of specialized discussions of Kant's philosophy of race that we find today. These discussions can be roughly divided between those investigations focused on issues related to racial taxonomy, and thus situated most clearly within the history of science, and those attentive to the connection between Kant's natural historical writings and his larger systematic concerns regarding the use of teleology when approaching both nature and history.[2] The research done in each of these versions can certainly be valuable, but it remains for the most part disconnected from any discussion of the socio-historical context within which discussions of racial diversity arose in the first place. It is at this point clear to many scholars that eighteenth-century discourse on political rights and personal freedom was framed by an increasing awareness on the part of its central interlocutors of the slave trade, and of the African and Amerindian dispossession this trade entailed. But we should also recognize that the fascination with natural history at the time and the creation of scholarship devoted to investigating »the varieties of mankind« were located within the same socio-political framework.[3] Contrary to a long-standing caricature, Kant was wholly abreast of the world events of his day, and he had ready access to the information coming out of Forster's Göttingen-connected network via the many journals and books produced by the university.⁴ Let us take a closer look then at the wealth of information that Kant would have had before him as he gathered his thoughts about the nature and specific vocation of mankind.

Now as we get started on this investigation, a key historical fact must be borne in mind throughout what follows: Göttingen University was an institution set up by the British to embellish King George I's German ›possession,‹ i. e., the Hannover Protectorate that was governed by a ›Personal Union‹ with England between 1737 and 1837. From the German-born monarch's perspective, Hannover was not just another British outpost, but the one closest to home and heart, and he thus spared no expense when furnishing first Münchhausen and then Heyne (Georg Forster's father-in-law) the funds for building a university with a library and a research faculty that would quickly rival the leading universities in Leyden and Paris on the European continent. This explains not just the enormous number of English-language volumes collected by Heyne for the university library, or the transfer of a large portion of the artifacts collected on Cook's voyages from Banks to Blumenbach in order to establish an ethnological museum, but why more than fifty percent of the students at the university were international, and indeed why King George III sent three of his own sons to study there.⁵

In the 1770s German readers thus received regular reporting via Göttingen on the events unfolding in Britain's American colonies. There might have been pervasive grumbling over the German conscripts being ›sold‹ to enrich certain noblemen in Kassel, but the main buildings in Göttingen were nonetheless lit up in celebration on news of Britain's victories in its campaign against the American rebels.⁶ Benjamin Franklin's immense popularity in Germany – Herder was an tremendous fan – did much to shift public opinion in favor of the colonists once the Treaty in Paris was concluded in 1783. After which Germans proceeded to read with curiosity and interest about the constitutional debates taking place in Philadelphia, even as they were learning of Britain's plans to establish a new ›thief colony‹ at Sydney Cove.

The idea for a new British settlement had been put forward as early as 1784 in light of the dire conditions being experienced by England's prisoner population. With no largescale prisons, convicts who were not to be hanged were primarily housed in floating barges along the Thames, and diseases like cholera were rampant. Up until the outbreak of the war for independence, some 120,000 convicts had been shipped to Britain's American colonies, with a fed-up Benjamin Franklin having reportedly announced at one point that he would like to send back a rattlesnake for every criminal dumped on American shores. The final push for the British decision, however, was the announcement by Russia's leader, the German-born Empress Catherine the Great, that all sales of flax to England would henceforth be subject to a significant tax hike. Flax was a critical import for Britain since it furnished materials for cordage and sails, both items in heavy demand for an empire built and maintained on the back of its ships.[7]

The travel narratives produced in the wake of Captain Cook's three expeditions to the Pacific had in fact carefully recorded the types of resources that might be suitable for colonial acquisition. This was as true for Georg Forster's famous account of the second voyage, as it was for the narrative of Cook's first visit to New Holland (Australia) in 1770. Compiled by John Hawkesworth, the naval report on Cook's first expedition included illustrations, maps, and detailed accounts of sites wherein ships might harbor for repairs. The volumes dedicated to the first voyage were published in 1773 and widely available in German translation the following year, with Kant, for example, making immediate use of them in his course on Physical Geography. It was the narrative's attention to an abundance of flax in the region, however, that seems to have tipped the balance in favor of the thief colony's location. Although Forster had not been to New Holland himself, Cook had made a stop at Norfolk Island, which lays some fourteen-hundred kilometers east of the mainland, with Forster aboard, and both men subsequently noted the potential advantages of the island as a stopover for ships needing to replace sails and masts – Norfolk pines are notably straight and tall – on their way from England to India. In November of 1786 Forster published a new essay on the advantages of Cook's initial landing site on the coast of New Holland, Botany Bay, as a site for a larger settlement and just two weeks later the British parliament formally passed its resolution to establish a penal colony there.[8]

The news on this was greeted with a level of enthusiasm that might seem surprising from our own historical vantage point. But it perfectly captures the widespread cultural belief at the time in the salutary effect of industry and labor. To understand this particular part of the story then is to focus on our main characters' faith in humanity's capacity for moral regeneration under the proper circumstances. Evidence of this for many was taken, on the one hand, from Rome's spectacular rise from inauspicious beginnings and, on the other, the success of the American »convicts« in having created a self-governing republic in their own right. As one observer put it in *The Public Advertiser* in October 1786: »It is an excellent thought on the part of the administration to people this new colony in the very same way their forefathers did America. […] But why mention the grandeur of America from an offspring of convicts, when we have all heard of Rome? Who peopled imperial Rome? Thieves, villains, robbers, and murderers.«[9] The author of this missive signed off as »Numa,« the legendary King of Rome, said to have been born on the day of Rome's founding, and successor to Romulus.

References to Rome, and indeed whole works devoted to the Roman empire, were certainly common in this period. The first volume of Gibbon's now-famous account of Rome's decline and fall (1776; vol. 2, 1781, vol. 3, 1788) appeared in German translation in 1779, with a complete set available in German by 1790. German scholars were of course active in this area as well. Kant owned a copy of Meiners's initial two-volume history of Rome which appeared in 1781 and 1782, but Meiners later came back to the topic in 1791 with a volume meant to serve as a companion to the complete set in German that had appeared the year before.[10] Herder's *Ideen zur Philosophie der Geschichte der Menschheit* (1784-1791) – the first two volumes of which were reviewed by Kant in a manner that effectively ended the friendship between him and his former student – also included long discussions of the history and lessons to be gleaned from the Romans. It should perhaps come as no surprise therefore to see references to the example provided by Rome appearing in German language news of British plans for the new colony. As one put it in the *Wiener Zeitung* of January 1787: the plan for the convicts »on the one hand exonerates the country of the outcasts of society, and perhaps at the same time works on the other hand through the betterment of these people to make them useful to humanity and the kingdom.« Indeed, one could hope that »eventually they may also erect a flourishing state, as did a band of not much better men a Rome and Roman Empire.«[11]

One particular class of English sentiment here was prepared to make the connection to Rome by way of William Hamilton's highly popular account of Etruscan art (1766). Hamilton had served as the British Ambassador to Naples, but his clear passion was Roman art and history. The potter Josiah Wedgewood was so taken by Hamilton's account that he named his new factory »Etruria« with the aim of creating jasper porcelain in emulation of Etruscan ceramics, and in 1769 the first products bore the stamp »Artes Etruriae Renascuntur« [The Arts of Etruria Reborn].[12] Wedgewood's great friend, the polymathic poet Erasmus Darwin, was similarly attracted to both the legends surrounding Rome and the model it provided for the planned colony. Thus when Joseph Banks sent batches of clay he had received from the newly established settlement to Wedgewood for testing (he also sent a batch to his friend Blumenbach in Göttingen), the two friends worked together, the one producing a series of clay medallions, and the other writing a commemorative poem to match, in honor of the new colony.

Wedgewood's »Sydney Cove« medallions demonstrated the utility of the clay samples for manufacturing earthenware goods, and therefore worked, as he saw it, as a model pathway for the convicts to emulate in their pursuit of moral uplift through labor. The medallion itself depicted four maidens in classical attire, with a ship in the distance, and »Etruria 1789« printed below the scene. The formal title read: »Hope encouraging Art and Labour, under the influence of Peace, to pursue the employment necessary to give security and happiness to an infant settlement,« with Darwin's poem echoing this in its title: »Visit of Hope to Sydney Cove.« This was in fact not the first effort on the part of the two friends to work together for what they saw as the betterment of society. Two years earlier, Wedgewood had designed a small cameo to be carried as identification for those committed to the abolition of the slave trade. The potter had produced and shipped dozens of the medallions at his own expense to abolitionist societies, including to Benjamin Franklin, who served as the President of the Philadelphia Society for the Abolition of Slavery. In this case, Darwin had again written a set of verses to match, with these eventually appearing as part of his long-form poem on the *Economy of Vegetation* (1791). Here Darwin explicitly drew a connection between Wedgewood's pieces – in the 1806 edition of *The Poetical Works of Erasmus Darwin* he would have images of both medallions printed on the facing page – writing: »The bold cameo speaks, the soft intaglio thinks. / Whether, O Friend of Art! The gem you mould / Rich with new taste, with ancient virtue bold; / Form the poor fetter'd SLAVE on bended knee / From Britain's sons imploring to be free; / Or with fair HOPE the brightening scenes improve, / And cheer the dreary wastes at Sydney Cove.«[13] The connection between these companion medallions was clear so far as the two friends were concerned: moral reform could be achieved, whether through industry on the part of the convicts facing seven to fourteen years of hard labor in the new Welsh colony, or via abolition of the slave trade.

The portrayal of New Holland as the site of a new Etruria appeared repeatedly in these years. Forster's father-in-law, C. G. Heyne, Professor of Eloquence and Poetry and, as noted already, head of the university library at Göttingen, gave an address on Roman deportation in relation to Botany Bay in 1791, and Forster's wife, Therese Heyne Forster, was at work on a book (published in 1801 under her second husband's name, Ludwig Ferdinand Huber), focused on the moral regeneration of a group of settlers on Norfolk Island.[14] In addition to the first artwork (Wedgewood), poetry (Darwin), and fiction (Huber) produced in connection to the newly established thief colony, there appeared in London *A New Moral System of Geography* (1790) for children. This would be the first educational work to make mention of the settlement, with the publishers explaining in an Appendix that »Botany Bay being now a part of the world allotted for civilization, we have collected the following particulars respecting the geography of this new world, from the most accurate and authentic accounts we could find.«[15] What followed were seven or so pages of ethnographic description of the native inhabitants, a discussion of the animals, fish, and climate, and a conclusion betraying the author's commercial instincts, so far as it remarked on the lack of minerals, gems, or furs (the latter having been seen as a key part of Cook's discoveries along the Pacific Northwest coastlines), and thus wondering out loud at the choice of the far-flung location in the first place.

At this point the »most accurate and authentic accounts« of the new colony would have been found in Robert Nares's compilation of the reports submitted by the colony's Governor, Arthur Phillip, and produced by John Stockdale in London in 1789. Published as *The Voyage of Governor Phillip to Botany Bay; with an Account of the Establishment of the Colonies of Port Jackson & Norfolk Island*, the book had an engraving of Wedgewood's Sydney Cove medallion on its frontispiece and included Darwin's poem after the publisher's brief account of Wedgewood's title of the vignette. Within months of its appearance, Georg Forster published a report on the book for German readers. At the time, Forster was undoubtedly best known for his narrative of Captain Cook's second voyage to the South Pacific, but from our own vantage point it might be plausibly argued that Forster's main contribution to the German reading public was the subsequent fifteen years spent by him translating and reviewing reports on the many activities undertaken in those years in service of science and empire. The busy year of 1789 was no different, with Forster publishing some twenty reviews, including, at Heyne's insistence, an anonymous review of his *own* collection of short pieces connected to his time in the South Seas. Forster's first review in 1790 was his account of Stockdale's *Voyage of Governor Phillip to Botany Bay*, which, given Forster's detailed attention in it to the flora and fauna of the region, functioned as something of a sequel to his 1786 essay on Botany Bay (reproduced in the 1789 collection).

Following some opening remarks, Forster took time to carefully describe the frontispiece to Phillip's *Voyage* for his readers. Wedgewood was already famous in Germany, enough so that it made news in Königsberg when Paul Collin, a former apprentice at the Etruria factory, had managed to replicate Wedgewood's black porcelain, »und schon die Bildnisse verschiedener Personen, als des Herzoges und der Herzoginn von Kurrland, des Oberpräsidenten von Damhard, des Hrn. Prof. Kant, u. a. m. darinn in basrelief ausgearbeitet, so daß jedermann nicht nur über die auffallende Aehnlichkeit, sondern auch über die Feinheit des Grabstichels gestaunt.«[16] Of Darwin's companion poem included in the *Voyage*, Forster wrote that it was »eine Prophezeihung von künftiger Herrlichkeit der neuen Colonie« (GFW 11: 215). Forster went on to briefly outline Cook's initial discovery of New Holland in 1770 before referring readers to his 1789 report on

Watkin Tench's unauthorized account of the new colony, which had appeared a few months ahead of the official one.

Here it is worth remarking on the intertextuality of Forster's method when approaching his writing projects. Starting with a published review, Forster would go on to develop his thoughts in his letter exchanges with Heyne and others. This would often enough lead to a decision to undertake a translation of a piece, with an added editorial apparatus in the form of both elaborative and corrective footnotes. At this point Forster would typically produce a reflective preamble or postscript, and in rare instances write an additional standalone essay. In this vein, for scholars working on Forster and Kant's dispute over racial determination, it is not enough to simply look at Forster's 1786 essay on the topic (GFW 8: 130-156), since Forster in fact brooded over the issue in multiple letters at the time and then continued to think through matters indirectly in his pieces on Botany Bay, and in the long biographical preface he wrote to accompany the publication of his translation of the official narrative of Cook's third voyage in 1787.[17]

In these texts Forster was optimistic regarding the promise afforded by Britain's Pacific expeditions, and he was, if not quite endorsing these as part of some kind of »civilizing mission,« certainly still hopeful regarding the advantages that could be gained for native inhabitants via a process of shared scientific and technological advancements. Forster was critical of what he took to be European romantic fantasies regarding the virtues and simplicity of Rousseau's »noble savage,« for while he insisted that happiness was a state achieved by each of nature's creatures in their own fashion – »the joy of life dwells to equal degree in the worm« (GFW 5: 161) – the merits of »civilized life« for comfort and thought could not be denied. As he put it in the essay on Botany Bay, »Cultural advancement is thus in the interests of mankind, and population of the whole earth with civilized inhabitants is the great goal which we above all see before us as worthy of our efforts« (GFW 5: 162). Forster's hero in this process was »the immortal Cook,« a modern-day Columbus who had opened commercial trade on both sides of the Pacific and led to the creation of a new thief colony at Botany Bay. »Certainly the first settlers of New Holland are villainous rabble,« Forster acknowledged, but »it is sufficiently proved by ancient and modern history that he ceases to be an enemy of society whenever he regains his full human rights and becomes a proprietor and cultivator of land« (GFW 5: 163). Forster's examples? Rome: »The robber band of the Seven Hills became through Numa's precepts the most eminent and most admired people on earth« (GFW 5: 163); and America, for »[t]he descendants of the offenders who James I first sent to Virginia now hold rank and voice among the nations and have become through Franklin and Washington free allies of the mightiest European states« (GFW 5:164). Here Forster echoed sentiments voiced on both sides of the Channel regarding the prospects for the new colony, before going on to a detailed description of the nature of the place taken up from both Hawkesworth's account, and whatever knowledge transfer had no doubt occurred during Forster's own long journey with Cook on the second voyage. Remarking that the »The savages on the coast are of medium size, well-proportioned and stout, but not especially lively and, like all savages, inactive and lazy« (GFW 5: 174), Forster still believed that the site was ideal given the low number of natives, the natural resources, and the deep harbors suitable for landing crews and supplies (GFW 5: 179).

This approach was continued in the following year's discourse on Cook, with the same optimism regarding the fruits of colonial commercial exchanges and settlement, and a firm belief in the advantages to be gained by a technology transfer from Europe to its colonies, with America cited once more as the proof of concept for this hope. Forster's report on Tench's unauthorized narrative stands out therefore, since here we see some wavering as Forster's text summarized an increasing sense that the native inhabitants might be incurably resistant to the settler's overtures: »Alle Bemühungen, ihr Vertrauen und ihre Freundschaft zu gewinnen, sind fruchtlos geblieben; Leichtsinn, Mißtrauen, Unbeständigkeit, Indolenz und vielleicht Geringschätzung derer, die ihre Übermacht nicht fühlen lassen, vereiteln bey ihnen jeden Versuch zur Annäherung« (GFW 5: 167). Even worse from Forster's perspective was the fact that the convicts had in some cases continued as before, stealing and wreaking havoc, such that a few had ultimately been hanged (GFW 5: 167).[18] Governor Phillip returned to England shortly after its founding with mixed feelings regarding the experiment. And the effort to maintain a colony on Norfolk Island would be abandoned within a decade: not only was flax *not* abundant, the colony never became self-sustaining, requiring ships to routinely navigate what were treacherous bays in all but the calmest ocean conditions. Forster's reserve after reading Tench, in other words, was in some ways prescient of the many difficult years ahead for the new Etruria.

As we bring this case study from Kant's time to a close, it should be clear by now that German audiences were deeply aware of the events happening in the broader world, and especially so with respect to Britain's geopolitical maneuvering. Even as readers reveled in tales of exotic lands and the plucky adventurers who visited them, the narratives themselves were in fact a serious business, offering not just life-saving information to ships looking for safe harbors with fresh food and water, but blueprints for colonial expansion. In this way natural historical reports became also texts of socio-political significance. Scientific descriptions did not simply add to botanical knowledge, they also informed governments of prospects for commercial exchange and, in the case of Britain's empire, of the possibilities for resource management across its many colonies. Joseph Banks's decision to transplant breadfruit – as an »ideal« food for the enslaved – from the South Pacific to the West Indies, is just one example of this among many. In light of this, it is all the more important that philosophers pay close attention to the context within which the figures we study both lived and worked. We should reject efforts to distinguish between so-called »abstract« philosophical positions and the context within which they were generated. There is no such thing as »a view from nowhere,« and the effort to maintain belief in one reveals a desire to maintain the status quo in a field that still looks very much like it did when Kant and his colleagues mounted their own lecterns each week, ready to explain the great business of the world to their students.[19]

Western Sydney University, Australia

---

1 The point has been made by Robert Bernasconi, Critical Philosophy of Race and Philosophical Historiography, in: Paul Taylor, et. al. (eds.), The Routledge Companion to the Philosophy of Race, London 2017, pp. 3-13.
2 I have produced work of both kinds myself, e.g., Species, Variety, Race: Vocabularies of Difference from Buffon to Kant, in: Dianoia-Rivista di Filosofia, vol. 39 (2024), pp. 155-179; From Crooked Wood to Moral Agent: Connecting Anthropology and Ethics in Kant, in: Estudos Kantianos, vol. 2.1 (2014), pp. 185-204.
3 See for example Silvia Sebastiani, The Scottish Enlightenment: Race, Gender, and the Limits of Progress, New York, 2013, Andrew Curran, The Anatomy of Blackness: Science and Slavery in an Age of Enlightenment, Baltimore, 2013, and Julia Jorati, Slavery and Race: Philosophical Debates in the Eighteenth Century, Oxford 2024.
4 Although Kant considered the *Göttingschen Anzeigen von gelehrten Sachen* – the venue where the bulk of Georg Forster's reviews appeared – to be essentially hostile to his own work, he followed it closely. For some evidence of this see my essay: »Kant and the Problem of Idealism: On the Significance of the Göttingen Review« in The Southern Journal of Philosophy, vol. 44.2 (Summer 2006), pp. 297-317. But we can also hear directly from Kant, who asked his publisher Friedrich Nicolovius to tell Forster: »Ich bitte Ihn meiner Seits meiner größten Hochachtung und zugleich der Dankbarkeit, für die mannigfaltige aus seinen interessanten Schriften gezogene Ergötzung und Belehrung, zu versichern« (18 November 1790), in: Kants gesammelte Schriften, vol. 11, Berlin 1902-, p. 235.
5 For Göttingen's scholarly impact see Thomas Biskup, The university of Göttingen and the Personal Union, 1737-1837, in: Brandan Simms and Torsten Riotte (eds.), The Hanoverian Dimension in British History, 1714-1837, Cambridge 2017, pp. 128-160, and Charles McClelland, State, Society, and University in Germany: 1700-1914, Cambridge 1980, pp. 34-149. Kant's estate catalogue includes multiple copies of Wieland's Weimar journal, *Der Teutsche Merkur* (1773-1790), but both Wieland (›Wylandt‹) and the *Merkur* are mentioned repeatedly

across Kant's letter exchanges, starting in 1774 with reference to Wieland and Goethe's relation to the new Philanthropinum school in Dessau. In 1786 the *Merkur* published the first of Reinhold's important »Letters on Kantian Philosophy,« but we might note rather that issue's inclusion of an article with a description of the famed Göttingen library and its liberal lending practices: Auszug eines Briefes über Göttingen, in: Der Teutsche Merkur von 1786, Erstes Vierteljahr, Weimar, pp. 90-96.

6 Two excellent resources here are Horst Dippel, Germany and the American Revolution: 1770-1800, Chapel Hill 1977, and Eugene Doll, American History as Interpreted by German Historians from 1770-1815, Transactions of the American Philosophical Society, Philadelphia 1949. Doll's piece discusses Forster at numerous points (Forster, like Herder and many others, was a member of the American Philosophical Society), but the text is best read with a copy of Baginsky's helpfully annotated bibliography nearby: Paul Ben Baginsky, Bibliography of German Works Relating to America, 1493-1800, Berwyn Heights, 2019 [1938]. For a sense of contemporary responses to conscription see: Henry Stafford King, Echoes of the American Revolution in German Literature, Berkeley 1929, and Albert Schmitt, Herder und Amerika, The Hague 1967.

7 Britain's thirst for this material added obvious motivation to Prussia's desire to takeover Silesia's large production of spruce linen. On the Silesian linen trade see: Anka Steffen and Klaus Webber, Spinning and Weaving for the Slave Trade: Proto-Industry in Eighteenth-Century Silesia, in: Felix Brahm and Eve Rosenhaft (eds.), Slavery Hinterland: Transatlantic Slavery and Continental Europe, 1680-1850, Cambridge 2021, pp. 87-108, and Anka Steffen, Silesia, Serfdom, and Slavery, in: Journal of Global Slavery, vol. 8 (2023), pp. 237-268.

8 Forster's essay was initially planned to accompany his translation of Cook's third voyage, but as events quickly unfolded – Arthur Phillip had already been named the prospective Governor of the new colony ahead of parliamentary debate – Forster published his account separately. See: Neuholland und die brittische Colonie in Botany-Bay, in: Georg Forsters Werke. Sämtliche Schriften, Tagebücher, Briefe, vol. 5, Berlin 1958, pp. 160-180. Subsequent references to Forster's Werke will be cited in-text as GFW followed by volume and page number, e.g., GFW 5: 160. The history here is told especially well by Robert J. King, Norfolk Island: Phantasy and Reality, 1770-1814, in: The Great Circle, A Publication of the Australian Association for Maritime History, vol. 25.2 (2003), pp. 20-41.

9 Cited by Robert J. King, www.australiaonthemap.org/index.html%3Fp=400.html, note 5.

10 For more on this see: Wilfried Nippel, Gibbon and German Historiography, in: Benedikt Stuchtey and Peter Wende (eds.), British and German Historiography 1750-1950: Traditions, Perceptions and Transfers, Oxford 2000, pp. 67-81.

11 Wiener Zeitung, 20 January 1787, pp. 149-150; cited in: Robert J. King, unpublished ms. notes, with thanks to author for permission to cite from them.

12 Much of this is recounted in Robert J. King's history of a seal for the new colony: Etruria, the Great Seal of New South Wales, in: Journal of the Numismatic Association of Australia, vol. 5 (October 1990), pp. 3-8.

13 Erasmus Darwin, The Poetical Works of Erasmus Darwin, London 1806, vol. 1, pp. 99-102. Emma Butler-Nixon has put together a nice narrative of this history,

with clear images of the medallions and the abolitionist cameo, for the State Library of New South Wales, see www.sl.nsw.gov.au/stories/moulding-eligant-impression-primitive-earth.

14 A translation of Heyne's Latin address by P. M. McCallum, alongside a careful comparison of the points raised by Heyne in tandem with Forster's 1786 essay on Botany Bay can be found in: E. A. Judge, C. G. Heine's Address on Roman Deportation: A 1791 Comparison with Botany Bay, in: Ancient History, vol. 29.2 (1999), pp. 118-158. Therese Huber's book has been translated by Rodney Livingstone with an introduction and notes by Leslie Bodi: Adventures on a Journey to New Holland, Sydney 1966. Huber's text drew from Forster's knowledge of the Pacific and especially Norfolk Island, and she was explicit in revealing the main character, Rudolf, to have been an avatar for Forster himself. A good starting point for further discussion of her work is Lisa O'Connell, Before *Frankenstein*: Therese Huber and the Antipodean Emergence of Political Fiction, in: Postcolonial Studies, vol. 23.3 (2020), pp. 348-359. Huber seems to have seen one of Wedgewood's slave cameos for the first time in 1818, an experience that had an immediate impact on her subsequent abolitionist activities. See Sarah Lentz, Abolitionists in the German Hinterland? Therese Huber and the Spread of Anti-slavery Sentiment in the German Territories in the Early Nineteenth Century, in: Felix Brahm and Eve Rosenhaft (eds.), Slavery Hinterland: Transatlantic Slavery and Continental Europe, 1680-1850, Cambridge 2021, pp. 187-212.

15 A New Moral System of Geography, printed by S. Hazard for G. Riley, Bath 1790, p. 181.

16 Physikalisch-Ökonomische Zeutung, 5ts Stück, Februar 1785, p. 97. Collin's portrayal of Kant can be seen here: users.manchester.edu/facstaff/ssnaragon/kant/helps/Life/IconData.html#1782Collin.

17 A concise account of Forster's position on race viz. Kant can be found in: Ludwig Uhlig, Georg Forster und Herder, in: Euphorion, vol. 84 (1990), pp. 339-366, with comprehensive treatments by Michael Weingarten, Menschenarten oder Menschenrassen. Die Kontroverse zwischen Georg Forster und Immanuel Kant, in: Gerhardt Pickerodt (ed.), Georg Forster in seiner Epoche, Berlin 1982, pp. 117-148, and Ludwig Uhlig, Die Südseevölker und Georg Forsters Rassenbegriff, in: Georg-Forster-Studien (2010), pp. 137-172.

18 As we read through Forster's letters to Therese only a few years later in war torn Paris, the Mainz Jacobin seems to have become thoroughly disillusioned, with all of his former optimism and faith in humankind's essential perfectibility gone. See on this especially: Christoph Bode, Georg Forster in Paris (1794/94), in: Litteraria Pragensia: Studies in Literature & Culture, vol. 29, no. 57 (2019), pp. 60-74.

19 My thanks to Corey Beckford for his insights regarding this; personal communication, 10 August 2024. For an approach to Kant that starts from this viewpoint see: Huaping Lu-Adler, Kant, Race and Racism: The View from Somewhere, Oxford 2023.

Classical Quotations in Georg Forster's Anthropological Essays: »Pausing on the Threshold«

Madhuvanti Karyekar

The name of German voyager, travel-writer, translator, naturalist, and revolutionary Georg Forster (1754-1794) has become increasingly popular in works on the history of Enlightenment anthropology. Forster scholars have written on his forward-looking intercultural awareness, cosmopolitanism, revolutionary spirit, and pioneering contributions to ethnography and travel writing. Through literary analysis of Forster's travel narratives, translations, critical essays, and book reviews, my research has focused so far on identifying distinguishing features of Forster's contributions to the practice of late eighteenth-century anthropology, which meant »doing ethnography« in its most literal sense – that is, by *writing* (*graphia*) about peoples from various cultures (*ethnos*). Hence, I have been equally interested in understanding the making of Forster's anthropological / ethnographic texts along with their content.[1] As James Clifford famously claimed in his introductory preface »Partial Truths« to the anthology of essays on »Writing Cultures,« one of the principal things ethnographers do is »write,« and writing is a crucial aspect of an anthropologist's work both during field research and afterward, putting textualization at the heart of the ethnographic experience.[2] In line with this argument, I see Forster's »völkerkundliche Anthropologie«[3] as his attempt to contribute to an empirical and scientific description of the world and its inhabitants, highlighting the narrative and performative aspect of how anthropological knowledge is created. Therefore, to understand the extent of Forster's writings, we need to work through the systematic and situational verbal structures that determine his representations of reality. The following reflection is one such attempt to critically engage with a consistent writing strategy embedded in Forster's ethnographic texts – the use of quotations from classical works. I am specifically interested in analyzing the quotations used by Forster that open an essay and resist easy recontextualization and interpretation for a hermeneutic reading of the text that follows the quotation, even though they serve as the »threshold« that readers must cross before engaging with the subsequent text.

Many of Forster's philosophical and anthropological essays, such as »O-Taheiti (1779),« »Neuholland und die brittische Colonie in Botany-Bay (1787),« »Cook der Entdecker (1787),« »Leitfaden zu einer künftigen Geschichte der Menschheit (1789),« »Über den gelehrten Zunftzwang (1792),« and »Über Leckereyen (1788),« open with classical quotations.

While the content of these essays has garnered much attention, the role of these introductory quotations has often been overlooked, perhaps because only sometimes these quotations seem to be linked to the ensuing content; at other times they seem disconnected, and their purpose appears to be elusive. The present paper seeks to redress this balance by looking less at the content of the essays and more at the relationship between Forster's quotations and the main text, using the theoretical framework provided by Gerard Genette for understanding the paratextual nature of these quotes and a rhetorical approach that examines how quotations work to enhance the persuasiveness of an argument.[4] During Forster's era, embedding quotations from classical literature in texts was a standard practice for establishing one's own intellectual credentials, which served to highlight the writer's education and familiarity with canonical sources and helped to affirm his/ her legitimacy and credibility. Forster's use of classical quotations, however, often transcends mere display of erudition. Scholars like Stefan Goldmann and Johannes Görbert have explored the function and purpose of quotations in Forster's various writings. Goldmann argues that Forster used quotations from classical authors to speak his mind while avoiding direct responsibility for his words, a function he terms »Entlastungsfunktion.«[5] Görbert understands the quotations Forster uses in his *Reise um die Welt* as »decorative clues« that highlight his educational background, serve as »loci communes« amidst the overwhelming foreign experience of new lands and people, and emphasize moral lessons from traditional voices throughout the world.[6] My essay argues, in contrast, that the quotations used by Forster to preface his critical essays go beyond the above-mentioned functions; these epigraphs – as Genette calls them – crucially influence the reader's interpretation and engagement from the outset, shaping the reading experience and amplifying the scholarly and rhetorical impact of Forster's work.

Moreover, to me, the authorial decision to open a crucial essay with a classical quotation in a language that most readers may not be familiar with is a bold one, as it could turn off readers' interest or may not serve its purpose in guiding the reading process. While Forster's intended audience likely included scientifically inclined readers familiar with classical languages and canonical works, it also encompassed a wider readership of travelogue enthusiasts, many of whom were laypeople. What impact from these quotations did Forster envision for his readers? For, as Genette observes, without editorial guidance, the ordinary reader often remains uncertain of the epigraph's purpose, left to guess its meaning or remain indifferent.[7] This uncertainty is further complicated by the fact that, as Meir Steinberg argues, quotations assume new meanings when transplanted from their original contexts.[8] Frederick E. Brenk expands on this idea, suggesting that quotations create a conflict or »seam« between themselves and their new contexts, potentially disrupting the coherence of the literary structure and the unity of perception.⁹ Building on these observations, this essay operates under the assumption that readers actively engage with epigraphs and that their meanings are products of readers' interpretive processes. It acknowledges that epigraphs can function as both »hermeneutic blinders« imposed by the author¹⁰ and as interferences that introduce foreign or unexpected elements, prompting readers to actively integrate them into their understanding of the text.

Considering the scope of this reflection, I have chosen to discuss the quotation that opens Forster's 1784 essay »Vom Brodbaum« [Of the Breadfruit Tree]. »Vom Brodbaum« as an essay, which Forster described as a »Beytrag zur Geschichte und Beschreibung eines in aller Absicht so wichtigen Naturproduktes,«¹¹ outlines not only the natural history of the breadfruit tree but also its cultural significance, blending diachronic and synchronic natural and cultural semantics to illustrate the tree's importance in various parts of the world. After publishing *Voyage Round the World* (1777) and its two-volume German version *Reise um die Welt* (1778/1780), along with many book reviews (mainly of travel literature) and translations, Forster had established his reputation as a renowned translator and reviewer in German academic circles. His scholarly work up until 1784 centered on writing about diverse cultures, appropriating foreign information, and using new anthropological information to write about various manifestations of the human race. Amidst these publications, »Vom Brodbaum« might seem an unusual entry, but it exemplifies Forster's interdisciplinary approach, weaving together botany, geography, social studies, economics, and natural science.

The essay consists of two parts – one philosophical or historical, inspired by Buffon, and the second taxonomic in nature in the spirit of Linné. In his characteristic style, Forster incorporates several important topics of his time in this essay, for example eighteenth-century European trade, its advantages and disadvantages, the voyages of discovery, and their implications for the science of man, the genre of travel writing, and the dissemination of knowledge about newly discovered parts of the world through travel literature. His comments on the natural history and cultivation of the breadfruit tree open discussions on how civilizations utilize natural resources, shape cultural practices around these products, and strategically transplant, adapt, and regenerate these products in new environments for the benefit of humanity. Forster conveys all this with his characteristic scientific and rational approach, employing rhetorical devices, wit, irony, sarcasm, and criticism to address significant contemporaneous issues such as the slave trade, the appropriation of newfound knowledge of non-Western civilizations, and the understanding of human diversity.

The essay begins with a Latin quotation from Horace: »at mihi cura; non mediocris inest, fontes ut adire remotos; atque haurire queam uitae praecepta beatae« (63).[12] Translated word-for-word, the quote reads in English as: »But in me, there is a not-moderate longing; that I may be able to go towards distant springs; and drink the lessons of a happy life.«[13] Immediately following these lines comes the first sentence of the essay: »Seit mehr als drittehalb hundert Jahren zieht Europa durch seinen alles verschlingenden Handel die asiatischen Naturgeschenke und die des vierten und fünften Welttheils an sich, und giebt ihnen durch neue Arten der Anwendung einen Werth, den sie in ihrem Vaterlande nicht hatten« (63). How should a reader, who has just crossed the threshold of Horace's quotation and is full of ideas about going to far-off distances to partake in philosophical teachings of a happy life, connect this initial sentence of the essay – one that simultaneously critiques and praises eighteenth-century European trade and commerce – with the themes of the quotation? Is Forster equating the act of seeking distant springs with European voyages of exploration? If so, how should we interpret »the lessons of a happy life« in this context? If European trade is described as »alles verschlingend,« how can it be justified by emphasizing that the natural products from non-European regions gained greater value when introduced to Europe? In cases like this, readers' desire for consistency in the author's ideas makes them first seek the context of the quotation.

Forster cites this text from Horace's satire 2.4, which is a part of the second book of »Sermones« (Satires), written between 33 and 30 BCE. This satire presents a humorous take on Epicureanism's emphasis on pleasure, particularly in the realm of food. Along with the other seven satires in Book 2, it employs philosophical dialogues, often compared to Plato's work, to satirize various schools of thought.[14] In this specific satire, Horace encounters Catius (an Epicurean philosopher, known to give lectures on various topics related to food), who appears to be in a great hurry to write down thoughts he just heard in a lecture on cooking. When probed further, Catius condescendingly agrees to share the great ›precepts verbatim from memory,‹ and breaks into a long monologue on creating a perfect meal. Through Catius's pretentious speech, Horace subtly mocks the absurdity of elevating culinary pursuits to the level of philosophy, suggesting that the focus on food pleasure overshadows true epicurean philosophy.[15] The satire concludes with Horace's ironic request to Catius to take him to the next lecture, giving the following reason: »nam quamuis referas memori mihi pectore cuncta, non tamen interpres tantundem iuueris. adde uultum habitumque hominis, quem tu uidisse beatus non magni pendis, quia contigit.«[16] This translates word-for-word as: »For however much you deliver (or report) the whole to me with remembering mind; yet as an interpreter you by no means please me just as much; add to this the face and bearing of the man, which, you lucky fellow, having seen, (you) weigh out not as important, because it has come (happened to you).« In Horace's satire, these lines get their meaning through the intended dramatic irony: instead of dismissing what Catius just said, Horace implies that he will need to hear this great gourmet talk, and he will need to do that because when anyone recounts the thoughts of a speaker, with whom one is familiar, one tends to not do justice to the original thoughts, because in all familiarity one tends to overlook certain things. Horace continues further that this is the reason why he is not afraid of going to distant springs and learn about the new knowledge directly from those sources. This is the original context for the lines Forster uses at the beginning of »Vom Brodbaum.« What possibilities of meaning and connection between the epigraph and the main body of the essay can readers explore then?

One possibility relates to Forster's emphasis on eye-witness accounts in travel literature. Forster is highlighting his distinct position among contemporaries as a man who traveled around the world, suggesting that readers can trust his information. This emphasis on direct experience and observation not only underscores his credibility but also positions him as a reliable source in an era where second-hand reports were common. In this interpretation, however, the original dramatic irony intended by Horace is completely lost. Alternatively, Forster might be emphasizing skepticism: One should not believe everything that one hears, and one should be skeptical of it until one confirms it through other means. This interpretation is plausible because it aligns with the motto of the Royal Society of London for Improving Natural Knowledge (to which Forster was admitted at the age of twenty-two) – *Nullius in Verba* (Take nobody's word for it). This motto also serves as the epigraph opening the literary monument Forster erected for Caption Cook in »Cook der Entdecker.« Through Horace's lines, Forster might be cautioning his readers not to get convinced too easily by everything they read, especially in travel literature. Or Forster might be targeting speculative philosophies attempting to explain human diversity using empty concepts and jargon, without placing them on the firm ground of experience.

Another possible interpretation of the quotation arises when we take into consideration the line that precedes the text quoted by Forster, which, although not explicitly included in his citation, influences its meaning and context: »non magni pendis, quia contigit.« As explained above, Horace uses these words to state that one tends to lessen the value of things with which one is very familiar. In the context of the breadfruit tree essay, Forster hints at the fact that the breadfruit tree is underappreciated by those who use it daily; and perhaps those who are overly familiar with it will not be able to value it as high as they should. And therefore, he implies that it could be valued more by outsiders who discover its richness through exploration. According to this interpretation, Forster argues that outsiders, who encounter the tree anew, are more likely to be impressed and appreciative of it than the locals who are accustomed to it. This perspective is supported by clues in the breadfruit tree essay, suggesting that Forster believes the tree deserves greater recognition from those who see its value from an external viewpoint.

At the beginning of the essay, Forster highlights that early European travelers recognized the breadfruit diet's effectiveness against scurvy and praised the tree as »one of the most beneficial natural products« in their reports from the late eighteenth century (63). He further notes that in the regions where the tree grows – across various islands from Java to the South Sea Islands – shelter and clothing, which are primary necessities elsewhere, are considered luxuries. And since their need for sustenance is so easily met through a nutrient-rich food, its value is not always recognized by those who profit from it most: »wie so vielen andern guten und in ihrer Art vortreflichen Dingen: sein großer Werth ward nirgends weniger, als in seinem ursprünglichen Vaterlande erkannt« (73). One might then assume that Forster aims to show that outsiders – i.e., non-native Pacific Islanders such as Europeans – are more likely to appreciate the breadfruit tree because natives take its use and worth for granted. Why would Forster, who criticized Eurocentric views on non-European worlds in his first travelogue and described European trade as »all-devouring« at the beginning of the breadfruit tree essay, want to urge Europeans to be the people who truly understand the worth of the breadfruit tree, specifically when Forster also notes that »[e]s [...] nicht zu leugnen [ist], daß sich kein unmittelbarer Nutzen für Europa von diesem Baum erwarten läßt« (64). The answer lies in what Forster was actually proposing through the breadfruit tree essay without explicitly saying it.

From the outset, »Vom Brodbaum« presents a structured argument: it describes the historical usefulness of the breadfruit tree as observed by European travelers, emphasizes its non-native status in its current locations – transplanted and cultivated successfully by human efforts on many Pacific islands – and contrasts this with unsuccessful attempts to cultivate the tree in European countries. These facts underscore several key points: the breadfruit tree thrives abundantly in warm climates, including regions where it is not indigenous. Efforts to cultivate it in Europe, even in the warmer southern parts of Italy and Portugal, met with failure as the tree struggled to survive winter months (64). Forster's exploration reveals the breadfruit tree as akin to a »wish-fulfilling« tree, utilized comprehensively to support various aspects of human life on the islands where it grows. Forster builds on this line of argument to impress on his readers that the breadfruit tree, a vital resource sustaining various island communities, is a remarkable discovery for those who encounter it through exploratory voyages. Therefore, so he implies, non-natives on the islands, such as European voyagers who can perceive the tree beyond its role in fulfilling daily needs, should consider how this resource can benefit humanity at large.

Forster reports that one such effort to make breadfruit tree useful to less fortunate humans still has been without any success. He refers here to the failure to implement the idea of cultivating the breadfruit tree in the West Indies for the benefit of Black enslaved (64). When expressing his discontent on the matter of enslavement and the inhuman conditions under which the enslaved are kept, Forster's tone assumes biting sarcasm when he says that despite the uncertainty about Black peoples' descent, they are humans, and we should therefore feel more strongly about their mistreatment. From this perspective, Forster writes further, the proposal to transplant and cultivate the breadfruit tree on the West Indies islands was rational and humanitarian, and should have been met with enthusiasm. But Forster then comments ironically, since when has greed not clouded the better judgment of human beings (64)? Since no action has been taken to implement the suggestion of cultivating the breadfruit tree for the benefit of enslaved Blacks, Forster implicitly proposes an alternative solution. It can be inferred from the overall argument of his essay.

After detailing the breadfruit tree's natural history across diverse regions – from Colombo to the Spice Islands to the South Sea islands – and noting its cultural adaptations, including some loss of awareness of its healing properties, Forster underscores the tree's enduring utility across all its parts. He then makes a key observation about the effects of daily breadfruit consumption on the people who rely on it. Forster notes the physical beauty, healthy appetite, and virtuous outlook of these people, emphasizing the positive effects of the breadfruit diet on their well-being. Cautiously he states, that we do not know with certainty now that eating such nutritious food has obvious effects on innate bearing – that will be a topic to be researched in the later years; however, »Wir wissen nur mit Zuverlässigkeit, dass Sanftmuth, Liebe und Fühlbarkeit des Herzens die hervorstehenden Characterzüge des Menschen sind, der von der Brodfrucht lebt« (79-80). This implies that if Europeans were to consume this breadfruit daily, it would not affect their innate character (as a form of degeneration); if anything, it would help bringing out the best in them. And therefore, establishing European settlements in the parts where the breadfruit trees grow in abundance can be beneficial. To support this unspoken claim, Forster cites Cook's observation that planting just ten breadfruit trees in one's lifetime could provide sufficient sustenance for one's own and the next generation, akin to the efforts of a European farmer who provides for his family and saves for future generations (79-80). Forster notes that a few breadfruit trees can yield enough to support multiple people comfortably, and they do not take up much land either. Forster suggests that Tahiti, with its ample land and the breadfruit tree's productivity, could support a larger population than its current inhabitants. Though not explicitly stated, Forster implies that European settlements on Tahiti and similar islands could be beneficial. The breadfruit tree, as both a vital food source and a settlement agent, would support new colonies. His argument is bolstered by historical examples of migration and settlement, where the breadfruit tree played a crucial role.

In other words, one can argue that »Vom Brodbaum« advocates for European colonial powers to look at the knowledge coming in from various travel reports and ethnographic accounts about the non-European worlds more critically and to use that knowledge to help the other parts of the world by establishing European settlements on these lands. As one can discern in the »Cook der Entdecker« and »Botany Bay« essays, Forster was indeed optimistic about European global expansion. He was convinced at least to some extent that European colonization of the Pacific will change the world. In this context, the opening quotation in »Vom Brodbaum« from Horace can be interpreted as a paratext that sets the stage for Forster's argument. Its choice and placement appear to be quite purposeful, because it talks about the narrator's strong wish to go to distant places, despite the dangers involved in the journey, for the sake of approaching the springs, which can be a source of happy, contented life. Forster might as well be saying to his readers at the very beginning that if one wants to live a »contended life,« then one should not be afraid of approaching the »distant springs,« thus encouraging them to look at his implicit proposal of new settlements positively.

The rationale behind this interpretative exercise is rooted in an overarching argument that seeks to understand Forster's writing strategies as an integral part of his anthropology. Just as George Marcus and James Clifford's »Writing Culture« advocated for redefining the ways in which anthropologists write and for reframing the perspectives through which such writings are understood, introducing a linguistic turn in anthropology, Gerard Genette's »Paratexts« redefined the act of reading by being more self-aware and critical of the constructional parts of the text, aiding readers in the conventional diegetic process of reading. It is important to analyze opening paratexts because they function as silent, open-ended gestures from the author that rely on the reader's interpretative skills to derive meaning. Situated *en exergue*, they are crucial in setting the reader's prospective relationship with the text, because, as Genette points out, such opening epigraphs can contribute to the overall literary construction as well as manipulate the reading experience, and even offer the opportunity to the reader to retreat from the text.[17]

The analysis of the opening quotation in »Vom Brodbaum« also sheds light on the inherent ambivalences in Forster's anthropology. Most of Forster scholarship will support the claim that Forster had a genuine interest in the advancement and fair treatment of non-European peoples and their cultures. Yet, we find him writing an essay that supports the purposeful migration of Europeans to non-European lands, fully aware of the negative impact such contact would entail for both sides. These essays showcase the ambivalence inherent to Enlightenment anthropology. They help us understand that we cannot really separate a »bad« (racist or colonial) from a »good« (anti-racist or anti-colonial) enlightenment.[18] And such analyses also help us understand the way power and history work through texts, in ways that their authors cannot fully control. How do we reconcile the insight that Georg Forster, an otherwise cosmopolitan and normatively good thinker, also advocates for settlement in non-European lands? He seemingly proposes this for the benefit of both sides, and yet he is aware that such contact will mostly lead to the exploitation of non-European natives. Both impulses are simultaneously present, and a literary analysis of Forster's ethnographic writings will help us contextualize his cultural conditioning and understand how he used this perspective to further his arguments.

Ultimately, if we understand anthropology as a discipline that helps us comprehend and appreciate the diversity of the world facing us, and if we see »ethnography« as an inherent part of anthropology shaping a culturally specific construction of reality, we cannot ignore the parts that make up the important contributions from unconventional thinkers like Georg Forster. These contributions have shaped the legacy of Enlightenment anthropology, which is a rich tapestry woven with a variety of materials from different times and places. Accordingly, our efforts to understand this legacy – such as this paper – should also reflect a variety of methodological perspectives mirroring the entangled web of Enlightenment anthropology.

Indiana University, Bloomington

---

1 I use *anthropology* as an overarching term here, in the sense of »all embracing anthropology«, a term that encompasses physical and cultural anthropology, and a term that includes a wide variety of discursive practices related to the reception of non-European cultures in the late eighteenth century. For the usage and interpretation of the term *Völkerkunde*, see Han F. Vermeulen, The German Invention of *Völkerkunde*: Ethnological Discourse in Europe and Asia, 1740-1798, in: The German Invention of Race, ed. by Sara Eigen and Mark Larrimore, Albany 2006, pp. 123-145.
2 James Clifford, Introduction: Partial Truths, in: Writing Culture: The Poetics

and Politics of Ethnography: A School of American Research Advanced Seminar, eds. James Clifford and George E. Marcus, Berkeley 1986, pp. 1-26, here p. 2.
3 Alexander Košenina, Literarische Anthropologie. Die Neuentdeckung des Menschen, 2. aktualisierte Auflage, Berlin/Boston, 2016, pp. 11-12.
4 Gerard Genette, Paratexts: Thresholds of Interpretation, Cambridge/New York 1997.
5 Stefan Goldmann, Georg Forsters Rezeption der Antike: oder Anmerkungen zur Affektstruktur des Zitats, in: Georg Forster in interdisziplinärer Perspektive, Berlin/Boston, 1995, pp. 325-338, here pp. 330-331. Psychologists Herbert Clark and Richard Gerrig, who view quotations as a distinct communicative device and accordingly developed the demonstration theory to explain their role in discourse, describe this as »dissociation of responsibility,« as quotations enable speakers to distance themselves from the language used, allowing them to avoid taking responsibility for their statements. See Herbert Clark and Richard Gerrig, Quotations as Demonstrations, in: Language, vol. 66 (1990), pp. 764-805, here pp. 792-793.
6 Görbert also argues that Forster's method of selecting and positioning quotations was distinctive for his time, as he frequently integrates them from both ancient and modern classics, showcasing his unique approach. See Johannes Görbert, Die Vertextung der Welt. Forschungsreisen als Literatur bei Georg Forster, Alexander von Humboldt und Adelbert von Chamisso, Berlin/München/Boston 2014, pp. 117-119.
7 Genette (note 4), p. 153.
8 Meir Sternberg, Proteus in Quotation-Land: Mimesis and the Forms of Reported Discourse, in: Poetics Today, vol. 3.2 (1982), pp. 107-156, here pp. 108, 131, and 152.
9 Fredrick E. Brenk, Voices from the Past: Quotations and Intertextuality in Plutarch's *The Oracles at Delphi*, in: Thomas S. Schmidt, Maria Vamvouri, Rainer Hirsch-Luipold (eds.), The Dynamics of Intertextuality in Plutarch, Leiden 2020, pp. 61-85, here p. 65.
10 I am borrowing the term »hermeneutic blinders« from: Jared A. Griffin, Common and Uncommon Quotes: A Theory and History of Epigraphs, Wilmington, DE/Malaga 2023, p. vii.
11 Georg Forster, Vom Brodbaum, in: Georg Forsters Werke. Sämtliche Schriften, Tagebücher, Briefe. Schriften zur Naturkunde, vol. 6.1, ed. by Klaus-Georg von Popp, Berlin 2003, pp. 61-92, here p. 65. All parenthetical page references in the text in the following refer to this text.
12 Horace, Satires. Book II, ed. by Kirk Freudenburg, Cambridge, UK/New York 2021, p. 35.
13 I am very much thankful to Lee Czerw, Ph.D.Candidate, Department of Germanic Studies; Kenneth Draper, Associate Professor, Department of Classical Studies; and Kristin Mann, Academic Advisor – all from Indiana University, Bloomington, for their invaluable insights and help in understanding the bare meaning of the quotation with focus on deconstructing the Latin grammar and providing me with the word-for-word translation for all the Latin quotations used in this essay.

14 For a critical analysis of Horace's satirical style in general, see: William S. Anderson, The Roman Socrates: Horace and his Satires, in: Essays on Roman Satire, Princeton, NJ 1982, pp. 13-49, here p. 46. Also, see: Deena Berg, The Mystery Gourmet of Horace's »Satires 2,« in: The Classical Journal, vol. 95.2 (Dec. 1995-Jan. 1996), pp. 141-151, for a specific analysis of Horace's second book of satires. Berg argues that the formal symmetry within the poems of Horace's second book reflects an ideological struggle between two fundamentally opposed views on the pursuit of happiness through eating. However, the book ultimately reveals inconsistencies in the poet's teachings through the use of dramatic irony. This dramatic irony, Anderson argues, is what makes the second book of satires a different reading experience from the first one.
15 Anderson (note 14), p. 45.
16 Horace (note 12), p. 35.
17 Genette, (note 4), here p. 149.
18 See Carl Niekerk, »Race« as an Enlightenment Problem, in: Goethe Yearbook, vol. 31 (2024), pp. 97-105, here p. 102.

Reflections on Translating Georg Forster's »O'Taheiti« (1779/1789), or: (What Is) Getting Lost in a Translation?

ANTJE KÜHNAST

At the beginning of the 1770s, following several exploratory journeys to the Southern Hemisphere, Europeans' awareness and imagination of the Society Islands, in particular Tahiti, were ignited. The resulting travel narratives (including those of Georg Forster and his father Johann Reinhard Forster) informed state, scientific, and public spheres alike. In the wake of Captain James Cook's first voyage to the South Seas, the Spanish also received word that the British were infringing on their dominion over the Southern Hemisphere. Soon, Don Domingo Boenechea set sail on the *Aguila* from Peru to the Society Islands by order of the Spanish Crown, in an attempt to secure Tahiti for later settlement and missionary pursuits. In 1772, Boenechea and his crew spent roughly a month on the island, making friendly contact with the locals and exploring the island and its surroundings.

In the following year he sent a report to his superior, the Peruvian viceroy Manuel de Amat, detailing the island's navigational location, natural phenomena, and providing insights into his crew's encounters with its inhabitants and their characteristics. In 1778, a version of his report was sent to Johann Reinhold Forster, who together with his son Georg had visited Tahiti shortly after Boenechea on board the *Resolution* during Captain James Cook's second voyage. Georg Forster had subsequently quickly risen to international acclaim on all matters South Seas. He felt great admiration for Tahiti and the Tahitians and aspired to present his German readership – »eager to learn and truth loving«[1] – with comprehensive and comparative information as to their characteristics and way of life. Thus, he immediately took the opportunity to translate and review Boenechea's account and thereby enrich his readers' knowledge and imagination through the Spaniard's perspective on Tahiti.

Both Forster's translation and evaluation of the Spanish account are now earmarked for a further rendering, this time addressing English-speakers.[2] A translation seems a straightforward exercise: Know the languages of the original source and its rendition, understand the source's meaning, apply your knowledge of both languages, done. The process of translating, however, has its twists and turns, many of which circle around gaining and losing meaning, especially when applied to historic texts. Basic questions of historical enquiry – *when, who, what, where, why?* – acquire center stage in almost every sentence of both the source and its rendition: Both texts are created at a certain point in time with their own specific, inherently multidimensional contexts; author and translator, too, exist in a specific location and situation, and they are at work with one or more particular aims in mind.

Similar to Forster's objective, it is my aim to enable those interested but not knowledgeable in the German language to engage with the views of a German Enlightenment traveler, naturalist, and philosopher – namely, Georg Forster. However, whereas Forster rendered a Spanish text into German as a contemporary of Boenechea, my challenge is to transform a translation that was created 245 years ago into one that speaks to today's readership. Forster had a contextualized understanding of how language was used in his times. Therefore, the phrases he employed, I must assume, most probably reflect the prose then commonly occurring in both German and Spanish. Notwithstanding, he would have made (conscious or unconscious) decisions about exactly which words and idiomatic expressions he applied to render the Spanish original into a truthful German interpretation.

This kind of decision making appears even more consequential when converting an already translated text into yet another language, and moreover at a historically distant point in time. Such an endeavor gives rise to many questions. For example: To which degree can a word's meaning be discerned in such a way that it reflects both its historical usage and our modern understanding of it? Can such a translation, as it takes us on a journey from the present to the past and back, ever be true to its source? Is it permissible to transform a historic text into a mix of older and modern language, or should the translation reflect language used at the time – sounding old-fashioned now and possibly conveying a meaning different from that actually intended at the time? To what extent am I able to understand the true intentions or perceive the tone of an author and translator such as Forster whose language is the same as mine yet not the same anymore? These questions are intricately connected to any translator's inclination (or rather requirement) for interpretation. My translation thus inevitably will be the result of many interpretations: It simultaneously represents my own interpretation of Forster's interpretation and evaluation of Boenechea's interpretation of his experiences in Tahiti. It's a situation compounded by the absence of the original Spanish texts.

As it turns out, an English rendition of Boenechea's report already exists, published in 1913 by Bolton Glanvill Corney. Based on another, presumably mostly identical, version of the Spanish account translated by Forster, Corney's translation thus potentially renders my own superfluous. Should I not include already existent scholarship into my own? This could be argued – I sure enough have had this internal debate as one of the constantly lurking instances of getting lost while translating. But his translation presents the same problem with regard to its temporal distance to both Boenechea's and Forster's late eighteenth-century and my own early twenty-first-century use of language. Further, Corney's source is one among other stand-alone documents in a collection of Spanish historical texts referring to Tahiti, whereas Forster not only translated his source but also imbedded it in his extensive discussion of its claims. His analysis of Boenechea's account is roughly double the length of his translation. To then imbed Corney's translation into my own would merely reproduce a translation of Boenechea, interpreted by Corney. It would disconnect Forster's translation from his analysis, not only in style but also in content. It has to be kept in mind that the subject of my translation is not primarily Boenechea's contribution to Enlightenment views on Tahiti but Forster's.

Even so, engaging with Corney's translation (i. e., interpretation) is not a loss. Getting lost in his rendering of Boenechea's report, getting distracted by his creation of context and usage of words – all of that leads to new questions and possible answers to previous ones. There are benefits for my own understanding of Forster's approach to and maybe even his own struggles with translating. How did he decide which German words and phrases to choose in order to reveal a Spanish word's or sentence's meaning? Where did he make interpretative assumptions? Was he concerned with rendering the text as closely as possible to its original wording, or did he focus on conveying the meaning in a more generalized sense? It was, after all, at his time common for translators not only to summarize rather than translate word by word, but to also add to, delete from or even »augment« original texts without referencing their interventions. This could and did lead to actual distortions of an author's original thinking. Was it Forster's objective to get the gist of the original rather than staying true to its words? And should this be my approach, too, diverting my thoughts towards an imagined analysis of Forster's adherence to the original Spanish text (which is unavailable to me)? Here's yet another way to get lost in a new direction.

To illustrate some of these intricacies I here offer a short but intimate insight into my approach to translating – a kind of productive and creative toing and froing. The following three text passages are renditions of parts of Captain Domingo Boenechea's Spanish reports: The first is taken from Georg Forster's 1789 translation; the second rendition is my own translation of Forster's translation, currently a work in progress; and the last is Corney's. They convey a general idea of differences and similarities in the tone emanating from each translation.

> [*Forster:*] Die Insulaner sind gelehrig, sehr verständig und geschickt. Sie lieben die Bequemlichkeit und den Müssiggang; sind schlau und diebisch, (ein Fehler dessen sich sogar ihre Vornehmen schuldig machten),

gierig im Essen, und ausschweifend in der Wollust, wovon die häufigen Statuen von schändlicher Gestalt im ganzen Bezirke der Insel ein Zeugniß gaben. Sie lassen sich von ihren Weibern gänzlich regieren; was sie an Bord der Fregatte bekamen, ward stets den Weibern zu Theil; ja sie bettelten in der Weiber Namen um alles was wir hatten mit grenzenloser Unverschämtheit, und fielen uns damit sehr beschwerlich. Sie boten uns mit großer Freymüthigkeit ihre Weibsbilder an, und verwunderten sich höchlich, daß wir dieses Darlehn nicht annehmen wollten. Das Frauenzimmer pflegte auch wohl selbst, jedoch mit einiger Zurückhaltung, sich anzubieten.[3]

[*Kühnast:*] The islanders are quick to learn, very intelligent and skillful. They love comfort and idleness, are cunning and larcenous (a flaw of which even their nobles were guilty), greedy when eating, and wild in their lust, to which the many statues of a shameful shape in the entire region of the island gave testament. They let themselves be governed completely by their women; whatever they got on board the frigate they gave to their women; indeed, they begged on their women's behalf for everything that we had, with boundless impertinence, and thereby became very burdensome to us. They offered us their women with great frankness and were greatly astonished that we were unwilling to accept this loan. The female too was in the habit of offering herself, albeit with a little reserve.

[*Corney:*] These islanders are tractable, very rational and sagacious, friends to their own interests, very astute, but likewise indolent and prone to thievishness – a defect which was observed even in those of the highest ranks. They are very voracious in regard to food, and wanton in the matter of sexual license, to which the many realistically carved figures they have in all their domains in the islands bear witness. The women carry the upper hand in everything, and whatever articles were obtained from us on board this Frigate were got for them: the others begged with exceeding importunity in the names of the women for whatever we had, so much so that they became a great nuisance to us. They tendered their women to us quite freely, and showed much surprise at our non-acceptance of such offers. The latter were also wont to make advances themselves, but with some show of coyness.[4]

To assist in producing a translation that is as close to the contemporaneous source as possible while concurrently conveying meaning according to today's understanding, I compile and compare pivotal words used in German and English based on current and historical dictionaries. I use

Corney's translation to check my own choice of words and understanding of Forster's prose. Here is an example: When comparing my rendition of Forster's first sentence (»Die Insulaner sind gelehrig, sehr verständig und geschickt«) with Corney's, the question arises whether my choice of the words »quick to learn, very intelligent and skillful« reflect Forster's wording more closely than Corney's »tractable, very rational and sagacious.« Accepting the compatibility of »intelligent« with »rational« and »skillful« with »sagacious,« I am inclined to consider Corney's »tractable« a less suitable term than »quick to learn« to translate Forster's *gelehrig*. According to Johann Christoph Adelung's contemporaneous German dictionary, *gelehrig* means to »be able and willing to easily learn something« (»fähig und bereit, leicht etwas zu lernen«).[5] »Tractable,« according to the Oxford English Dictionary, meant and still means »That can be easily managed; docile, compliant, manageable, governable. (Of persons and animals, or their dispositions, etc.).«[6] This, to my ear, rings differently than Forster's prose: *gelehrig* denotes a person being able and willing to do something with ease (i. e., that person is active) and »tractable« denotes a person receiving some sort of treatment by another person that has agency over them (i. e., the described person is passive).

Therefore, Forster seems to present the Tahitians in a more pleasing way than Corney, but can this be attributed to interpretation? And if so, whose interpretation: Forster's, Corney's or my own? Or, does that discrepancy merely reflect different wording in their sources? A comprehensive parallel reading of Forster's and Corney's translations suggests that they worked from very similar but nevertheless distinct sources. Forster provides more details in some respects, Corney in a few others. In the paragraphs cited above, their prose appears different in other instances, pointing to two separate documents. Referring to Boenechea's citing of Tahitian statues, for example, Forster denotes them as being *von schändlicher Gestalt* (i. e., in my rendering »of a shameful shape«), whereas Corney refers to »realistically carved figures.« This difference could imply several scenarios. Boenechea may have used the Spanish term for »shameful« in Forster's copy but used another Spanish word translatable as »realistic« in Corney's. We do not know if this was so or what the reasons may have been; arguably different addressees of his reports could explain it. If, however, Buenechea used the same term in both reports, one of his translators interpreted it differently than the other. There is much room for speculation here, another path on which I can get lost while translating as only a comparison of the Spanish sources could verify the circumstances.

Returning to the questions of *when, who, what, where* and *why?* outlined above, they help to gain clarity and meaning at the same time as they create a puzzle in a maze of paths towards a finished translation. Seen in the most simplistic but surely not exhaustive way, *when* is fourfold – 1772/1773, 1778/1779, 1913, 2024. *Who* also comprises four authors and translators – myself, Corney, Boenechea, and Forster. *Where* can be associated with many locations, but the geographical settings alone include Tahiti, Germany, and former Spanish and British dominions. The answer to *where* also points to specific cultural spaces. *What* does the translation deal with? That would be many intertwined things, among them travel narratives, military and scientific reports, investigations and ruminations, translations and information. Finally, *why* asks about motivations for these texts such as improving navigation, securing dominions, providing education, undertaking scholarly enquiry and gaining prestige, a career, or income for any of the participating *whos* and their associated institutions.

I have come to think of the process of translating as identifying and collecting these pieces of a scattered whole which may have been thrown by history into sometimes apparently inaccessible places. This puzzle's trails – those interpretative thought journeys – can lead to dead ends in that maze. They can feel like a loss (of time, focus, energy perhaps) but need to be followed, encountered and pondered to eventually gain access to one of possibly many ways out.

A rather exhausting endeavor, it may seem. However, piecing together the puzzles created by Forster's translation, following some of the many paths through that maze is exciting and highly rewarding. It allows me to get a glimpse of the vibe of those exploratory journeys – as actual travels and those of the mind – when a lot seemed at stake, nothing was settled, and everything could be open to interpretation. Any translation is the result of, among other things, making many tiny decisions on word choice, the immersion in context, and allowing oneself to get lost, to imagine different scenarios and thereby finding one's way, or at least one way.

Still, for practical reasons and depending on the context, it could be argued that it suffices to use quick digital translation services. An automatically performed, word for word translation, however, may garner results that are ignorant of context. It can produce partly non-sensical content or, worse, convey the exact opposite meaning especially when applied to historic texts written in older languages. I have experienced this many times in the not so distant past, when one of my dear friends, also a scholar, would send me Google Translate's renderings of German historic texts for comment and correction. It has become more accurate recently – I presume with AI in the mix – as the below rendition of the paragraph cited above shows. I invite the reader to compare my own translation with the following (and as a sidetrack maybe ponder about the translation of *Weiber*, *Weibsbilder* and *Frauenzimmer*):

> The islanders are docile, very intelligent and skillful. They love comfort and idleness; they are cunning and thieving (a fault of which even their nobles were guilty), greedy in food and excessive in lust, as is evidenced by the frequent statues of shameful appearance throughout the whole district of the island. They allow themselves to be completely ruled by their women; what they got on board the frigate was always given to the women; indeed, they begged in the name of women for everything we had with boundless impudence, and thereby became very burdensome to us. They offered us their wives with great frankness, and were very surprised that we did not want to accept this loan. The women also used to offer themselves, although with some reticence.[7]

Google Translate's interpretation of Forster's German translation seems close enough to my own. Relying on translation machines for historic texts, however, not only diminishes context of both the text and its translation. It also threatens to simplify and eventually standardize our understanding of history, historic events, the evolution of ideas, and the adventure of trying to understand our ancestors and their lives. Were we to use machines for translating historic texts, meaning across time would be simplified and the creative intellectual act of interpretation would be lost in translation.

Wondering, if AI could (or should?) be used for translating, I entered Forster's German paragraph into ChatGPT, asking for its English translation. This is what happened: After translating the first sentence, my own text field (asking for the translation) as well as ChatGPT's answer field turned blank, both immediately displaying the following message: »This content may violate our usage policies.« Typing in every sentence as a separate translation request clarifies which sentences (or words within them?) seem problematic for ChatGPT: While it translates every sentence when typed in separately, it still finds that the content of two of my requests for translation »may violate usage policies.« Accordingly, the machine is upset by specific German descriptions of Tahitians which it nevertheless then translates to English: »They are cunning and thieving (a fault even their nobles were guilty of)« and »they allow themselves to be completely ruled by their wives.«[8] Separating those supposedly problematic sentences into even smaller entities poses no problem, whereas several sentences in one go again prompt the flagging of possible policy violation. While ChatGPT does not specify why these particular German sentences may violate its usage policies, I assume it may have to do with the content or rather the context the machine construes, possibly the way Tahitians are depicted in Forster's text. The question arises then, on what basis this machine interprets the text it has been given; which principles and context are being assumed to be permissible by those programming the machine?

This seems to me to be a chilling test of the possible impact of AI on translating historic texts especially. If certain contexts are being banned, particular words not permitted or only to be translated in a certain way and we come to rely on machine translations, this form of AI will eventually narrow our horizon of intellectual debate. Programmed in this way it not only poses a threat to historical scholarship but also to academic freedom and creativity in general. It deprives us of getting lost in translation, while we are losing meaning and context. The knowledge, time, and consideration invested in translating historic texts remains an important and utterly rewarding labor of love for what makes us inherently human: the capacity and urge for intellectual enquiry.

Independent scholar

1 Georg Forster, O-Taheiti, in: Georg Forsters Werke. Sämtliche Schriften, Tagebücher, Briefe, vol. 5, ed. by the Akademie der Wissenschaften der DDR, Berlin 1985, pp. 35-71, here p. 35. Forster published his text initially in 1779 and then, with minor changes, again in 1789: O-Tahiti, in: Göttingisches Magazin der Wissenschaften und Litteratur, vol. 1.1 and 1.3 (November 1779/1780), pp. 69-104, 420-58; O-Taheiti, in: Kleine Schriften. Ein Beytrag zur Völker- und Landeskunde, Naturgeschichte und Philosophie des Lebens, gesammelt von Georg Forster, vol. 1, pp. 275-354. The Werke edition uses the 1789 publication.
2 Georg Forster, O'Taheiti, translated by Antje Kühnast, in: Key Texts in the History and Philosophy of the German Life Sciences, 1745-1845: Generation, Heredity, Race, London 2025, forthcoming. I would like to thank Jennifer Mensch and Michael Olson for the opportunity to contribute to their volume.
3 Forster, p. 44.
4 Don Domingo de Boenechea, Description of the Island, part of The Journal of Don Domingo Boenechea, in: The Quest and Occupation of Tahiti by Emissaries of Spain in 1772-1776, Told in Dispatches and Other Contemporary Documents, vol. 1, trans. and compiled by Bolton Glanvill Corney, London 1913, pp. 326-41, here p 333.
5 Johann Christoph Adelung, Grammatisch-kritisches Wörterbuch der Hochdeutschen Mundart, mit beständiger Vergleichung der übrigen Mundarten, besonders aber des Oberdeutschen, Leipzig, 1811, lexika.digitale-sammlungen.de/adelung/lemma/bsb00009132_2_1_1078.
6 Tractable, Adj., in: Oxford English Dictionary, Oxford, June 2024, www.oed.com/dictionary/tractable_adj?tab=meaning_and_use#17858135.
7 Google Translate, 25 June 2024.
8 ChatGPT, 4 July 2024. »[Sie] sind schlau und diebisch, (ein Fehler dessen sich sogar ihre Vornehmen schuldig machten)« [They are cunning and thieving (a fault even their nobles were guilty of)]; and »sie lassen sich von ihren Weibern gänzlich regieren« [They allow themselves to be completely ruled by their wives]. English text in square brackets denote ChatGPT's translations.

Proximity and (Dis)Comfort with Georg Forster's »O-Taheiti«

Heather Morrison

Georg Forster is finally getting the recognition he always thought he deserved. In his lifetime, he bemoaned being distracted and diminished by insufficient money, positions, patronage, and recognition. This relatable academic from the past appeals to us today due to a global turn in scholarship, because Forster traveled around the world and engaged in comparative ethnography. As a result, more and more monographs, edited collections, and even popular histories are appearing that thematize his life and work.[1] The eagerness to read and discuss Georg Forster was also tangible in the 2023 German Studies Association Seminar, »Translating the Pacific.« As seminar conveners Jennifer Mensch and Michael Olson divided responsibilities for each of the core texts, Forster's essays were most coveted. Immanuel Kant did not generate such enthusiasm. Participants claimed the less prominent and more terrible Christoph Meiners's works last and most reluctantly. At the conference in Montréal itself, we were eager to discuss Forster, had to force ourselves to move on to Kant, and barely left time for the horrid Meiners and his racist writings. Forster got the attention he always wanted, and his ideas battling essentializing racial categories outplayed his bigoted contemporaries.

Here I will happily continue to ignore the founders of European scientific racism and talk about the not-so-bad Georg Forster. His essay »O-Taheiti« (1780)[2] is fascinating in its work to bring people closer to other people through print and by means of a sympathetic but critical understanding. The essay's publication history reveals the same underlying intentions. Forster centered multi-lingual and multi-cultural exchange. In this essay I explore proximity and comfort when faced with Forster's thinking on race and how he worked. To close, I discuss productive discomforts with Forster's self-conscious schtick.

Georg Forster first published »O-Taheiti« in the inaugural issue of a periodical he founded in Göttingen with the physics professor Georg Christoph Lichtenberg (1742-1799). Seeking intellectual friendships after a recent move for a teaching position, Forster found in Lichtenberg a fellow Anglophile with a great interest in non-European cultures. Publishing a journal was a popular endeavor around 1780, and their *Göttingisches Magazin der Wissenschaften und Literatur* did not aspire to innovation. They instead sought to share ideas from abroad in German-reading Europe and provide a venue for their own writing and that of their friends. Alessa Johns argues that work like theirs made Göttingen »a node of expanding internationalization and especially anglicization.«[3] Forster hoped the *Magazin* and time spent with Lichtenberg would keep him connected to England and relieve his fears of marginalization since moving to Kassel in 1778.

Through their periodical, Forster and Lichtenberg publicly displayed their engagement in knowledge work. Stefanie Stockhorst and Sotirios Agrofylac see the journal projects of German Enlightenment thinkers as a call to action akin to Kant's emphatic *Sapere Aude* in »What is Enlightenment?« Expanding the social experience of knowledge sharing from small milieus to print, periodicals were »how the intellectual ›doers‹ of the enlightenment succeeded in their efforts to influence society.«[4] Journals' regular recurrence made possible new forms of exchange. This practice continues in some forms in academia. Just as the GSA seminar in Montréal extracted me from my small college town to discuss texts with scholars from a variety of disciplines and all over the world, the resulting forum's publication in an Anglo-German international yearbook distributes ideas generated in person across the globe. Periodical publications reflect and reflected for broader audiences what social intellectual practice produced.

Typical for these sorts of endeavors, the *Göttingisches Magazin* appeared for only a few years.[5] Forster and Lichtenberg filled its pages with works reflecting the quick pace of periodical publication. Lichtenberg signed the preface in the first days of January 1780. Forster mentions having written the »O-Tahiti« essay a month before publication. In the same journal, Forster's father, Johann Reinhold Forster (1729-1798), reviewed Buffon's 1779 *Les Époques de la Nature* in the form of a letter to Lichtenberg.[6] Lichtenberg and Forster published their thoughts on recent intellectual developments from further afield, initially shared with each other, and then presented to the reading public within months after that. The publication extended their conversations to readers' studies and parlors and invited responses back. The fluidity between intellectual conversations and written work in the journal was generative, intended to codify these men's thinking and then produce more thought. Similarly, this article, now validated in print by the *Lessing Yearbook*, would never have been produced without shared conversations with experts in the field. However, publications today typically downplay benefits from in-person connections, whereas Enlightenment era publications highlighted them. When I could not access an article on »O-Taheiti« through my university's library, its author Madhuvanti Karyekar generously emailed me a copy. We then had rich conversations in the seminar, where I learned even more from her. Yet it is customary not to platform such interactions behind our intellectual work, save a footnote of appreciation like the one below. Back in the eighteenth century, Forster began his work naming the hands through which a manuscript came to him.

»O-Taheiti« encapsulates the *Magazin's* focus on the movement of ideas from spoken to written language and/or from one language to another. The essay is a strange hybrid of translation, critical review, and independent argument. It centers on a Spanish author and traveler's description of Tahiti. Now known to be by Don Domingo Boenechea, the essay came to Forster through outreach to his father from the director of Madrid's Royal botanical gardens. Before publication he deprecated the essay to a friend as a »rag« and derided himself in the process with the complaint, »I am such a translating machine [*Uebersetzmaschine*], that I unfortunately! can think nothing.«[7] I get the sentiment. At the GSA seminar, when I contributed a point that directed the conversation away from the philosophy being discussed to the eighteenth-century social setting, I experienced self-doubt. I like working in the social history of ideas, and yet in Montréal and now in a journal forum being accompanied by philosophers and Germanists diving into the ideas themselves, I question my ability to think. I will continue to wade into the waters of historical journal production, though – impostor syndrome or not. Forster's concerns that translation kept him from original thought would also recur.

Forster wrote »O-Taheiti« in December 1779. This was not long after the publication of his *A Voyage Round the World* in English in 1777 and the first volume of the German translation in 1778, with the second volume of the German edition about to appear in print. He did more than translate his own writing. He had gotten ready for his journey on Cook's ship by preparing Bougainville's *Voyage* in English.[8] In Kassel he worked on translating Buffon's *Époques*.[9] Forster most identified with the English, German, and French languages as these efforts illustrate. But he extended his practice to the work of a Spaniard to compare another's reports of Tahiti with his own. Forster's ability to work in about a dozen languages during his life is impressive. Rather than merely sharing content, though, Forster used these translations to explore how one's identity has an impact on understanding others. Translating allowed him to expand his own comparative observations and develop his ideas on empiricism's flaws. Yet he remained plagued by concerns about his intellectual work.

His mixed feelings about translation work and the »O-Taheiti« essay persisted. Forster once wrote »you have to consider that translating adds nothing to one's reputation, nor to one's pleasure, nor to one's intellectual stimulation, which one's own work *can* do.«[10] Enjoying this mode of self-deprecation, I shared the quote at the GSA, not thinking about seminar organizer Michael Olson's monumental work to translate key texts on race for a forthcoming anthology. The group responded with giggles and grimaces as they saw the parallels across centuries. Forster's tendency to complain about his work is ever relatable for academics. Given that he kept at his translation efforts, one wonders how serious he was about his disgruntlement.

Forster expressed dissatisfaction with many things, including the ephemerality and limited distribution of his journal publications. Already in mid-February of 1780 he lamented to a friend how the *Magazin's* first issue, containing »O-Taheiti,« »does not make much of an impression.«[11] He always needed more money, so he frequently collected and republished older work. The republication of the essay »O-Taheiti« in the first volume of his *Kleine Schriften* joined it with his »Brodbaum,« »Cook der Entdecker,« and other texts. His introduction informs readers that the five essays in this volume together reflect his approach to studying peoples and places, reporting, »[w]ith the vivid impressions that only an unmediated view of objects, and nothing else, can give, I went to the sources for regional geography and ethnology, simultaneously drawing on and interrogating them.«[12] This preface argues that Forster's previous proximity to his subjects of study gave him a clarity of understanding when reading the scientific observations by others. Despite his private dismissal of »O-Taheiti« after he had written it, he wanted readers for the essay's comparative critique of what Europeans can learn about other cultures.

»O-Taheiti« begins by reconstructing the origins of a Spanish written travel report. Forster assumes his readers' familiarity with his time in Tahiti, neither referring to ›my father‹ by name nor introducing their participation in James Cook's second voyage before relaying what he had heard about the arrival of the Spanish from Tahitians. The focus of his writing is not to tell stories from personal experience, though. He instead hopes to make readers aware that observations are always subjective and subject to chance, so reading more than one viewpoint is needed. To seek the truth about Tahiti, he demonstrates that even he as a firsthand observer needed to rely on reports with other observations to confirm, contradict, or round out his own knowledge. He models this in attempting to date the Spanish traveler's visit. The essay's first mentions of Tahitians name them and relay their accounts. Forster then weighs the reliability of these narrators against one another, against his own observations, and against Spanish port authorities elsewhere, deeming them ›more reliable‹ than the Tahitians. In the bulk of the essay, though, written reports represent the true science he wants to test. Their observations reveal no truth because of the limits placed on the observer, but multiplying observers and reading each while trying to understand the cultural lens through which they observe brought more knowledge. Thus »O-Taheiti,« as Karyekar argues, is not just a translation and commentary on Spanish observations about the island, it also reflects Forster's desire to ensure that readers know that any supposedly empirical observations are just temporally specific and only provisionally true.[13]

Forster practiced multiplication. The layers of comparative observation in this essay transcend time and space. In one passage comprising just over two lines and a footnote of »O-Taheiti,« a German born in Poland who went on an English voyage analyzes a Spaniard's description of Tahitian costumes in comparison with the Peruvian and Chilean dress described in a French publication. And then 240 years later I commented on it in Montréal, and now I report on it again in a dual German and U.S. publication. As Forster was so self-conscious about the relationship between observer and observed, my self-consciously awkward alternating between intellectual cultures of today and the 1780s is an homage but also a probe.

The 2018 *Lessing Yearbook* reported on existential questions raised at another conference about scholarship in our fact-denying times. Mary Bricker and Carl Niekerk introduced essays from that gathering by stating, »today we long for enlightened actors who believe in the value of the concept of truth as a way to manage the discontent, lessen the insecurity, and stop the systematic chaos that so often have come to dominate our view of the world.«[14] Georg Forster is that enlightened actor we long for. He shared the truth of his overseas experiences of difference to counteract the invented racializing theories of Kant and others who offered reasons for systematic violence and the oppression of non-westerners. That a debate occurred and people disagreed is reassuring. Forster thus adds to what makes him sympathetic to contemporary scholars by being so congenially disgruntled about the working conditions and limited institutional support and readership of an academic. He laments distractions and insufficient focus on the most important things. Importantly, he makes transparent the research process of ethnographic work in the late eighteenth century. Though famous for his observations and the experience of proximity to distant places and peoples, he critiqued the limits of observation and the categorization of people thus observed. He sought more effective, humane ways of thinking through human difference. Forster is an academic's academic. I am comfortable with him. Kant promotes a forceful intellectual confidence and the duty of self-regard while I prefer Forster's tendency to wallow in self-recrimination. Forster is less foreign too in that Kant and Meiners lived in homogenous places and times (without traveling much), confidently writing theories about peoples of a variety of ethnic backgrounds. At least Forster wrote about human difference after being exposed to different humans. Sure, he still had the chauvinist's air about him. In »O-Taheiti« he defends Tahitians from negative European comparisons but treats the Ni-Vanuatu and Fuegian peoples horribly based on Euro-centric standards. Even with this bigotry, I feel I can talk about him without constantly expressing discomfort; this is not so with Meiners. It is easier to discuss and connect with not-as-racist Georg Forster. Yet, much about him tests that proximity, like the hidden labor he relied on and the entitlement he felt for recognition.

Shift the lens from fawning over his proximity to diversity, and I see grounds for distance. Despite his airs of suffering, he and his father were among the first to be paid as researchers.[15] He had patrons from the ruling class and the sorts of teaching positions that undergirded research, and yet he felt under-supported, under-appreciated, and exiled. Tahitians gave him prominence. He spent his life piggybacking on Cook's fame. He profited from the work of others, like the then unnamed Boenechea in »O-Taheiti.« For all that he got regular ego-stroking praise and admiration. All this happened while he whinged about how little reward he received. Georg Forster's use of literary journals and his republishing of his papers in essay collections show intellectual networks and the ability to reach for resources and financial support based on prior work. Lichtenberg took on most of the work for their journal though. By the second and third year, Forster had mostly disappeared from its pages, and even in its early days Forster privately acknowledged he did little for it. No one would wish such a coeditor, although Lichtenberg's personal history limits my sympathy. The eighteenth century was different, without gender equity or statutory rape laws. Yet looking back at Forster's coeditor Lichtenberg's life, I resist comfort and any feeling of proximity to a man who had a sexual relationship for two years with Maria Dorothea Stechard (1765-1782) that lasted until her early death at age seventeen. In 1959, one of Lichtenberg's biographers romanticized the scientist's meeting her as a twelve-year-old in 1777 and lamented the cruelty and crassness of August von Kotzebue for publicizing this case of predatory pedophilia.[16] Scholars should not do that anymore. While Forster is no Lichtenberg, keeping his abuses and privilege in sight is important. Forster's comment on being an *Uebersetzmaschine* was before he relied on his wife to complete work and turned his machine into a factory employing women to work on the translations that he sold to a print shop under his name.[17] When male colleagues have put their names at the bottom of texts I wrote, it was in an academic culture where intellectual property is better defined than in Forster's day. This was just university service work though, not ›real publications.‹ Perhaps I should not blame Forster for the appropriation of women's labor and be more forgiving of him even than I am of my colleagues' transgressions. And yet, I resent. There are patterns in Forster's' work worth questioning.

I am not the only one questioning the importance of my research and writing on white men who have long been dead in response to contemporary reckonings. Our seminar at the German Studies Association in the Fall of 2023 explored eighteenth-century ideas ordering humans into races. The history of racialization is important to document, but to produce such scholarship is difficult. To be comfortable with Forster and repulsed by Meiners leads to an existential dilemma of the sort on which Forster would have loved to dwell. If scholars stay close to the writers from the past we are comfortable with, and avoid those we despise, then we lose some justification for our central European studies. We cannot explain quite as well how and why Europeans harmed people of color in the short and long term systematically and globally. Meiners explained slavery and imperialism. Kant's racism held sway. So why did I still want to talk and write about Forster rather than about Meiners? Knowledge of the damage of Europeans' writings about race repulses me even as my feelings of sympathy for Forster pull me toward him. In one of his most self-reflective moments of a life spent reflecting on himself, Forster wrote, »feeling was always my first desire, knowledge only the second. And how much effort it cost me to sacrifice my feelings in times of sad fanaticism and bigotry.«[18]

Here, then, is a justification for this essay's focus on Forster, »O-Taheiti,« and my act of writing it. It costs to put aside sensibility in favor of knowledge in an era of injustice. Feeling might just have been why Forster in my mind is not-so-bad compared to others of his time. His empathy, not his reason, made him the one best able to counter Kant. His former proximity to Tahitians lingered in his sensibility so he could question knowledge on distant populations no matter how authoritative Kant's tone or sweeping his theory. However contested and resisted, my empathy for a historic actor, if explored, can add to my understanding of the person in the past. I enjoy reading Forster's well-phrased complaints about the stunted life of the mind and my feelings of proximity to that sensation could generate knowledge. This is an ego history, but I hope not egoistic. I will not unduly praise Forster. Though Forster may be less racist because he managed to be in proximity to people of color in his lifetime, that is not enough. Georg Forster might be a good egg in comparison to some of the writers and thinkers of his time, but he should be irreverently criticized as well from my perspective.

Scholars exploring ego histories today deal with complex questions on the discipline and academic practice. Exploring the self and emotional connection to one's field, rather than adopting a false objective voice, could create strong critical reflections on the past.[19] I have attempted to reflect here on my perspective, as Forster did with Europeans who studied Tahitians. Forster's insistence in »O-Taheiti« that the position of the observer influences the content of the observation also applies to historians observing the people of the past. We too should examine feelings of distance or proximity resulting from our identities and try to figure out how they influence our observations. As Sally Hatch Gray explores in this forum, Forster's attacks on Meiners concerned both his ideas and his person because these were interrelated. My identity shapes my way of understanding; my written ideas here reflect my personality and position as a scholar. Forster wanted more and more observers to write about those he had observed and test the influence of his perspective. Lichtenberg's hagiographer presented himself as an objective, scientific historian. Yet this western, white man's connection with his topic resulted in a backwards understanding of a victimizer as a victim. As Forster receives more attention and those attending to him come from, acknowledge, and reflect on the influence of different backgrounds, we will start to see something more truthful about this imperfect and interesting figure.

SUNY, New Paltz

1 Aided by the completion of the eighteen-volume *Georg Forsters Werke*, the past seven years has seen the publication of four works that have Georg Forster as the title proper: Todd Kontje, Georg Forster: German Cosmopolitan, College Station, PA 2022; Jürgen Goldstein, Georg Forster: Voyager, Naturalist, Revolutionary, trans. Anne Janusch, Chicago 2019; Frank Vorpahl (ed.), Georg Forster: From the South Seas to Wörlitz, Munich 2019; and Helmut Peitsch, Georg Forster. Deutsche ›Antheilnahme‹ an der Europäischen Expansion über die Welt, Berlin 2017.
2 Georg Forster, O-Taheiti, in: Georg Forsters Werke. Sämtliche Schriften, Tagebücher, Briefe, vol. 5, ed. by the Akademie der Wissenschaften der DDR, Berlin 1985, pp. 35-71 (cited in the following as GFW + volume and page numbers).
3 Alessa Johns, The Book as Cosmopolitan Object: Anna Vandenhoeck, Publisher, and Philippine Charlotte of Brunswick-Wolfenbüttel, Collector, in: Bluestocking Feminism and British-German Cultural Transfer, 1750-1837, Ann Arbor 2014, pp.17-38, here p. 6.
4 Stefanie Stockhorst and Sotirios Agrofylac, »Sapere aude!« Praxisformen der Aufklärung im Spiegel editorischer Abgesänge auf Zeitschriftenprojekte, in: Lessing Yearbook, vol. 49 (2022), pp. 15-37, here p. 15.
5 Stockhorst/Agrofylac (note 4), p. 17.
6 Göttingisches Magazin der Wissenschaften und Literatur, ed. by Georg Christoph Lichtenberg and Georg Forster, Göttingen 1780. Digitized at gdz.sub.uni-goettingen.de/id/PPN353258334.
7 I would like to thank Madhuvanti Karyekar for the reference and sharing a copy of her paper: Comparative Anthropology in Travel Literature: Georg Forster's ›O-Taheiti‹ (1779), in: Colloquia Germanica, vol. 46.3 (2013), pp. 211-228.
8 Kontje (note 1), p. 26.
9 Forster, Letter to Johann Reinhold Forster, 29 December 1779, GFW 13: 265.
10 Cited and translated by Kontje (note 1), p. 36.
11 Forster, Letter to Friedrich Heinrich Jacobi, 14 February 1780, GFW 13: 282.
12 »Vorrede zu: Kleine Schriften GFW 5:345-8, here 346.
13 Karyekar (note 7), pp. 218-219.

14 Mary Bricker and Carl Niekerk, Introduction: The Wit and Wisdom of Lessing's Laughter, in: Lessing Yearbook/Jahrbuch, Bd. 45 (2018), pp. 157-160, here p. 157.
15 Horst Bredekamp, Georg Fosters Bilderfahrzeuge, in: Weltensammeln. Johann Reinhold Forster und Georg Forster, ed. by Elisabeth Décultot, Jana Kittelmann, Andrea Thiele, and Ingo Uhlig, Goettingen 2020, pp. 15-42, here p. 17.
16 J. P. Stern, Lichtenberg: A Doctrine of Scattered Occasions, Reconstructed from his Aphorisms and Reflections, Bloomington, IN 1959, p. 61.
17 Klaus-Georg Popp, Einführung. Entstehungs- und Wirkungsgeschichte der einzelnen Texte, GFW 6: 86-87.
18 Georg Forster, Letter to Samuel Thomas Sömmering, Vienna, 26 and 28 August 1784, GFW 14: 170.
19 Enzo Traverso, Singular Pasts: The »I« in Historiography, New York 2022.

Aufklärung as Vocation in Georg Forster's »Cook, der Entdecker«: Reality, Mirror, or Rorschach Test?

Joseph D. O'Neil

Why do we read Georg Forster? Please note: The question is not »Why *should* we read Georg Forster?« What do we look for, and what do we think we find? The recent answers seem to be: a little bit of everything, and nothing in particular. At the same time, Forster has become a sort of figurehead for the politically and ethically good (or at least the less bad) in scholarship informed by the imperatives of diversity and inclusion on a global scale. Recent scholarship on his South Seas voyages emphasizes his openness to diversity and non-European perspectives, and Forster's similarly open and essayistic style seems to allow for a similar openness to interpretation and modification of his ideas.[1] Jonathan Israel goes so far as to rank Forster among the »radical Enlighteners.«[2] Nonetheless, a more comprehensive view of Forster's less fluid positions seem to yield a *Weltanschauung* that makes him less of an egalitarian, defying the simplistic Radical Enlightenment paradigm of »a carefully defined binary classification of ideas and reform projects into socially endorsing and socially oppositional blocs, differentiating those backed by state and church from those rejected.«[3] As David Blackbourn points out, not only were German scientific travelers sponsored by states (the Forsters, Georg and his father Johann Reinhold, by Russia and Britain; Chamisso by Russia; Alexander von Humboldt by Spain); they were also purveyors of a certain notion of human equality based on emerging European social and political norms: »Through the end of the eighteenth century, the language of most naturalists still reflected the instrumental, Enlightenment view that the natural world was something to be ›conquered‹ in the interests of humankind.«[4] For Forster, as I shall also discuss in what follows, Enlightenment is a global development in which Europeans move out into the world to stimulate less-developed cultures by contact, colonization, and the transplantation of European *mores* – and flora and fauna –, especially into the Pacific. So far, so predictable: the script one might also be familiar with from nineteenth-century imperialism with its forced openings of Japan and China or, post-1945, the ideology of Third World development. That exposure has for better or worse resulted in the world we live in, and that is perhaps the most compelling reason to read Forster.

Forster's version of science and politics culminates in his understanding of *Aufklärung* in psychological and anthropological terms. If *Aufklärung* is the name for the spot where knowledge claims and political claims intersect,

Forster might just be the man for our moment, when ecology and public health are two of the main idioms of the political. However, if we want to understand what Forster has to say to us, I think we should begin with Max Weber's attempt at a separation of science and politics. Weber's model of vocation will be a useful foil in understanding how Forster's understanding of Enlightenment is similarly passionate and similarly precarious.

In his intellectual biography of Forster, Jürgen Goldstein presents Forster's reading of Tahiti as a relatively egalitarian society in terms that allude to later sociological language. Forster experiences directly and not just in principle that, as Goldstein puts it, »Inhaber der Herrschaft« are »Funktionsträger,« unlike European monarchs, who are instances of a political theology that sets them apart.[5] Goldstein refers to Habermas at this point and relates Forster throughout his study to the ideals of the French Revolution. In what follows, however, I want to read Forster's essay »Cook, der Entdecker« (1787) in terms of another sociological concept, that of vocation, which yields a more formalized version of what it means to be a *Funktionsträger*, and in trans-Atlantic terms, as Forster's historical model is the American Revolution, not the overthrow of the state or its rulers on its own territory but a colonial uprising against a monarch who rules from overseas. Even though Forster's putatively radical side results in what are for us fairly conventional assumptions, however humanitarian in character, about human development, he does advance a theory of modernity that begins to use the conceptual tools that come into play around 1800: not the assumption of a universal and generic humanity in which equality means similarity but the transition from a stratified to a functionally differentiated society. I do not want to argue that Forster presents a fully-fledged sociology of modernity or a sociological history of early modernity from the point of view of a transition to a later modernity. Indeed, his categories are much fuzzier and more rudimentary. At the same time, Forster's rough divisions of people – not just Europeans – into different roles resemble Max Weber's choice of a highest value distinction as defining social roles *qua* vocations (*Berufe*). Unlike Weber, Forster does not make Calvinist or Pietist notions of religious calling the foundation of a worldless attitude such as that of Christian ethics or a this-worldly (*innerweltlich*) asceticism. Like Weber, Forster sees a drive to action in the world as somehow fated and inevitable, finding in »Cook, der Entdecker« a collective subject that, as Weber puts it, »den Dämon findet und ihm gehorcht, der *seines* Lebens Fäden hält.«[6] The quandary faced by members of Weber's student audiences at the end of the *Kaiserreich* is individual, if still fated – one does not choose, but one finds one's guiding spirit. Enlightenment as a value choice is for Forster almost a genetic fact of Europeanness, an echo of or reduction to the cultural particularity of Euro-Atlantic modernity.

While one might reproach Weber from a Forsterian point of view for creating a world in the mirror image of late Kantianism, Forster's account of the world in his essay »Cook, der Entdecker« also sees action in the world as shaped by the drive of the discoverer (*Entdecker*) to Enlightenment. He contrasts this quality in Captain Cook with the violence of imperialism and colonial exploitation, which he denounces as the work of conquerors, *Eroberer*. Implicitly in »Cook« and explicitly in his essay »O-Taheiti,« Forster introduces two more vocational categories, *Erfinder* and *Erhalter*, as examples of a »wohltätige Anlage zur Vervollkommnung«[7] (GFW 5: 52) – not quite as demonic as Weber, perhaps, but still an example of the connection between activity and progress. In the latter, he addresses the question of whether the Tahitians found the breadfruit tree in their environment and discovered uses for it and the other plants (making them *Erfinder*) or brought the breadfruit tree from another island where its use was known, conserving it as *Erhalter*, and transplanted it against all odds (the sea voyage, the chancy nature of transplantation as such, and so on).

Why these four categories? In lieu of an answer, I want to offer the heuristic fiction that Forster presents a four-cornered sociology of modernity here. This fiction will of course break down as other determinants of Forster's world view are considered, but they become more visible when set against the pleasingly symmetrical *Entdecker – Eroberer – Erfinder – Erhalter*. The conceptual yield from this fourfold figure might also explain why Forster recurs to these figures as not-quite-ideal types. Forster completed »Cook, der Entdecker« in 1787 as the preface to his translation of the official report on Cook's third voyage. While not a public speech or lecture, the »Cook« essay has in common with Weber's vocation lectures that it is an address to German youth – not yet at a moment of crisis but at a moment of immense promise. Forster's and Cook's world seems as full and varied and warm as Weber's is empty and cold, the metaphorical »polar night of icy darkness and hardness« of defeat and crisis[8] that would not be escaped simply through the leadership and skill Cook showed in Antarctic waters. Forster's apostrophe to the youth of his nation and time is as follows:

Deutscher Jüngling! Auch Du lasest *Cooks* unvergeßliche, thatenvolle Entdeckungsgeschichte. Sprich! Wurdest Du nicht belehrt, aufgeklärt, zum Nachdenken erweckt, jezt unwillkürlich durch Züge von erhabener Größe erschüttert; dann zu sanftem Mitleid, zur Tugend- und Menschenliebe hingerissen oder zum edlen Selbstgefühl und zum Streben nach nützlicher Betriebsamkeit entflammt; und von Dank und Bewunderung für den Entdecker durchdrungen? (GFW 5: 297)

Forster certainly asks a lot of his ideal listener. The story of Cook's voyage – whether Forster means in his own version, in Cook's account of the second voyage, or in the report translated by Forster for which »Cook, der Entdecker« serves as a preface – contains the whole philosophical-psychological-aesthetic-affective curriculum of German letters in the decades from Lessing's early work to the time of Forster's writing. It is hardly a concise sketch of the one or very few values to which one might orient an awareness of one's calling in the world, but it does resemble the plethora of expectations placed upon the post-post-modern pedagogical subject as well: intellectual motivation, emotional intelligence, empathy, self-optimization, and of course gratitude for such a complete ego-ideal. One longs for Weberian specificity and concision, also for therapeutic reasons: Freud would not have been surprised to hear that the author had been on a boat with his real father and his fantasy father-substitute for three years.

Jürgen Goldstein indicates that »Cook« was for Forster an intense confrontation with his own beliefs and values.[9] Goldstein also focuses on the vocational element of the essay's title as a reflection of Cook's »aufklärerische Entdeckungstaten« in implicit contrast to Christopher Columbus's deeds and motives: the title is after all »Cook, der Entdecker,« not »Cook, der Eroberer.«[10] This contrast is as simple and appealing as it is wrong, at least in that form. As Todd Kontje points out, Cook as ›discoverer‹ is intimately connected to the process of conquest in one form or another, from the ecological devastation of the Pacific to the depopulation of Tahiti that followed on the heels of Cook's voyages.[11] While the British might not have inflicted the cruelty Forster attributes in »Der Brodbaum« to the Spanish conquest of the Mariana Islands, that conquest eludes some of the typological functions of the *Eroberer* as it causes decline and not flourishing (GFW 5: 80). Are conquest and devastation, not to say genocide, justifiable when they are Anglo-Protestant in origin and, as Forster imagines it, conducive to human progress?

From the other end of this distinction, Forster does not consider Columbus to be an *Eroberer* in the sense of a strong typological opposition to *Entdecker*. Rather, he sees Cook as a latter-day Columbus, whose voyage was driven and supported by the same complex motivations:

> Die Abwechselung der Jahreszeiten kann, *in moralischer Beziehung*, in der That nicht gleichgültiger seyn, als jene Revolutionen, (so wichtig sie übrigens für subjektive Bildung seyn mögen) wodurch ruhende Kräfte wirksam werden *müssen*, und die Gränzen der Erkenntniß durch den Drang der innern und äußern Verhältnisse sich *nothwendig* erweitern. Der Zeitpunkt kam, wo ein heller Kopf den Gedanken hatte, die runde Erde müsse sich umschiffen lassen; er fand einen König, der in der Hoff-

nung zu einem Gewinste einen Versuch wohl der Mühe werth hielt, – und Amerika ward entdeckt. (GFW 5: 197-198)

Whatever else one might say about Columbus, this brief passage expounds the fundamental monism at the heart of Forster's account of nature, human agency, and the term »revolution.« The feeling of urgency (*Drang*) is no simple scientific curiosity, and it is not separate from political power or economic gain. There is no *Entdecker* who is not potentially an *Eroberer*. More philosophically, Forster sees freedom and necessity not as separate or regulatively distinct regions (for Kant, we must at least act *as if* our actions were not empirically constrained, and we are aware in reflection that we do not have direct knowledge of phenomena) but as being of one piece in explaining how and why human beings are motivated to act and to effect change in the world. The »ruhenden Kräfte« are in the subject's potential; they are actualized by chance, fate, and circumstance; and action is made possible more often than not by base motives.

While it might be tempting to engage in preemptive critique of the Enlightenment as the triumph of instrumental reason or the destructive desire for human control over nature (and over the less rational parts of human nature), Forster's location of Enlightenment in the Pacific is perhaps not as susceptible to such a critique beyond the most general level. The term »Aufklärung« appears repeatedly in »Cook, der Entdecker« in a sense perhaps deliberately contrary to what Kant meant by it: there is no separation of public and private activity, no deference to a wise monarch who concedes freedoms to an elite of *Wissenschaftler*, so long as they stay in their own sphere. For Columbus and Cook as well as the scientific voyages of German travelers circa 1800 (e.g., Humboldt, Chamisso), it is the monarch's self-interest and even venality that drive *Aufklärung*. There is no moment of »sapere aude« as a decision to leave the unfreedom of one's self-inflicted circumstances »durch eigene Bearbeitung [sein]es Geistes.«[12] »The limits of knowledge« are expanded »necessarily« by the urgency of circumstances or relations, creating the tension and at times the *lack* of distinction among those vocational terms.

How then, if at all, is anything or anyone *liberated* in Forster's version of Enlightenment? His focus in 1787 is on another revolution. While one might read references to »Revolutionen« (almost always in the plural) in »Cook, der Entdecker« as an anticipation of events in Paris, as Goldstein does, the primary revolutionary reference point in »Cook, der Entdecker« is the United States of America.[13] American independence had been recognized by Britain in 1783, and Forster's references to »Länder [...] wo Freyheit der Person, des Eigenthums, des Gewissens, des Denkens, jede Art von Betriebsamkeit im höchsten Grade befördert« seem to include the new country. He continues: »Diese wenigen Züge sind gewiß hinreichend, um jedermann einen Staat ins Gedächtnis zu rufen, der sie alle in sich vereinigt« (GFW 5: 287). These cryptic references to countries and then to a single state are to the *status quo* as of 1787; that the second is to the United States becomes more probable in a subsequent reference to »die Freystaaten in Amerika.« As for Weber with the Protestant ethic, capitalism, and his meditations on education in *Wissenschaft als Beruf*, it is the Atlantic that serves Forster as a model for modernity, the kind of modernity that can emerge in the Pacific.

As he considers the American revolution, Forster is not a thinker of principles and institutions – his American Revolution is not Hannah Arendt's – but of biological processes, entropy, and self-organization. Rot can afflict states and reduce them to the level of »Schimmel und Bilze,« only to encounter a »bildenden Trieb« infused (»eingehaucht«) by Promethean figures, »Menschen von größerer Seele,« such as, implicitly, the American founders. The *bildender Trieb* leads to development and self-organization (GFW 5: 289) – an indication of the biological foundation of Forster's political thinking, in which *Revolutionen* are part of the cycle of nature. As, implicitly, a *Mensch von größerer Seele*, it is not so much Cook's egalitarian example as his role as discoverer that is so important to the *revolutions* that mark human history, as the discoverers spread revolution in this particular sense from Europe to the rest of the world. Even after the violence of conquest, a return to culture in »Revolution« is inevitable, as the victor, the »Eroberer,« enjoying his victory, will experience more needs (*Bedürfnisse*): »Luxus, Kunst, und Wissenschaft, die Kinder einer Geburt, bringen eine neue Brut – Ungeheuer und Genien – zur Welt« (GFW 5: 197). The alternate Enlightenment seemingly echoed here is that of Bernard Mandeville in *The Fable of the Bees, or Private Vices, Publick Benefits* (1714), in which putatively immoral pursuits such as gambling and prostitution create national wealth. This increase in real and artificial needs is what leads, for Forster, not just to GDP growth but to political organization in the first place.

Beyond the basic rights Forster mentions, his conception of the political is fundamentally a global biopolitics of population dynamics informed by the genetic theories of his time. Within the scope and language of »Cook, der Entdecker,« I note that Forster's very bourgeois charter of basic rights – private property was especially important to him – is also a means to an end: the increase of *Betriebsamkeit*, busyness. In Forster's understanding of *Anlagen*, virtual human capacities, on a global scale, *Betriebsamkeit* is the central European quality:

> Auf derjenigen Stufe der Kultur, die der Europäer insbesondere nun einmal erstiegen hat, ist die Kenntniß der eigenthümlichen Beschaffenheit

aller Gegenden der Erde so in sein Bedürfnis verwebt, daß eine nähere Untersuchung nothwendig wird um seiner Betriebsamkeit Luft zu machen. (GFW 5: 201)

The *Trieb* in *Betriebsamkeit* is cognate with the *bildender Trieb* of renewed political organization, i. e., of revolution. As *Betriebsamkeit*, it is particular to the insatiable European desire for knowledge and commercial activity. As *bildender Trieb*, it is an anthropological constant, a general part of »revolution« as the cycle of human nature in its political form; the latter enables Forster to generalize to a universal human need for European influence.[14] Forster sees any »vermeintlicher Kontrast zwischen der physischen und der sittlichen Bestimmung des Menschen« as a product of »Abstraktion« (194). Nonetheless, biology and politics intersect in the idea that spontaneous self-organization is not sufficient. European *Betriebsamkeit*, or the person »of greater soul,« or the »heller Kopf« (i. e., Columbus, above) seems to take the place of the *qualitas occulta* that informed Blumenbach's *Bildungstrieb*. An influence that is simultaneously inside the human species and outside of the particular cultural group, whether Tahitians, Fuegians, Maori, Indians, or Chinese, is necessary to trigger the hitherto latent *Anlagen* for development.

While Forster sees a need for Europeans to release their own potential for *Betriebsamkeit* by giving up their cultural and political inertia in the French Revolution (a position he sketches out in 1790 in *Ansichten vom Niederrhein*), his take on the next great revolution (or set of *Revolutionen*) in 1787 has to do with sovereign freedom (as he said of the USA), not personal freedom, and with a distant future: the potential of the projected penal colony at Botany Bay to grow into a flourishing, continent-sized land, including New Holland, i. e., Australia, »ein ungeheures Land [...], unbebaut und unbewohnt« – a common colonizing myth, even though he is perfectly aware that there are people there – and New Zealand (289-290). These »Pflanzstädte« are the real agents of revolutions in »Cook, der Entdecker« because they bring the European *Betriebsamkeit* of white-majority colonies to – as Forster sees them – static civilizations such as China and India or contented places such as Tahiti that seem to be disconnected from the demand for *Entwicklung*.

But we knew that Forster wouldn't be the hero of our particular political moment. We might even take his address to the »Deutscher Jüngling« as a foil for our own preferences and priorities, what moves us, how we react to it, what we think we should do. But, thinking with Forster, this calling is not a free ethical choice; it is not even a tragic decision. Where Weber articulates vocations almost as ideal types, heuristic means of self-discovery surrounded with the conceptual apparatus of the sociology of knowledge and post- or neo-Kantian conditionality, Forster simply uses metaphor:

mold and fungi represent entropy; modern society and politics are certainly not the steel cage they seemed to Weber but a mixing of virtual and actual characteristics, a machine that is at the same time a »beseeltes organisches Ganzes« (GFW 5: 287), one in which we can now intervene in amazing ways even as we label both biological and media phenomena »viral.«

As we think with Forster, we might ask ourselves where our own *Drang* comes from, if we are so lucky to sense it at all rather than be consumed by anxiety or apathy. Kant's »free your mind« bootstraps approach even seems risky because those freethinkers or *Querdenker* who are »doing their own research« on social media didn't do their homework. How do we even tell the difference between a *heller Kopf* or a *Mensch von größerer Seele* and a fabulating techbro-edgelord-disruptor? Adrian Daub points out that the pop-academic media theory of Marshall McLuhan provided the tech industry with a »narrative of historical inevitability« that privileges the medium over content.[15] Forster's understanding of biological codes and historical processes has the same veneer of inscrutability and inevitability as Silicon Valley's cult of innovation and technological determinism. It seems to me that we are living in Forster's world, whether we want to admit it or not, paying the price for hypotheses, abstractions, and systems while having to admit that the feedback loop between us and our environment, or even between the future and the past of our Anthropocene age, is tightening.

In other words, there is no mere animal state of nature (GFW 5: 280) and not even a Tahiti of the mind where »das Barometer weder steigt noch fällt, wo die Winde und die Jahreszeiten einer unabänderlichen Regel unterworfen sind,« and where, as Forster writes, one can do without »Wetterpropheten« (GFW 5: 294). Where, after the twentieth century, we are accustomed to the end of Enlightenment in political matters, Forster's warning about too much harmony applies both to *Wissenschaft* and to *Politik*. While we might not imagine we are entering an age of »eine zukünftige allgemeine Übereinkunft des Menschengeschlechts« (unless, of course, we find Steven Pinker's *Enlightenment Now* credible), that would also be a negative development for Forster, since, where there is no risk and no change, only harmony and consensus, thinking is also not necessary; we would have nothing better to do than to usher thinking into retirement (»die Denkkraft feiern zu lassen«; GFW 5: 294).

With the consequences of our romance with *Betriebsamkeit* becoming clear to us, we are not, with Weber, wondering who will be the next ghost-in-the-machine occupant of the steel cage of modernity. Instead, we are tracking the mad loops and vortices that have replaced Alexander von Humboldt's orderly climate zones, wondering which thoroughly globalized set of pathogens will arrive next in our vicinity, looking anxiously out of the window – scratch that, we're looking at our phones – as we check our own temperature. Never mind that wars and conquests hardly seem to be advancing the human cause, if they ever did. As Forster tells us, Enlightenment is chancy, fragile, precarious. To adapt Astra Taylor's title, we might not agree about what it is, but we'll miss it when it's gone.[16] As we are reminded every day, in nature, in culture, in politics, there is no infinite utopian trajectory, no necessary permanence, only the guarantee of transformative change upon change, *Revolutionen*.

Miami University, Ohio

1 See for the former point: Madhuvanti Karyekar, Comparative Anthropology in Travel Literature: Georg Forster's »O-Taheiti« (1779), in: Colloquia Germanica, vol. 46.3 (2013), pp. 211-228; and Chunjie Zhang, Transculturality and German Discourse in the Age of European Colonialism, Evanston 2017, ch. 1. For the latter, among others, Carl Niekerk's recent observations on the Kant-Forster debate: Carl Niekerk, Enlightenment Anthropology: Defining Humanity in an Era of Colonialism, University Park, PA 2024, p. 132.
2 See for example Jonathan Israel, The Enlightenment that Failed: Ideas, Revolution, and Democratic Defeat, 1748-1830, Oxford 2019, pp. 435-440.
3 Israel, The Enlightenment That Failed (note 2), p. 2.
4 David Blackbourn, Germany in the World: A Global History 1500-2000, New York 2023, pp. 171-172.
5 Jürgen Goldstein, Georg Forster. Zwischen Freiheit und Naturgewalt, Berlin 2015, p. 96. Goldstein relates the idea to Habermas's notion of »horizontale Vergesellschaftung.«
6 Max Weber, Wissenschaft als Beruf, in: Weber, Gesammelte Aufsätze zur Wissenschaftslehre, ed. by Johannes Winckelmann, 7th ed., Tübingen 1988, pp. 582-613, here p. 613.
7 Georg Forster, O-Taheiti, in: Georg Forsters Werke. Sämtliche Schriften, Tagebücher, Briefe, vol. 5, Berlin 1958-, pp. 35-71, here p. 52. Further references to Forster's *Werke* will be cited parenthetically as GFW followed by volume and page number.
8 Max Weber, Politics as Vocation, in: Weber, The Vocation Lectures, ed. by David Owen and Tracy B. Strong, trans. Rodney Livingstone, Indianapolis 2004, pp. 32-94, here p. 93.
9 Goldstein (note 5), p. 131.
10 Goldstein (note 5), p. 131
11 Todd Kontje, Georg Forster: German Cosmopolitan, University Park, PA 2023, pp. 83-84.
12 Immanuel Kant, Beantwortung der Frage: Was ist Aufklärung?, in: Gesammelte Schriften, vol. 8 (Berlin / Leipzig 1923), pp. 35-42, here p. 36.
13 Eugene Edgar Doll notes a letter from Forster to his wife dated 21 August 1793, in which Forster praises the Americans in hindsight compared to the Continental revolutionaries. Eugene Edgar Doll, American History as Interpreted by Ger-

man Historians from 1770-1815, in: Transactions of the American Philosophical Society, vol. 38.5 (1948), pp. 421-526, here p. 473. I thank Jennifer Mensch for this reference.
14 Forster's version of epigenesis in relation to Blumenbach's *Bildungstrieb* and the larger question of self-organization is too complicated a topic to address here. Blumenbach's first publication on the *Bildungstrieb* was in 1780 in the *Göttingisches Magazin* edited by Forster and Lichtenberg: Johann Friedrich Blumenbach, Über den Bildungstrieb (*Nisus formativus*) und seinen Einfluß auf die Generation und Reproduction, in: Göttingisches Magazin der Wissenschaften und Litteratur, vol. 1.5 (1780), pp. 247-266. Scholars including John Zammito have studied this moment in the history of science intensively. See for example John H. Zammito, Between Reimarus and Kant: Blumenbach's Concept of *Trieb*, in: Manja Kisner and Jörg Noller (eds.), The Concept of Drive in Classical German Philosophy, Cham (Switzerland) 2022, pp. 39-60.
15 Adrian Daub, What Tech Calls Thinking, New York 2020, pp. 47-48.
16 Astra Taylor, Democracy May Not Exist, But We'll Miss It When It's Gone, New York 2019.

Kant's Reviews of Herder:
»Es mag ihn wohl ein *böser* Mann gesagt haben«

JEFFREY JARZOMB

Despite the universalizing teleological implications and long reaching influences associated with eighteenth-century attempts to formulate a philosophy of history, Johann Gottfried Herder's introduction to his four-volume magnum opus *Ideen zur Philosophie der Geschichte der Menschheit* (Ideas on the Philosophy of the History of Humankind, 1784-1791) denotes a hesitancy regarding the possibility of any singular narrative. He claims instead that such a philosophy cannot yet be written in his time and may indeed remain an impossible task until the end of the millennium.[1] Looking back from a perspective beyond that millennium – a perspective similar to that of Walter Benjamin's angel of history – one might be inclined to put off the uncovering of any universal narrative of human history for another thousand years. Nonetheless, alongside Herder's faith in the continued development of *Humanität* there is a notable decentering of European modes of reason and hierarchy, overtly calling for an end to colonial exploitation and slavery, even though these thoughts are preceded by a lengthy section of broad and demeaning racialization of non Europeans. His understanding of a historical narrative, his philosophy of history, is thus that all people are both culturally determined and capable of learning. Although Herder attests to a fundamental progress in the cultivation of knowledge and development of humanity, this can only be seen through culturally determined perspectives that inherit both faults and virtues.[2] The modest skepticism Herder holds for his »Grundlage« for future research, however, seems to be forgotten in Immanuel Kant's harsh reviews of his former student's first two volumes of *Ideen*. While Kant points out notable contradictions in Herder's attempted synthesis of empirical approaches to nature combined with spirituality, he largely ignores or misrepresents Herder's pluralist approach to anthropology, particularly the dismissal of the term *Rasse* and the concept of happiness as culturally determined.[3] Moreover, he almost entirely excludes the multiple incisive criticisms Herder makes of European states and their violent tyranny across the globe, sections which question the confident progression of Kant's own ideas of universal history.

Kant's reviews on the first and second volumes of *Ideen* were written at the request of Christian Gottfried Schütz and published anonymously in January and November of 1785 in the *Allgemeine Literatur-Zeitung*. He declined to review the third volume when it was published. The dismissive tone of these reviews, which Gregory Martin Moore describes as »schoolmasterly censures« in the introduction to his recent English translation of the *Ideen*, had a negative impact on the reception of Herder and his works, especially given Kant's prominence.[4] Both of these reviews include brief and sometimes inadequate summaries of the volumes under review, using paraphrased quotations that are occasionally lacking in accuracy or misconstrue Herder's arguments. Notwithstanding these inaccuracies, Kant levels effective criticisms of Herder's arguments on epigenesis, claimed abstention from metaphysics, and apparent favoring of lyrical eloquence over cold reason. Although Herder was evidently surprised at the vehemence used against him, such criticisms are indeed reactive to many aspects of the *Ideen* that seem to assault Kant's system. As both Sonia Sikka and John Zammito have pointed out, many of Herder's writings before and including the *Ideen* contained an alternative to Kant's philosophical categories and framework.[5] One particular disagreement on which Kant focuses in his second review is the concept and teleological function of happiness, *Glückseligkeit*. In critiquing Herder's individual and pluralist approach, Kant employs the example of the native Tahitians to demonstrate the necessity of an ostensibly higher, or European, rational reflection to achieve a form of happiness acceptable to Kant.

This invocation of Tahiti was the initial impetus for this essay's exploration of Kant's general dismissal and misrepresentation of Herder's criticisms of European hegemony, and even the term *Rasse* itself. Kant's example implies an inferiority of the Tahitians contrasted by an enlightened Europe in an attempt to undermine Herder's approach to happiness as culturally and historically determined. Shortly before his reference to the south Pacific, Kant accuses Herder of selectively reading the travelogues and accounts of ethnographers, claiming that the inconsistencies of the research available at the time enables one to make almost any argument regarding the various peoples around the globe. Although such accounts are indeed often wildly inaccurate and speculative, Herder repeatedly cites the need for further and better anthropological studies and often specifically avoids the type of universal claims central to Kantian thought. Interestingly, one of the most likely sources for both Kant and Herder's information on the Tahitians, Georg Forster's *A Voyage Round the World* (1777), apparently had already directly addressed and contradicted Kant's criticisms. This disagreement on the definition and role of happiness derives in part from Kant's understanding of race, which Herder, who almost certainly references Kant's *Von den verschiedenen Racen der Menschen* (1775), regards as fundamentally invalid. While Kant briefly mentions Herder's problems with this conception of race, he essentially misrepresents the latter's wider arguments on the topic. The following readings examine passages on happiness and race from Kant's review, contrasting them with the arguments presented in Herder's

Ideen and venturing briefly into Forster's account to contextualize the discussion of Tahiti. The scope of certain misrepresentations in these reviews reveal how the anti-imperial arguments excluded by Kant expose gaps in his own teleological vision of history.

The opening lines of Herder's chapter on happiness in book eight immediately acknowledge how his approach does not seek any universally applicable notion of happiness, but rather embraces the necessity of its inherent subjectivity. The very word *Glückseligkeit*, Herder claims, indicates that »der Mensch keiner reinen Seligkeit fähig sei,« since the perception thereof is determined »nach dem Lande, der Zeit, der Organisation, den Umständen« in which a person lives (HW 6: 327). Despite his condemnation of any attempts at projecting singularizing European conceptions of happiness onto different cultures, calling it »[u]nsinnig-stolz« (327), the manner in which he does so reads as somewhat obtuse today. Herder examines the shared human prerequisites of happiness – adequate health, presence of mind, and the acceptance of mere existence as an end in itself – by contrasting other cultures with the cold indifference of European states. This process, however, relies on what reads today as demeaning and arrogant accounts of the foreign other, for instance his claim that »kein Wilder mordete sich selbst, so wenig ein Tier sich selbst mordet« (HW 6: 330). Two aspects of this section, particularly with Kant's criticisms in mind, are important to note. First, Herder acknowledges the likely inaccuracy of many of the accounts upon which he relies several times in the *Ideen* for instance at the start of book eight when he speaks of »fremde, mangelhafte, und zum Teil unsichere Nachrichten« (HW 6: 286). Second, he uses these rather problematic »einfachen Voraussetzungen« to highlight the dehumanized relations of a supposedly more civilized Europe (HW 6: 332). It is from this contrast between a cruel civilized Europe and the so-called savages that Herder ends his section with a condemnation of the artificial and highly abstracted model of the European state which, he claims, functions based on the suffering of its own population. The notion that tens of thousands must face death and persecution to make it possible that »Ein gekrönter Tor oder Weiser seine Phantasie ausführe« is thus the context in which Herder claims that human happiness is not in any way derived from a state (HW 6: 334). From this Herder goes on to argue in book nine that the notions of progress and enlightenment are similarly culturally determined, and that it is the folly pride of »so manches Europäischen Pöbels« to see their technological might as indicative of an inherent superiority (HW 6: 358).

Contrary to what a reader might derive from Kant's review, Herder's investigation of happiness here aims more at a criticism of the widespread suffering and alienation of European society rather than the delineation of a precise universal category. While Kant acknowledges the necessary subjectivity of happiness and its relation to the »Umstände, darin es [das Geschöpf] geboren und erwachsen ist,« he immediately disregards this formulation as inadequate, a »Schattenbild der Glückseligkeit,« that cannot be compared because of its interiority.[6] He goes on to question the validity of individual happiness by replacing it with a telos of a constantly growing and progressing »Thätigkeit und Cultur« enabled through constitutional rights. He follows this model of productive statehood with the probing question:

> Meint der Herr Verfasser wohl: daß, wenn die glücklichen Einwohner von Otaheite, niemals von den gesittetern Nation besucht, in ihrer ruhigen Indolenz auch tausende von Jahrhunderten durch zu leben bestimmt wären, man eine befriedigende Antwort auf die Frage geben könnte, warum sie denn existiren und ob es nicht eben so gut gewesen wäre, daß diese Insel mit glücklichen Schafen und Rindern, als mit im bloßen Genusse glücklichen Menschen besetzt gewesen wäre? (AA 8: 65)

Kant then relates this question back to Herder's specific indictment of mankind's need for a master in his sixth proposition of »Idee zu einer allgemeinen Geschichte in weltbürgerlicher Absicht« (Idea for a Universal History with a Cosmopolitan Purpose, 1784), ostensibly claiming that the Tahitians require a master to save them from their own base impulses, or perhaps that they need foreign entanglement to properly progress. This rebuttal demonstrates Kant's general unwillingness to entertain Herder's pluralist approach to history. He not only misrepresents one of Herder's central aims in the section he quotes from, that European imperial ambitions cannot force a singular vision of happiness upon the world, but also implicitly denies any inherent value to non-European lives.

Despite one of Kant's other central criticisms of the *Ideen*, that the travelogues and reports Herder relies on often contradict one another, Georg Forster's account of his experience on Tahiti during Cook's second voyage (1772-1775) comes to essentially the opposite conclusion regarding the state of the natives. In reflecting upon the friendly and unequivocally happy disposition of the Tahitians, Forster predicts that the interference of Europeans, particularly their introduction of novel luxuries will instigate a marked increase in inequality and bring inevitable strife. This observation casts doubt upon the very purpose of Cook's voyage, lamenting that if anthropological knowledge »can only be acquired at such a price as the happiness of nations, it were better for the discoverers and the discovered, that the South Sea had still remained unknown to Europe and its restless inhabitants.«[7] Indeed, rather than seeing the Tahitian society as inferior to Europe, excepting their overindulgence in the »impulses of nature,« Forster observes the general well-being of the population as an indictment of

»the miseries of the lower class in some civilized states,« resulting from the »unbounded voluptuousness of their superiors.«[8] It would appear therefore that Forster might answer Kant's question regarding the Tahitians by saying that it would certainly make a great difference to those »rational beings« whether or not they were sheep and cows.[9] Indeed, the question Kant raises regarding the Tahitians appears to prefigure his eventual dismissal in *Anthropologie in pragmatischer Hinsicht* (1798) of non-Europeans as capable of true philosophy and therefore incapable of pure moral thinking.[10]

Given the role that concepts of ›race‹ play in his own historical teleology and philosophical system – a connection thoroughly explored in Lu-Adler's *Kant, Race, and Racism* (2023) – it is curious how dismissive Kant is of Herder's brief exploration of the term. In his review, Kant briefly mentions how Herder disagrees with the »Eintheilung der Menschengattung in *Racen*,« particularly on the basis of inherited skin color, and presumes that this is because the »Begriff einer Race ihm noch nicht deutlich bestimmt ist« (AA 8: 62). This does somewhat accurately describe Herder's position on inheritable skin tone, as he notes how such colors »verlieren sich in einander« and are all »nur Schattierung eines und desselben großen Gemäldes« (HW 6: 256). Furthermore, it seems that Kant's frustration that Herder is simply unfamiliar with the term stems in part from the shared arguments for monogenesis by both authors. Herder's disapproval of previous categorizations of humans into four or five races references wider debates on such divisions by a wide range of authors: Carl Linnaeus, Johann Friedrich Blumenbach, Voltaire, Hume, and Kant. Kant's own essay, *Über die verschiedenen Racen der Menschen* (1775/1777), concentrates foremost on skin color as the most identifiable heritable trait in his division of four races.[11] However, one central aspect of Herder's disapproval of the term stems from his rejection of polygenesis, that the term assumes a »Verschiedenheit der Abstammung« (HW 6: 255). This is precisely not the case in Kant's essay, and was even the basis for his later conflicts with Forster's proposal of polygenesis in *Noch etwas über die Menschenraßen* (1786), as Kant explicitly constructs the term as a subcategory of a singular, monogenetic species. Alongside their agreement on a singular human origin, Kant compares his own notion of *Keime* to Herder's description of genetic forces that enable the development of variations.

While Kant's frustration certainly stems in part from what could be a misrepresentation of his application of ›race‹ in the *Ideen*, he excludes the conclusions Herder connects with this shared singular origin. The dismissal of ›race‹ as a viable category is preceded by, and draws from, an overt condemnation of imperial and colonial exploitation on the basis of shared humanity. Not only does Herder see it as wrong to violently oppress Americans and Africans, »denn er ist ein Mensch wie du bist« (HW 6: 255), but the »Haß der Amerikaner gegen die Europäer« is rendered as a wholly justified reaction to the misdeeds of colonizers (HW 6: 261-262). Unlike Kant's essay, Herder connects his monogenetic arguments with behavioral prescriptions, condemning not just polygenesis, but also the dehumanization that is often interwoven in racialism. Following the same pattern as the criticism of Herder's shadowy form of happiness, Kant ignores the prescriptive conclusions in the *Ideen* regarding European behavior on a global scale and strongly favors rebuttals against assaults on his own ideas over any exploration of critical self-reflection on Western perspectives.

Herder's examinations of the widespread suffering and exploitation of European states both by their populations and through colonial violence do not appear in Kant's review because they expose significant gaps in his own proposed teleological view of human history. Kant's idea of historical progress, as explained in »Idee zu einer allgemeinen Geschichte in weltbürgerlicher Absicht,« is intertwined with the development of western models of political states that, he claims, are continuously developing onto a higher stage of moral enlightenment. In what makes for a rather humorous line in historical hindsight given the anonymity of his review, Kant defends the propositions from his own essay without discounting the possibility that the author – Kant himself – may be evil: »Es mag ihn wohl ein *böser* Mann gesagt haben« (AA 8: 65). However, his clever quip does not cover up the problems Herder discusses regarding slavery, colonial exploitation, and the hitherto omnipresent suffering in European nations. Like Forster's observations on the future of Tahiti, Herder finds that if historical progress is measured through the achievements of abstract forms of states, it is often purchased with catastrophic human suffering. He sees throughout history how the supposedly cultured empires of his present are repeating the »destruction, imbalance, and, ultimately, implosion« of the past.[12] Although the *Ideen* express a faith in the inherent capacity of people to further *Humanität*, he has somewhat less confidence in the »regelmäßige Gang der Verbesserung« of those European states inflicting imperial violence across the globe.[13]

If there is one thing unequivocally true in Kant's criticisms of Herder, it is that his »poetischer Geist« does indeed occasionally impact the comprehensibility of his arguments. This stems in part from the radical difference in the two authors' approaches, particularly after Kant's critical turn. Unlike Kant, almost all of Herder's writings constitute an assault on the possibility of any closed philosophical system, described succinctly as a lifetime of writings »largely hostile towards any systematicity in philosophy.«[14] As is clear from his introduction to the *Ideen*, Herder is not opposed to being wrong nor insistent that his words should ever be final – not that this prevented him from strongly influencing or even establishing a range of disciplines, including hermeneutics, linguistics, and anthropology. These differences in outlook between Kant and Herder are particularly clear in their competing views regarding the philosophy of history, something that becomes evident in Kant's reviews. While Kant's notion of progress is enabled by legal constitutions derived from states, »nur das Product einer nach Begriffen des Menschenrechts geordneten Staatsverfassung« (AA 8: 64). Herder's hermeneutic thought and methods make him naturally suspicious of a codification and closed system of laws.[15] Though Kant addresses this aspect of his disagreement with *Ideen*, he does not engage with nor accurately present the persistent problems of political states Herder identifies.

These problems that Herder elucidates in the *Ideen* include strong indictments of European colonialism that undermine core aspects of Kant's historical teleology and prefigure later criticisms of imperialism. Regarding the then ongoing institution of slavery embedded in the spread of European power, not addressed by Kant until a decade later, Herder asks: »Und was für Recht hattet ihr Unmenschen, euch dem Lande dieser Unglücklichen nur zu nahen, geschweige es ihnen und sie dem Lande durch Diebstahl, List und Grausamkeit zu entreißen?« (HW 6: 261) Such immoral and despicable acts are not merely portrayed as the selective errors of a few bad actors; Herder identifies the pervasiveness of such systems in the mode of European life. Just like the sugar and coffee one drinks while philosophizing are connected to a chain pulled mechanically by slaves, so too is »unsre Vernunft und Lebensweise, unsre Gelehrsamkeit und Kunsterziehung, unsre Kriegs- und Staatsweisheit ein Zusammenfluß fremder Erfindungen und Gedanken« (HW 6: 358). Herder's faith in *Humanität* is therefore tempered with a profound acknowledgement of both the interdependence of eighteenth-century systems of knowledge and production as well as Europe's exploitative position in such systems. It is for these reasons that he concludes that Kant's claimed necessity of a master over human beings and confidence in the progress of states are evil propositions. With this in mind, it comes as little surprise that Kant seldom presents the breadth and implications of these aspects in his review.

What Kant excludes from his review and summaries is the incisive examination of the human cost hidden within particular conceptions of historical progress, an analysis that remains relevant today and seems incompatible with his conclusions regarding regular progress. Though contemporary scholarship has largely shied away from teleological narratives, Herder's belief in an inherent human capacity for growth, rather than an inevitable and regular pace of improvement, is not necessarily incompatible with such approaches. Indeed, Herder's harsh rebuke of those who equate technological might with human development, the notion that such knowledge is anything more than the confluence of historical factors, has only grown more relevant in an era infatuated by technologically bound concepts of progress. What Herder says to the colonizer who sees his mastery of warships and gunpowder as indicative of his own superiority remains relevant to the technology-obsessed sophists today: that one has bought an EV or learned to write effective prompts for AI is no more remarkable than a dry sponge absorbing the water around it.

University of Washington

1 Johann Gottfried Herder, Ideen zur Philosophie der Geschichte der Menschheit, in: Werke in zehn Bänden, vol. 6, ed. by Martin Bollacher, Frankfurt a. M. 1989, p. 18. Hereafter cited parenthetically as HW + volume and page numbers.
2 See for a concise summary of Herder's notion of progress: Vicki Spencer, In Defense of Herder on Cultural Diversity and Interaction, in: The Review of Politics, vol. 69.1 (Winter, 2009), pp. 79-105, here p. 88-93.
3 For an explanation of debates around description of Herder as a relativist or pluralist, see: Vicki A. Spencer, The Pluralist Alternative, in: Herder's Political Thought: A Study on Language, Culture and Community, Toronto 2012, pp. 96-128.
4 Gregory Martin Moore, introduction to: Ideas for the Philosophy of the History of Mankind, by Johann Gottfried Herder, trans. and ed. by Gregory Martin Moore, Princeton 2024, p. xvi.
5 Sonia Sikka, On the Value of Happiness: Herder contra Kant, in: Canadian Journal of Philosophy, vol. 37.4 (December 2007), pp. 515-546, here p. 518; John Zammito, Herder and Historical Metanarrative: What's Philosophical about History?, in: A Companion to the Works of Johann Gottfried Herder, ed. by Hans Adler and Wulf Koepke, Rochester 2009, pp. 65-91, here p. 82.
6 Immanuel Kant, Recensionen von J. G. Herders Ideen zur Philosophie der Geschichte der Menschheit, in: Kants gesammelte Schriften, vol. 8, Berlin 1923 [Akademie Ausgabe], p. 64. Hereafter cited parenthetically as AA + volume and page numbers.
7 Georg Forsters Werke. Sämtliche Schriften, Tagebücher, Briefe, vol. 2, ed. by Gerhard Steiner, Berlin 1965, p. 217. Hereafter cited parenthetically as GFW + volume and page numbers.
8 GFW 2: 215-216.
9 GFW 2: 215.
10 Huaping Lu-Adler, Kant, Race, and Racism: Views from Somewhere, Oxford 2023, pp. 66-71.
11 Kant, Von den verschiedenen Racen der Menschen, AA 2: 430.
12 Sankar Muthu, Enlightenment against Empire, Princeton 2003, p. 252.
13 Kant, Idee zu einer allgemeinen Geschichte in weltbürgerlicher Absicht, AA 8: 29.
14 John Zammito, Karl Menges, and Ernest A. Menze, Johann Gottfried Herder Revisted: The Revolution in Scholarship in the Last Quarter Century, in: Journal of the History of Ideas, vol. 71.4 (October 2010), pp. 661-684, here p. 671.
15 Michael N. Forster, Herder and Human Rights, in: Herder: Philosophy and Anthropology, ed. by Anik Waldow and Nigel DeSouza, Oxford 2017, pp. 224-239, here p. 229.

Kant contra Herder: Persius and Tahiti

PETER GILGEN

1. Persius

At the opening of Kant's reviews of the first two volumes of Herder's *Ideas for a Philosophy of the History of Mankind*[1] we encounter a significant detail that hitherto has been overlooked. A quotation serves to put in relief Kant's disagreement with his former student on the question concerning the vocation and destination of humankind. Moreover, it demarcates the territory of their dispute – namely, the question of what man is – and thus points to »the birth of anthropology« out of the collaboration and conflict between Kant and Herder.[2]

Kant's review appeared in the fourth issue of the newly founded *Allgemeine Literatur-Zeitung* (*ALZ*). Intent on surveying the entire production of scholarly and literary books in Germany and beyond, the editors of this groundbreaking journal recruited a remarkable roster of outstanding specialists as reviewers. All reviews were published anonymously.[3] Appearing on 6 January 1785, Kant opened his review with the customary title and bibliographical data. However, he deviated from standard practice when he also included a Latin quotation in his bibliographical note: »Quem te Deus esse jussit et humana qua parte locatus es in re disce« [Learn what God has ordained you to be and what part of humanity you are placed in].[4]

The quoted passage constitutes the epigraph of the first volume of Herder's project, where it is printed in verse form, as composed by its author, Persius, whose name Kant omits. Terence's proverbial words »Homo sum, humani nihil a me alienum esse puto« [I am human, I consider nothing human to be alien to me] serve the equivalent purpose at the opening of the second volume of Herder's *Ideas*. Yet Kant abstained from including these in his second review. Moreover, none of his other reviews of writers as diverse as Peter Moscati, Johann Heinrich Schulz, and Gottlieb Hufeland begin by citing an epigraph taken from the respective text. By including Persius's verses in his review, Kant intended to make a point.

Aulus Persius Flaccus (34-62 CE) was an author with whom Kant was intimately familiar. He liked to quote the Roman satirist regularly in entries written for a wide variety of *libri amicorum*. Thus, he used a particular verse credited to Persius, but actually a montage of two passages by Horace (*Epist.* I.11.29) and Persius (*Sat.* I.7), the former unacknowledged, on at least ten occasions ranging from 1777 to 1795[5]: »Quod petis in te est – – Ne te quaesiversis extra./ Persius« (AA 12: 416). It is no exaggeration to claim that this concocted verse became Kant's personal motto: »That which you seek within you – – do not search for it elsewhere.«[6]

An entry of 25 August 1780 in the *liber amicorum* of Johann Christoph Dittmann quotes the concluding verse of Persius's fourth *Satire*: »Tecum habita et noris quam sit tibi curta supellex« [Dwell in your own house, and you will know how insufficient your furnishings are] (AA 12: 417).[7] Soon afterwards, Kant used this quotation again, this time in the preface to the first edition of his *Critique of Pure Reason* (Ax; AA 4: 13). There, it concludes a lengthy paragraph in which Kant asks the reader to join in taking inventory of all the mental possessions that we have acquired through reason. As the terse verse by Persius makes clear, this will be mainly a project of curtailing our tendency to overstep our natural limits.

It is not Persius's last word in the *Critique*.[8] In its second-to-last paragraph, Kant quotes the Roman satirist again: »Quod sapio, satis est mihi, non ego curo esse quod Arcesilas aerumnosique Solones« [What I know is enough for me. Personally, I have no desire to be like Arcesilas or those troubled Solons] (*Sat*. III.78-79; quoted at A855/B883; AA 3: 552). Persius has a sweaty and ignorant centurion speak these words. In Kant's adaptation, they characterize proponents of the naturalist approach who simply invoke »healthy« or »common reason,« rather than adhering to the more onerous scientific method. Kant makes short shrift with such »misology« (A855/B883; AA 3: 552). In his concluding paragraph, he then briefly reviews the twin dangers of dogmatism and skepticism that threaten (philosophical) science and states famously: »Only the critical path is still open« (A855/B883; AA 3: 552). The biting criticism contained in Persius's verses is thus the obverse of the Persius quotation in the first preface. There, at the outset of Kant's radical (self-)examination of reason, his readers were cautioned not to overestimate their own capacities, whereas by the end of the book, the absurdity of those who forego the critical reflection and limitation of allegedly »natural« insights of »healthy reason« lies exposed.

In Persius's satires, Kant found pithy gnomes that could be deployed as suggestive poetic summaries of his dense philosophical arguments. The verses that Herder placed at the opening of his *Ideas*, and which Kant subsequently quoted at the head of his review, served this very purpose, not without bringing to the fore the deep disagreement between Kant and his erstwhile student concerning the epistemological and ontological status of the human.

Persius's verses at the head of Kant's unfavorable review esoterically communicate several things at once. In the first place, quoting the quotation back to Herder is very much the gesture of a teacher: Kant rubs the passage in his former student's face, as if to say: here, read it again, and this time, read it better! The condescension that Herder perceived in Kant's reviews is hardly the misperception of an especially touchy former student who had hoped for more sympathy and understanding. On the contrary, it is there from the beginning, even before Kant voices his reservations in his own words.

It is important to keep in mind that Kant wrote the reviews at a time when the fate of his philosophical enterprise was far from certain. Only after 1787 did it become apparent that his critical philosophy had established itself as a de rigueur touchstone of the discipline.[9] The situation was different in 1783, when Hartknoch, the publisher of both Kant and Herder, told the latter that »Kant believed [that] the lack of attention to the first *Critique* was the result of Herder's influence.«[10] An echo of this anxiety can be heard in Kant's response to a refutation of his first review, which was authored by Reinhold, but published anonymously. There Kant justifies his negative review by claiming grudgingly that he passed his judgment »with all due respect and even sympathy for the author's *fame* [Ruhme] and even more his *future reputation* [Nachruhme]« (AA 8: 58).

Kant had taught and supported Herder when the latter was his student from 1762 to 1764. During those years, Kant experienced a dramatic shift in his thinking.[11] It was brought about by his close study of Rousseau and the sudden recognition that the »moral capacities of humanity [...] have a fundamentally higher value than even the achievements of modern society, philosophy, and science.«[12] Kant undoubtedly recalled that the quotation from Persius had also been quoted by Rousseau at the end of the preface of his second *Discourse*, and before him by Pufendorf.[13] As Rousseau makes clear, it is of the utmost importance to learn what the place of the human is in the world (and thus, of course, also of the reader whom Persius addresses in the second person). In fact, as long as an understanding of »natural man« eludes us, »we shall in vain try to ascertain either the Law he has received or that which best suits his condition« (Rousseau 132). In order to establish a proper political theory and, *a fortiori*, a philosophy of history we have to remove »piles of quicksand« to find the needed »unshakable base« (Rousseau 134). In short, for Rousseau the Persius quotation is nothing less than a poetic shorthand for the vast project at stake, and arguably that is precisely how Herder and Kant understood it as well.

Dedicating the concluding parts of his published *Anthropology* lecture to determining the character of the human species, Kant develops his conception in close dialogue with Rousseau. He addresses the latter's »three works on the damage done to our species by 1) leaving nature for *culture*, which weakened our strength, 2) *civilization*, which caused inequality and mutual oppression, 3) presumed *moralization*, which brought about unnatural education and the deformation of our way of thinking« (AA 7: 326), only to point out that the three unnamed works in question – presumably the two *Discourses* (1750 and 1755, respectively) and *Julie, ou la nouvelle Hé-*

loïse (1761) – ought to be read in conjunction with the *Social Contract* (1762) and *Émile* (1762). Although, the position derived from the three earlier works – namely, that the state of nature is »a state of *innocence*« – is frequently identified with Rousseau's considered view, it ought to be supplemented, as Kant rightly insists, by the insight that it serves merely as a »guiding thread« for the *Social Contract* and *Émile* »for finding our way out of the labyrinth of evil with which our species has surrounded itself by its own fault« (AA 7: 326). Unlike Rousseau who argued that society was the root of human evil and therefore has often been misunderstood as propagating a return to nature, Kant recognizes »an innate evil tendency in our species [that] may be censured by common human reason, and perhaps also restrained, but it will thereby still not have been eradicated« (AA 7: 327). Overcoming this tendency is the moral task of humanity: an infinite task for finite embodied rational beings who are always torn between duty and their own inclinations.

Kant's reiteration at the opening of his review of Persius's exhortation to learn the place one has been assigned while seemingly directed at all humans in general is aimed most of all at Herder himself. Putting his former student in his place, Kant by means of quotation turns Herder, philosophically speaking, into the heir of the Rousseau of the second *Discourse*, a primitive thinker or philosophical *Naturmensch* akin to the South Sea Islanders about whom he wrote, in contrast to Kant, with interest and compassion.

2. The Happy Inhabitants of Tahiti

For Herder human history is a direct continuation of the history of nature. The specific character of a people and the conditions of the local »climate« mutually influence and interact with each other. As a result, numerous different cultures have developed over time. Herder considers all of them equally valid expressions of humanity. They cannot be condensed into one linear universal history of progress that defines the destiny of humankind. Rather it would seem that the many branches deserve to be considered on their own terms and ought not to be pruned prematurely in the interest of a philosophy that arrogates to itself the ability to judge all instances of human history in moral terms without so much as ever having observed, let alone experienced, the distinct forms of life that differ from its own.[14] Although Kant is not wrong when pointing out that Herder is prone to detours and distractions, his barbed advice that »our spirited author [...] should curb his lively genius somewhat« in order to live up to the standards of philosophy »which is more concerned with pruning luxuriant growths than in growing them« (AA 8: 55) is of a piece with his dismissal of the South-Sea Islanders as a negligible dead-end of human history.

Needless to say, Herder ignored Kant's advice. He never ceased to be fascinated by the plurality and multifariousness of human societies. In fact, many of the descriptions of different peoples and cultures in his *magnum opus* can be read as momentous precursors to modern anthropology. That is not to say that Herder never resorts to Eurocentric value judgments when native practices do not find his personal approval. Yet unlike Kant, he is not pursuing a transcendental inquiry into the conditions and limits of human reason as such. His epistemological interest is of a different kind. He is curious about real existing peoples of whose divergent cultural practices he aims to give *thick descriptions*.[15] In fact, as Michael Forster notes, for Herder »the empirical exploration of the realm of mental diversity« is central. The title of his *magnum opus*, *Ideas*, signals his anti-systematic intent, based on his conviction that system-building »leads to a premature closure of inquiry, and in particular to a disregarding or distortion of new empirical evidence.«[16]

Herder's insight into the tremendous cultural variations that affected values, beliefs, and concepts, »his principle of *radical mental difference*,« as Forster calls it, was coupled with respect for otherness. The result of this combination was a »pluralist cosmopolitanism« (Forster) that unlike more traditional versions homogenized neither psychological nor moral diversity.

Averse to all apriorism, Herder sees the human world as a large canvas of different cultural formations. To draw any conclusions about universal, invariant features a comprehensive comparative method must be applied to all the empirical evidence available. Hence the enormous bibliography on which his work relies, consisting largely of travelogues and proto-ethnographic reports on remote and unfamiliar cultures. As he puts it in an unfinished work on Baumgarten's *Aesthetica*, it is time to »der Natur ablernen, daß unser Anfang im Denken, nicht Vernünfteln, sondern Sammeln ist« [learn from nature that the beginning of our thinking lies not in ratiocination but in collecting] (HW 1: 672).

A decisive moment in the reviews of the first two volumes of *Ideas for a Philosophy of the History of Mankind* occurs when Kant takes exception to Herder's criticisms of a couple of propositions that are recognizably derived from his own rival project of a philosophy of history, the »Idea for a Universal History with a Cosmopolitan Aim« of 1784. Not only does Herder disagree with his erstwhile teacher on how the purpose of humanity is to be realized, but in the process he also postulates his own »ideas« that are freewheeling conjectures rather than Kantian concepts of reason. Whereas the stern singular in Kant's title implies »a theoretical idea, that is, an a priori conception of a theoretical program to maximize the comprehensibility of human history,«[17] Herder's plural signals from the start a more open, pluralistic enterprise that frequently runs counter to Kant's views. Noticeable disagreements run through the entire text of the *Ideas* but come to a head, as Kant clearly sensed, when Herder takes aim at the questions of whether the human animal needs a master to develop morally and whether human progress is tied to the development of the species in its entirety rather than the individual.

Herder's thoughts on the importance of human happiness [*Glückseligkeit*] are central to both of these criticisms. Although happiness is an essential part of the highest good, as Kant acknowledges, it is the part over which rational beings have no control, and of which they have to become worthy by proving themselves morally (AA 5: 110). Turning happiness itself into the principle of the will, Kant warns, would be tantamount to »destroying morality altogether« (AA 5: 35). A major reason why happiness cannot be the principle of morality is precisely that »it does not prescribe the same practical rules to all rational beings« and thus, unlike the moral law, cannot be conceived »as objectively necessary« (AA 5: 35).

Herder draws a rather different conclusion. In the terms of his »narrow expressivism,« every philosophical concept depends for its expression on its linguistic embodiment.[18] Scrutinizing »Glückseligkeit,« he concludes that the word first of all indicates that humans are »not capable of pure bliss [*Seligkeit*],« but rather are dependent on luck and good fortune [*Glück*], which largely determines their degree of happiness. Thus, the place, time, and general conditions within which a particular human comes to be are all matters of luck, on which depends the respective »ability to enjoy« and thus »the kind and measure of [a human being's] joys and sufferings« (HW 6: 327). For Herder, this observation sufficiently demonstrates that it would not only be arrogant, but also downright absurd to assume that humans in all parts of the world »would have to be Europeans in order to live happily« (HW 6: 327). Rather, human happiness is »an individual good« that depends on climatic and organic conditions as well as on »routine, tradition, and habit« (HW 6: 327). The fickleness of happiness is not a random whim but rather a sign of different natural-cultural formations within which a specific individual is always already placed. There is thus a communal, collective aspect to happiness that Kant completely neglects, yet which for Herder constitutes the basis of the binding ethos of a community.

To be sure, Kant has no patience with such talk of happiness. Adapting a mocking tone as his second and final review of Herder is drawing to a close, he asks:

Does the author really mean that if the happy inhabitants of Tahiti, never visited by more cultured nations, had been destined to live for thousands of centuries in their tranquil indolence, one could give a satisfying answer to the question why they exist at all, and whether it would not have been just as good to have this island populated with happy sheep and cattle as with human beings who are happy merely enjoying themselves? (AA 8: 65)

This dismissal of the inhabitants of Tahiti is not a one-off occurrence. Time and again, from notes dating to the 1770s (AA 15: 785-788) to the *Groundwork*, Kant chastises the South Sea Islanders as people who »let [their] talents rust,« which, as he is quick to point out, contradicts the Categorical Imperative (AA 4: 423).[19] He argues that »unsociable sociability« (AA 8: 20) is the motor of human historical development, and that in the presumed absence of unsociability no civil associations, including the modern state, »but at most only the arcadian life of a shepherd« would have arisen. The result of such lack of tension is thus »a life full of laziness« as it is to be found »in Tahiti where laziness dominates all the inhabitants« (AA 25: 1422-1423).[20] For Kant, the Tahitian form of life and Herder's philosophy of history have something in common: they are both dead ends that deviate and detract from the necessary course of human history that can be determined a priori by the true philosopher who is in the business of pruning all unnecessary and superfluous branches of history.

If, however, we take into consideration more recent developments in anthropology, would it not be more advantageous to understand Herder's critical remarks as a reminder that Kant's moral philosophy, including the state as the necessary external condition of human moral development, is too narrowly, too Eurocentrically conceived? That it does not duly consider other possible socio-political formations that might also ultimately lead to peaceful arrangements among a people and among different peoples and thus make possible their moral development? In fact, it may well be the case that we ignore such unfamiliar arrangements at our own peril. For they may offer alternatives to the exploitative and extractive social, political, and economic practices that are so deeply ingrained in modern western societies. Rather than being dismissed out of hand as dead ends of history, they ought to be seen as roads not taken that may hold considerable potential for contemporary world society, faced as it is with such global problems as the impending ecological collapse, for which Kant's metaphysics of moral autonomy does not provide sufficient solutions that would lead to the reduction and ultimately the abandonment of our environmentally harmful habits.

Considering his harsh criticism of Herder's project and his narrow-minded view of Tahitian culture, Kant would have done well to recall his own parody of yet another verse by Persius in a footnote in his *Anthropology*, which reads: »Naturam videant ingemiscantque relicta« [May they see nature and pine away for what they relinquished] (AA 7: 133n.). It is no small irony that Kant replaces the »virtue« [*virtutem*][21] that was juxtaposed to the decadence of seemingly cultured people in Persius's original verse with »nature« to indicate originary, unspoiled demeanor. According to Persius, the unfulfilled longing for the virtue they have abandoned is the worst punishment for the offenders. Kant's substitution signals a Rousseauian lapse, a momentary suspension of the rigor of Kantian reason. As if to make an echo of Rousseau's dialectic of enlightenment audible in Persius's verse, Kant's rewriting implies an imaginary return to nature itself: a longing for a »still unspoiled nature,« which he discovers in people who are inexperienced in the »evil [...] art of semblance« [bösen [...] Kunst zu scheinen] (AA 7: 133).

Does not Kant's lapse, then, draw attention to the need for a view of the histories and types of development of diverse human communities that cannot be accommodated within the impoverished framework of linear progress? And could such *rêverie* ultimately not have led the philosopher to a more considered and just treatment not only of Herder, but also of the happy inhabitants of Tahiti far away in the South Sea?

Cornell University

---

1 All references to Kant are to: Kants gesammelte Schriften, Berlin 1902– (Akademieausgabe or AA; in the case of the Critique of Pure Reason, the page references of the first edition of 1781 [A] and the second edition of 1787 [B] are also given); references to Herder are to Johann Gottfried Herder, Werke in zehn Bänden, ed. by Martin Bollacher et al., Frankfurt a. M. 1985-2000, cited parenthetically as HW + volume and page numbers.

2 To quote the seminal study on the birth of the discipline out of the encounter and subsequent disputes between Kant and Herder by John Zammito, Kant, Herder, and the Birth of Anthropology, Chicago 2002. As Zammito points out, Kant is not considered a crucial predecessor, whereas »Herder is and will remain a major figure in the emergence of [anthropology]« (p. 344). His importance lies not so much in »the *rejection* of Kant« but in »the *mutation* that Herder insinuated into the evolution of Kantianism and of *Aufklärung* more generally« (p. 347).

3 See the *Vorbericht* of the ALZ, which was published separately in December 1784, before the actual journal began publication on 3 January 1785.

4 Generally, the reviews in the ALZ do not mention the epigraphs of the reviewed publications. However, in the case of an *Erotika Biblion*, reviewed on 4 January 1785 (no. 2), the two opening epigraphs were cited at the head of the review (p. 12). On 20 January (no. 16), the review of a history of the papacy also contained the epigraph by Vergil, although apparently not in its entirety since it ends with »etc.« (p. 70). During the first month of publication with 25 issues of on average four to five reviews, these are the only two quotations of epigraphs besides Kant's own.

5 The last of these *Stammbuchblätter* is not contained in AA. It was sold at auction by Bonhams in June 2020.

6 By 1795, Kant had replaced the two dashes with a simple comma.
7 Persius's verse (*Sat.* IV.52) reads: »tecum habita: noris quam sit tibi curta suppellex.«
8 I thank Jennifer Mensch for pointing out that Kant quotes Persius in the first *Critique*.
9 Manfred Kuehn, Kant's Critical Philosophy and its Reception – the First Five Years (1781-1786) in: The Cambridge Companion to Kant and Modern Philosophy, ed. by Paul Guyer, Cambridge 2006, p. 631.
10 Kuehn, p. 642.
11 Zammito provides the most comprehensive and judicious treatment of these years. Kant's complex reception and rewriting of Rousseau is discussed in detail by Richard L. Velkley, Freedom and the End of Reason: On the Moral Foundation of Kant's Critical Philosophy, Chicago 1989; Ernst Cassirer, Kant and Rousseau, in: Rousseau, Kant, Goethe: Two Essays, trans. James Gutmann et al., Princeton 1945, is perceptive and still useful.
12 Karl Ameriks, Kant's Elliptical Path, Oxford 2012, p. 221.
13 As Victor Gourevich points out, Rousseau's reference to the inscription on the Temple at Delphi and the Persius quotation at the beginning and end of his preface, respectively, both occur in the same paragraph within a few lines of each other in Pufendorf's work (Bk.II, ch.4, §v). The French translation of this work by Barbeyrac served as one of Rousseau's main sources for information concerning political history and theory. See Jean-Jacques Rousseau, The First and Second Discourses, together with the Replies to Critics and Essay on the Origin of Languages, ed. and trans. by Victor Gourevitch, New York, 1986, p. 332, n. P[1]. Cf. also Samuel Pufendorf, Le droit de la nature et des gens, 5th ed., trans. Jean Barbeyrac, Amsterdam 1734, p. 263.
14 For a detailed argument that Kant's philosophy of history could be beneficially supplemented by a genuinely anthropological perspective, see: Peter Gilgen, In der Wildnis des Denkens. Kant mit Lévi-Strauss, in: Das wilde Denken. Liechtensteiner Exkurse 5, Eggingen 2004.
15 See Clifford Geertz, Thick Description: Toward an Interpretive Theory of Culture in: The Interpretation of Cultures, New York 1973, pp. 3-30.
16 Michael Forster, Johann Gottfried von Herder, in: *The Stanford Encyclopedia of Philosophy* (Winter 2023 Edition), ed. by Edward N. Zalta and Uri Nodelman, plato.stanford.edu/archives/win2023/entries/herder/.
17 Allen W. Wood, Translator's Introduction, in: Immanuel Kant, Anthropology, History and Education, ed. by Robert B. Louden and Günter Zöller, Cambridge 2007, p. 107.
18 See Forster (note 16) who here relies on Charles Taylor.
19 For a penetrating treatment of Kant's utterances on Tahiti and the South-Sea Islanders see Jennifer Mensch, Kant's Four Examples: On South Sea Islanders, Tahitians, and Other Cautionary Tales for the Case of »Rusting Talents« in: Goethe Yearbook 31 (2024), pp. 115-126. On the fundamental disagreement between Kant's and Herder's conceptions of »happiness« see Sonia Sikka, On the Value of Happiness: Herder contra Kant in: Canadian Journal of Philosophy 37.4 (2007), pp. 515-546.
20 This passage from the student notes of Kant's anthropology course is quoted in:

Huaping Lu Adler, Kant, Race, and Racism: Views from Somewhere, Oxford 2023, p. 101.
21 Neither AA nor the Cambridge edition reference the original passage in Persius, *Sat.* III.38.

Vieh, or Humans as Domestic Animals: On a Dispute between Herder and Kant

Daniel Purdy

This short reflection concentrates on the Enlightenment characterization of humans as domesticated animals, or beasts of burden. The common German words would be *Vieh* or *Lasttier*. When applied to people, these terms took on moral and political connotations that moved well beyond their agricultural designation.[1] They became metaphors to describe colonial slavery and feudal serfdom, because it is presumed that domestic animals are always under the control and direction of some overseer; they have no purpose on their own and for themselves.

When in 1784 Kant characterized his dualistic understanding of subjectivity to state that humans were animals that required a master, Herder was quick to object that he was not merely pointing to the importance of reason in controlling human instincts, but that Kant was also providing a legitimation of monarchical domination. This debate occurred as Herder had begun publication of his major work, *Ideen zur Philosophie der Geschichte der Menschheit* [Ideas for a Philosophy of the History of Humanity] in 1784, to which Kant responded with an openly critical book review and his own essay, *Idee zur einer allgemeinen Geschichte in weltbürgerlicher Absicht* [Idea for a Universal History with a Cosmopolitan Purpose], also published in 1784. The question of where to draw the boundary between humans and animals arose as thinkers responded to competing materialist designations of animals and humans as machines in the work of Descartes and La Mettrie.[2]

Immanuel Kant argued against such materialist accounts of subjectivity by defining moral character in terms of freedom. However, Kant's schema did imply that animals represent the absence of freedom. As David Baumeister notes in his excellent study, Kant never wrote on the nature of »animality.«[3] In his singular concentration on freedom, Kant treats its lack as a failure to be completely autonomous and rational (*selbst verschuldete Unmündigkeit*). The condition of a human becoming an animal, domestic or wild, provides a metaphorical shorthand for Kant and others to reflect on »unfreedom.« There are of course many insightful ways in which the Enlightenment referred to humans as animals, most importantly as an object of natural history. Kant's *Von den verschiedenen Racen der Menschen* [On the Different Races of Humans] from 1775 begins with the words »Im Tierreich« to indicate that he is no longer treating humans as spiritual beings with individual souls, but rather as natural phenomena that can be grouped and analyzed within abstract concepts. His implicit rejection of the Genesis creation story in which humans are raised above animals with the power to name them would have been well understood by contemporaries. Kant also intended to treat humans according to their general classification apart from any social particulars – as a species, rather than as self-aware individuals.

Imprecise and often highly metaphorical terms define the range of meanings in Kant's grey zone between humans as rational beings capable of moral freedom and humans as beings living according to their nature. In the midst of this metaphorical imprecision emerged a strong disagreement between Kant and his most famous student, Herder, who took exception with the political and social connotations of Kant's describing humans as animals. At stake is the question of what it means to refer to humans as animals. Does such a comparison entail a degradation that goes beyond stripping them of their souls? To treat humans as empirical objects does not mean that they should be treated as things. At what point does referring to humans as animals suggest that many people are less than completely human, that they exist at some stage below rationality and freedom, that they have become stripped of these qualities to become beasts, brutes, or in the German, *Vieh*.

For a society based on an agricultural economy, such comparisons were so commonplace that they hardly stood out as metaphors. David Brion Davis points to how slavery was frequently, and always incompletely, equated with the domestication of farm animals over the course of human history.[4] Aristotle sees little difference between slavery and domestication: »And indeed the use made of slaves and of tame animals is not very different; for both with their bodies minister to the needs of life.«[5] The Grimm *Woerterbuch* includes several definitions delineating how *Vieh* serves as an insult for a person who has debased themselves, but it does not consider how the word is used as a means of debasing others. The political strategies implied by referring to people as *Vieh* are not included, nor are the word's increasing use during the eighteenth century to make intercultural comparisons. *Vieh* as an anthropological designation, as the lowest level in the hierarchy of races and civilizations, and not just a word for someone who has drunk themselves into a stupor.

The German words, *Vieh* and *Lasttier* figure in the eighteenth-century debates about humans that were considered to not yet have risen to the stage of European Enlightenment: serfs, slaves, and primitive people. On the one hand, *Vieh* is used to describe oppression. The designation of humans as animals delivers a moral condemnation of political forces that strips humans down to weakest minimum of existence. Johann Heinrich Voss, perhaps the only eighteenth-century German poet to directly confront serfdom, compares the downtrodden with animals, except that beasts know to steal food to survive: »Aehnlich dem Vieh an dumpfem Begriff, nur daß sie den Hunger / Durch sinnreicheren Raub oft bändigen oder davongehen.« Only when the master remembers his own self-interest in keeping his laborers alive, does he provide them with food: »Daß der Entmenschenden doch sich erinnerten, eigener Vortheil / Nöthige, wohl zu nähren und blank zu erhalten das Lastvieh!«[6] Kant makes the same point succinctly in his notebook: »Die Leibeigenschaft ist der Tod der Persohn aber das Leben des Thiers.«[7]

By holding a person to the level of a domesticated animal, they are kept alive for the sake of their labor, yet they lose or have never gained a civil identity, certainly not within European conventions. To this extent we can connect the designation of a person as a *Vieh* with broader theoretical discussions of »social death,« in which a dominated person is kept alive within the machinery of work and discipline at the most minimal level.[8] If Giorgio Agamben describes the bare life of the concentration camp as the degradation of humans to the lowest, almost animal-like, state, the eighteenth-century description of humans as *Lasttiere* or *Vieh* refers to humans who have not yet risen to the Enlightenment's standard of rational autonomy.[9] *Vieh* in its critical sense refers to the stark conditions of forced laborers under the brutal biopolitics of feudalism and conquest colonialism. The connotations of this »human as animal« comparison were used to affirm the domination of an absolute power. Serfs and slaves were described by aristocratic landlords as beasts of burden incapable of thinking or acting freely, and thus undeserving of emancipation. Alternatively, colonial slavery could be condemned because it reduced free people to domesticated animals. A few examples follow:

In his *Reise um die Welt*, Georg Forster reiterates one of the first European arguments against colonialism, namely that the first European conquerors of the New World were rightfully condemned as cruel because they treated the indigenous people as unthinking animals: »Die ersten Entdecker und Eroberer von Amerika, haben oft und mit Recht den Vorwurf der Grausamkeit über sich ergehen lassen müssen, weil sie die unglücklichen Völker dieses Welttheils nicht als ihrer Brüder sondern als unvernünftige Thiere behandelten.«[10]

In its widest formulation, *Vieh* applied to serfs, slaves, and non-European primitive peoples equally. This triangular link becomes obvious in Georg Forster and Theresa Huber's reactions as they traveled eastwards from Göttingen to Vilnius for his professorship at the university. They are both shocked by the pathetic, servile existence of Lithuanian serfs. Drawing on her husband's travelogue, Huber compares them to naked Patagonians living at the southernmost tip of the Americas, a people whom European travelers repeatedly judged to live at the lowest level of human society. Huber extends the three-way comparison when she describes the downtrodden rural Lithuanians: »das Volk, vom Bauer bis zum Edelmann, ist ein Mittelding zwischen Sklaven und Vieh.«[11] Forster reiterates the comparison in a letter to the anatomist Samuel Thomas von Soemmerring when he laments that the ordinary Polish lord is accustomed to treating his serfs as domestic beasts (»der gewöhnt ist mit seinem Leibeignen wie dem Vieh umzugehen«).[12]

The German translation of Buffon's *Natural History* uses the term *Vieh* to compare two different Central Asian peoples, raising the question of which population is more animal-like: »Die Tartaren, welche sich langs der Wolga, unter dem fünf und fünfzigsten Grade aufhalten, sind bey merklicher Unförmlichkeit ungemein dumm und viehisch, fast wie die Tungusen, weil sie, gleich diesen, von Religionsbegriffen fast gar nichts wissen.«[13] The French terms in the original text are »Grossiers, stupides & brutaux.«[14] The Enlightenment pedagogue, Joachim Campe, provided two connotations for *Vieh* in one sentence describing African society: once to indicate irrationality and the second time to characterize the political mastery of a tribal king over his subjects: »In Afrika also, wo die Mohren wohnen, sind die meisten Menschen noch so roh und ungesittet, wie das liebe Vieh. Ihre Anführer oder Könige, die selbst nicht viel kluger sind, gehen dann auch mit ihnen um, als wenn sie wirkliches Vieh wären.«[15] Herder underscores how little Europeans actually know about African societies when he argues in volume two of the *Ideen* that they have not studied the national histories of Africa because they have viewed the people there as brutes: »Man betrachtet sie wie Vieh und bemerkt sie im Kauf nur nach den Zähnen.«[16]

On the other hand, some Enlightenment race theorists could classify humans while insisting that they not be treated like animals. In his preface to the German translation of Johann Friedrich Blumenbach's *Über die näturlichen Verschiedenheiten im Menschengeschlechte* [On the Natural Differences in the Human Species], Johann Gottfried Gruber asserted a moral obligation to identify with other humans when he cautions against treating people in other parts of the world as mere beasts of burden (*Lasttiere*). In this regard his attitude aligns with Herder's sympathetic approach to distant and oppressed peoples, hardly a surprise given that Gruber dedicates his translation to Herder.[17] Gruber considers it an intellectual failure to not recognize the similarity between humans, a failure to think through the relationship between humans so as to recognize the possibility that any one person could be in the same position as a less fortunate. Gruber positions Blumenbach somewhere between Kant and Herder. Herder rejects the use of racial categories altogether in favor of an empathetic reading of foreign cultures, while Kant asserts an epistemological need to classify people according to skin color and to arrange the races in a cultural hierarchy. By translating Blumenbach, Gruber endorses the investigations of physiological differences between human populations while insisting on a universal brotherhood of mankind. While Herder eschews all racial groupings, Gruber insists that any physiological classification be accompanied with a strong sense of humanity's unity and the common similarities in human fates, such that any person under the wrong conditions might have become a slave in the Americas or a serf in Europe.

The problem of domesticating humans comes to a philosophical head in the shadow boxing match between Kant and Herder in the middle of the 1780s.[18] Responding to the first volumes of Herder's *Ideen*, Kant pens his own remarkable account of principles underlying social history. While Kant wrote cautiously against serfdom in his later moral works, he provided what would seem to be a full legitimation of the Prussian state's absolutist rule in the sixth section of his *Idee zu einer allgemeinen Geschichte in weltbürgerlicher Absicht*. Here he makes unequivocally clear that the human animal requires total domination, in order to live among others: »der Mensch ist ein Thier, das, wenn es unter andern seiner Gattung lebt, einen Herrn nöthig hat« (AA 8: 23). Kant argues that even though humans possess reason and a moral law, they will abuse their freedom against other people. Kant then offers his harshest account of this authority »Er bedarf also einen Herrn, der ihm den eigenen Willen breche und ihn nöthige, einem allgemeinen Willen, dabei jeder frei sein kann, zu gehörchen« (AA 8: 23). Here Kant writes in a most Prussian manner by insisting on the necessity of discipline that breaks the individual down. He could be describing serfdom or the commands of the Prussian army, famous for its insistence on absolute obedience. Kant furthermore leaves no question that this master is not some philosophical principle, such as the moral law, but rather it must by necessity be another human being: »Das höchste Oberhaupt soll aber Gerecht für sich selbst und doch ein Mensch sein« (AA 8: 23).

As Eva Piirimäe explains, Herder was furious when he read Kant's essay, for he felt strongly that Kant had swiped the central idea that he had laid out in the first two volume of his own *Ideen*.[19] Unloading his dismay to Hamann, Herder characterizes Kant's position succinctly as »der Mensch ist ein Tier, das einen Herrn braucht: der Mensch ist nicht für sich, sondern für die Gattung: in der Gattung developirt er alle Kräfte und wie zuletzt alles auf einen politischen Antagonismus und eine vollkommste Monarchie, ja auf eine Coexistenz vieler vollkommensten Monarchien, die die reine Vernunft in corpore regieret, hinausgeht etc, etc.«[20] In essence, Herder argues, Kant is giving an ethical and political rationale for feudal domination over peasants. His argument is not far removed from the standard aristocratic attitude toward serfs. Indeed, Kant explains that within society each class lords it over those below while at the same time having a superior class above them. The biggest challenge then remains for the highest authority, namely the monarch, is to maintain rational ethical principles even though he does not have an authority looming above him. Kant does not even mention the convention that kings are accountable to God, a principle that royalty has always invoked.

Herder's response to Kant's »Allgemeine Ideen« carries over to his strongest anti-colonial writing in *Briefe zur Beförderung der Humanität* [Letters on the Furtherance of Humanity] where he starts the 114th letter with a rejoinder to Kant's fourth thesis in *Allgemeine Geschichte*. Kant had claimed that competitive drives between people lead to human progress, producing thereby an »ungesellige Geselligkeit der Menschen.« Herder rolls out an array of historical examples of societies fighting each other to counter Kant's claim: »Aber warum müssen Völker auf Völker wirken, um einander die Ruhe zu stören? Man sagt [here Herder means Kant], der fortgehendwachsenden Kultur wegen; wie gar etwas anders sagt das Buch der Geschichte!«[21] Herder then uses an example that every German living in the eastern periphery would have felt – did the invasion by central Asian nomads improve the lives of those they conquered? He proceeds then to list off a succession of such incursions.

Herder's basic position maintains that any moral and historical philosophy must preserve the concept of humanity. As Tilman Borsche concludes, Herder oriented his questions not according to the internal order of the philosophical discipline, but rather in the interests of people who have philosophical questions.[22] Referring to humans as domestic animals, that have been tamed by a farmer, or in this case a monarch, sends an immediate political message to eighteenth-century readers that without a sovereign to rule over them, they would regress to a violent and chaotic state of nature. Not only does the phrase legitimize absolute monarchy. Kant's analogy also appears to confirm the domination implicit within the feudal class system that degraded the overwhelming majority of humans in Europe to agricultural labor without any personal freedoms. Particularly in the Baltic territories, such as East Prussia, Latvia, Courland, Estonia, and Lithuania, serfdom entailed an absolute condition in which laborers were denied any personal freedoms, property, mobility, or control over their own work. Their children were born into the same condition, forced to labor for an aristocratic owner of the land to which they were forever bound.[23] As indigenous inhabitants, Baltic peasants were both legally and historically defined as belonging of the land on which they lived, as if they were local fauna. Indigeneity in this case was used to justify the feudal rule that owning land included the inhabitants upon it. Herder described the reorganization of the Baltic tribes after the Northern Crusades much like the dispersion of cattle between ranchers, or booty among Homer's Greeks: »Die alte Preußische Nation ward vertilget, Litthauer und Samojiten, Kuren, Letten und Esthen wie Herden dem Deutschen Adel verteilt.«[24] Garlieb Merkel, the Baltic abolitionist carried the metaphor forward in to the 1790s arguing that Baltic lords still treated their serfs as cattle to be slaughtered: »Nach der Vorstellung der meisten Adlichen sind ihre Rechte über den Leibeigenen noch immer nicht die Lehnsherrn über den Dienstmann, sondern die des Schlachters über die erkaufte Heerde.«[25] The long history of the Baltic colonization – the region both Kant and Herder grew up in – shows that the feudal principle that the people living on the land are a natural resource no different than animals was sharpened into a general tactic so that indigenous people Europeans conquered elsewhere often became subject to the same treatment as beasts of burden.

Pennsylvania State University

---

1 Deutsches Wörterbuch von Jacob Grimm und Wilhelm Grimm, digitalisierte Fassung im Wörterbuchnetz des Trier Center for Digital Humanities, Version 01/23, www.woerterbuchnetz.de/DWB. The Grimm dictionary describes a rank order in which humans are placed between angels and animals, but sometimes degrade themselves to the lower level. The originally neutral designation of »Vieh« as a farm animal becomes thereby a negative comparison for humans in this usage. The Grimm definitions refer to situations in which humans are themselves responsible for their animalistic condition. The dictionary does not of course offer a more critical view of politics to argue that humans can be reduced to the level of animals by oppressive political and military force.
2 John H. Zammito, Herder between Reimarus and Tetens: The Problem of an Animal-Human Boundary, in: Herder: Philosophy and Anthropology, ed. by Anik Waldow and Nigel DeSouza, Oxford 2017, pp. 127-146.
3 David Baumeister, Kant on the Human Animal: Anthropology, Ethics, Race, Evanston 2022.
4 David Brion Davis, In the Image of God: Religion, Moral Values, and Our Heritage of Slavery, New Haven 2001, p. 127
5 Aristotle, The Complete Works of Aristotle. Bollingen Series LXXI, Princeton 1992, online Database, 1254a24-1255a3; Carlo Ginzburg, The Soul of Brutes, Calcutta 2022. Thanks to James Kopf for this reference.
6 Johann Heinrich Voss, Die Erleichterten, in: Poetische Werke, vol. 2, Berlin 1867, p. 23.
7 Immanuel Kant, Reflexionen zur Moral-, Rechts-, und Religionsphilosophie, in: Kants gesammelte Schriften, vol. 19, Berlin 1902-, p. 545 (in the following cited as AA + volume and page numbers).
8 The classic study remains: Orlando Patterson, Slavery and Social Death, Cambridge, MA 2018.

9 Giorgio Agamben, Homo Sacer: Sovereign Power and Bare Life, trans. Daniel Heller-Roazen, Stanford 1998.
10 Georg Forster, Reise um die Welt, in: Georg Forsters Werke. Sämtliche Schriften, Tagebücher, Briefe, vol. 3, Berlin 1958–, p. 16
11 Therese Huber, Fragmente über einen Theil von Polen, in: Erzählungen, vol. 4, Leipzig 1831, p. 325.
12 Georg Forster, Werke, vol. 14, p. 343 [22 Mai 1785 to Sömmerring].
13 Herrn von Büffons Allgemeine Naturgeschichte, eine freye mit Anmerkungen vermehrtes Uebersetzung, vol. 6, Berlin 1774, pp. 16-17.
14 Histoire Naturelle, Générale et Particulière, vol. 3, Paris 1749, p. 379.
15 Joachim Heinrich Campe, Robinson der Jüngere, zur angenehmen und nützlichen Unterhaltung für Kinder, vol. 2, Hamburg 1780, p. 235, cited in: Jürgen Overhoff, Slavery and the Slave Trade in German Children's Picture Books (1714-1827) (forthcoming).
16 Herder, Ideen zur Philosophie der Geschichte der Menschheit, in: Sämtliche Werke, vol. 13, ed. by Bernhard Suphan, Berlin 1887, p. 232 [vol. 2, Book 6].
17 Johann Friedrich Blumenbach, Über die natürlichen Verschiedenheiten im Menschengeschlechte, trans. Johann Gottfried Gruber, Leipzig 1798, p. vii.
18 For a thorough overview, see John H. Zammito, Kant, Herder, and the Birth of Anthropology, Chicago 2002.
19 Eva Piirimäe, Human Rights, Imperialism and Peace among Nations: Herder's Debate with Kant, in: Intellectual History Archive, vol. 2 (2018), pp. 3-4.
20 Johann Gottfried Herder, Briefe, vol. 5, September 1783–August 1788, Weimar 1979, p. 109 [28 February 1785 to Hamann].
21 Herder, Briefe zu Beförderung der Humanität, in: Werke, vol. 7, ed. by Hans Dietrich Irmscher, Frankfurt a. M. 1991, p. 671.
22 Tilman Borsche, Vorkritisch oder metakritisch? Die philosophische Aktualität Herders. Die philosophische Kontroverse zwischen Kant und Herder und ihre gemeinsame Grundlage, in: Herder im Spiegel der Zeiten. Verwerfungen der Rezeptionsgeschichte und Chancen einer Relektüre, ed. by Tilman Borsche, Munich 2006, pp. 126-141, here p. 132.
23 For further historical evidence, see Daniel Purdy, Human Bondage Compared: The Enlightenment Discourse on Baltic Serfdom and Atlantic Slavery, in: Colonialism and German Enlightenment: The Legacies of Race Theory, co-edited with Bettina Brandt, Oxford, forthcoming.
24 Herder, Ideen zur Philosophie der Geschichte der Menschheit, in: Werke, vol. 6, ed. by Martin Bollacher, Frankfurt a. M. 1989, 6: 878 [vol. 4, book 20]. This passage does not appear in the Suphan edition.
25 Garlieb Mekel, Die Letten vorzüglich in Liefland an Ende des philosophischen Jahrhunderts. Ein Beytrag zur Völker- und Menschenkunde, second edition, Leipzig 1800, p. 83.

Forster's Critique of Slavery in Meiners's Natural History: On Objectivity and Cultural Creativity

Sally Hatch Gray

In 1790, Christoph Meiners (1747-1810), an established professor of natural philosophy at the University of Göttingen, published two articles in the *Göttingisches historisches Magazin*. The first, »Historische Nachrichten über die wahre Beschaffenheit des Sclavenhandels und der Knechtschaft der Neger in West Indies« [Historical Report on the True Quality of the Slave Trade and the Servitude of the Blacks in the West Indies], argued in support of slavery, and the second, »Von den Varietäten und Abarten der Neger« [Of the Varieties and Deviate Forms of Blacks], approached the topic of Blackness from the perspective of his natural history.[1] His main conclusion in these two articles, well known at the time, was that darker complexioned African people could be improved through their enslavement. An attack on the idea of shared humanity, his work was largely forgotten until the 1930s and 1940s when the Nazis revitalized interest in Meiners's work in their study of the invention of »scientific« race categories found in classical German thought.[2] Similar to them, Meiners maintained that parentage was determinate, seeing any Black descent going back generations as grounds to enslave a person (VAN 642, 206). However, unlike the Nazis, Meiners concluded that Europeans can better others by interbreeding with them, supporting the slave owners' mixing with, or raping of, their Enslaved. Children of the fairer European colonists and their darker Enslaved, whose skin color became indistinguishable from that of other Europeans after a generation or two, he claimed, are in Meiners's view still justly enslaved. Meiners's organizational chart divides all of the earth's peoples into two major groups: the Caucasians and the Altaic. In Europe, he claims, only the Celts (who are Caucasians) are capable of the highest moral perfectibility, and not the Slavs (who are not Caucasians).

One year after Meiners, in 1791, Georg Forster, a naturalist who had published a narrative on his travels aboard the *Resolution* with Captain James Cook as part of the latter's second circumnavigation of the world from 1772 to 1775, wrote a condemnation not only of Meiners's work, but also of his character, in a review also published in the *Göttingisches historisches Magazin*. Here Forster recognizes the necessity for a natural science of humankind, as in other kinds of empirical science, to find a hypothetical model to organize the endless variety of human cultural groups (GFW 11: 237-238).[3] At the same time that he acknowledges this, Forster himself demonstrates a racial prejudice by stating that dark skin is ugly and white skin more beautiful, seeing a correlation between skin color and social hierarchy.[4] However, his review of Meiners also illustrates his objections to static categorical race theories based on skin color, focusing instead on development and change.[5] Also, Forster believed in human freedom, joined the Mainz revolution acting on his radical egalitarian politics, and was adamantly against slavery of any kind.[6] In his review, he objects to Meiners's assumption that physical differences are demonstrative of bad character, finding Meiners's »harsh« descriptions to be a reflection of the man himself (GFW 11: 243-244). My discussion in the following will highlight how Forster turns Meiners himself into a subject for his anthropology, employing what resembles a Goethean model of science based on radical empiricism and including the interaction between the scientist and nature.[7]

First, Forster outlines how Meiners's argument is circular, that he develops the proof of his classification system from the system itself, and that this »künstliche Cirkelbewegung« [artificial circularity] is no longer acceptable in philosophy (GFW 11: 243). Forster argued that Meiners in his scientifically indefensible system harshly judges black Africans to be endowed with »teuflischen Anlagen« [devilish aptitudes] and »einer unverbesserlichen Unsittlichkeit« [unimprovable bad morals, customs, or behavior] (GFW 11: 244). Acknowledging that part of the problem is Meiners's source material, he writes, »Vielleicht ist es nicht ganz seine Schuld, wenn er überall nur das Schlechte, Hässliche, Ekelhafte, Verabscheuungswürdige sieht« [Perhaps it is not entirely his fault if he sees everywhere only the bad, ugly, disgusting, [and] detestable] (GFW 11: 245).[8] Reports from slavers and planters could account for this prejudice.[9] Meiners had not visited the peoples he describes, Forster notes, but his detailed descriptions of geographic locations where immoral behavior took place, underpinning his measurement of the absolute worth of people, are his own invention (GFW 11: 245).

Meiners's hierarchy of groups in Africa suggests that the more various peoples mixed with those of lighter complexion, as the peoples of Northern Africa supposedly had done, the more human they supposedly became. He then describes how the »original form« of Blacks is to be found in the remote interior of the continent:

> Die Neger aus dem Innersten von Afrika sind fast ohne Ausnahme Menschfresser, haben ein fürchterlich tigerartiges kaum menschliches Ansehen, und spitzige, oder zackigte Zähne, die wie Fuchs = Scheeren, oder das Gebiß von Füchsen in einander schliessen. (VAN 631)
> [Blacks from innermost Africa are almost without exception cannibals. They have a horrible tiger-like, hardly human look and pointed or jagged teeth that close together like pinking shears or [like] the teeth of foxes.] (VAN 201)

In the interior, where far fewer Europeans ventured, Meiners's descriptions become more fantastic and more beastly. Still, Meiners emphasizes here that these conclusions are based on several centuries of data (VAN 631, 201). In Meiners's geography of the varying traits of the peoples of Africa, it appears that where European colonists have made more inroads, he sees Africans as more human. Here the residents would be more readily captured, and so would be more profitable for the slavers and planters. All enslaved Blacks shipped to the West Indies, in Meiners's view, however, are »übelartig« [nasty] and »verdorben« [depraved], such that they need to be »gezähmt« [tamed] and »entwildert« [domesticated] (VAN 637, 203-204). Refusing to obey even the mildest command, Meiners charges, feral Africans should be domesticated by breeding them with »Creoles,« children of Blacks and Europeans, who, he alleges, are proud of their colonial origins (VAN 637, 204). Detailing his extensive source material for his theory of race varieties, he argues that slavers and planters were especially empowered to great discernment due to their extensive experience subduing a variety of Blacks from central and southern Africa (VAN 633, 202). Much like the way a breeder can spot the characteristics of a promising racehorse, the slavers and planters, in Meiners's view, were experts on people they deemed as black.

Offensive and wrong, Forster easily disproves Meiners's fundamental binary division between Caucasians and everyone else, for all one would need to do is to find Europeans behaving badly or people anywhere else demonstrating admirable moral behavior. Forster argues,

> [...] dass man bei gehöriger Aufmerksamkeit auch Züge zu vortheilhaften und angenehmen Schilderungen von sehr vielen, sogar den wildesten, Völkern, bey den glaubwürdigsten Schriftstellern aufgezeichnet findet. (GFW II: 247)
> [that one when sufficiently attentive can also find traits enabling favorable and even pleasant portrayals of very many, even of the wildest, peoples, written up by the most credible authors.]

On the one hand, Forster argues, there are many reports even among the »wildest« groups of agreeable character traits. On the other hand, for evidence of morally lacking Europeans, Forster trains his eye on slavers and those who support them, attempting to legitimize an analysis of Meiners's humanity, or lack thereof, as evidence for his own study of humans of color. Describing Meiners while also describing a characteristic of this group, Forster writes,

> Fast scheint es, wenn Hr. M. es rechtfertigen kann, dass er zuerst zwey Menschenstämme durch wesentliche, angebohrne Unterschiede charak-

terisiert, und sodann den einen mit allen Ausdrücken des Abscheues und der lieblosesten Verwerfung überhäuft, weil er *das* nicht ist, was er vermöge der Definition nicht seyn sollte und konnte. (GFW 11: 246).
[It appears almost as though whenever Mr. M. can justify it, that he characterizes first off two human stems by way of existential, inborn differences, and then showers one with all expressions of abomination and the most uncharitable dismissal, because he is not *that*, what he, by definition, neither should nor could be.]

Here Forster describes Meiners's method of knowing what he is not, and then casting those with whom he does not identify in the worst possible light. In so doing, Meiners's own character – how he identifies what he is versus what he is not – becomes fundamental to his work. This then gives Forster the opening to include the character of an authority, in this case that of Meiners, in his critique of anthropology. Forster argues that when a planter or slaver observes »abomination« in Black African people as justification for potential profit, their conclusions reflect their own character, while the people who suffer from the way they are characterized remain unknown to them. While scientific attempts to discover classification systems for peoples, which continued in academia well into the twentieth century, were scientifically of dubious value, their use for economies of slavery and exploitation was not. Forster's critique demonstrates how tying science to economics, to the extent that successful science became that which was instrumental to the success of economic structures in place, revealed an early-on a problem with the methodology itself. That is, what is not useful, or considered part of an objective analysis for the purposes of the study, could be omitted. This lack of knowledge or understanding of the objects of study beyond economic goals meant that the traditions, languages, culture, and arts of African people were assumed to be unworthy of attention or non-existent. The practice of enslavement was based on useful fictions and built out of an image of European superiority, and it implanted this structure into social reality and empowered the most extensive, longest continuing crime against humanity in modern history.

Unlike Meiners, Forster worked from experience, having observed many different lands, customs, societies, and peoples during his long voyage. And he had written a travel narrative, *Voyage 'round the World*, 1777, published as *Reise um die Welt* in German translation in 1778 and 1780, to document his findings. He had observed the slave trade and the Dutch colony on the Cape of Good Hope in South Africa first-hand when ported there during the journey into the South Pacific and again on his trip back to England. His first time there in 1772, he wrote that while the houses looked to be the result of a prosperous industry, there was, however, only one small church. Comparing, then, the Dutch colony with Holland he writes, »Der Duldungs-Geist, welcher den Holländern in Europa so viel Nutzen verschaft hat, ist in ihren Colonien nicht zu finden« (GFW 2: 27) [That spirit of toleration, which has been so beneficial to the Dutch government at home, is not to be met with in their colonies] (VRW 47). He points out that the conditions aboard the slaving ships were so horrible, that eighty to one-hundred captives out of eight hundred aboard would die just from the journey alone, and another two to three hundred arrive so sick that they must be hospitalized (GFW 2: 77; VRW 48). For Forster, there is no justification for such barbary.

Witnessing the realities of slavery in Cape Town, Forster writes that there is little to learn by observing or meeting the Enslaved, as they have been kidnapped and removed from their home. They are not free to be themselves, to be observed, as Forster describes in his narrative. That is, they are not free to speak their own languages, to visit or share a meal, to practice their customs, religions, or to express themselves creatively. Instead, he trained his observations on those who could do these things, those who enslaved, and found the whole settlement diminished by the practice of slavery, such that human life for everyone was less valued (GFW 2: 77; VRW 48). Indeed, Forster writes,

> Nichts ist hier und in andern Holländischen Colonien gemeiner, als Soldaten in der Compagnie Diensten zu finden, die öffentlich gestehen, daß sie in Holland ›weggestohlen‹ sind. (GFW 2: 77-78)
> Nothing is more common, in this and other Dutch colonies, than to meet with soldiers in the company's service who, upon enquiry, acknowledge that have been kidnapped in Holland. (VRW 48)

Militarized across the whole society and armed by soldiers who were often themselves ›kidnapped‹ from Holland and made to serve the East Indian Company, the colony was held together by force. Forster discusses how the state of education, healthcare, religion, and a sense of community, which would contribute to the quality of life in any settlement, were degraded (GFW 2: 83-86; VRW 53-56). Unlike Holland, he writes, the settlement was not a commonwealth, but rather the East India Company alone was amassing a great deal of wealth (GFW 2: 87; VRW 56). The colony had been set up inefficiently for the settlers, who lived great distances apart, in part due to law, but also by choice for their own safety from the company and town, he observed. Walking up into the mountains, away from the port town, Forster's group encountered the Khoikhoi, called »Hottentots« by the Europeans; he describes them as secretive, trading in livestock, and technically adept miners (GFW 2: 89; VRW 57). He remarks that little is known about them. The implication of this reticence to say more contrasts with Meiners's readiness to condemn all Africans with dark skin and view them only from the perspective of potential profit.

The principle of a »general philanthropy« must be the basis of scientific observations of peoples, Forster explains in his preface to volume 1 of the *Reise um die Welt* in 1778. Kidnapped, starved, chained in their filth, and surrounded by death for months at sea, no wonder that the Africans were not cooperative upon arrival in the West Indies. Forster does not fault them here. He himself would later join the Mainz revolution against tyranny in his own country. He states the goal of the project, as outlined by his father, under whom he had apprenticed:

> Mit einem Wort, man erwartete von ihm eine philosophische Geschichte der Reise, von Vorurtheil und gemeinen Trugschlüssen frey, worin er seine Entdeckungen in der Geschichte des Menschen, und in der Naturkunde überhaupt, ohne Rücksicht auf willkürliche Systeme, blos nach allgemeinen menschenfreundlichen Grundsätzen darstellen sollte; das heißt eine Reisebeschreibung, dergleichen der gelehrten Welt bisher noch keine war vorgelegt worden. (GFW 2: 8)
> [It was to be] a philosophical history of the voyage, free from prejudice and vulgar error, where human nature should be represented without any adherence to fallacious systems, and upon the principles of general philanthropy; in short, an account written upon a plan which the learned would had not hitherto seen executed. (VRW 5-6)

»Free from prejudice« and from »any adherence to fallacious systems,« Forster believed their work to be ground-breaking, scientific observation. The reasons for the observations, the background of the observer, as well as their feelings all contribute to the colored lenses through which they observe. While he cannot cast away all of the color from his own lenses, Forster concludes, »Wenigstens bin ich mir bewußt, daß es nicht finster und trübe vor meinen Augen gewesen ist« (GFW 2: 13) [Of this at least I am certain, that a gloomy livid tinge hath never clouded my sight (VRW 9)]. After traveling around the world aboard an English ship, Forster concludes that everywhere the inhabitants were worse off for their contact with European explorers (GFW 2: 186-187; VRW 121). Watching the English sailors rape women and girls, spread venereal disease, and kill people, Forster became very concerned with how they and he himself saw the world.[10]

Forster's turning of his trained eye on Meiners, in the position of the observer, and on the interaction between the observer and the observed, as well as his critique of static classification systems, aligns his practice of anthropology with a Goethean practice of natural science.[11] Forster's practice of scientific observation of humankind resembles that of Johann Wolfgang von Goethe (1749-1842), in that it is based on evolution, interconnectivity, and creativity.[12] Forster's review of Meiners also fits a Goethean model, such that the living, connected, and creative scientist is not apart from, but part of a living changing environment. Thus, the act of observation must also be subject to inquisition. In the final chapter of his book, *The Wholeness of Nature: Goethe's Way of Science* (1996), entitled, »The Possibility of a New Science of Nature,« physicist Henry Bortoft explains how human sensory experience itself does not deliver objective reality to us. Instead, in a process of defining what objective reality is, we are choosing what we will consider as such.[13] The more static our definitions become, the more blind the scientist turns out to be regarding diversity and change. In Goethe's view of the *Urpflanze*, a living and real archetype of a plant, a whole is brought about by on-going perceptions of a living plant made up of each individual plant's participation in being that plant.[14] Similarly, Forster demonstrates how both he and Meiners participate in what humankind is, as a part of natural history. For Forster, scientists also participate in an understanding of the being that is human. This model allows for both the individual and for the whole, but it disallows transcendence of cultural perspective. One's own cultural perspective must be part of the examination. Fundamental to Forster's idea of the necessity of *Sittlichkeit* is the ability to appreciate other human beings as free, creative individuals. That is, a scientist must be open to this idea that humans who they see as »other« are also individuals like themselves deserving of respect in order to do this work. It follows that the essential problem with Meiners's work for Forster is his community with slavers.

In his review, Forster grapples with a creative, culturally specific, and yet seemingly necessary element to the practice of natural history, that a natural historian must demonstrate highly developed *Sitten*, a specifically German idea of proper behavior, manners, and mores.[15] While every cultural group develops their own *Sitten*, Forster believes a highly developed »mechanism of morality« has empowered Europeans more than others, and Germans more than the British, through a long history of arts and science and by collecting knowledge from different cultures in other parts of the world.[16] He writes,

> In Europa sind die Wissenschaften und die Künste bis zu einer anderwärts nicht erreichten Stufe der Vervollkommung gelangt; wir haben einen Mechanismus der Sittlichkeit vor andern Völkern voraus, der nur aus langer Gewöhnung an durchdachte Grundsätze entspringen kann; wir endlich herrschen auch in andern Weltheilen, und umfassen mit unserer vollkommneren Erkenntniss die ganze Erde. (GFW 11: 239-240)

[The sciences and arts have attained a level of perfection in Europe not achieved elsewhere; we have an advantage over other peoples in a mechanism of morality that can only arise from long habituation to well thought out principles; finally, we also rule over other parts of the world and encompass the whole world with our more complete knowledge.]

Forster shared a commonly held belief during the Enlightenment period that the arts and technology that developed together with globalization have led to the advancement of Europe, but he attributes this to European mores and customs. He then continues to write that Europe has gained a tremendous amount of knowledge and culture from other parts of the world. »Sittlichkeit« can be anywhere or may be lacking in any individual. For Forster, a foundational, culturally defined, and moral outlook is a prerequisite for the practice of natural history, including the scientific study of humans, such that a study of an anthropologist, too, must be included in this work.

Forster's employment of culturally specific German *Sitten* is a double-edged sword, which enables the prejudice that Europeans are the most beautiful and moral people in comparison to the rest of the world. Forster's aesthetics reflect a widely held, but also increasingly problematized belief during the classical period of a transcendental link between beauty and moral goodness.[17] While acknowledging that this aesthetics is one of White supremacy, this discussion turns to an examination of how Forster's idea of German *Sitten* also demonstrates an important element in Forster's view of scientific theory. Against Meiners, he argues that physical and cultural differences are not existential characteristics that justify condemnation or oppression (GFW 11: 246). The word »mechanism« in his idea of a »*Mechanismus der Sittlichkeit*« signals a scientific or systematic energy composed of complex cultural and environmental realities. Forster uses Meiners's conclusions to expose that not all Europeans or all Germans have *Sittlichkeit*. Thus, it is not brought about by simply being a member of a privileged group, but learned, or not, through experience. Every individual, who is free to do so, plays a role in its development, such that freedom and cultural creativity must be accounted for too. Forster's critique here, then, demonstrates the willingness to form a structure that can be a basis for objectivity in science, such that objectivity becomes the product of a shared practice among an infinite number of disinterested, well-meaning, and self-reflective individuals (GFW 2: 7).[18] Furthermore, while the idea that cultural mores are a mechanism among Europeans itself seems to be overly reductionist, it points to a fundamental assumption from which an anthropologist must work, in Forster's view, that no one person or group enjoys a privileged view from a separate, objective platform. Knowing the complications, Forster accepts here that culture is part of a science of humankind. Thus, it becomes important to examine from which cultural perspective one works. With this awareness, Forster's idea of science becomes much more complex. It follows from his review, that there is a necessary creative cultural element in a study of natural history, such that any isolated and fixed classification systems are insufficient to capture the great multitude of cultural and natural environments.

Meiners, an influential scholar, participated in some of the worst behaviors of humans. His inability to understand the limitations of systematic thinking and of his own reduction of science to industry leave him blind to the necessary status of cultural context. Aligning Forster's eighteenth-century critique of the parameters of natural science with that of twenty-first century physicist Henri Bortoft demonstrates how when Enlightenment-aged natural science collapsed into technological development in pursuit of wealth and property, it limited possibilities for human understanding. Indeed, the history of Forster's critique offers insight into how science can still be practiced today.

Mississippi State University

1 Christoph Meiners, Von den Varietäten und Abarten der Neger: in Göttingisches historisches Magazin 6 (1790), pp. 625-645, here p. 642. Of the Varieties and Deviate Forms of Negroes, in: Kant and the Concept of Race: Late Eighteenth-Century Writings, trans. and ed. by Jon M. Mikkelsen, New York 2013, pp. 195-207 (hereafter cited as VAN followed by page references first in German and then in English translation).
2 See Britta Rupp-Eisenreich, Christoph Meiners' »New Science« (1747-1810), in: The Invention of Race: Scientific and Popular Representations, ed. by Nicolas Bancel, Thomas David, and Dominic Thomas, New York 2014, pp. 68-83. See also Jonathan Hess, Jewish Emancipation and the Politics of Race, in: The German Invention of Race, ed. by Sara Eigen and Mark Larrimore, New York 2006, pp. 203-212. Hess shows how Meiners's race theory was instrumental in creating new definitions of Jews as an inferior race.
3 Georg Forster, Rezension von Christoph Meiners, in: Georg Forsters Werke. Sämtliche Schriften, Tagebücher, Briefe, vol. 11, Berlin 1958, pp. 236-252. Further references to Forster's Werke will be cited parenthetically as GFW followed by volume and page number.
4 For an analysis of the role of aesthetics in Forster's work, see Reinhard M. Möller, Sakontalas Reise oder »Individualitäten vergleichen,« in: Ästhetik, Kulturpoetik und weltliterarische Bildung bei Forster, Herder und Friedrich Schlegel, in: Komparatistik. Jahrbuch der Deutschen Gesellschaft für Allgemeine und Vergleichende Literaturwissenschaft (2016), pp. 113-130. See also: Sally Hatch Gray,

Aesthetics, Anthropology, and the Limits of Enlightenment Cosmopolitanism in Georg Forster's Reise um die Welt, in: New Perspectives on the Eighteenth Century, vol. 9.1 (Spring 2012), pp. 31-51.

5   Forster published a critique of Immanuel Kant's race categories in 1786; see: Noch etwas über die Menschenraßen, GFW 13: 130-156; Something More about the Human Races, VAN 143-167. Möller (note 4) discusses the multifaceted dynamics in Forster's anthropology.

6   See Gordon A. Craig, Engagement and Neutrality in Germany: The Case of Georg Forster, 1754-1794, in: The Journal of Modern History, vol. 41.1 (1969), pp. 1-16. See also Todd Kontje, Georg Forster: German Cosmopolitan, University Park, PA 2022, pp. 143-171, and Yomb May, Georg Forsters Literarische Weltreise, Berlin 2011.

7   For a discussion of this idea of science featuring a combination of empiricism and the creative role and moral responsibility of the human subject, see Dalia Nassar, Romantic Empiricism: Nature, Art, and Ecology from Herder to Humboldt, Oxford UK, 2022.

8   For translations of Forster's review, I am indebted to Michael Olson, who translated this piece for the German Studies Seminar, Translating the Pacific: Georg Forster and the Order of Nature in Meiners, Kant, and Herder, 2023, that he and Jennifer Mensch organized at the annual meeting of the GSA, and which made this essay possible. I am referencing Michael Olson's working draft, while also adding a some of my own edits. I owe a debt of gratitude to Jennifer Mensch and Michael Olson for their vision and work, and to the seminar participants for their contributions to this forum.

9   For an analysis of the source materials that were referenced in eighteenth-century anthropology, see Huaping Lu Adler, Kant, Race, and Racism: A View from Somewhere, New York 2023.

10 See May (note 6), pp. 28-40, on cultural reflection in Forster's work. For a discussion of Forster's aesthetics, see Möller (note 3). For a discussion of this tension more broadly across Forster's life's work, see Kontje (note 6). See also Helmut Peitsch, Georg Forster. Deutsche ›Antheilnahme‹ an der europäischen Expansion über die Welt, Berlin 2017.

11 See Renata Schellenberg, Goethe's Scientific Approach to Nature: Innovation and Imagination, in: Lessing Yearbook, vol. 50 (2023), pp. 157-175, and Nassar (note 7), pp. 146-175.

12 For an analysis of creativity in Goethean science, see; John A. McCarthy, Remapping Reality: Chaos and Creativity in Science and Literature (Goethe – Nietzsche – Grass), New York 2006, pp. 169-230.

13 Henri Bortoft, The Wholeness of Nature: Goethe's Way of Science, Edinburgh 1996, pp. 321-330.

14 For an analysis of Goethe's idea of the »Urphänomen,« a way of seeing the individual and the whole, as well as his concept of the perspective on the scientist, see Nassar, pp. 104-145 (note 7). See also Henri Bortoft (note 13).

15 See Peitsch (note 10), pp. 77-80, on how Forster elevates German culture in his argument against Meiners.

16 See Susanne Zantop, Colonial Fantasies: Conquest, Family and Nation in Precolonial Germany, 1770-1870, Durham, NC 1997. Zantop focuses on precolonial

Germans reading travel narratives and their fantasies about being better colonialists who would be kind to others.
17 Perhaps the most influential and developed discussion of this belief may be found in Immanuel Kant's *Kritik der Urteilskraft* (Critique of Pure Reason, 1790), where Kant argues that beauty is a symbol of morality. Kant also sees the color white as a symbol of fineness of character and moral goodness. See Sally Hatch Gray, Kant's Race Theory, Forster's Counter, and the Metaphysics of Color, in: The Eighteenth Century: Theory and Interpretation, 53.4 (2012), pp. 393-412.
18 Yomb May discusses phenomenology in Forster's anthropology (note 6), pp. 28-40.

Slavery and Enthusiasm in the German Enlightenment: The Case of Christoph Meiners

Michael Olson

The question of how we should understand the relationship between the principles and aspirations of the Enlightenment and all manner of institutionalized injustice has become familiar territory in the nearly eighty years since Adorno and Horkheimer published *Dialektik der Aufklärung* (1944/1947). More recently, this question has been pursued in the pages of both scholarly publications and prominent newspapers specifically in relation to race, racism, and the legacies of Atlantic slavery. So far there is little consensus to be found, but even those authors most inclined to conclude that Immanuel Kant and others bear some culpability for the history of racism in the centuries after their deaths do not argue that these authors advocated for slavery on the basis of Enlightenment principles. It can thus be surprising to stumble across the Göttingen philosopher and historian Christoph Meiners (1747-1810) wrapping himself in the mantle of the Enlightenment while arguing:

> No person has ever doubted that children and imbeciles can rightly be subjected to the will of more sensible people. [...] Experiences of a thousand different kinds make it no less undeniable that Blacks [*Neger*] and innumerable other peoples become happier and better when they are under the power and discipline [*Zucht*] of more rational Whites than when they remain left to their own indolence and wickedness.[1]

In this essay, I want to make sense of the historical reality that in at least some cases German authors that positioned themselves as proponents of enlightenment were also defenders of slavery and staunch critics of abolitionists. In order to do this, I will reconstruct two conceptions of enlightenment in late-eighteenth-century German thought with specific attention to how these views relate to slavery.

1. *Enlightenment and Liberation*

The first conception of enlightenment is familiar, and the attitude toward slavery it often engendered is predictable. On this view, enlightenment involves some form of liberation from ignorance. The metaphoric connections of enslavement to ignorance or tradition of course incline proponents of this view to oppose other forms of more literal enslavement. More than this, however, the rational insights many of these authors take as illustrative of their liberation from ignorance include the recognition of some form of natural rights or basic dignity for all people. This recognition was a crucial element of the case against the dehumanization at the core of Atlantic slavery.

Authors that linked enlightenment with liberation vary widely on how explicitly they articulate their opposition to slavery and how metaphorically they conceive of the slavery to which their notion of enlightenment is opposed. Perhaps the most famous version of this view comes from Kant, who wrote, »Enlightenment is the human being's emergence from its self-imposed immaturity.«[2] Kant's interest in that essay lies in defending the right to argue one's views in the public sphere, and not in opposing slavery.[3] Others, however, saw an incompatibility between this kind of intellectual freedom and a metaphorical enslavement to ignorance. One anonymous author, for example, concluded, »Freedom and enlightenment are sisters, just like foolishness and slavery: but there is neither enlightenment nor truth where one may not speak the *truth* without being punished.«[4] Here, the importance of intellectual freedom for the pursuit of truth stands in opposition to a very general sense of servitude. Other authors presented enlightenment as incompatible with a less abstract notion of slavery that reflected at least some historical reality. In his comparative history, the Hamburg politician Christian Eggers (1758-1813) argues that the progress of enlightenment in Europe is a bulwark against forms of slavery in Muslim north Africa, where, he writes, »[h]umanity has no value [...]. Unlimited slavery of all subjects with respect to the regents and among themselves; complete lack of enlightenment: perpetual stasis of culture to the point where the human being satisfies only bodily necessities in civil society.«[5] On this view, slavery is an historical remnant that survives only in the absence of the progress characteristic of entlighenment. The head of the Habsburg imperial secret police, Johann Anton von Pergen (1725-1814), similarly remarked in an anonymous pamphlet that, because of the general suppression of the spirit under despotic governments, »fear alone still maintains some empires in the yet uncivilized parts of the world and slavery persisted over so many centuries in nearly the whole world, and still exists in the Orient. But the enlightenment of Europe – where everyone's intellectual powers (even the common man's) are developed from youth – is irreconcilable with this condition.«[6] Slavery is antithetical to intellectual maturity, and as enlightenment and civilization spread to other parts of the world, what practices of enslavement remain will gradually disappear.

It is clear that authors writing in the Holy Roman Empire commonly presented enlightenment as antithetical to slavery. The examples we have seen to this point invoke notions of slavery that are either entirely abstract or related to Old World slavery. Since the German lands were not involved in overseas colonization in the eighteenth century, one might conclude, German-language authors were simply uninterested or unaware of debates about slavery and abolition in England, France, and their American colonies. This would be a mistake. There was robust German-language cultural engagement with Atlantic slavery and calls for its abolition, and this engagement targeted both scholarly and popular audiences.[7] Indeed, there were also authors who defended ideas about enlightenment specifically opposed to the inhuman practices characteristic of Atlantic slavery. The pastor and publisher Andreas Riem (1749-1814), referring to an anecdote made famous by Hector St. John de Crèvecoeur's *Letters from an American Farmer* (1782), writes:

> When an English barbarian hangs a Black slave [*Negersklave*] up in an iron cage in the deepest forest so that for days birds of prey eat him alive piece by piece, turning his torment into infernal torture – would it not be better for humanity if Carolina, where this occurred, were more enlightened and would learn to honor the rights of humanity?«[8]

And Gottlob Tittel (1739-1816), who is remembered today as a critic of Kant's moral philosophy, concluded a brief discussion of racial slavery like this: »All friends of humanity are united in the wish that slavery, that dishonorable yoke, had never been known to human beings, or indeed would like it to be cease entirely. Philosophy, the mother of enlightenment, has already brought this wish, in large part, to fulfilment.«[9] This shows that proponents of the view that enlightenment is fundamentally liberatory did not only conveive of it as opposed to concrete instances of slavery but in at least some cases presented it as a motive force in the abolition of earlier historical forms of servitude.

2. Enlightenment as anti-Enthusiasm

The idea that *the* Enlightenment was a monolithic philosophical or cultural movement that spread throughout Europe in the long eighteenth century has been undermined by historians and replaced with a splintered vision of the Enlightenment as essentially contested. It is thus not surprising to find that notions of enlightenment within the German Enlightenment were also a subject of debate. Indeed, there are many cases where we find scholars contrasting their own understandings of enlightenment with an alternative they argue is mistaken or misleading. The Mainz historian Nicolas Vogt (1756-1836), for example, presented his own vision of a patient enlightenment in opposition to the ways enlightenment can go astray: »The best means of attaining enlightenment and spiritual freedom are thinking for oneself, publicity, and book printing. All secret or violent or hasty enlightenment leads back to slavery.«[10] The central contrast in such cases is not between enlightenment and ignorance but between proper and improper pursuits of a growing interest in enlightenment.

Christoph Meiners similarly calls upon his reader to differentiate between true enlightenment and inopportune or false enlightenment.[11] »In the most general sense of the word,« he writes, »enlightenment means any measure of beautiful and beneficial knowledge through which the human mind is educated or the heart of the human being is ennobled.«[12] In the wake of the French Revolution and English debates concerning the abolition of slavery and the slave trade, Meiners noted a tendency for people to appeal to enlightenment in support of a variety of political causes, many of which he took to in fact be contrary to true enlightenment. In the opening lines of an essay defending slavery, he writes:

> The growing enlightenment and the growing humanitarianism that unfailingly grows with true enlightenment and the cultivation of the mind have in recent times not only spread better concepts of the rights and duties of human beings but have also to a great extent increased the sense of atavistic or continuing injustice, indignation at all oppressors, and sympathy for the oppressed.[13]

Calls for increased civil and political rights for Jews, women, Blacks, and others are misguided, he claims, because these peoples do not possess the qualities that would warrant more egalitarian treatment. Legal equality must be rooted in natural equality, Meiners argues, and the empirical knowledge characteristic of enlightenment indicates that nature has not made all individuals equal. As such, Meiners writes:

> [...] just as subjects and their rulers, children and adults, women and men, servants and their masters, lazy, ignorant people and active, educated people, or declared villains and innocent, laudable citizens will never obtain the same rights and freedoms, Jews and Blacks [*Neger*], as long as they are Jews and Blacks [*Neger*], cannot ask for the same rights and privileges as the Christians and Whites among whom they live or whom they obey.[14]

If a misguided sense that enlightenment amounts to a universal opposition to oppression led »to a febrile enthusiasm [*Enthusiasmus*] for an equality of all classes and all peoples,« »[c]onsistent progress in useful knowledge and free investigation will also correct these noble but misled passions.«[15] As the knowledge characteristic of enlightenment advances, then, calls for social change based on what Meiners took to be mistaken attributions of equality to all people will gradually fall away.

Meiners thus articulates a second conception of enlightenment active in German-language discussions of slavery and abolition. On this conception, real enlightenment is »most of all opposed to superstition and enthusiasm.«[16] Though the understanding of enlightenment as an antidote to or shield against enthusiasm was not as prevalent as the first view we considered, Meiners was far from the only author to advance it.[17] The German discussion of enlightenment and enthusiasm, which gained speed with the French and Haitian Revolutions, was particularly influenced by English authors.[18] In addition to Edmund Burke's strident writings on French political events, Meiners and others appear especially indebted to David Hume (1711-1776) on this point.

In 1741, Hume identified superstition and enthusiasm as important sources of the corruption of true religion. Superstition, which Hume takes to spring from fear, melancholy, and ignorance, subjects people to the tyranny of the priestly caste it elevates to provide protection against mysterious threats. The enthusiast, on the other hand, believes themself to have divine insight or inspiration to a degree that »Human Reason, and even Morality are rejected as fallacious Guides.«[19] Since enthusiasm dismisses social custom and tradition, it is »naturally accompanied with a Spirit of Liberty« that »begets the most extreme Revolutions.«[20] Hume's examples of enthusiastic sects include English Quakers and Levellers, German Anabaptists, and Scottish Covenanters. One crucial commonality across these religious sects is their egalitarian rejection of the power of those whose claim to be naturally superior to the common person.

When the distaste for disruptive egalitarian religious and political movements is combined with a white supremacist anthropology, the connection between Atlantic slavery, enthusiasm, and enlightenment comes more fully into view. For his part, Meiners had spent much of the 1780s developing just such an anthropology. In the preface to the first (1785) edition of the textbook he prepared for his classes on the topic in Göttingen, the *Grundriß der Geschichte der Menschheit*, Meiners concludes by highlighting the central point of his history of humanity:

> [...] the present human species consists in two primary stems [*Hauptstämme*], the stem of the fair-colored and beautiful, and that of the dark-colored and ugly peoples; [...] the latter is not only much weaker in body and mind, but also much more foul-natured and devoid of virtue than the former.[21]

According to Meiners, the natural superiority of Europeans, and Celtic peoples in particular, explains the histories of human migration, of the development of science, culture, and government, and of conquest and colonial expansion. With this anthropology in hand, Meiners writes:

> A great deal has been won against the heated opponents of slavery just by having proven that Blacks [*Neger*] do not possess the same senses, the same powers, and the same mental facilities as Europeans; that they are not capable of the same duties and accomplishments, and that they thus cannot demand the same rights and freedoms.[22]

Calls for the abolition of slavery, on this view, are the products of enthusiasm rather than healthy reason because they make broad claims about human equality that fly in the face of what Meiners takes to be the wealth of empirical evidence of human inequality and White superiority.

This speculative anthropology was further supplemented by contingent historical events that reinforced the sense that abolition was a species of religious fanaticism. That the religious advocates of abolition included the Quakers – whom Hume names as primary agents of enthusiasm – and the Swedenborgians in England – whose founder Kant made a representative of enthusiasm in his *Träume eines Geistersehers* (1768) – bound abolitionism more tightly to criticisms of enthusiastic overreach. Moreover, other liberatory political movements appealing to human equality began in the early 1790s to exhibit just the propensities to violence and social upheaval that Hume associated with enthusiasm and Meiners and others took to be antithetical to the measured reforms of true enlightenment.

We can thus make sense of Meiners's initially confusing claim that European colonial slavery – and not its abolition – is consistent with enlightenment. Beyond the antiquarian, however, what interest does this hold for us today? We would do well to recall that the principles and legacy of the Enlightenment are as contested as they are today at least in part because the meaning and political implications of enlightenment was just as contested in the eighteenth century. Modern authors have appealed to the principles of the Enlightenment to criticize a wide range of political movements and phenomena: nationalism, anti-Semitism, Islamophobia, identity politics, isolationism, wars of territorial expansion, and many more. Resisting social or political movements we judge to be misguided and supporting those we judge to be promising demands more than wrapping ourselves in the abstract notion of the Enlightenment. The complexity and capaciousness of just the German Enlightenment, to say nothing of the Enlightenment as an international phenomenon, are precisely what account for its enduring historical interest. The polysemy of the Enlightenment makes many modern political invocations of its legacy into a shibboleth in a culture-war approach to politics that asks us to pledge allegiance to the Enlightenment as a metonym for the accomplishments of ›European culture‹ or ›Western civilization.‹ Perhaps Meiners's insistence that ›true‹ enlightenment defends Atlantic slavery will remind us of the importance of being more precise and nuanced when we invoke the principles of the Enlightenment in modern political debate.

Marquette University

1 Christoph Meiners, Geschichte der Ungleichheit der Stände unter den vornehmsten Europäischen Völkern, vol. 1, Hannover 1792, p. 18.
2 Immanuel Kant, Beantwortung der Frage: Was is Aufklärung?, in: Kants gesammelte Schriften, vol. 8, Berlin 1902-, pp. 35-42, here p. 35.
3 Christian Garve argued that the principle of Kantian moral philosophy clearly prohibited slavery in a way Kant never did so directly. See: Uebersicht der vornehmsten Principien der Sittenlehre, Breslau 1798, p. 251.
4 Anonymous, Französische Bemerkungen über Aufklärung und Reformen unsrer Zeit, Berlin/Stockholm 1786.
5 Christian Ulrich Detlev Eggers, Skizze und Fragmente einer Geschichte der Menschheit in Rücksicht auf Aufklärung und Volksfreiheit, vol. 1, Flensburg/Leipzig 1786, p. 111.
6 Friedrich Schilling (ed.), Betrachtungen über Die Revoluzion, und das neue sogenannte Demokratische System in Frankreich, n. p. 1790, pp. 82-83.
7 Examples of the former include: Paul Erdmann Isert, Reisen nach Guinea und den Caribäischen Inseln in Columbien, in Briefen an seine Freunde beschrieben, Copenhagen 1788; Johann Ernst Kolb, Erzählungen von den Sitten und Schiksalen der Negersklaven, Bern 1789; and Johann Jacob Sell, Versuch einer Geschichte des Negersclavenhandels, Halle 1791. More popular products include plays – Friedrich Döhner, Des Aufruhrs schreckliche Folge, oder Die Neger. Ein Original-Trauerspiel in fünf Aufzügen, n. p. 1792; Carl Freyherr von Reitzenstein, Die Negersklaven. Ein Trauerspiel in fünf Aufzügen, n. p. 1794; August von Kotzebue, Die Negersklaven. Ein historisch-dramatisches Gemählde in drey Akten, Leipzig 1796, and Andreas Georg Friedrich von Rebmann's satirical novel: Hans Kiekindie-Welts Reisen in alle vier Welttheile, Leipzig/Gera 1794.
8 Andreas Riem, Ueber Aufklärung, Berlin 1788, p. 8. See also: Hector St. John de Crèvecoeur, Letters from an American Farmer, Dublin 1782, pp. 189-191. This specific anecdote was widely translated into German, including in: Beschreibung von Charles-Town, und einige Nachrichten von den dortigen Neger-Sclaven, in: Journal aller Journale 2 (1786), pp. 270-278; Neue Litteratur und Völkerkunde, vol. 2.2 (1788), pp. 213-217; and Kolb (note 7), Erzählungen, pp. 59-63.
9 Gottlob August Tittel, Erläuterungen der theoretischen und praktischen Philosophie nach Herrn Feders Ordnung, Frankfurt a. M. 1786, p. 334. For his discussion of Kant, see: Ueber Herrn Kant's Moralreform, Frankfurt/Leipzig 1786.

10 Nicolaus Vogt, Ueber die Europäische Republik, vol. 4, Frankfurt 1789, p. 237. Other examples of authors warning against false or improperly employed enlightenment include Moses Mendelssohn, Ueber die Frage: was heißt aufklären?, in: Berlinische Monatsschrift, vol. 4.9 (1784), pp. 193-200, esp. p. 199; and Johan August Eberhard, Über die wahre und falsche Aufklärung, wie auch über die Rechte der Kirche und des Staats in Ansehung derselbern, in: Philosophisches Magazin, vol. 1.1 (1788), pp. 30-77.
11 Christoph Meiners, Ueber wahre, unzeitige, und falsche Aufklärung und deren Wirkungen, Hannover 1794. This text was originally published as chapters 12-14 of Meiners, Historische Vergleichung der Sitten, Verfassungen, der Gesetze, und Gewerbe, des Handels, und der Religion, der Wissenschaften, und Lehranstalten des Mittelalters mit denen unsers Jahrhunderts, vol. 3, Hannover 1793-1794.
12 Christoph Meiners, Ueber wahre, unzeitige, und falsche Aufklärung (note 11), p. 2.
13 Christoph Meiners, Ueber die Natur der Afrikanischen Neger, und die davon abhängende Befreyung, oder Einschränkung der Schwarzen, in: Göttingisches Historisches Magazin, vol. 6.3 (1790), pp. 385-456, here p. 385.
14 Meiners, Natur der Afrikanischen Neger (note 13), pp. 386-387.
15 Meiners, Natur der Afrikanischen Neger (note 13), p. 386.
16 Meiners, Aufklärung (note 11), p. 6.
17 Other authors that oppose enlightenment to enthusiasm include: Friedrich Gentz, Einleitung, in: Betrachtungen über die französische Revolution, vol. 1, Berlin 1793; Leopold Alois Hoffmann, Neueste Wirkungen der Pöbel-Aufklärung in Paris, in: Wiener Zeitung, Vienna 1792, pp. 201-232; and J. L. Ewald, Über Revolutionen, ihre Quellen und die Mittel dagegen, Berlin 1792. Melchior Adam Weikard later satirizes this view in his Philosophische Arzneykunst, Frankfurt 1799, 152.
18 Accordingly, the history of this line of thought has been written by authors interested in the English and Scottish Enlightenment. See J. G. A. Pocock, Enthusiasm: The Antiself of Enlightenment, in: Huntington Library Quarterly, vol. 60.1/2 (1997), pp. 7-28; and Richard Whatmore, The End of Enlightenment: Empire, Commerce, Crisis, London 2023.
19 David Hume, Of Superstition and Enthusiasm, in: Essays, Moral and Political, Edinburgh 1741, pp. 141-151, here p. 143. Though Meiners cites English editions of Hume, this essay appeared in German translation in 1756: David Hume, Von dem Aberglauben, und der Enthusiasterey, in: Herrn David Hume, Moralische und Politische Versuche, Hamburg/Leipzig 1756, pp. 128-137.
20 Hume, Of Superstition and Enthusiasm, pp. 150, 144.
21 Christoph Meiners, Grundriß der Geschichte der Menschheit, 2nd ed., Lemgo 1793, pp. 29-30
22 Christoph Meiners, Historische Nachrichten über die wahre Beschaffenheit des Sclaven-Handels, und der Knechtschaft der Neger in West-Indien, in: Göttingisches Historisches Magazin, vol. 6.4 (1790), pp. 645-679, here pp. 645-646.

Book Reviews

Edited for the Lessing Society by
Thomas Martinec

The section is arranged as follows:

I. Books on and editions of Gotthold E. Lessing
II. Books on and editions of eighteenth-century authors
III. Books on general topics of the eighteenth century

I.

LESSING, GOTTHOLD EPHRAIM, *Nathan der Weise*, hg. von Bodo Plachta. Stuttgart: Hiersemann (2023) (= Stuttgarter Studienausgabe, Bd. 5). 256 S.

Die einzige historisch-kritische Ausgabe von Lessings Schriften ist in die Jahre gekommen. Der Abschluss der von Karl Lachmann begründeten und in der 3. Auflage von Franz Muncker besorgten Edition jährt sich 2024 zum 100. Mal. Alle Werkausgaben seither hatten unterschiedliche Vermittlungsanliegen. In textkritischer Hinsicht überzeugten sie allein schon deswegen nicht, weil in ihnen munter modernisiert wurde. Dieser Umstand bildet nicht nur den Ausgangspunkt für das Projekt *Lessing digital*, an dem der Verfasser dieser Rezension beteiligt ist.[1] Vor allem hat er dazu geführt, dass Leserinnen und Leser, die eine textkritisch zuverlässige Ausgabe wünschen, inzwischen bei einigen wichtigen Dramen Lessings besser zu Studienausgaben greifen. Bodo Plachta etwa – das wird den meisten Leserinnen und Lesern des vorliegenden Jahrbuchs bekannt sein – publizierte im Reclam-Verlag eine sehr gute Studienausgabe von *Minna von Barnhelm* und zusammen mit Elke Bauer eine ebenso gelungene von *Emilia Galotti*. Beide sind Lachmann-Muncker textkritisch deutlich überlegen. Vor diesem Hintergrund ist die hier anzuzeigende, von Plachta im Hiersemann-Verlag herausgegebene Studienausgabe von *Nathan der Weise* zu beurteilen.

Gegenüber den Studienausgaben von *Minna* und *Emilia* hat die neue *Nathan*-Ausgabe den zusätzlichen Vorteil, dass die Darlegung der Editionsgrundsätze, die Ausführungen zur Entstehung und Überlieferung, die Hinweise zur Textgrundlage und -gestaltung sowie schließlich zur frühen Wirkungsgeschichte im insgesamt rund 60 Seiten langen Anhang weit ausführlicher erfolgen. All diese Paratexte sind informativ, präzise und zuverlässig. Wenn man den Ausführungen im Anhang überhaupt etwas vorwerfen kann, dann vielleicht, dass die Forschungsliteratur etwas eklektisch wahrgenommen wird und manche Sachverhalte etwas häufiger hätten nachgewiesen werden können. Gerade Studierende, die mit der Materie nicht vertraut sind, erhal-

---

1 Vgl. www.hab.de/lessing-digital/.

ten zwar alle wichtigen Sachinformationen, bekommen aber angesichts des schlanken Nachweisapparats nur selten die Möglichkeit, gezielt in der Forschungsliteratur weiterzulesen. Lessing-Liebhaber und -Kenner aber werden wie professionelle Leserinnen und Leser begeistert sein, wie akribisch und ausführlich etwa Manuskriptentwicklung und Druckverlauf rekonstruiert werden.

Plachta folgt mit seiner neuen Studienausgabe den Editionsprinzipien, die ihn bereits bei den Reclam-Ausgaben geleitet haben, indem er den Erstdruck zugrunde legt. Da bei *Nathan der Weise* anders als bei *Minna von Barnhelm* und *Emilia Galotti* keine vollständige Hand- oder gar Reinschrift vorliegt, ist seine Entscheidung hier noch naheliegender als bei seinen anderen beiden Studienausgaben.

Dass die Entscheidung für den Erstdruck in der Lessing-Philologie gleichwohl alles andere als selbstverständlich ist, deutet sich im Anhang lediglich an. Plachta begründet, warum er sich gegen die auf den Erstdruck folgende zweite Ausgabe entschieden hat. Nur kurz wird erwähnt, dass letztlich drei Ausgaben 1779 erschienen sind, die von Lessing autorisiert wurden. Lachmann-Muncker hatten die dritte und damit letzte Ausgabe, an der Lessing – wie auch immer – beteiligt war, als Textgrundlage gewählt, auch wenn schon Muncker eine gewisse Unzufriedenheit mit dieser Entscheidung andeutet. Im editorischen Vorbericht zum *Nathan* weist er etwa auf die »zahlreichen Druckfehler« (LM 3: 1) in der dritten Ausgabe hin. Gleichwohl haben erst Klaus Bohnen und Arno Schilson 1993 in Bd. 9 der DKV-Ausgabe mit dieser Tradition gebrochen und den Erstdruck als Textgrundlage gewählt – freilich ohne diesen erneut einer kritischen Kollationierung zu unterziehen.

Vor diesem Hintergrund publizierten Dieter Neiteler und Winfried Woesler 1999 in dem vorliegenden Jahrbuch einen Artikel, der die Vorbehalte gegen die dritte Ausgabe bestätigt. Sie formulierten außerdem Argumente gegen den Erstdruck, indem verschiedene Faktoren (u. a. Lessings Beteiligung am Druckprozess und offenkundige Druckfehler) bilanziert wurden, und plädierten letztlich dafür, die zweite Ausgabe als Textgrundlage für weitere Editionen zu wählen. Diese Überlegungen versuchten Valerie Hantzsche und der Verfasser der vorliegenden Rezension in der kritischen Studienausgabe des *Nathan* zu berücksichtigen, die bei Reclam erschienen ist und mittlerweile in einer überabeiteten zweiten Auflage vorliegt.

Plachta stellt in seinem Nachwort ausführlich und außerordentlich präzise Lessings Konzeption des »dramatischen Gedichts« dar. Er schildert klar und kenntnisreich Textgenese und Druckverlauf. Herrschende Annahmen widerlegt er unaufgeregt, indem er sie überzeugend historisch kontextualisiert. So erklärt er – leider ohne weiterführenden Nachweis, welche »Forschungsliteratur« gemeint ist – beispielsweise:

> Die Drucklegung von *Nathan der Weise* dauerte fünf Monate. In der Forschungsliteratur wird diese kurze Zeitspanne immer wieder mit einem Zeitdruck gleichgesetzt, der auf der Herstellung des Buches gelastet habe. Zu dieser Einschätzung dürfte Lessing selbst beigetragen haben […]. Sieht man sich jedoch vergleichsweise die Zeiträume an, in denen *Minna von Barnhelm* oder *Emilia Galotti* sowohl als Einzelausgabe als auch mit anderen Texten in einer Sammelausgabe gesetzt und gedruckt wurden, dann haben wir es im Fall von *Nathan der Weise* mit völlig normalen Abläufen zu tun. (225)

Die Ausführungen zur Druckgeschichte schließt Plachta mit Hinweisen zur vorgenommenen Kollationierung und den konsultierten Ausgaben ab. Sie machen deutlich, dass seine Studienausgabe ohne jeden Zweifel als die textkritisch zuverlässigste *Nathan*-Ausgabe gelten darf, die aktuell verfügbar ist.

Dass der Erstdruck, den Lessing als Subskriptionsausgabe konzipiert und publiziert hat, gewählt wird, begründet Plachta zum einen mit der »durchdachte[n] und kompromisslose[n] Werkpolitik«, die bei der Vorbereitung des Druckes zu beobachten sei, und zum anderen mit der »geringere[n] medienhistorischen Bedeutung« der beiden Folgedrucke, die auch nicht dadurch aufgewogen werde, dass – zumal der zweite Druck – »in textueller Hinsicht [...] Verbesserungen« (200) biete. Plachta ordnet letztlich die Argumente, die Neiteler und Woesler angeführt haben, rezeptionsästhetischen Überlegungen unter.

Wie dargelegt, ist diese Entscheidung vor dem Hintergrund von Plachtas bisherigen Studienausgaben schlüssig. Das gilt zumal, da die Abweichungen gegenüber dem zweiten Druck direkt nachgewiesen werden. In der Summe sind sie auch nicht zahlreich und meistens nicht besonders bedeutend.

Es finden sich aber auch Eingriffe wie die folgende Äußerung des Tempelherren gegenüber Nathan in V,5:

[...] Nathan, Nathan!
Was hattet Ihr für einen Engel da gebildet,
Den Euch nun andre so verhunzen werden. (V. 3491-3493)

Ein Blick in das Variantenverzeichnis informiert alle aufmerksamen Leserinnen und Leser rasch, dass V. 3492 im zweiten Druck zu »Welch einen Engel hattet Ihr gebildet«, korrigiert wurde. Die Abweichung vom Blankvers in V. 3492 in der Subskriptionsausgabe dürfte also eher nicht als eine bemerkenswerte Akzentuierung, sondern schlicht als Versehen zu deuten sein, das vielleicht Lessing, vielleicht aber auch einer seiner Vertrauten in Berlin korrigiert hat. Insgesamt finden sich im zweiten Druck einzelne Eingriffe, die mal fehlerhafte Blankverse wie V. 3492 korrigieren oder missverständliche Verse (z. B. V. 3797-3798) vereindeutigen. Es lässt sich nur nicht sicher sagen, ob diese Eingriffe persönlich von Lessing veranlasst wurden oder von einer Person, die eigenverantwortlich, jedoch in seinem Auftrag handelte. Wer also auch immer den Text überarbeitet hat – ihm muss attestiert werden, dass er insgesamt um Korrektur kleiner sprachlicher Schnitzer in der Subskriptionsausgabe bemüht war. Gerade die zeitgenössischen Rezensionen haben sich in den meist eher knappen Hinweisen auf das Drama nicht zuletzt über dessen sprachliche Qualität geäußert. Die hat der zweite Druck zu verbessern versucht. Vor dem Hintergrund der zeitgenössischen Wirkung und Lessings Werkpolitik hätte sich Plachta also auch für den zweiten Druck als Textgrundlage entscheiden können.

Doch ist dieses Plädoyer für die Argumentation von Neiteler und Woesler letztlich ein Detail, das an Plachtas außerordentlichen Studienausgabe abperlt. Allein der Aufwand, den er für sie betrieben hat (nicht weniger als 13 Exemplare der Subskriptionsausgabe wurden kollationiert), macht sie nicht nur zur besten *Nathan*-Ausgabe, die derzeit erhältlich ist. Die Ergebnisse von Plachtas textkritischen Überprüfungen sind zugleich Wasser auf die Mühlen all derer, die eine kritische Neuedition von Lessings Schriften fordern. In Folge der Kollationierung zeigt seine Ausgabe, wie komplex der

Druckprozess war und wie variantenreich allein schon die Subskriptionsausgabe ist. Bodo Plachtas Studienausgabe ist also nicht nur an sich eine beeindruckende und überzeugende Edition. Sie lässt zugleich erahnen, dass weitere textkritische Untersuchungen zu Lessings Schriften nicht nur die Textbasis für die Forschung deutlich verbessern werden, sondern auch versprechen, neue Einblicke in die Entstehungs- und Druckgeschichte von Lessings Werken bereit zu halten.

Freie Universität Berlin *Kai Bremer*

NIEFANGER, DIRK, *Lessing* divers – *Soziale Milieus, Genderformationen, Ethnien und Religionen*. Göttingen: Wallstein (2023). 394 S., 15 Abb.

Reading Dirk Niefanger's *tour-de-force* monograph *Lessing ›divers,‹* one encounters a new Lessing. Not the idealized figure of *Toleranz* and *Mitleid*, not the polemicist *per se*; instead, we are introduced to a Lessing whose works offer a wide range of perspectives, not all of them tolerant and empathetic, on categories of difference. The book explores Lessing's writings, often (though not exclusively) focusing on lesser-known literary texts with an eye to shaking up rigidified and ideologically informed notions of Lessing and his *oeuvre*, to offer »eine Erweiterung, eine Relativierung unseres Lessing-Bildes« (244). This project includes not only mining marginalized works and fragments for unexpected representations and perspectives, but also presenting truly fresh, historically contextualized interpretations of often overlooked aspects of Lessing's canonical works. In a series of riveting interpretations informed by a dazzling combination of philological, cultural, and historical contextualizations, the study sheds light on multiple instances in Lessing's works of unexpected engagements with questions of class and gender hierarchies as well as with queer sexualities, disability, and aging. By the time I was finished reading this page-turner, I was utterly convinced of the thesis that it is not empathy and tolerance but *diversity* and its cousin »Mehrdeutigkeit« (346) that characterize Lessing's *oeuvre*.

Niefanger is quick to point out that diversity does not neatly correspond to tolerance and empathy. Though tolerance and empathy can certainly result from literary and theatrical encounters with »others,« they need not. Niefanger shows, for example, how Lessing's representation of aging characters in *Der Schlaftrunk* and in some of the fables invite and model empathy for decaying male figures; but he also points out how the aging female figure in *Die alte Jungfer* is ridiculed. Lessing, as we are reminded, uses ethnic stereotypes in particular in the early comedies and fables, though also in later works, such as *Minna von Barnhelm* (for example, Minna's comparison of Tellheim to the »ugly Moor« Othello). Niefanger contextualizes these uses of stereotypes, though he does not negate their racist, classist, sexist, and ableist implications. As he points out, within the genre of satire, Lessing seems to have followed the dictum that »die Herabsetzung des Anderen« (253) is acceptable.

He likewise explores unflinchingly Lessing's representation of Jewish characters in a stated attempt temporarily to look away from »nachgeschalteten Diskursen« (284). There are obvious reasons why Germany needs Lessing to be the Enlightenment spokesperson for the rights of Jews. And Niefanger does not propose that Lessing was not explicitly concerned with this cause; he simply offers historically contextualized, new readings of Lessing's Jewish characters that render them more realistic and less ideal. For example, an oft-neglected piece of the narrative presented in *Die Juden* is highlighted. At the outset of the play, the Traveler, who is not immediately coded as Jewish, rescues a baron from robbers. This is the catalyst for a rethinking of antisemitic stereotypes within the play. Niefanger does not negate this dominant reading, but he reminds us of the Traveler's needlessly violent behavior toward the robbers: the Traveler shoots at the robbers as they are running away, hoping to kill them. The text makes clear that these robbers had not become violent and were likely members of the lower class hoping to benefit from a relatively petty crime. Yet, as is pointed out, the Traveler behaves unnecessarily violently toward these fleeing ruffians. Offering here an elegant intersectional interpretation, Niefanger shows how the Traveler is, despite his Jewish identity, himself a member of the elite and hence enacting behaviors linked to class hierarchies. This is just one example of how the Jewish figure in *Die Juden* (and in this context, we find a fascinating discussion about the use of the plural in the title of Lessing's play) is a product of Lessing's realism. Niefanger also contextualizes and underscores his reading with an eye to legal discourses of the period. It is this kind of deep historicization combined with a contemporary eye to structures of othering that makes reading *Lessing ›divers‹* so exciting.

It is made clear that Lessing's use of stereotypes and sometimes critical representations of cultural Others cannot be attributed exclusively to the young Lessing. Just as the Jewish Traveler in Lessing's 1749 play *Die Juden* is a »gemischter Character,« so, too, we are reminded, is the Jew Nathan, the product of Lessing's late work. Nathan, like the Traveler, belongs to the elite in Saladin's Jerusalem. Within the hierarchy of the period, Jews were integrated as trading partners. It is actually the Christians who are the least powerful figures in Saladin's Jerusalem. And, as is proposed in another nuanced intersectional reading, Nathan utilizes his authority as a rich and powerful member of the elite to buy and silence his Christian servant, Daja. The study is likewise sensitive to the gendered power structures in this relationship, highlighting Nathan's status as rich, powerful, and male vis-à-vis the Christian, female Daja. Again, Niefanger's goal is not to undermine the importance of *Nathan der Weise* within the German canon; instead, he argues that a more nuanced reading of Lessing's engagement with diversity is a gesture of respect toward »dem großen Autor« (347). Rather than trying to excise uncomfortable elements from Lessing's works, we would do well to follow the reminder to look closely and, to the extent that it is possible, without preconceived expectations of what we will find in Lessing's wide and varied *oeuvre*.

The book is divided into three chapters: »1. Soziale Milieus;« »2. Gender-Formationen,« »3. Ethnien und Religionen.« Each chapter traverses a wide variety of literary works, occasionally referencing Lessing's theological, philological or theoretical writings. Despite the chapter framings, the topics treated reflect the intersectional approach: a reading of *Minna von Barnhelm* is included in the »Gender-Formationen« chapter, but this analysis frequently focuses on class, race, and even disability. As a reader, I was not in the least disturbed by these thematic shifts; this is the nature of intersectional analysis. The analyses flow in a manner that is both organic and associative. For example, the »Gender-Formationen« chapter focuses frequently on sexual orientation, on homoeroticism and homosexuality. As is rightly pointed out, Lessing has not been sufficiently queered, and Niefanger's interpretations of texts such as »Rettungen des Horaz«, in which Lessing discusses the polymorphously perverse

»Spiegelkabinett-Passage« (185) in Horace, help to further open up this line of analysis. Scholars like Alice Kuzniar, Robert Deam Tobin, and Daniel Wilson began the process of queering Goethe in the 1990s, but corresponding approaches to Lessing have been few and far between.

Niefanger's monograph is by no means short, but it is light in the best sense. He uses the term »Verve« (132) as an invitation to approach Lessing anew, and this is precisely the energy that emanates from *Lessing ›divers‹.* Niefanger's approach is likewise transnational in a manner that will be refreshing to contemporary readers; he fluidly uses terminology emerging from the North American context and engages both Anglo-American and German-language scholarship on Lessing. Niefanger clearly brings his authoritative knowledge about Lessing and about the early modern period to his work; this is apparent in his fluid methodology. His close interpretations of literature are elegantly contextualized historically and philologically. Indeed, Niefanger frequently looks to eighteenth-century receptions of Lessing's work and to archival manuscripts to underscore his analyses. He likewise often explores the history of editions of Lessing's writings, as these offer insights into complex reception histories. In this way, he is able to situate contemporary concerns about representations of diversity in a manner that is truly generative. In short, *Lessing ›divers‹* is a brilliant »Erweiterung, eine Relativierung unseres Lessing-Bildes« (244) and is from cover to cover a delight to read; the book presents a novel, rich, and exciting intellectual journey through Lessing's works that invites the contemporary reader to turn to them with fresh eyes. It truly deserves a wide and diverse readership.

University of Illinois, Chicago *Heidi Schlipphacke*

TRAVANTI, ELEONORA, *Lessings exoterische Verteidigung der Orthodoxie. Die Wolfenbütteler Beiträge gegen die Aufklärungstheologie (1770-1774)*. Berlin, Boston: de Gruyter (2023). (= Frühe Neuzeit, Bd. 251) 352 S.

Wie hielt es Lessing mit der Religion? Diese Frage hat Mitwelt und Nachwelt gleichermaßen beschäftigt. Die hier anzuzeigende Studie nähert sich ihr, indem sie sich einem »Stiefkind« (27) der Forschung zuwendet: Lessings widersprüchlich anmutenden Beiträgen zur Aufklärungstheologie. Den Schlüssel zu ihrem Verständnis findet die Verfasserin in einer Unterscheidung, auf die Lessing selbst hinweist. In der Abhandlung über die Ewigkeit der Höllenstrafen betont er, Leibniz habe »die Lehre von der ewigen Verdammung sehr *exoterisch* behandelt« und würde »sich *esoterisch* ganz anders darüber ausgedrückt haben« (zit. n. 72). Lessing, so Travantis These, verfährt in seiner Verteidigung der Orthodoxie selbst exoterisch; esoterisch glaubte er »keineswegs an das alte Religionssystem« (258). Wie Leo Strauss, auf dessen Spuren sie sich bewegt (vgl. Kap 8.2), geht sie davon aus, dass Lessings wahre Lehre nur »between the lines« (zit. n. 27) zu finden sei. Wie diese wahre Lehre aussieht, ist die Frage, der ihre Bemühungen gewidmet sind.

Travanti verfolgt sie mit großer Sorgfalt und nimmt weite Wege auf sich. In einem ersten Durchgang rekonstruiert sie die Geschichte dieser Unterscheidung, die zu Aristoteles zurückführt und im Aristotelismus der Frühen Neuzeit fortgeschrieben wurde (Kap. 3). In einem zweiten Schritt bereitet sie die theologischen Debatten auf, die Lessing in seiner Wolfenbütteler Zeit führt; sie porträtiert ihn als herzoglichen Bibliothekar (Kap. 4) und stellt die Gelehrten vor, deren Schriften in den *Beiträgen zur Geschichte der Litteratur* zur Diskussion stehen (Kap. 5). In einem dritten Schritt kommentiert sie diese Debatten detailliert. Im Zentrum ihrer Rekonstruktion stehen Lessings Leibniz-Lektüren: *Leibniz von den ewigen Strafen* und *Des Andreas Wissowatius Einwürfe gegen die Dreieinigkeit* (Kap. 6). In einem vierten Schritt schließlich wendet sie sich Lessings Spinozismus zu, von dem in den vorangegangenen Kapiteln beiläufig die Rede war (Kap. 7).

Lessing hat die Unterscheidung zwischen einer exoterischen und einer esoterischen Schreibart nicht systematisch entwickelt. Dass er mit der Begriffstradition vertraut war, steht außer Zweifel: Er kommt auf sie im zehnten *Literaturbrief* zu sprechen (dort verweist er auf die *Noctes Atticae* von Gellius), und er dürfte ihr auch bei Leibniz selbst begegnet sein (vgl. Kap. 3.5). Wenn Lessing sie in Erinnerung ruft, dann nimmt er Leibniz gegen die Unterstellung in Schutz, »er sei in Ansehung der Lehre selbst mit sich nicht einig gewesen; indem er sie öffentlich mit den Worten bekannt, heimlich und im Grunde aber geleugnet habe« (zit. n. 72), *und* er nimmt diese Rettung zum Anlass, auch die »esoterische große Wahrheit selbst« zur Geltung zu bringen, die Leibniz in der orthodoxen Lehre entdeckt und gegen ihre Kritiker verteidigt hatte: Es ist die Erkenntnis, »daß in der Welt nichts insulieret, nichts ohne Folgen, nichts ohne ewige Folgen« ist (zit. n. 168), so dass die sogenannten ewigen Strafen mit den natürlichen Folgen allen Handelns identisch sind. Ähnlich verfährt Lessing im Falle von Leibniz' (exoterisch anmutender) Verteidigung der Trinitätslehre gegen die Einwürfe Andrzej Wiszowatys. Er betont, dass es Leibniz lediglich darum zu tun war, die Lehre von der Dreieinigkeit »gegen den Vorwurf des Widerspruchs, mit sich selbst, und mit unleugbaren Wahrheiten der Vernunft, [zu] retten« (zit. n. 175), *und* er erkennt in der Zurückweisung dieses Vorwurfs die (esoterische) »Seele« (zit. n. 177) von Leibniz' Philosophie wieder: die Annahme eines göttlichen Grundes der Wirklichkeit, die es Leibniz unmöglich machen musste, die Argumente gegen die Trinitätslehre ernst zu nehmen, obwohl er diese selbst philosophisch nicht zu begründen vermochte.

Travanti begreift Lessings Parteinahme für Leibniz als Verteidigung der Philosophie gegenüber der Theologie und identifiziert seine Kritik an der neologischen »Rationalisierung des Christentums« als »heimliche, aber radikale Förderung der Freiheit des Denkens« (259). Damit aber bleibt die Frage nach Lessings esoterischer Religionsphilosophie unbeantwortet. Und fast hat es den Anschein, als ließe sich diese Philosophie gar nicht finden, wenn man sie zwischen den exoterischen Zeilen sucht. Vielleicht bürdet die beeindruckende philologische Rekonstruktion der Begriffsgeschichte Lessings beiläufiger Verwendung des Begriffspaars zu viel an Gelehrsamkeit auf. Er selbst spricht im Kontext des Fragmentenstreits davon, dass er genötigt sei, sich nach seinem Gegner zu richten, und deshalb nicht *dogmatisch*, sondern *gymnastisch* zu argumentieren habe – eine Unterscheidung, die ihm aus der patristischen Tradition (Origenes, Hieronymus) vertraut gewesen sein dürfte und die Travanti, begriffsgeschichtlich durchaus zu Recht, mit der Unterscheidung zwischen exoterischer und esoterischer Rede identifiziert (vgl. 257-258). Lessing aber akzentuiert hier weniger die »Verschiedenheit der Lehrart« (zit. n. 72) als die Bindung der Argumentation an den Gesprächszusammenhang, in dem sie entwickelt wurde. Auch an Leibniz schätzte er die Souveränität, mit der dieser »sein System willig bei Seite«

setzte und »einen jeden auf demjenigen Wege zur Wahrheit zu führen« suchte, »auf welchem er ihn fand« (zit. n. 160-161).

Diesem dialogischen Prinzip von Lessings Denken ist es zuzuschreiben, dass ihn die Theologen für einen Freigeist und die Freigeister für einen Theologen hielten.[1] Er war keines von beiden, weil er erkannt hatte, dass die Sprache der Bibel eine Sprache der Bilder und Gleichnisse ist, deren dogmatischer Gehalt in lebendige Erfahrung übersetzt werden will, wenn er denn irgendeinen Wahrheitsgehalt haben soll. Die eigentliche Pointe von Lessings Religionsphilosophie liegt in der Einsicht, dass auch die Bibel *exoterische*, an das Fassungsvermögen ihrer Entstehungszeit angepasste Rede ist, und in der Gewissheit, dass es in ihr eine *esoterische* Wahrheit zu entdecken gibt. Weil sie das einzige Buch ist, »welches im eigentlichen Verstande, für die Wahrheit der Bibel jemals geschrieben worden«, darf sich »die gemeine Lehre« rühmen, »daß sie so lange noch nicht richtig verstanden ist, als sie einer einzigen [Vernunftwahrheit] zu widersprechen scheinet« (zit. n. 178).

Was soll man also von diesem Aufklärer halten, der so quer zu allem steht, was im achtzehnten Jahrhundert in Religionsangelegenheiten gedacht wurde? Für einen Moderaten ist er Travanti zu radikal; für einen Radikalen zu traditionsbewusst (vgl. 259). In den Freimaurergesprächen bekennt sich Lessing dazu, dass es »Wahrheiten« gibt, »die man besser verschweigt« (zit. n. 237), weil sie leicht missverstanden werden könnten. Travanti bezeichnet ihn deshalb (mit Strauss) als einen »esoterischen Aufklärer«, der das Licht der Vernunft »nur vorsichtig verbreiten und das Volk langsam erziehen« möchte (260). Aber davon kann nur mit Vorbehalt die Rede sein. Lessing hat öffentliche Debatten geradezu programmatisch angestoßen und hatte als Dramatiker wie als Publizist nicht das Volk, sondern die »Erleuchtesten und Besten seiner Zeit« im Sinn.[2] Aufklärung war für ihn (nicht anders als für Kant) ein kultureller Lernprozess, der mit dem öffentlichen Gebrauch der Vernunft und den von ihm genährten »Geist der Prüfung« identisch ist.[3]

Deshalb hat auch der Gedanke, dass die publizistische Anstrengung, die Lessing unternimmt, um »die mißverstandene Religion«[4] zu retten, auf eine »Trennung von Theologie und Philosophie, Religion und Vernunft, Glauben und Wissen« (259) hinauslaufen soll, etwas Missliches – verdankt sich doch die christliche Dogmatik selbst schon dem Versuch, eine ursprüngliche Erfahrung mithilfe der philosophisch geschulten Vernunft zu erfassen. Das gilt insbesondere für die Lehre von der Dreieinigkeit Gottes, an der sich Lessing zeit seines Lebens abarbeitete: Sie ist selbst schon das Ergebnis der frühchristlichen Bemühungen, eine liturgische Formel theologisch auf den Begriff zu bringen.[5] Wenn sich Lessing einen »Liebhaber der Theologie« nennt, dann geht es ihm nicht um eine Grenze zwischen Offenbarung und Vernunft,

---

1 Vgl. Gotthold Ephraim Lessing, Werke und Briefe in zwölf Bänden, hg. von Wilfried Barner, Frankfurt a. M. 1985-2003 [im Folgenden mit der Sigle *WB* abgekürzt, gefolgt von Band- und Seitenangabe], Bd. 12, S. 69.
2 *WB* 6: 191.
3 *WB* 6: 717.
4 *WB* 6: 778.
5 Vgl. Jörg Lauster, Der Heilige Geist. Eine Biographie, München 2021, S. 95-97 u. S. 107-109.

sondern um die Freiheit, sich in Religionsangelegenheiten zu äußern, ohne auf ein »gewisses System schwören [zu] müssen«.[6]

Nur ein denkend gelebtes Leben war für Lessing ein bewusst geführtes Leben.[7] Sein Credo galt der rechten Praxis, die aus der rechten Einsicht erwächst: »Komm! übe, was du längst begriffen hast; / Was sicherlich zu üben schwerer nicht, / Als zu begreifen ist«,[8] lässt er seinen Nathan in der Hiob-Szene sagen. Das charakterisiert zugleich sein Verhältnis zur Offenbarung. Nicht erst im vierten *Anti-Goeze* polemisiert er gegen die »Namenchristen«, »die ihr undenkendes Leben so hinträumen«: Die »letzte Absicht des Christentums«, heißt es da, ist »nicht unsere Seligkeit«, sondern »unsre *Seligkeit, vermittelst unsrer Erleuchtung*«.[9]

Solche Einwände ändern freilich nichts daran, dass Travantis mustergültige Studie der Forschung neues Terrain erschließt und sich nicht nur in der Lessing-Philologie als unverzichtbares Referenzwerk etablieren wird.

Universität Graz   *Robert Vellusig*

VELLUSIG, ROBERT, *Lessing und die Folgen*. Berlin: Metzler (2023). VIII + 270 S.

In this relatively small book, Robert Vellusig undertakes a large task. Not only does he offer studies of Lessing's major works within a biographical framework, but in the second part of the book (163–259) he surveys Lessing's posthumous reputation, going into particular detail about the reactions to Lessing by Goethe, Schiller and Hebbel.

The book begins well, with a vivid account of how Lessing fell out with his scandalized parents when he neglected his theological studies in favor of the theatre, and, instead of pursuing a clerical career, joined his cousin Christlob Mylius in making a career in journalism. Here Vellusig establishes the image of Lessing that he develops throughout the book: a combative intellectual who insists on examining for himself the assertions put forward by ecclesiastical and political authorities, who neither expects nor desires to arrive at any final truth, and who is motivated by an intense ethical concern. In this light, he gives concise presentations of Lessing's best-known writings, beginning with the early comedies and including such major critical works as the *Rettungen*, the correspondence on tragedy with Mendelssohn, the *Literaturbriefe* (naturally with emphasis on the seventeenth), *Laokoon*, the controversial theological writings, *Ernst und Falk*, and *Die Erziehung des Menschengeschlechts*. The student readers for whom this book is presumably intended will obtain a handy (albeit sometimes too compressed) account of Lessing's literary career, and be able to move on to the more comprehensive accounts by Monika Fick, Hugh Barr Nisbet, and Friedrich Vollhardt.

---

6 *WB* 9: 57.
7 Vgl. *WB* 8: 137.
8 *WB* 9: 596.
9 *WB* 6: 196, Hervorhebung durch Lessing.

Vellusig's presentation of Lessing is unified by the conviction that both the fables and the dramas are rationally constructed to display »die Kunst der moralphilosophischen Reflexion« (66). Hence, quite appropriately, the chapters on the dramas are longer than the others. Moreover, in Vellusig's view, Lessing's plays are »Literatur aus Literatur« (108). Here he is referring specifically to *Minna*, which is for him »ein Musterbeispiel für eine dramatische Produktion, die sich ganz und gar der Kritik verdankt« (108). It is certainly true that Minna warns Tellheim against misanthropy and cites *Othello*, but does that justify Vellusig in affirming that Lessing has ingeniously combined Shakespeare's play with Molière's *Le Misanthrope*? Such a schematic account of the play rests on conjecture about Lessing's method of writing; and it underrates Lessing's success in creating relatable and even, on occasion, lovable characters.

Turning to *Emilia Galotti*, Vellusig asserts that the catastrophe combines the myth of Virginia from Livy with the tragedy of *Othello* (125), and interprets Odoardo as the tragic hero. He suggests that Odoardo is misled by prejudice into calling the Prince a »Wollüstling,« because the latter is innocently in love with Emilia (121-122). Odoardo's very name suggests »*odio ardo*,« »I burn with hatred« (125). I have to differ: to me the Prince seems a compelling portrait of a character who combines libertinism, sentimental self-pity, hypocritical polish, and spinelessness, allowing Marinelli to manipulate him and even to address him as »er« (see Act IV, scene 1), while Odoardo blusters but goes to pieces in a crisis. Once again, Lessing receives too little credit for his understanding of human psychology, an understanding surely derived from experience of the world more than from books.

Vellusig finds many other unexpected classical sources. In *Miß Sara Sampson*, both »Sara und Marwood sind Medea-Figuren« (48), though Sara also corresponds to Medea's victim Kreusa (51) and suffers the death of Socrates (52). Marwood as Medea is based not only on Euripides and Seneca but also on Hypsipyle in Ovid's *Heroides* (50). *Philotas* is said to be based on Sophocles's *Ajax*, *Nathan* on his *Oedipus*. Readers must decide for themselves how plausible these claims are.

To do so, they should return to the work of the eminent Lessing scholar Gisbert Ter-Nedden (1940–2014), to whom this book is dedicated. Vellusig has already paid homage to his former colleague by editing the latter's unpublished papers as *Der fremde Lessing. Eine Revision des dramatischen Werkes* (Göttingen: Wallstein, 2016). In the book under review, Ter-Nedden is the only Lessing scholar cited more than once: among the parenthetical abbreviations used for references, »GTN« occurs thirteen times (or fourteen, if that is the meaning of the otherwise inexplicable »GNT 4« on p. 50). It is from his work that Vellusig takes the multiple Medea sources, the resemblance of Odoardo to Othello, the combination of Molière and Shakespeare in *Minna*, the presence of *Oedipus* in *Nathan*, and much else. Some material (*Philotas* and *Ajax*; Odoardo's misjudgment of the Prince) was already presented in Ter-Nedden's *Lessings Trauerspiele. Der Ursprung des modernen Dramas aus dem Geist der Kritik* (Stuttgart: Metzler, 1986). The difference is that in his two substantial books, Ter-Nedden had scope to pursue his philological source-study in appropriate detail, anticipate possible objections, and engage with other commentators, whereas the limited space available to Vellusig obliges him to present his case in a terse and apodictic manner, without reference to the full range of critical opinion. That is particularly unfortunate, since for Lessing, as Vellusig reminds us with an apt quotation from *Wie die Alten den Tod gebildet*, truth can be approached only through argument (167). A mono-perspective account of Lessing already misrepresents him.

The section on »[d]ie Folgen« offers a bird's-eye overview of Lessing's literary reception from his earliest readers down to the facile negativism of George Tabori and other parodists. It surveys skeptically a number of well-known attempts to characterize Lessing which are among the clichés of Lessing reception: the precursor of classicism, the militant *Aufklärer*, the unpoetic or untragic *Dichter*, the critical lawgiver. Readers may gain much stimulus from the sections on Goethe and Schiller in relation to Lessing. Vellusig notes that in *Iphigenie*, in particular, Goethe is following in Lessing's footsteps, and that while Schiller's concept of sympathy, seen in the *Philosophische Briefe*, in *An die Freude*, and elsewhere, has affinities with Lessing, the concept of the tragic sublime, which Schiller analyses in theory and represents in his dramatic practice, is remote from Lessing. No less remote is Hebbel, who detects »dämonische Kräfte« (quoted 208) lurking within Emilia and argues for a conflict – imaginary, in Vellusig's opinion – between her piety and her sensuality; Vellusig also hints at a resemblance between the two rough-mannered fathers, Odoardo and Meister Anton. He seems to lose sight of Lessing when discussing Fontane's conception of realism, but finally links the two by attributing to both a method of perspectival representation. The comparison deserves to be explored at greater length.

While this wide-ranging reception history contains much of interest, it presupposes that Lessing's reception has been »eine Geschichte der Missverständnisse« (169). But could one not reverse this approach and see Lessing's reception (and the reception of any complex author) as a series of partial interpretations? Even when wrong-headed, these can be recuperated, not as mistakes, but as contributions to an ongoing conversation in which nobody has complete authority?

The book has some technical faults. The system of referencing is reader-unfriendly. If it was imperative to save space, why not use the author-date system (e.g., »Ter-Nedden 2016, p. 45«)? The copy-editor has overlooked two incoherent sentences (14, 129-130). A quotation from *Hamlet* appears as »von des Gedankens Blässe nicht angekränkelt« (70): why has »nicht« been inserted? »Bogen« is misprinted as »Boden« (63). The author of *Das Erlebnis und die Dichtung* is called »Friedrich« Dilthey (222). It is a pity that these slips have been allowed to disfigure a book which opens up many possibilities for fruitful debate.

The Queen's College, Oxford   *Ritchie Robertson*

ZIMMERMANN, DANIEL, *Göttliche Zufälligkeiten. G. E. Lessings Vernunftkritik als Theodizee der Religionen*. Tübingen: Mohr Siebeck (2023) (Collegium Metaphysicum, Bd. 29). XVI + 324 S.

Das Buch von Daniel Zimmermann ist durch eine Leidenschaft für das Erklären geprägt. Zielpunkt der Arbeit, einer Dissertation an der Evangelisch-Theologischen Fakultät der Universität Tübingen, ist die Reihe von Reflexionen und Spekulationen unter dem Titel *Die Erziehung des Menschengeschlechts*, die als Lessings »religionsphilosophische Hauptschrift« klassifiziert wird (281-282, vgl. schon 236 und bes. 245, Anm. 222). Indessen will der Autor die Schrift nicht mit Bezug auf einzelne Traditionen von Judentum und Christentum studieren, sondern in einer Fokussierung auf das »blank[e] Grundgerüst« von Lessings »religionsphilosophischer Konzeption«, das in der »Bestimmung des Verhältnisses von Vernunft und Offenbarung« (247) greifbar sei. Der Untertitel des Buches ist insofern irreführend, als nicht die »*konkrete* Gestalt« der postulierten »Theodizee dieser beiden geschichtlichen Religionen« (247) Thema sein soll, die Frage nach dem Islam offen bleibt (vgl. 271, Anm. 340) und die Frage nach dem Zoroastrianismus oder weiteren positiven Religionen erst gar nicht gestellt wird. Lessing wird als ein Kritiker des »Absolutheitsanspruch[s] der Vernunft« gedeutet, weil er die Vernunft »in ihrer Unvollkommenheit« entlarve (247), einer Unvollkommenheit, die – so ist es offenbar zu verstehen – darin liege, dass die Vernunft ihre Aufgabe, eine »*absolute* Wahrheitsgewissheit« in Bezug auf »geoffenbarte Glaubenswahrheiten« zu erzeugen (243), noch nicht erfüllt habe (vgl. auch 287).

Das Spektrum der Quellen schließt unter dem Titel »Die Suffizienzthese in der Krise« (157-189) Lessings Herausgebernotizen von 1770 bzw. 1773 zu Berengar von Tours und zu Andreas Wissowatius ein, während sich der erste Teil des Buches unter dem Titel »Wanderjahre« (11-154) Ausführungen in den frühen Schriften und Skizzen widmet: *Gedanken über die Herrnhuter* (1751), *Rettung des Hier. Cardanus* (1752), die Thesenreihen *Das Christentum der Vernunft* (1752/53) und *Über die Entstehung der geoffenbarten Religion* (1763/64) sowie eine Kontroverse mit Bezug auf Klopstock im 49. *Literaturbrief* (1759).

Wie der Buchtitel andeutet, werden im Sinne einer postulierten »Theodizee der Religionen« die »zufälligen Geschichtswahrheiten« aus Lessings Kontrastierung der christlichen (!) mit der natürlichen Religion zu »göttlichen Zufälligkeiten«; ob und wie weit dieser Deutungsansatz ein Gewinn für die Lessing-Interpretation ist, wäre zu fragen (vgl. bes. 238-242). Lessing wehrt sich dagegen, die christliche (!) Religion mit einer vernünftigen, natürlichen Religion und deren Universalitätsanspruch gleichzusetzen, doch hätte er wohl keine Einwände dagegen, die eine neben der anderen Option von Religion stehen zu lassen. Wo die zwei Texte zu Fragen der Interpretation von Aspekten der christlichen (!) Religion – die Deutungen des Abendmahls und der Trinitätslehre – vorgestellt werden (157-189), bleibt es ein reines Postulat, dass damit die Option einer Beschränkung auf eine vernünftige, natürliche Religion überwunden werden solle.

Das Buch ist mit der Frage zu lesen, ob das Konzept einer natürlichen Religion in Lessing einen interessanten Vertreter im achtzehnten Jahrhundert hatte oder nicht. Aus dieser Perspektive ist es zu bedauern, dass z. B. die gemeinsame Beschäftigung von Lessing und Mendelssohn mit Alexander Pope (*Essay on Man*) oder Lessings anzunehmende gute Kenntnis von Voltaire (*Zaïre, Poème sur la loi naturelle, Le Fanatisme* usw.) unberücksichtigt bleiben. Denn das Verhältnis von natürlicher Religion und positiver/offenbarter Religion ist in den Schriften dieser im achtzehnten Jahrhundert geläufigen Autoren intensiv und differenziert erörtert worden. Die Freundschaft zwischen Lessing und Mendelssohn, die, soweit sie sich zu einer positiven Religion bekannten, zwei verschiedenen Bekenntnistraditionen angehörten, sollte dabei nicht unterbewertet werden; insofern ist die Erläuterung von Lessings Bemerkungen in einem Brief an Mendelssohn von 1774 unbefriedigend (179, Anm. 121). Die Versuchsanordnung für eine Erklärung von Lessings Schriften im Themenfeld der Religion wäre in jedem Fall eine andere, wenn *Nathan der Weise* als Lessings religionsphilosophische Hauptschrift gelten würde. Es wäre dann nämlich der Opal, »der hundert schöne Farben spielte«,[1] in seinen verschiedenen möglichen Ringfassungen zu betrachten.

Unter dem Titel »Gipfelschau« (193-284) rückt Teil 3 die »Gegensätze« Lessings zu seinen Reimarus-Fragmenten (218-236), seine Abhandlung *Über den Beweis des Geistes und der Kraft* (238-242) sowie die Thesenreihe *Die Erziehung des Menschengeschlechts* (244-281) ins Licht. Die Unklarheiten, die in Teil 2 durch den Ausschluss einer »Suffizienzthese« als Folge einer Beschäftigung mit klassischen *articuli fidei* entstehen, werden in Teil 3 fortgeschrieben: Zimmermann vermischt den Diskurs über die christliche (!) mit dem über die natürliche Religion, um zu der Schlussfolgerung zu gelangen, dass es ohne die (welche?) Traditionen oder Mysterien der christlichen Religion als Offenbarung bei Lessing keine natürliche Religion als Modell oder Erkenntnisleistung der Vernunft geben könne. Für diese Konstruktion wird der Begriff einer »Geschichtlichkeit« der Vernunft eingesetzt (vgl. z. B. 236, 244, 260, 274) – und die Lesenden dürfen sich fragen, inwiefern etwa bei Aristoteles der Gebrauch der Vernunft unter der Bedingung einer »Geschichtlichkeit« im Sinne eines Angewiesenseins auf eine positive Offenbarung gestanden hat.

Mit einem Zitat aus den Erklärungen zu Lessings »Gegensätzen« kann das Problem verdeutlicht werden. Im Sinne von Arno Schilson geraten einzelne »Gegensätze« in den Fokus, und es heißt dazu:

> Hier gelingt es Lessing, als Antwort auf Reimarus – und in kritischer Korrektur des *ungeschichtlichen* Vernunftoptimismus der Aufklärung insgesamt – *Notwendigkeit, Möglichkeit* und *Wirklichkeit* einer *göttlich* veranstalteten Offenbarung *in der Geschichte* zu begründen. Ihre philosophiehistorische Brisanz besteht dabei in der »fundamentalen Kritik der aufklärerischen Vernunft und ihres mangelnden Verständnisses für die Positivität geschichtlich gewachsener Gestaltungen« [Zitat Schilson, Kommentar in: *WB* 8: 906]. (224, Hervorhebung im Original; vgl. schon 202, Anm. 46)

Dieser Lektüreansatz führt in einem – von Schilson angeregten – Vergleich mit Kants Abhandlung *Beantwortung der Frage: Was ist Aufklärung?* (1784) zu der Erklärung:

> Was [...] Kant [...] von einer wesentlich als autonom verstandenen Vernunft *selbst* zu leisten fordert, nämlich im Zuge ihrer Selbstaufklärung ›aus ihrer selbstverschuldeten Unmündigkeit auszugehen‹, ebendies kann in der noch kritischeren Perspektive Lessings unmöglich von der wesentlich als *geschichtlich* zu verstehenden Vernunft (bzw. vom Menschen) gefordert werden: Anstatt sich an die eigene Hand zu nehmen und sich »ohne Leitung«, lediglich dem inneren Kompass folgend, auf den Weg zu begeben, bedarf die noch *unvollendete* Vernunft vielmehr der Lenkung von außen. Diese Lenkung aber wird ihr durch Offenbarung zuteil. In diesem Sinne dokumentiert die Religionsgeschichte den Weg, welchen Gott die menschliche Vernunft bis hierher geführt hat. (235, Hervorhebung im Original)

---

1 Gotthold Ephraim Lessing, Werke und Briefe in zwölf Bänden, hg. von Wilfried Barner, Frankfurt a. M. 1985-2003 [im Folgenden mit der Sigle *WB* abgekürzt, gefolgt von Band- und Seitenangabe], *WB* 9: 555; III/7, V. 398.

Ersetzt man probeweise den Begriff »Geschichtlichkeit« durch den Begriff »Narrativ«, wird Lessing hier als ein Philosoph präsentiert, für den es vernünftiges Denken nicht anders als unter der Voraussetzung eines Narrativs geben kann, und dieses Narrativ ist die Entwicklungsgeschichte der biblischen Offenbarung *ab orbe condito*. Dass dieses Narrativ eine Option ist, wird man nicht bestreiten wollen, dass sich nur durch dieses Narrativ ein Begriff der Vernunft gewinnen lasse, wird umstritten bleiben. Ein logisches Problem liegt darin, dass es die Vernunft ist, die das Narrativ kritisch konstruiert, etwa bei der Frage, ob der Monotheismus oder der Polytheismus am Ursprung der Religionsgeschichte steht.

Für die Lektüre der sog. *Erziehungsschrift* (244-288) stützt sich Zimmermann u. a. auf Ingrid Strohschneider-Kohrs' *Vernunft als Weisheit. Studien zum späten Lessing* (Tübingen 1991) sowie Arno Schilsons *Geschichte im Horizont der Vorsehung. G. E. Lessings Beitrag zu einer Theologie der Geschichte* (Mainz 1974). Auch Helmut Thielickes *Offenbarung, Vernunft und Existenz. Studien zur Religionsphilosophie Lessings* (Gütersloh 1936 und weitere Auflagen) wird mehrfach zitiert, wobei Thielickes *Kritik der natürlichen Theologie* (1937 als Heft in einer Schriftenreihe der Bekennenden Kirche) unbeachtet bleibt. Doch was lässt sich so über das Modell der natürlichen Religion als Thema bei Lessing lernen? Für Lessing – wie in seiner Zeit auch für Mendelssohn oder für Herder – ist es ungenügend, die aus der *theologia polemica* erwachsenen Etiketten »Deismus« und »Neologie« nur negativ zu gebrauchen; Zimmermann selbst notiert dieses Problem in einer Anmerkung (193, Anm. 4). Um es in Anlehnung an *Nathan der Weise* zu sagen: Man wüsste doch gerne, was Nathan Recha gelehrt hat, wenn er ihr von Gott »nicht mehr, nicht weniger« vorgetragen hat, »als der Vernunft genügt«[2] und wie Rechas Unterhaltung mit Sittah aussehen würde, wenn er ihr von Mose, Jesus und Muhammad mehr vorgetragen hätte.[3]

Die Vorstellung der Reflexionen in der sog. *Erziehungsschrift* bleibt insgesamt eigentümlich farblos, obwohl Zimmermann zurecht die Paragraphen 77 und 80 auszeichnet. Auf dem Erziehungsweg zu wahrer Frömmigkeit wird das klassische Modell von Lohn und Strafe – diesseitig oder jenseitig – ausgehebelt, indem nach § 77 »bessere Begriffe«[4] von Gott, vom Menschen und vom Verhältnis des Menschen zu Gott kommuniziert werden (264-265). Nach § 80 wird als Ideal der Frömmigkeit eine »Reinigkeit des Herzens« erreicht, die den Menschen »die Tugend um ihrer selbst willen zu lieben, fähig macht« (270).[5] Das korrespondierende Gottesbild jenseits des Lohn-Strafe-Modells lässt sich aus einer Anrede Gottes durch die Titelfigur in *Nathan der Weise* ergänzen: »der du allein den Menschen nicht / Nach seinen Taten brauchst zu richten, die / So selten seine Taten sind«.[6] Die hierbei vorausgesetzte klassische – priesterlich-rituelle – Versöhnungstheologie wird von Lessing als Aussicht auf »die Zeit eines *neuen ewigen Evangeliums*« (§ 86) ausgemalt,[7] womit zugleich jeder Dualismus der traditionellen Apokalyptik aufgehoben ist. Wenn überhaupt im Bereich der Religionsphilosophie eine Offenbarung die Vernunft lenkt, dann

---

2 *WB* 9: 578; IV/2, V. 179-180.
3 Vgl. *WB* 9: 614-618; V/6.
4 *WB* 10: 95.
5 *WB* 10: 95.
6 *WB* 9: 607; V/4, V. 180-182.
7 *WB* 10: 96, Hervorhebung im Original.

hier, wo die Vernunft bei der Vergeltungslogik von Lohn und Strafe stehenbleiben würde. Nach §§ 4 und 77 (dazu 272-281) darf man fragen, ob eine völlige Konsistenz zwischen den Themen Monotheismus und Satisfaktionslehre existiert.[8]

Zimmermann zitiert Nisbets auf die sog. *Erziehungsschrift* ausgerichtete Frage, »whether the work's basic character is poetic, philosophical, rhetorical, or a combination of these elements« (245, Anm. 221). Wer seiner Studie folgt, wird vielleicht auch noch die Option »visionary« hinzufügen: Was bleibt aus der Religionsgeschichte, wenn es um die religiöse Erfahrung von »innigster Ergebenheit in Gott« geht?[9]

Universität Erfurt   Christoph Bultmann

II.

ADLER, HANS / ESSEN, GESA VON / FRICK, WERNER (Hg.), *Der ›andere Klassiker‹. Johann Gottfried Herder und die Weimarer Konstellation um 1800.* Göttingen: Wallstein (2022). 386 S., 32 Abb.

Unsurprisingly, Goethe looms large in studies on Weimar Classicism and the relationship among the main representatives. It is therefore long overdue that Johann Gottfried Herder as the other »Classical Poet« – presumably besides Goethe, Schiller, and to a lesser extent also Wieland, Anna Amalia or Charlotte von Stein – is placed at the center of this critical and successful inquiry into the »Weimar Constellation« of poets and thinkers.

Instead of an introduction, Ulrich Gaier revisits the term Classicism (»Klassik?«). It is then followed by ten chapters, addressing a wide-cast net of topics, from Herder's difficult relationship with Goethe and Schiller to his philosophy of history to his accomplishments in pedagogy. The volume concludes, quite fittingly, with three chapters on today's representations of Herder in Weimar: Martin Kessler's overview of spaces of commemoration (»Weimarer Orte der Herder-Erinnerung. Kirche – Wohnhaus – Grab«), Hellmut Seemann's examination of »Das Herderzimmer im Stadtschloss zu Weimar« (»Herder, kein Günstling der Zeit«), and Andreas Beyer's discussion of Herder sculptures (»Herder-Plastiken«).

In »›Katzbalgereien‹. Herder im Wechselspiel mit Goethe und Schiller,« coeditors Gesa von Essen and Werner Frick effortlessly introduce readers to Herder's difficulties of realizing his own place in the »Denkraum« Weimar (30). Specifically, Goethe and Schiller as both Herder's intellectual friends and subsequent rivals constitute the focus of this chapter. Undeniably, readers find complex and interesting interdependencies of the three competitors in this and the following chapters. Gerhard Sauder's contribution »Herders ›Früchte aus den sogenannt-goldnen Zeiten des achtzehnten Jahrhunderts‹ (›Adrastea‹). Erinnerung an Aufklärung« highlights Herder's reflection on the Enlightenment scrutinizing the previous century with apparent disdain. In *Adrastea*, Herder presents side by side, critical reconsiderations and pessimistic foreboding; be they the many wars and the rulers with tyrannical tendencies, be

---

8 Vgl. *WB* 10: 75 und 95.
9 *WB* 9: 559; III/7, V. 531.

they Herder's resentment toward the intellectual movements of the new century: the Kantians, the Jena Romantics Schlegels, Schelling, and Fichte (cf. 77), or – again – his discontentment with Goethe's and Schiller's literary developments and surpassing accomplishments (cf. 82).

»Herders Position in der deutschen und europäischen Ideengeschichte ist zwar gesichert, aber nicht gut verankert« (93), declares coeditor Hans Adler at the beginning of the next chapter regarding Herder's »Wünsche und Visionen« (»Offenheit und Ordnung«). Adler outlines Herder's philosophy of history pertaining to knowledge, rationality, self-education, and self-enlightenment, as well as to the concept of *Humanität*: Herder's anthropology finds the human core in the universal whole of mankind as the sum of human deviation (cf. 110). Adler corroborates that the complexity of Herder's thoughts and vision for the future was indeed attainable and not mere utopian speculation, and as such was not as different from Schiller's and Goethe's. Daniel Fulda (»Erziehung des Menschengeschlechts. Der Geschichtsdenker Herder – ein Klassiker des Historismus?«) pursues the question of Herder's purported historicism and his use of the concept of the education of the human race. Here, Fulda proposes that Herder's understanding of revelation and history is not as close to that of Lessing as it is often claimed. And this in turn excludes the former from the cannon of Weimar Classicism (cf. 142). It is commonly known that Herder is not a political thinker; his reflections on state and government are limited and widely scattered throughout his works. But »ohne Relevanz bleibt der Staat bei Herder nicht« (149), judges Jonas Kahl in his contribution »Staatskonzepte und Französische Revolution. Johann Gottfried Herders politische Reflexionen im Problemfeld historischer Empirie.« Kahl's chapter sketches a development of Herder's political thought focusing on two texts – the chapter on governments in the *Ideen* and a draft for the *Humanitätsbriefe* – as well as an outlook into texts written after the French Revolution. According to Kahl, Herder's political deliberations generally help to understand his status as a classical poet and thinker in Weimar (cf. 187-188). John Noyes's intriguing chapter »Herder als ›Geograph der Schönheit‹« insinuates that the problem of German Classicism is also one of a politics of beauty (cf. 211). His chapter follows fittingly Marion Heinz's »›Kalligone‹. Interpretationen zu Herders Ästhetischem Humanismus.« Like Noyes, she encourages readers to reconsider established ideas about the dynamics and development of the Weimar constellation. While Herder is correctly credited for being an initiator of German Idealism during the first phase of his work in Weimar, the Herder after he discontinued the *Ideen* should not be merely seen as a disqualified philosopher (cf. 193). Both Heinz and Noyes thus attempt to shed a new light on Herder's anthropology, aesthetics, and philosophy of nature and human life. Central for their arguments is Herder's notion of the human being as an artist. Humans can only through aesthetic practices realize themselves as beings of nature determined by mind and understanding thus pursuing perfection (cf. Heinz 204). Art lifts the individual as much as the human race above the division of nations (cf. Noyes 232).

Any wide-ranging inquiry into Herder demands a discussion of his philosophy of religion, as his ideas and thoughts on history, language, education, or on beauty and art attest to the inextricable nature of Herder's holism. Appropriately, Christoph Bultmann (»Herder über ›natürliche Religion‹ und die Pluralität der Religionen«) revisits Herder's position on natural religion, a commonplace in Herder scholarship.

Bultmann points out that, at the time, any defender of natural religion could be easily accused of deism. But he sees in Herder's skillfully crafted idea that rationality and revelation are not to be seen as contradictions a successful circumvention of such judgement. Herder understands scripture as the book of nature and thus the history of nature as traditions of revelation (cf. 245). Accordingly, Christianity does not need to defend itself against Judaism or Islam – since Herder sees other religions as archetypes of »National-Gottesdienste« (254) that had been long surpassed by Christianity – but against positive religion, critique of Christianity from a moral-philosophical position, as it may be represented by Kant and his followers (cf. 233, 242). Bultmann, with reference to Lessing, repeats the view that Herder, however, was unable to overcome his own (religious and philosophical) believes to be more open toward the plurality of religions. Rainer Wisbert and Kaspar Renner then pick up, now systematically, the reoccurring topic of education (cf. Sauder's *Adrastea* chapter). The former presents Herder's concept of self-education within the context of Weimar, whereas Renner locates Herder's role for the development of modern pedagogy in the school speeches as the principle of Weimar's Wilhelm-Ernst-Gymnasium. Both articles portray Herder as a pedagogical reformer and instigator and find much common ground: Just as the human being cannot rely entirely on one's own inner self-education (cf. Wisbert 270), schools and teachers only model education as a preparation for life-long learning. In the process, pedagogical autonomy and educational dependency demand a balance, since self-practice (cf. Renner 286) and self-motivation to learn must be acquired, just as educating students must be learned.

Der ›andere Klassiker‹ is the result of an international symposium of the 2016 meeting of the Research Centre for European Classicism (Klassik Stiftung Weimar). All contributions are in German and have been revised and expanded. Still, the lecture-format is at times noticeable; sometimes in refreshing ways – for example Adler's plea for more integrated research on the Enlightenment, Goethe, Schiller, and Herder (cf. 113). Sometimes however, it feels more peculiar for a scholarly publication like this. For example, Gaier's opening lines may not be as insightful for readers as it may have been for participants six years ago: »Mit dem Begriff *Der ›andere Klassiker‹* war unsere Tagung überschrieben, und er hielte es nicht für angemessen, sich in Weimar darüber Gedanken zu machen?« (9) Or, Renner's framing of his chapter (cf. 279-280 and 300) would be more appealing during an oral presentation, possibly accompanied by images of the inscription above the entrance of the Wilhelm-Ernst-Gymnasium. This intermediate position between popular-scientific and academic writing presents some challenges for users, like the many and sometimes extensively long footnotes or the absence of a comprehensive bibliography. In addition to the index of names, an index of subjects would also have benefited scholars and Herder enthusiasts alike. On the other hand, some of Herder's lesser-known works and ideas take a more dominant role which attests to a far-reaching and mature Herder scholarship in Europe and North America. A volume like this can and will not make the claim for completeness; and thus readers might see the success of this publication as an invitation to pursue certain topics further, for example expanding the Weimar constellation to include female representatives, or expounding Herder's literary production and poetry in relation to Goethe or Schiller.

Still, six years after the symposium and a pandemic later, this reviewer had hoped for chapters to include more of the current state of Herder scholarship. Especially in those cases where recent publications could have presented a more differentiated view. With a few notable exceptions – for example Noyes's and Wisbert's contributions[1] – a slight bias toward European-German Herder research surfaces at times. As an example, I would like to point to Sonia Sikka's important argument concerning Herder's »relativism.« Bultmann's discussion concerning the plurality of religion(s) could be extended by Sikka's notion of Herder as a »relativist,« which – as she proposes – »captures facets of Herder's positions that the term ›pluralism‹ does not.«[2] For her, Herder accepts the idea of a multiplicity of religions when their cultural contexts are considered. She contents, Herder »is a strong advocate of religious toleration within states, as well as between them. However, his support for political toleration of internal religious diversity is not only accompanied by, but actually grounded in, his belief that the proper language of religion is national, in a cultural rather than political sense.« She thus calls for a much further differentiated view that allows both for Christianity to thrive in Europe, while at the same time allowing religions of other cultures to flourish: »Herder's understanding of religion as culturally embedded would need to be supplemented by a more complex analysis of how religious traditions adapt themselves to various cultures.«[3] Likewise, Vicki Spencer's discussions of Herder's »anti-dualism«[4] or Anik Waldow and Nigel DeSouza's (erroneously listed as »de Souza« in the index of names) edited volume *Herder. Philosophy and Anthropology* – first published in 2017 – could have provided additional context not only for Bultmann's contribution but also others. The point here is not that these views oppose those in this volume, but rather that they often present amplifying or augmenting perspectives. This slight European bias would not be as conspicuous if the reliance on some more dated scholarship from the 1970s and 1980s were not as apparent. To be fair, several of Frederick Beiser's important contributions to Herder find a positive echo in chapters by Fulda (cf. 121, 139), Kahl (cf. 186), Heinz (cf. 192 f.), and Noyes (cf. 212). Yet, most other references to North-American Herder scholarship are relegated to the footnotes; whereas Beate Allert,[5] Katherine Arens,[6] Sabine Groß,[7]

1 Noyes points to Sonia Sikka in the context of racism and racialism (pp. 220-221); Wisbert points readers to Isaiah Berlin (pp. 220, 276) and Charles Taylor (pp. 257, 276).
2 Sonia Sikka, Herder on Humanity and Cultural Difference. Enlightened Relativism, Cambridge a. o. 2011, p. 4.
3 Sikka, p. 237.
4 Cf. Vicki A. Spencer, Herder's Political Thought: A Study of Language, Culture, and Community, Toronto 2012; and: Unity and Diversity: Herder, Relativism, and Pluralism,« in: Martin Kusch (ed.), The Emergence of Relativism, New York 2019, pp. 201-215.
5 E. g., Herder's Mental Imprinting: Cognition and ›Gestalt‹ Formation, in: Beate Allert (ed.), J. G. Herder: From Cognition to Cultural Science, Heidelberg 2016, pp. 105-119.
6 E. g., Rereading Herder as Heritor of Idealism: Robert von Zimmermann's Aesthetics, in: Herder Yearbook 13 (2016), pp. 129-146.
7 E. g., Malen, Dichten, Schildern, Sehen: Lessing und Herder im Streit über Homer und Vergil, in: Hans Adler, Sabine Gross (eds.), Anschauung und Anschaulichkeit. Visualisierung im Wahrnehmen, Lesen und Denken, Paderborn 2016, pp. 107-130.

Michael Forster,[8] John McCarthy,[9] Karl Menges,[10] Ernest Menze,[11] John Noyes,[12] Charles Taylor,[13] John Zammito,[14] or Rachel Zuckert[15] are mentioned not at all or only marginally.

Regardless, the volume continues and highlights a long tradition of Herder scholarship, and it will thus attract the interest of a wide audience, especially those with only limited familiarity with Herder's life and works. Scholars seeking to be introduced and get acquainted with his ideas and thoughts on philosophy, theology, pedagogy, aesthetics, and his philosophy of history will find the entire volume highly beneficial. It is a particularly good contribution for those readers more familiar with Goethe and Schiller than with Herder, successfully bridging the gap between existing cursory introductions to Herder or Classicism and deeply specialized academic journals and monographs.

Clemson University   *Johannes Schmidt*

ADLER, JEREMY, *Goethe. Die Erfindung der Moderne. Eine Biographie*. Aus dem Englischen von Michael Bischoff auf der Grundlage der Übersetzung überarbeitete und erweiterte Fassung. München: C. H. Beck (2022). 655 S.

Jeremy Adler's book is an old-school paean to Goethe: it is erudite and sweeping, operates from an almost entirely positive evaluative perspective, demonstrates a profound mastery of Goethe's works across the spectrum (literary, scientific, theoretical, autobiographical, etc.) as well as of the traditions and thinkers that influenced Goethe and those that he then went on to influence. In short, the book explores Goethe's biography through an analysis of his major works and then traces the impact of those works across various fields, including science, sociology, psychology, economics, philosophy, and political theory. The book offers an expansive overview of Goethe's life and works that seeks both to contextualize Goethe within the intellectual *milieu* of his own time and then to illustrate Goethe's influence until the present day. In the course

---

8 After Herder: Philosophy of Language in the German Tradition, Oxford 2010.
9 E. g., The Old / New Enlightenment: From the Compossible to the Complex, in: German Quarterly 94/1 (2021), pp. 49-66.
10 Here principally: Particular Universals: Herder on National Literature, Popular Literature, and World Literature, in: Hans Adler, Wulf Koepke (eds.), A Companion to the Works of Johann Gottfried Herder, Rochester, N.Y. 2009, pp. 189-213.
11 E.g., Herder's Relationship to American Transcendentalism, in: Beate Allert (ed.), J.G. Herder: From Cognition to Cultural Science, Heidelberg 2016, pp. 197-207.
12 Aesthetics Against Imperialism, Toronto 2015.
13 Cf. especially: The Importance of Herder, in: Edna and Avishai Margalit (eds.), Isaiah Berlin: A Celebration, Chicago 1991, pp. 40-63.
14 E.g., Herder and Naturalism: The View of Wolfgang Pross Examined, in: Staffan Bengtsson et al. (eds.), Herder and Religion, Heidelberg 2016, pp. 13-24.
15 Herder's Naturalist Aesthetics, Cambridge, UK 2021.

of his study, Adler traces the overt threads of Goethe's influence (i. e., through those writers who directly cite Goethe as an influence) as well as those threads that are more remote (works or traditions where Adler finds echoes or sympathies with Goethe's thought and work without any direct textual evidence of those influences). While the core of this book may have begun as a translation of Adler's 2020 biography, *Johann Wolfgang von Goethe*, which appeared in the *Critical Lives* series of Reaktion Books (London), this current biography goes well beyond Adler's earlier one: *Die Erfindung der Moderne* is more than twice as long, covers a great deal more historical ground, and gives a great deal more detailed context – especially in respect to the influence of Goethe's thought and works.

Adler himself, in the beginning of his book, admits that its old-school approach of singing Goethe's praise within a national backdrop is not part of current academic fashion, but he emphasizes the relevance of this approach. As he argues, the Greeks have their Homer, the Italians Dante, the Spanish Cervantes etc., and the Germans Goethe:

> Selbst unter den genannten Autoren hat Goethe etwas Besonderes. Tatsächlich übertrifft er die Mehrzahl seiner künstlerischen Mitstreiter so sehr an Breite und Tiefe, dass er als einer der beachtlichsten Künstler aller Zeiten gelten darf – auf einer Stufe mit Michelangelo und Mozart. Diese Gestalten dachten die menschliche Identität neu. (11)

And while Goethe may be broadly enough known for his literary accomplishments, Adler hopes to establish Goethe's significant influence well beyond the literary sphere:

> Während seine Stellung in der Weltliteratur gut belegt ist, wird meines Erachtens noch nicht ausreichend gesehen, wie nachhaltig er die Entwicklung der modernen Zivilisation mitgeprägt hat. […] Ich möchte Goethes Rolle bei der Herausbildung der westlichen Zivilisation – und in gewisser Weise der modernen Zivilisation schlechthin – aufzeigen. (27)

The first part of the book resembles a traditional biography: Goethe's major life events are contextualized within greater world events and his own literary output. The latter part of the work treats topics more thematically and is more forward looking. The focus on the last third of the book is on Goethe's influence in various interdisciplinary spheres.

The book is a remarkable resource for anyone interested in Goethe, whether in his life, his interdisciplinary corpus, or the afterlife of Goethe's influence across different disciplines. Adler is a Goethe scholar *par excellence* – and one who has profound and wide-ranging knowledge of the Western tradition as a whole – and as such is able to draw on many interesting parallels as he tells Goethe's story and tracks his influences. He offers nuanced interpretive readings of many of Goethe's seminal texts and provides important historical background for Goethe's life and influence in the nearly two hundred years after his death. The book also does an excellent job in sketching out Goethe's complex relationship to the major figures of his day – Adler's analysis of Goethe's relationship with Napoleon and Beethoven, for example, provide new insights and information.

The book is at its best when it is rooted in Goethe's works themselves and when tracing direct textual evidence of Goethe's impact. Adler's arguments about Goethe's influence that he bases on similarities of ideas, however, can at times seem like a stretch, as when he argues for Goethe's stance as a proto-feminist, his influence on modern German politics, or as a forerunner of globalization. One further wonders whether the book might have been more effective in its stated goal of finding new readers of Goethe had some of the extolling language been toned down. (See, for example, »Goethe lehrte das moderne Europa, wie es in intelligenter Weise denken und fühlen sollte«, 212, or »Goethe veränderte das Gesicht der Welt durch die Kraft seines Genies«, 218, or »Goethe wurde nicht nur für die neuzeitliche Dichtung, sondern auch für die gesamte wissenschaftliche Welt der Moderne zur Schlüsselfigur. Er inspirierte die Geschichtswissenschaft und die Psychologie wie auch die Soziologie und die Philosophie«, 452). Perhaps, however, it is unfair to read a book meant for a more general audience through the eyes of an academic scholar. Luckily for the scholar, however, Adler has also provided rich textual sources and a wealth of ideas to contribute to the ongoing conversation about Goethe and the impact of his corpus.

University of Illinois Chicago *Astrida Orle Tantillo*

BOHNENGEL, JULIA / KOŠENINA, ALEXANDER (Hg.), *Joseph Marius von Babo (1756-1822). Dramatiker in Mannheim und München. Mit einem Lexikon der Theaterstücke.* Hannover: Wehrhahn (2023). 226 S.

Theaterleute der Sattelzeit, wie August von Kotzebue, August Wilhelm Iffland oder August Klingemann, die nicht eigentlich mehr Teil des Kanons jenseits von Germanistik oder Theaterwissenschaft sind, wurden in den letzten Jahren vergleichsweise intensiv beforscht und teils mittels umfassender Werklexika neu erschlossen.[1] Insbesondere der Wehrhahn Verlag hat sich durch die Neuausgabe etlicher Texte Verdienste um diese Autoren erworben. Dies geschah sicherlich nicht mit der Absicht, dem Gegenwartstheater neue Spielideen zu vermitteln, sondern in der Erwartung, dem theatergeschichtlichen Bild der Goethezeit mehr Breite und Tiefe zu verleihen. Dasselbe lässt sich auch für den Dramatiker Joseph Marius von Babo (1756-1822) in Anspruch nehmen, denn er zählt zu den in jenen Jahren ausgesprochen populären Autoren, die einbezogen werden müssen, um ein angemessenes Bild der Bühnenwelt zu gewinnen. Babo repräsentiert maßgeblich das süddeutsche Theaterleben, zunächst ab 1774 als Geheimer Sekretär des Mannheimer Komödienhauses, dann durch seine Tätigkeit am Münchner Nationaltheater, wohin er im Herbst 1778 wechselte, so dass er wohl Mozarts dritten Mannheimer Aufenthalt verpasst haben wird (47).

1 Siehe z. B. Mark-Georg Dehrmann, Alexander Kosenina (Hg.), Ifflands Dramen. Ein Lexikon, Hannover 2009; Johannes Birgfeld, Julia Bohnengel, Alexander Košenina (Hg.), Kotzebues Dramen. Ein Lexikon, 2. Aufl., Hannover 2020; Nils Gelker, Manuel Zink (Hg.), »Meister in der Kunst des Amalgamirens«. Untersuchungen zu August Klingemanns Werk, Hannover 2020; Manuel Zink, Musealisierung als wirkungsästhetisches Prinzip. Studien zu August Klingemann, Göttingen 2022.

Der von Julia Bohnengel und Alexander Košenina herausgegebene Band erfüllt eine doppelte Funktion: Der erste Teil (1-174) bietet im Stil eines üblichen Sammelbandes Einzelinterpretationen von Stücken, die zu verschiedenen Dramentypen im Werk Babos gehören. In der Rubrik *Schauspiel und Komödie* werden drei Dramen besprochen, und die Dimension des Musiktheaters wird in zwei Beiträgen dokumentiert, die sich mit den melodramatischen Stücken befassen; das Gros der Dramen Babos gehört dem Typus der Geschichts- und Militärdramen an, die in fünf Beiträgen näher analysiert werden.

Bernhard Jahn untersucht z. B. Babos Melodrama-Libretto *Armida und Rinaldo* (1793) auf der Basis des ungemein populären Stoffes aus Tassos *Gierusalemme liberata* im Kontext anderer Armida-Opern und fragt nach den spezifischen Leistungen des Melodramas im Vergleich zur Opera seria. Während in dem Lustspiel *Das Fräulein Wohlerzogen* (1783), wie Irmtraud Hnilica zeigt, eine regelrechte »Weiberpolitik« (3) inszeniert wird, in deren Rahmen auch erotische Dienstleistungen zur Förderung der Karriere des Ehegatten erbracht werden, verzichtet das explizit als »militärisches Drama« qualifizierte Stück *Arno* ganz auf die Präsenz von Frauenfiguren; dies war im damaligen Schauspielbetrieb ungewöhnlich und habe dem Drama Originalität verliehen, wie Johannes Birgfeld unterstreicht, auch wenn mit dieser Einseitigkeit für den »zeitgenössischen Theaterbetrieb mit seiner Rollenfachlogik« (92) ein Defizit gegeben war. Babo hatte zudem in Frage gestellt, dass eine Frau im Gefolge der Armee ein »artiges Frauenzimmer« (91) sei, das auf der Bühne präsentiert werden solle. Timm Reimers greift das frühe Stück *Die Römer in Teutschland* (1780) heraus, um Babo nicht so sehr als »Kleinmeister und Epigonen im Schatten größerer Dramatiker seiner Zeit« zu behandeln, sondern als Schöpfer eines charakteristischen Werkes, das sehr wohl das Interesse der Germanistik verdiene, weil hier ein Autor sichtbar werde, der kontinuierlich an »Formen und Problemgehalten« (146) gearbeitet habe. Hans-Joachim Jakob untersucht dann mit *Otto von Wittelsbach, Pfalzgraf in Bayern* (1782) ein besonders erfolgreiches Stück Babos: Das Trauerspiel ereilte zwar unmittelbar nach der zweiten Aufführung ein Aufführungsverbot, aber es konnte dann bis in die 1840er Jahre einen festen Platz auf den Spielplänen der Theater verteidigen.

Immer wieder ergeben sich in den Analysen spezifische Bezüge zu Lessing. Im Kontext der Soldatenstücke lesen Thomas Wortmann und Johannes Birgfeld etwa *Minna von Barnhelm* als Prätext zu *Das Lustlager* (1778), da es hier gleichfalls um Geld und Schulden geht. Ein anderer Bezug ergibt sich in dem von Anke Detken analysierten Drama *Die Maler* (1783), denn da Maler in zeitgenössischen Dramen selten auftauchten, ist es um so auffälliger, dass sowohl bei Lessing (in *Emilia Galotti*) als auch bei Babo Frauenporträts eine wichtige Rolle spielten. Anders als bei Lessing, wo das Gemälde in der Exposition wichtig ist, komme ihm bei Babo »eine handlungsbestimmende und sogar handlungsauslösende Funktion zu« (18), und während der Maler Conti bei Lessing nur eine Nebenrolle spielt, rücke Babo gleich zwei Maler ins Zentrum des Geschehens, wobei zu konstatieren sei, dass bei Babo »im Gegensatz zu *Emilia Galotti* nicht allein die auf den Gemälden Abgebildeten von Bedeutung sind, sondern auch die Hersteller der Requisiten, die Maler« (32).

Der zweite Teil des Bandes (175-226) bietet ein hilfreiches Lexikon des dramatischen Gesamtwerks von Babo, in dem die vollständigen bibliographischen Angaben sowie Zeit und Ort der Uraufführung, soweit sie ermittelt werden konnten, geboten werden. Teilweise kamen Stücke entweder nicht zur Aufführung oder wurden nicht gedruckt; auch diese sind mit Lemmata vertreten, so etwa ein verschollenes Jugendwerk mit einem Thema aus der römischen Geschichte Triers und das bayerische Trauerspiel *Tassilo*, das Babo für den Wettbewerb zur Eröffnung des Münchner Hoftheaters 1818 einreichte, dann aber wegen seiner Ernennung zum Preisrichter zurückzog.

Ergänzend wird auch die von Babo gemeinsam mit Johann Baptist Strobel und Lorenz Hübner von 1782 bis 1783 in wenigen Heften herausgegebene Theaterzeitschrift *Der dramatische Censor* berücksichtigt, die, ganz der Aufklärung folgend, den einzigen »Endzweck jeder Theatererrichtung« (225) in der Moralität erblickte. Vor dem Hintergrund von Konzeptionen Lessings geht es den Zeitschriftenherausgebern zugleich um die Verbesserung des Theaters und der Sitten, außerdem um eine spezifisch bayerische Ausrichtung des Theaters, die zugleich mit einer antifranzösischen Spitze (Kritik am Ballett) verbunden war. Ein Stück, *Der Physiognomist*, ist von zweifelhafter Autorschaft und wird nur deshalb aufgenommen, weil es im Katalog der Österreichischen Nationalbibliothek Babo zugeschrieben wird – eine notorisch unsichere Angelegenheit (209); es ist jedoch auch inhaltlich von Interesse, weil hier in theatralischer Form an der von Lavater inaugurierten Mode des dilettierenden Physiognomierens Kritik geübt wird.

Mit seinen Einzelanalysen und dem lexikalischen Teil verbessert der Band insgesamt die Informationslage zur Theatergeschichte der Aufklärung und demonstriert die weiterhin große Ergiebigkeit personenbezogener Forschungsansätze.

Technische Universität Berlin *Till Kinzel*

BOHNENGEL, JULIA / WORTMANN, THOMAS (Hg.), *»Die deutsche Freiheit erdolcht«. Neue Studien zu Leben, Werk und Rezeption August von Kotzebues.* Hannover: Wehrhahn (2023). 378 S., mit Abb.

Die Beiträge des vorliegenden Sammelbandes gehen, bis auf eine Ausnahme, auf eine Tagung zurück, die aus Anlass des 200. Jahrestages der Ermordung August von Kotzebues 2019 in Mannheim stattfand. Im Vorwort schreiben die Herausgeberin und der Herausgeber, dass dieser Jahrestag Anlass gewesen sei, an »einen vergessenen Autor« zu denken, der im »kulturellen Gedächtnis nur noch als Opfer jenes politischen folgenreichen Attentats präsent« (xi) sei. Diese Ansicht und der darin enthaltene Forschungsüberblick verwundern, denn tatsächlich ist August von Kotzebue längst kein vergessener Autor mehr, war es wohl nie, zumal er als Antipode in der klassisch-romantischen Literaturgeschichtsschreibung gebraucht wurde. Die Literatur- und Theaterkritik um 1800 baute ihn als Goethes Gegenspieler auf. Im *Brennus* schreibt 1803 ein Kritiker anlässlich einer Aufführung der *Iphigenie auf Tauris* im Berliner Nationaltheater: »*saure* Wochen, *frohe* Feste, sey unser künftig Zauberwort! Das heißt, Kotzebue in Ueberfluß, und alle Tage, bald rein sauer, bald säuerlich, bald verwässert und schaal, bald mit Zucker und pikantem Gewürz versetzt, – und Göthe zum frohen Feste; Kotzebue der weite, bunte Markt für Alle, Göthe das Allerheiligste für die Erwählten«.[1] Seither wurde auf Kotzebues Werk als Negativfolie

---

[1] Brennus. Eine Zeitschrift für das nördliche Deutschland, 3 (1803), Merzheft, S. 336.

verwiesen, wenn über das Theater um 1800 gesprochen wurde. Geändert hat sich allerdings seit einigen Jahren der Gesichtspunkt, unter dem Kotzebue und sein Werk betrachtet werden. Schon 2002 zeigte Thomas Betzwieser in seiner Habilitationsschrift *Sprechen und Singen. Ästhetik und Erscheinungsformen der Dialogoper* (Metzler) ganz unvoreingenommen, dass Kotzebues dramaturgisches Konzept der motivierten Musik der Librettistik und der romantischen Oper wichtige Impulse gab. Spätestens seitdem 2012 der von Mari Tarvas herausgegebene Band *Von Kotzebue bis Fleming* (Königshausen & Neumann) erschien, ist in der Forschung eine Neubetrachtung der Person und des Werkes auszumachen, die sich kontinuierlich fort- und durchgesetzt hat. Schließlich finden seit 2012 in Kooperation mit der estnischen Botschaft in Berlin, der estnischen Akademie für Musik und der Berlin-Brandenburgischen Akademie der Wissenschaften jährlich in Berlin und Tallinn »Kotzebue-Gespräche« statt, die ein breites Publikum anziehen und aus denen bereits zwei Sammelbände hervorgegangen sind, der erste unter Beteiligung des Rezensenten, der zweite unter Beteiligung Alexander Košeninas herausgegeben. Angesichts dieser Forschungslage, die durch eine Fülle von Publikationen über Kotzebue zu ergänzen wäre, von einem »vergessenen Autor« zu sprechen, ist nicht nachvollziehbar.

Unter diesen Umständen den vorliegenden Band unbefangen zu rezensieren ist dem Rezensenten nicht möglich, weil ihm leicht Befangenheit unterstellt werden könnte. Dessen ungeachtet soll der bisher von der Kritik noch gar nicht zur Kenntnis genommene Band hier vorgestellt werden, um die Forschung darauf aufmerksam zu machen, wenngleich der Rezensent sich darauf beschränkt, die Beiträge anzuzeigen.

Der Tagungsband ist in vier Abschnitte gegliedert. In »Der Dramatiker im europäischen Kontext« finden sich Beiträge von Anke Detken, Johannes Birgfeld, Irmtraud Hnilica, Thomas Wortmann, Julia Bohnengel und Axel Schröter, die sich mit dem Phänomen des Seriellen, des Bearbeitens und Umdeutens fremder Stücke und Vorlagen durch Kotzebue beschäftigen. Die hier vorgetragenen Thesen zu einer »Ästhetik der Professionalität« (26) oder zu einer »Dramaturgie der Kommunikation« (28) laden zu weiterführenden Überlegungen ein. Rezensent ist der Auffassung, dass Kotzebue weniger Dichter als vielmehr Dramaturg war, der den Hauptzweck eines dramatischen Textes in der Aufführung sah.[2] Daher gestaltete Kotzebue seine Texte so, dass sich die Schauspielerinnen und Schauspieler möglichst virtuos auf einer Schaubühne entfalten konnten, die eine andere Funktion als die heutigen subventionierten Staatstheater erfüllte.

Der Abschnitt »Schriftstellerisches Engagement jenseits der Bühne« enthält Beiträge von Max Graff, Alexander Košenina und Albert Meier. Dass Kotzebue die Technik der Fremdaneignung, die er bei seiner Dramenproduktion so virtuos anwendet und die Gegenstand der Betrachtung im ersten Abschnitt war, schon bei seinem Erstlingswerk, dem Prosaband *Er und Sie*, gebraucht, exemplifiziert Graff in seinem in die Tiefe gehenden Aufsatz.

Der Abschnitt »Kotzebues Ermordung. Kontexte – Folgen – Rezeption« versammelt Beiträge von Sarah Pister, Sylvia Schraut, Rolf Haaser, Wilhelm Kreutz, Sandra Beck, Hiram Kümper und Hermann Wiegand. Aus diesen Beiträgen sticht Haasers

---

2 Vgl. René Sternke, Performative Moralistik. Sinn und Unsinn in Kotzebues *Wirrwarr*, in: Klaus Gerlach, Harry Liivrand, Kristel Pappel (Hg.), August von Kotzebue im estnisch-deutschen Dialog, Hannover 2016, S. 213-237.

Aufsatz heraus, da er neue Quellen aus dem Staatsarchiv Darmstadt vorstellt und damit die Verbindung Karl Sands mit dem Theologen und Schriftsteller de Wette aufarbeitet. Darüber hinaus zeigt er auch, dass Kotzebues Persönlichkeit und Werk so nachhaltig Unbehagen in der soziokulturellen Verfasstheit vieler Intellektueller um 1800 in Deutschland hervorriefen, dass sie zu Gegenreaktionen motivierten.

Abschnitt IV enthält Abbildungen und eine Übersicht der von Kotzebue in Mannheim gespielten Stücke. Ein Personenregister des so heterogenen Bandes fehlt leider.

Auffällig an dem Sammelband ist, dass sich nur gut die Hälfte der Beiträge mit Kotzebues Werk, sogar weniger als die Hälfte mit seinem dramatischen Werk befasst. Die im Vorwort geforderte Schwerpunktverschiebung weg vom Interesse am Mordopfer und seinen Folgen hin zum literarischen Werk wird somit nicht eingelöst, zumal der Band auf dem Buchdeckel mit einem Bildnis von Kotzebue mit blutroter Brust, in der ein Dolch steckt, wirbt und mit einem Graphikzyklus schließt, der die Ermordung des Dichters und die Hinrichtung des Mörders als Bildgeschichte erzählt.

Berlin-Brandenburgische Akademie der Wissenschaften　　　　　　　　*Klaus Gerlach*

KOTZEBUE, AUGUST VON, *Ich, eine Geschichte in Fragmenten*. Mit einem Nachwort herausgegeben von Max Graff. Hannover: Wehrhahn (2021). 102 S.

Karl, a 23-year-old Straßburg student who regards himself as a genius, writes his great aunt a series of letters describing his travels through Germany in search of any woman worthy of becoming his bride. Miffed at the difficulties he encounters in his quest, he vents his spleen in a series of episodic fragments with the intention of alerting young men to the risks of falling in love with women, whom he regards as duplicitous.

Notable among the twenty-one fragments that constitute the main body of *Ich* is a debate between a defender of women (a *Magister*) and a skeptic (a *Kandidat* similar to Karl), in which neither is able to convince the other; apart from Karl's great aunt, the *Magister* is the sole supporter of women who is given a voice, though the male chauvinist gets the last word. Also featured in this narrative is Kotzebue's survey of recent love-literature, particularly novels by Johann Martin Miller and above all Goethe's *Leiden des jungen Werthers* and the many imitations it inspired. Karl, who views Werther as a martyr to female infidelity and cruelty, actually has little direct experience with women, as his knowledge of them is chiefly derived from his reading. »Ich habe viel gelesen, ich weiß, wie's in der Welt zugeht,« he proudly announces (18). Female authors in particular draw his ire: »Meine Frau, sagt ich, darf kein Buch schreiben« (28).

His quest to find a woman who suits him having met with failure, Karl informs his great aunt that he intends to write a booklet, or rather a folio, containing all he has learned regarding female shortcomings. *Ich* thus amounts to an epistolary travelogue about the book the narrator claims he was unable to write – a rather meta performance. Eventually, marriage being a necessary evil, Karl resolves to take a wife after all, and so sets sail to the recently discovered Tahitian Islands, whose women were conceived of as innocent and free in their love. There his quest is successful, and he returns in triumph with a native bride, thus revealing that he does not reject women in general, but only modern European – and especially German – ones.

In a »Patriotischer Nachtrag« which parodies Wieland, the author proposes the creation of a »Damenakademie [...] woselbst zwölf, von verständigen Männern wohlunterrichtete Frauen, als Professorinnen bei den vier Fakultäten anzustellen sind. Drei in der Kochkunst, drei in der Hebammenkunst, drei in der Geschiklichkeit [sic], statt der zeitherigen unbequemen Moden, neue und bessere zu erfinden« (57). The students of this academy are to be single women imported from Tahiti, who after graduation can enter the marriage market; in exchange, women from Germany will be shipped to the South Pacific.

Five short items are attached in the appendix. *Ich* was the initial item published in *Ganymed für die Lesewelt* (Eisenach, 1781). The publisher of that work, Johann Georg Ernst Wittekindt, explains in a »Vorrede« the journal's title, declaring that his purpose is not to provide the strong nectar that Ganymede once served the gods (that could make the reader's head spin), but rather to offer a good glass of Franconian or Rhine Wine, or Malaga, or Burgundy. He begs our indulgence if there should be a bad bottle in the mix. After all, we should keep in mind that the god Mercury had his troubles, and in the present instance our server is Ganymede, who is but a demi-god. The current editor, Max Graff, attributes this lighthearted preface not to Wittekindt but to Kotzebue himself, who not only suggested the title *Ganymed* but also sought to make his mark by indirectly lampooning Wieland via the name of his journal, *Der Teutsche Merkur* (87). Be that as it may, an argument can be made that this »Vorrede« should come first, where it was originally placed, instead of being consigned to the appendices. That way, it would alert readers in advance to the frivolous tone of what follows. Also questionable is the editor's decision to omit the original vignette showing a youthful Ganymede in a pastoral setting, raising a glass of wine he has just drawn from a barrel, as he convivially toasts an unseen gathering and invites them to imbibe. Instead, the cover for the present edition shows the frontispiece from an entirely different work, Goeckinck's »Lieder zweier Liebenden« (2nd ed., Leipzig, 1779).

The second item in the appendix contains a brief but apt review from the *Allgemeines Verzeichniß neuer Bücher mit kurzen Anmerkungen* (Leipzig, 1781): »[*Ich*] soll witzig und satyrisch seyn, ists aber nicht, wenigstens in dem Grade, wie der Autor zu glauben scheinet« (62). The third is a review that appeared in the *Allgemeine Deutsche Bibliothek* (51, 1. St., Berlin/Stettin, 1782):

> Der V. sucht in einer ängstlich gesuchten Laune über die Untreue des weiblichen Geschlechts zu spotten; die Anspielungen aus Litterair- und Natur-Geschichte verrathen eine verunglückte Nachahmung der physiognomischen Reisen; wird er [der Verfasser] der Laune künftig nicht so ängstlich nachjagen, sich nicht selbst kitzeln, um nur lachen zu können, so könnten dergleichen Fragmente wohl in Zukunft der Lesewelt einen Zeitvertreib schaffen. (63)

The fourth item contains an excerpt from Kotzebue's autobiography, *Mein literärischer Lebenslauf* (Leipzig, 1796), in which he says that in *Ich* he was attempting to copy the originality and vocabulary of the *Physiognomische Reisen* (Altenburg, 1788) of Johann Karl August Musäus, his uncle and mentor. The last item documents the authorities' inspection of Würzburg bookstores in 1781; among other works, they confiscated *Ich* on the grounds that it was both tasteless and obscene. This charge would be echoed a century later, when Hugo Hayn mentioned it in his study of literary erotica, describing it succinctly as the »Erstes u. zwar sehr liederliches Opus Kotzebue's« (*Bibliotheca Germanorum erotica*, 1885). Kotzebue had quoted, for example, Matt. 7:7 (»Klopfet an, so wird euch aufgetan«) and given it a sexual connotation.

The reissue of *Ich* is part of publisher Matthias Wehrhahn's ongoing efforts to remind the public that the *Goethezeit* could with equal justification be called the *Kotzebuezeit*. While this is a worthy goal, one must ask, does *Ich* represent a significant contribution to this undertaking, and can such a dubious work be rehabilitated? Contemporary journals were skeptical, including one not mentioned here: the *Neueste Critische Nachrichten* merely lists the complete contents of the volume, commenting dismissively, »Mehr zu sagen würde überflüßig seyn.«[1]

At first blush, *Ich* seems to live up to its reputation of being little more than a footnote to the discussion of the nature of women and their proper role in marriage. No previous commentator has ever devoted more than a few sentences to this work, and in his Afterword, which borrows Hayn's heading »Erstes u. zwar sehr liederliches Opus Kotzebue's,« Max Graff observes that some critics may have done so without having actually read it (92). »*Ich* ist kein literarisches Meisterwerk« (92), he concedes, before arguing that it is worth reexamining because doing so may help to revise Kotzebue's reputation as primarily the prolific author of trivial dramas. Incidentally, Graff has since updated his comments on this work in an essay for *Kotzebue International*.[2]

Graff reconsiders *Ich* from three angles: Its formal aspects (including the use of framing devices), its self-reflexive, inter- and paratextual character, and its treatment of the topics of love and sexuality. While regretting »das [...] mehr als problematische Frauenbild« (92) in Kotzebue's text, Graff argues that *Ich* should be seen as a web of quotations and allusions, composed of fragments that are hybrid in nature – both narrative and dramatic, epistolary and diaristic, culminating in a parody of a *Bildungsroman*. »Was Kotzebues Text aber auszeichnet, ist das lustvolle, humorvolle und selbstreferenzielle Spiel mit dem Vorgang des Erzählens« (96). It is these modernist, formal elements that most interest the editor, though he also deals with the work's ostensible topic: »Tatsächlich ist das Frauenbild, das der Erzähler entwirft, zutiefst misogyn; dass er dabei natürlich satirisch übertreibt, kann nicht wirklich als milderner Umstand gelten« (100).

While Graff claims that Kotzebue's text is partly ironic, partly parodistic, and partly satiric, *Ich* contains its own best description when the author himself in his prefatory motto calls it an »Ufer-Aas« or »Eintagsfliege« (8). Though Kotzebue laments the ephemeral life span of such works in the current literary marketplace, *Ich* itself is laden with references to just such one-day wonders. He flatters his readers by assuming they are up to the minute when it comes to the latest German, French, English and Italian publications and their authors – Graff uses the term »Namedropping« advisedly (97).

Though at times one is tempted to say that »Sie« (»They« or »Them«) would be a better title, Karl's true subject proves to be himself in all his egotism, so *Ich* is appropriate after all. One could perhaps venture an apology for this work by saying

---

1 Neueste Critische Nachrichten, Bd. 7, Greifswald 1781, p. 296.
2 Max Graff, »Eine Frau ist ein nothwendig Uebel«. Zu Kotzebues früher Erzählung »Ich, eine Geschichte in Fragmenten«, in: *Kotzebue International*, 05/08/2023, kotzebue.hypotheses.org/4099.

that while it appears to fan the flames of women hating, the misogynist's exaggerated self-portrayal instead exposes his own shortcomings. While prejudice does not automatically become subverted by being expressed in clichés, Karl's loathing of women is so over-the-top as to become self-parody. The reader comes to realize (though Karl never does) that his diatribe – written, as the subtitle says, »zu Nuz [sic] und Frommen der mannbaren Jugend, an's Licht bracht von mir selbst« – reveals more about male self-absorption than it does about female duplicity.

In sum, while the title may suggest that *Ich* is a work of radical *Sturm und Drang* subjectivity, what it amounts to in practice is a pastiche of prejudices gleaned from books the narrator has read, all of which confirm him in his view that the current generation of European women takes satisfaction in driving their hapless worshipers to imitate Werther. Kotzebue mouths misogynist opinions at length, then winks as if to suggest that anyone who disapproves has failed to realize that his performance has all been one elaborate joke.

Independent Scholar *Hamilton Beck*

LA ROCHE, SOPHIE VON, *Erscheinungen am See Oneida*. Hg. von Claudia Nitschke und Ivonne Pietsch. Mit einem Nachwort von Claudia Nitschke. Hannover: Wehrhahn (2022). 528 S.
LA ROCHE, SOPHIE VON, *Mein Schreibetisch*. Hg. von Bodo Plachta. Hannover: Wehrhahn (2022). 325. S.

Die beiden Bände, die hier anzuzeigen sind, enthalten zwei Texte aus dem Alterswerk Sophie von La Roches, die 1797/98 bzw. 1799 im Verlag Heinrich Gräff in Leipzig erschienen. La Roche lebte zu dieser Zeit als mittlerweile professionelle Schriftstellerin in Offenbach. Beide Werke, die formal ganz verschieden sind, beschäftigen sich unter anderem mit Gender-Fragen, geben Einblick in die Lesekultur der Zeit und erhellen einige wichtige Grundkategorien im Denken der Autorin, wie zum Beispiel Natur und Naturphilosophie oder ihre kritische Haltung zum zeitgenössischen politischen Hintergrund, zur Pädagogik und zum Wert von Familie und Freundschaft.

Der Roman *Erscheinungen am See Oneida* erzählt multiperspektivisch die Geschichte des adligen Ehepaares Wattines, das vor der Französischen Revolution, in der einige Familienmitglieder den Tod gefunden haben, nach Nordamerika flieht und sich dort eine neue Existenz aufbaut. Nach anfänglichem Aufenthalt in Baltimore und Philadelphia ziehen Carl und Emilie Wattines auf eine Insel im Lake Oneida und werden später Mitglieder einer neuen von Holländern und Deutschen getragenen Kolonie, die in der Nähe der Insel entsteht. In die Zeit des Inselaufenthalts fällt die Geburt des Sohnes Carmil, bei der indigene Frauen helfen, deren ausführliche Beschreibung Aufschluss über eine Kultur gibt, die in Kontrast zur europäischen gesetzt wird. Die Familie ernährt sich von Obst- und Maisanbau, Hühnerhaltung und Honigernte, wobei das ruhige bäuerliche Leben auf der Insel, das von Tugend und harter Arbeit geprägt ist, dem geschäftigen Großstadtleben im Sinne Rousseaus vorgezogen wird. Gleichwohl wurde eine aus 300 Bänden bestehende Bibliothek in die Einsamkeit mitgenommen, die u. a. Werke der europäischen Naturwissenschaft und -philosophie (Georges-Louis Leclerc, Comte de Buffon; Bernardin de Saint-

Pierre; Jean-Jacques Rousseau; Johann Gottfried Herder), Bände der *Encyclopädie* und historische Werke von Guillaume Thomas François Raynal enthält; Wissen wird in diesem Zusammenhang als Charakteristikum einer progressiven Fortschrittskultur gesehen. Später geben die Wattines ihr Inselleben auf und schließen sich einem kolonialen Siedlungsprojekt an.

Wie Claudia Nitschke in ihrem umsichtigen und erhellenden Nachwort hervorhebt, gehört dieser Roman zu den Robinsonaden, die sich seit Campes Bearbeitung von Daniel Defoes *Robinson Crusoe* großer Beliebtheit erfreuten, aber: »Anders als es Campes Einwand gegen den ›Putz‹ vermuten lassen mag, ist La Roches Roman ein ungewöhnlich ambitioniertes Kompendium zeitgenössischen Wissens, und ein selbstbewusster Beitrag zu heute noch zentralen gesellschaftlichen Themen wie Gender, Kolonisierung und Umwelt(schutz), mit denen sich La Roche als intellektuelle Frau des achtzehnten Jahrhunderts – an alte Stärken anknüpfend – neu platzierte« (478). Yvonne Pietsch geht in ihrem kurzen Nachwort auf die zeitgenössische Rezeption des Werkes, über die nicht viel bekannt ist, ein. Interessant ist dabei, dass Johann Heinrich Campe eine gekürzte französische Übersetzung des Stoffes in *Voyage d'un Allemand au Lac Oneida* veröffentlichte, die La Roches Original »mehr oder weniger vom Markt« (526) verdrängte.

Mit *Mein Schreibetisch* führt La Roche die Leserschaft in ihren persönlichen geistigen Raum ein. Symbolisch repräsentieren der »Schreibetisch«, der die Autorin von ihren Anfangsjahren in Warthausen bis zur letzten Lebensstation in Offenbach begleitet hat, und der Raum, in dem er steht, die kontinuierliche geistige und schriftstellerische Tätigkeit. Der »Schreibetisch«, auf dem Briefe, wichtige Werke, Bilder und Erinnerungsstücke liegen, und das Arbeitszimmer werden ausführlich beschrieben und bieten damit nach Bodo Plachta »eine Inspektion des Lebens- und Schreiborts« (305). »Sammeln, Aufbewahren, Inventarisieren und Erinnern gehen Hand in Hand,« was »dem enzyklopädischen Denken des 18. Jahrhunderts nicht fremd« sei. (313) Gewidmet ist dieses Werk dem Freund Johann Friedrich Christian Petersen in Darmstadt. Die Titelvignette des Kupferstechers Christian Schule zeigt die Autorin in zeitgenössischer Kleidung mit der Feder in der Hand.

Formal kann man diesen in zwei Bänden erschienenen Text als Collagenwerk bezeichnen, in dem Sophie von La Roche persönliche Erinnerungen festhält, Lesefrüchte mitteilt und literarische, philosophische, historische und pädagogische Bücher sowie Reiseberichte vorstellt. Einen besonderen Platz nehmen dabei Werke von herausragenden französischen, englischen und deutschen Autorinnen ein, denn, so hebt die Autorin hervor, »ich liebe alles, was aus der Feder einer Person meines Geschlechts abstammt« (46). Dazu gehören zum Beispiel Madame de Sévignés *L'Éloge* über das Schreiben von Briefen, Caroline von Wolzogens *Agnes von Lilien* oder Charlotte Smiths *The Wanderings of Warwick*. Der zweite Band enthält Auszüge aus Briefen von der Schweizer Philosophin und Schriftstellerin Julie Bondeli, mit der Sophie von La Roche über viele Jahre korrespondierte, ohne sie persönlich kennengelernt zu haben. Im Mittelpunkt dieser Korrespondenz stehen Mitteilungen über Jean-Jacques Rousseau, Gedanken über dessen *Julie, ou La Nouvelle Héloïse* sowie über La Roches *Geschichte des Fräuleins von Sternheim* und Kommentare zum weiblichen Schreiben sowie zum Glück der Freundschaft.

Die jeweils auf dem Erstdruck beruhenden Ausgaben sind mit informativen Nachworten versehen, die die Werke vor dem zeitgenössischen Hintergrund und innerhalb des Gesamtwerks Sophie von La Roches verorten. Orthografie und Interpunktion wurden dem heutigen Gebrauch vorsichtig angeglichen; kleine Fehler wurden berichtigt. Die Ausgaben enthalten außerdem Frontispize, Titelvignetten und mehrere Abbildungen und sind ansprechend gestaltet. Diese Editionen leisten einen wichtigen Beitrag zur Verfügbarkeit der Werke von einer Autorin, die einem größeren Publikum immer noch nur wegen ihres Erstlingsromans bekannt ist. Doch auch der La Roche-Forschung, die dem Alterswerk der Schriftstellerin in den letzten Jahrzehnten größere Aufmerksamkeit gewidmet hat, bieten sie eine solide und leicht zugängliche Textgrundlage.

University of Memphis *Monika Nenon*

LEE, DAVID E. / OSBORNE, JOHN C. (Hg.), »*mein lieber deutscher Horaz*«. *Der Briefwechsel zwischen Johann Wilhelm Ludwig Gleim und Karl Wilhelm Ramler*. Heidelberg: Winter (2022) (= Wieland im Kontext. Oßmannstedter Studien, Bd. 1). 685 S.

Um den Jahreswechsel 1744/45 herum begegneten sich Johann Wilhelm Ludwig Gleim und Karl Wilhelm Ramler in einer Buchhandlung in Berlin. Der 25-jährige Gleim hatte zu diesem Zeitpunkt schon seine berühmt gewordenen *Scherzhaften Lieder* in eben jener Buchhandlung verlegt und sich als »deutscher Anakreon« einen Namen gemacht. Ramler ging später durch seine Prosa-Übersetzung der Horazischen Oden als »deutscher Horaz« in die Literaturgeschichte ein. Ab Mai 1745 sind erste Briefe zwischen Gleim und Ramler überliefert, wobei die Korrespondenz bis in das Jahr 1765 reicht.[1] Der Abbruch des Briefwechsels 1765 verwundert, hat doch Ramler bis 1798 und Gleim bis 1803 gelebt. Allerdings kam es 1765 aufgrund literarischer Meinungsverschiedenheiten zu einem Freundschaftsbruch, der endgültig sein sollte.

Der vorliegende erste Band, den David E. Lee und John C. Osborne erarbeitet haben,[2] umfasst die Briefe aus der Anfangszeit der Korrespondenz von Mai 1745 bis März 1752. In diesen Zeitraum fällt die Suche nach einer Anstellung der beiden Korrespondenten sowie erste gemeinsame literarische Projekte. Gleim wurde Privatsekretär des Fürsten Leopold von Anhalt-Dessau in Oranienbaum, nachdem er sich in einem Bewerbungsverfahren gegen einen »Nebenbuhler« (1) durchgesetzt hatte. Ramler hatte indessen auf Vermittlung Gleims eine Anstellung als Hofmeister in Löhme erhalten. Nachdem Gleim kurz nach Berlin zurückgekehrt war, erhielt er Ende 1748 schließlich den Posten als Domsekretär in Halberstadt, den er bis 1797 innehatte. Die finanziell einträgliche Stelle war Grundlage für sein Wirken als einer der bedeutendsten Literaturmäzene des achtzehnten Jahrhunderts. Ramler verdingte sich ab August 1749 als Lehrer für Philosophie an der Kadettenanstalt in Berlin, was ihm nur ein Leben in bescheidenen Verhältnissen einbrachte. Sein Wohnort Berlin

---

1 Es sind noch jeweils zwei Briefe aus den Jahren 1769 und 1790 überliefert, de facto war der Briefwechsel da jedoch bereits abgebrochen.
2 John Osborne verstarb 2002. Neben den beiden Herausgebern wird auch noch die inzwischen ebenfalls verstorbene Gerlinde Wappler, langjährige Leiterin der Handschriftenabteilung des Gleimhauses, als Mitwirkende der Edition aufgeführt.

ermöglichte ihm dafür jedoch Eingang in literarische Kreise der Stadt und war maßgeblich für sein Wirken als Kritiker, Herausgeber und Übersetzer.

Die Edition beginnt mit einer kenntnisreichen Einleitung der Herausgeber, die den Briefwechsel in den Kontext seiner Zeit stellt. Darüber hinaus wird sogleich ein Ausblick darauf gegeben, was die Forschung in den geplanten zwei Folgebänden zu erwarten hat. Ein zentrales Thema des Briefwechsels ist die Freundschaft, zuweilen auch ihre Nichterfüllung, denn »die Briefe erhellen Konflikte, die eine solche Beziehung nicht auszuhalten vermochte« (xix). Ein wiederkehrender Vorwurf Gleims war die mangelnde Schreibfreudigkeit Ramlers. So beklagt er sich am 25. April 1748: »Ich muß mir in der That nach gerade etwas einbilden, daß ich würcksamer bin, als alle meine Freunde, nemlich in Absicht auf die Pflichten der Freundschaft. Denn ich schreibe freylich weniger bücher als h. langen aber ich plaudre desto mehr in briefen« (255). Ramler antwortet in einem Brief vom 7. Mai 1748 mit Humor auf solche Vorwürfe: »Solch *Recept* [Augen schonen, indem man nicht liest und schreibt, C. B.] kommt recht mit meinem Charakter überein weil sie mich doch für faul halten« (260). Auch die Überarbeitung von Ewald Christian von Kleists Gedicht »Der Frühling« durch Ramler, welche Gleim selbst angeregt hatte, gestaltete sich nicht konfliktfrei, denn angesichts von weitreichenden Änderungen bemerkte Gleim: »Wenn sie aber fortfahren, wie sie angefangen haben, so wird nicht viel übrig bleiben« (334). Nicht ohne Grund besorgte Kleist den Druck seines Gedichts letzten Endes selbst.

Carl Schüddekopf hatte bereits 1905/1906 die Briefe Gleims und Ramlers aus dem Zeitraum von 1745 bis 1759 in zwei Bänden veröffentlicht, wobei der dritte Band mit den Briefen bis 1765 und dem Kommentar zu allen Briefen nie erschienen ist. Als Lee und Osborne 1970 mit der Arbeit an ihrer Edition begannen, wollten sie ursprünglich diese Lücke schließen und nur die ungedruckten Briefe von 1759 bis 1765 edieren sowie den Kommentar zu allen Briefen nachliefern. Die Absicht, »nach mehr als 100 Jahren alle Texte zu überprüfen und die Orthographie und Interpunktion genau abzubilden« (xi), führte dann jedoch zu dem Entschluss, alle 517 Briefe der Korrespondenz abzudrucken. Das war eine gute Entscheidung, denn Schüddekopf hatte in seiner Ausgabe zahlreiche Anpassungen in Hinblick auf den Brieftext vorgenommen. So hatte er beispielsweise Textstellen, insbesondere solche, die den kommunikativen Teil der Briefe widerspiegeln, gekürzt. Darüber hinaus sind bei Schüddekopf nicht konsequent Gemeinschaftsbriefe wie der von Ramler, Hempel, J. G. Sucro und Sulzer an Gleim vom 11. Oktober 1749 (390-392) abgedruckt. Eben jener kommunikative Charakter der Briefe und das sich darin widerspiegelnde Netzwerk sind es jedoch, die die Forschung in den letzten Jahren immer mehr in den Mittelpunkt gerückt hat.[3] Insofern stellt die Ausgabe von Lee und Osborne einen echten Mehrwert dar.

Aus editorischer Sicht ist es zudem begrüßenswert, dass nunmehr »eine orthographisch getreue Wiedergabe des jeweiligen Originaltextes der Briefe« (xlix) vorhanden ist. Auf die Wiedergabe aller Varianten und Lesarten wird aufgrund des Platzmangels verzichtet. Nur Streichungen werden im Brieftext wiedergegeben, da deren Weglassungen »eine unverständliche Lücke in der Syntax hinterlassen würden« (xlix).

---

3 Als Beispiel sei genannt: Hannes Fischer, Erika Thomalla, Literaturwissenschaftliche Netzwerkforschung zum 18. Jahrhundert, in: Zeitschrift für Germanistik 26.1 (2016), S. 110-117.

Signifikante Änderungen werden am Anfang des Kommentars mit dem Hinweis auf die Seitenzahl in den Originalbriefen vermerkt, was mitunter das Auffinden der Textstelle erschwert. Positiv hervorzuheben ist, dass erschlossene Briefe sowohl im Briefteil (mit Erläuterungen) als auch im Briefverzeichnis grau hinterlegt sind, was Aufschluss über Überlieferungslücken gibt. Der Kommentar zu den Briefen ist sehr umfassend und gründlich, lediglich ein systematischer Nachweis über vorhandene Abschriften und Drucke wäre noch wünschenswert gewesen, insbesondere wenn man sich mit der Editionsgeschichte auseinandersetzen möchte.

Alles in allem ist es ein großer Gewinn für die Forschung, dass diese vorzügliche Edition vorliegt. Es bleibt zu hoffen, dass die fehlenden zwei Bände mitsamt Register bald erscheinen und das höchst verdienstvolle Lebenswerk von David E. Lee, inzwischen Emeritus an der University of Tennessee, damit vollendet wird – zumal sich am 25. Februar 2025 der Geburtstag von Karl Wilhelm Ramler zum 300. Mal jährt.

Gleimhaus Halberstadt *Claudia Brandt*

POTT, UTE (Hg.), *Plötzlich Poetin!? Anna Louisa Karsch – Leben und Werk.* Göttingen: Wallstein (2022) (= Schriften des Gleimhauses Halberstadt, Bd. 12). 289 S.

The tercentenary of Anna Louisa Karsch's birth in 2022 has been marked by a number of publications, including a new edition by Claudia Brandt and Ute Pott, bringing together a selection of Karsch's letters and work. The present, handsome produced volume was published as an accompaniment to the exhibition of the same name that opened in the *Gleimhaus* in Halberstadt on 2 December 2022, the day of Karsch's birth. The volume features two interacting halves, neatly reflecting the research and public-facing function of the *Gleimhaus*. The first collects a selection of papers from the 2021 conference on *Anna Louise Karsch. Werke – Netzwerke – Öffentlichkeiten*, and the second offers a richly illustrated exhibition catalogue. Karsch is both a media phenomenon historically speaking – exemplified, for instance, by Sulzer's famous and stubbornly persistent stylization of her work as a »Naturgenie« (59) – and in scholarly reception of the past few decades, given the attention garnered by Karsch's distinctive »Tränenbrief« following the exhibition *Brief – Ereignis & Objekt* at the *Freies Deutsches Hochstift* in Frankfurt am Main in 2008. In both sections, the volume draws on and complicates the received image of Karsch as a media phenomenon, emphasizes the importance of attending to material and archival objects, and points toward the transnational appreciation of Karsch in her time and beyond.

The first part can be roughly divided into two sections, with articles that offer close readings and literary-historical contextualization of Karsch's works, letters, alongside those examining Karsch's canny self-presentation in the public sphere. There is some conceptual loss on account of a third of the papers from the original conference, all on the topic of »Öffentlichkeiten,« having been published separately in *Das achtzehnte Jahrhundert* in 2022.[1] The effect of the articles presented is nonetheless coherent, as

---

1 See the section: Anna Louisa Karsch: Edition und Öffentlichkeit, in: Das achtzehnte Jahrhundert 46/2 (2022), pp. 131-218.

they demonstrate how differentiated Karsch's literary production and engagement were alongside her fame in salons as a »Stegreifdichterin« (129). Regina Nörtemann's article re-reads the »Tränenbrief« in the context of Sappho's love epistles to Phaon, arguing for a reciprocal relationship between writing and the expression and control of emotion. Maria Düfert offers a sustained analysis of the autobiographical poem »Belloisens Lebenslauf,« whose truncated and initial, posthumously published version omitted Karsch's familiarity with seventeenth-century poetry, folk songs and Paul Gerhardt and Johann Rist's church hymns, thereby reinforcing the received image of Karsch as a natural talent. Ulrike Leuschner presents a thorough examination of Karsch's reception of Homer, with a focus on the critical letters on the *Iliad*, which reflect the classicizing literary play of the Gleim circle. Formal questions come to the fore in Christoph Georg Rohrbach's contribution on Karsch's occasional odes. Here, Karsch emerges as a transitional figure, since her work holds on to forms favored by the Anacreontics and became obsolete once Klopstock's Horatian innovations with the ode became the norm. May Mergenthaler also attends to Karsch's religious odes, which deploy the aesthetics of the sublime, as well as drawing on church hymns and devotional literature. A detailed analysis of »An Gott als sie bey hellem Mondschein erwachte« offers an assessment of Karsch's distinctiveness, whose use of the sublime anticipates tendencies in Romantic lyric poetry. Inka Kording examines the expressive potential of *lacunae* in Karsch's correspondence with Gleim by looking at the use of catachresis.

A broader social focus is given through the articles that focus on Karsch's position within literary networks. Nikolas Immer analyses Karsch's complimentary verse epistles on *Emilia Galotti* and *Die Räuber*, although neither led to sustained contact with Lessing or Schiller. Reimar F. Lacher's article offers a survey of Karsch's iconographic representations and demonstrates a self-reflexive aspect of Karsch as a media phenomenon, since portraits acted as stimuli for Karsch's own verse-writing. Claudia Brandt provides insights into Karsch's agency in supporting others through her (formally creative) use of letters of recommendation. Karsch's presence in Berlin as a poet and performer of panegyric verse is the subject of a nuanced investigation by Maximilian Bach, in which Karsch's poetic extemporising found considerable favour – in multiple senses – compared to Karl Wilhelm Ramler's declamations in private circles. The last two contributions provide a broader scope for an appreciation of Karsch. Thomas Assinger's article explores the positive reception of Karsch in the Austrian Enlightenment, and traces how a fascination with Karsch's unlikely biography persisted, particularly among female readers, into the nineteenth century. Baptiste Baumann and Jana Kittelmann's article offers a complement to Assinger by exploring Karsch's reception in Switzerland and France, with an initial and unsurprising focus on Sulzer and Bodmer's support of Karsch, before moving on to Michael Huber's introduction of Karsch to the Francophone world.

The second part of the volume is devoted to the exhibition itself, offering an illustrated panorama depicting Karsch's life from her early years onward. The high-quality illustrations are an edited selection of the items exhibited, including unauthorized editions of Karsch's poems as well as prestige editions, alongside Daniel Chodowiecki's etching of her audience with Frederick the Great. Karsch's ability to swiftly produce poetry based on given end-rhymes at social gatherings is represented by manuscript reproductions. This section is usefully rounded off by a list of Karsch's publications, including those anthologized, in addition to a chronological list of Karsch's knowledge of literary works.

Overall, the volume is a vital and substantial contribution to scholarship on Karsch, and Wallstein should be commended on designing it extremely well. Whilst the structure necessarily does not give rise to a unifying thesis, the contributions, taken together, shed light on Karsch's own agency and her ability to navigate the social complexities of her contemporary literary world. Given the breadth of material present in the volume, both scholarly and bibliographical, it deserves to be essential reading for scholars of Karsch and the material and visual aspects of literary culture of the period.

Università degli Studi di Verona   *Joanna Raisbeck*

REEMTSMA, JAN PHILIPP, *Christoph Martin Wieland. Die Erfindung der modernen deutschen Literatur.* In Zusammenarbeit mit Fanny Esterházy. München: C. H. Beck (2023). 704 S., 34 Abb.

Mit dem immer weiter voranschreitenden Erscheinen der maßgeblichen historisch-kritischen Werk-[1] und Studienausgaben[2] und dem nun schon länger vorliegenden *Wieland-Handbuch*[3] ist der Boden für eine Wieland-Renaissance in der Literaturwissenschaft und darüber hinaus bestens bestellt. Alles, was nun noch fehlt, um diesen zwar nicht vergessenen, aber eben als halb-vergessen kanonisierten Autor, Übersetzer, Kommentator und Herausgeber von der Peripherie in die Mitte des literarischen Austauschs zu befördern, ist eine Anregung, ihn auch zu lesen. Diese Anregung kommt in Form einer großen Biographie, mit der Jan Philipp Reemtsma, einer der besten Wieland-Kenner unserer Tage, zweierlei versucht: Gegen das überkommene Bild eines Dichters, der *vor* dem eigentlichen Höhenkamm der deutschen Literatur schrieb, setzt er Wieland provokativ als den Beginn der Moderne, wie der vielversprechende (vielleicht auch: zu viel versprechende) Untertitel »Die Erfindung der modernen deutschen Literatur« bereits markiert; und er versucht die Lust zu wecken, Wieland zu lesen.

Die Darstellung eines so langen und produktiven Lebens in so bewegter Zeit und mit so vielen prägenden Zeitgenossen fordert die Ordnung des Biographen; dasselbe gilt für die Darstellung von Wielands Werk. Kapitel zum Leben Wielands und zu seinem Werk wechseln sich ab und funktionieren wunderbar als geschlossene Essays. Wer Wieland entdecken möchte, kann einfach das Kapitel aufschlagen, das gerade interessiert, sei es zum *Agathon* (jenem revolutionären Individualroman, der Christian Friedrich von Blanckenburg zur ersten Romanpoetik in Deutschland anregte), zum Singspiel (in dem Wieland mit seiner *Alceste* Geschichte schrieb) oder

1 Klaus Manger, Jan Philipp Reemtsma, Hans-Peter Nowitzki (Hg.), Wielands Werke. Historisch-Kritische Ausgabe, Boston, New York 2008-.
2 Hans-Peter Nowitzki, Jan Philipp Reemtsma (Hg.), Wieland. Studienausgabe in Einzelbänden. Kritische Ausgabe, Göttingen 2022–.
3 Jutta Heinz (Hg.), Wieland-Handbuch. Leben – Werk – Wirkung, Stuttgart, Weimar 2008.

zur Liebschaft mit Sophie La Roche. Andererseits verliert die Gesamtlektüre durch diese Struktur mitunter gegenüber dem punktuellen Schnuppern, denn bis zu 200 Seiten können zwischen der biographischen Verortung eines Textes und seiner Kommentierung liegen (so beim *Goldenen Spiegel*), und Wielands Auseinandersetzung mit den Philosophen Rousseau und Kant steht etwas verloren im hinteren Teil der Biographie. Freilich ist Vorblättern nicht verboten, aber dann reißt doch der Faden ab, den Reemtsma spinnen möchte, um die Biographie als Geschichte zu erzählen.

Reemtsma begleitet den übermütigen Jungpoeten, den unglücklich Verliebten, den von Religions- und Politikquerelen geplagten Biberacher Kanzleisekretär, den berühmten Literaten, den (wie Reemtsma korrigiert: umsichtigen) Hofbesitzer und schließlich den gealterten, arbeitsamen Routinier. Oft einfühlsam, manchmal auch etwas boshaft und ohne Wieland je zu verklären, stellt Reemtsma ihn mit jener Umsicht dar, die Werturteile über eine Person aus einer anderen Zeit und Welt ermöglichen.

Anders als im Untertitel der Biographie angekündigt, stellt die Kommentierungen des Werks dieses dann größtenteils nicht unter den Begriff der beginnenden Moderne. Denn dort, wo Reemtsma Wieland abstaubt, geht es *grosso modo* nicht um die vielfältigen Schattierungen dessen, was man als moderne Deutsche Literatur bezeichnen könnte. Stattdessen geht es in erster Linie um Sound: Wieder und wieder zitiert Reemtsma ausführlich Wielands Verse und Sätze und fordert zu lautem Lesen auf, zählt Silben, vergleicht Reime, Textstufen, Wortwahlen und zeigt damit die künstlerische Gemachtheit von Texten, die über weite Strecken des Werks genau diese Gemachtheit verschleiern. Eine enthusiastischere Einladung zur Wieland-Lektüre hat es vielleicht seit Arno Schmidt nicht mehr gegeben.[4] Wo Reemtsmas Expertise in Verbindung mit seinen klugen Lektüren anregend ist, hat die Begeisterung des Kenners doch auch ihre Schattenseiten. Denn die Freude an der Sprache führt mitunter zu einer Phänomenologie, der man nicht immer folgen kann. Wer Wielands Sound liebt, der wird gern mitschwelgen; wer nicht, der wird von manchen Kapiteln weniger profitieren.

Wie Wielands Verse scheint auch diese Biographie für ein lautes Lesen geschrieben. Reemtsma schießt immer wieder kleinere und größere Bemerkungen zwischen Briefstellen, schüttelt den Kopf, macht einen Scherz. Damit setzt sich der Sound dieses Buchs vom Gros der germanistischen Forschung ab und markiert diese Distanz deutlich: So kommt es zu Sticheleien gegen das Fach, das allerdings in der Weise, in der es hier dargestellt wird, schon gar nicht mehr existiert. Wo ist es noch »Triumph der Germanistik« (34), das biographische Klein-Klein eines Liebesgedichts zu sondieren? Auch die mit polemischer Schärfe geführte Abwicklung der Wieland-Biographie von Friedrich Sengle irritiert,[5] als ob die Germanistik noch das Fach Sengles wäre.

4 Arno Schmidt, Wieland oder Die Prosaformen, in: Das essayistische Werk zur deutschen Literatur. 4 Bde., Bd. 1: Barthold Heinrich Brockes. Johann Gottfried Schnabel. Friedrich Gottlieb Klopstock. Christoph Martin Wieland. Johann Gottfried Herder. Johann Karl Wezel, Zürich 1988, S. 121-149.
5 Friedrich Sengle, Wieland, Stuttgart 1949. Auf Zarembas neuere Darstellung geht Reemtsma an keiner Stelle ein: Michael Zaremba, Christoph Martin Wieland. Aufklärer und Poet, Köln, Weimar, Wien 2007. Dass der Klappentext von »der ersten [Biographie Wielands] seit siebzig Jahren« spricht, ist irritierend.

Nachvollziehbar ist indes die Kritik an einer teleologischen Literaturgeschichtsschreibung, die für die Vernachlässigung Wielands verantwortlich ist; die Vorreiter haben es im Kanon eben nicht besser als die Epigonen. Aber gerade mit Blick auf diese Kritik ist Reemtsmas eigener Umgang mit Teilen von Wielands Werk doch erstaunlich: Das von religiöser Schwärmerei geprägte Frühwerk klammert er über weite Strecken aus, übergeht Texte, die er nicht für lesenswert hält, und erzeugt damit ein Bild von Wielands Werk, das selbst einer gewissen Teleologie nicht entbehrt. Nachdem Reemtsma z. B. Sengles Fehleinschätzung von *Klelia und Sinibald* harsch kritisiert (405), geht er selbst fast kommentarlos an den *Dschinnistan*-Märchen vorbei (407-408). Auch das Kapitel zu Wielands langjähriger literarisch-politischer Zeitschrift *Der Teutsche Merkur* fällt überraschend knapp aus. Dabei hätte der gleichzeitig einschmeichelnde und kaufmännisch-direkte Stil in der Korrespondenz des Zeitschriftenherausgebers größere Aufmerksamkeit verdient, so etwa der kurze Brief an den Theaterautor Friedrich Wilhelm Gotter (1746-1797), in dem Wieland den Empfänger nicht nur zu einem großen Schriftsteller erklärt und ihn um Beiträge zum *Merkur* bittet, sondern auch zeitlich unter Druck setzt, Themen für Texte unterbreitet und um die Anbahnung eines Kontakts zu Gottfried August Bürger in Göttingen bittet.[6] Wie jeder Biograph setzt auch Reemtsma eigene Schwerpunkte, und für die wertneutrale Beschreibung einzelner Werke gibt es das *Handbuch*; aber gerade mit Blick auf die wichtige Rolle, die diese Biographie und Werkschau auf absehbare Zeit spielen wird, ist nicht nur bedeutsam, was Reemtsma rettet, wie etwa das von ihm verteidigte Alterswerk *Aristipp* (ab 1800),[7] sondern auch das, was er der Rettung nicht für wert befindet.

Im Fach und darüber hinaus wird Reemtsmas *Wieland* auf lange Sicht der Standard für eine Annäherung an diesen Autor sein: an sein Leben, an sein Werk und besonders an seinen Sound. Man folgt dieser so fundierten wie engagierten Einladung gerne.

Leibniz Universität Hannover   *Nils Gelker*

III.

BACHLEITNER, NORBERT with Chapters by PÍŠA, PETR / SYROVY, DANIEL / WÖGERBAUER, MICHAEL, *Censorship of Literature in Austria 1751-1848*. Translated by Stephan Stockinger. Leiden / Boston: Brill (2022). 435 pp.

This exemplary study of censorship from the enlightenment period to the bourgeois age is the culmination of twenty years of pioneering research. Over the course of more than two decades, Norbert Bachleitner and his team have completed two major research projects,[1] published numerous articles, and built a fully searchable

---

6 Wieland an Gotter, 29. Januar 1773, in: Wielands Briefwechsel, hg. von Siegfried Scheibe, Hans Werner Seiffert, 20 Bde., Bd. 5, Berlin 1983, S. 68-69.

7 So schon früher: Jan Philipp Reemtsma, Das Buch vom Ich. Christoph Martin Wielands »Aristipp und einige seiner Zeitgenossen«, Zürich 1993.

1 Censorship in Austria (1999-2002); Records of Banned Books in Austria 1780-

database[2] on books, journals, and periodicals that fell victim to Austria's censorship apparatus from its establishment by empress Maria Theresa in 1751 to the March Revolutions of 1848. »The study presented in this book,« Bachleitner explains, »is based primarily on analysis of this database and the extensive archival studies undertaken in the course of its compilation« (xi). *Censorship of Literature in Austria* enriches these studies with insights from the fields of politics, sociology, history and media studies, creating a valuable reference work for diverse students and scholars of Austrian culture.

In a very instructive introduction, Bachleitner explores »old« and »new« (1) notions of censorship, from the Vatican's religiously motivated prohibitions in the early modern period to contemporary approaches that consider censorship as one of many »mechanisms of canon generation« (5). For the project on hand, he opts for a narrow definition of censorship, meaning that his »study deals with formal, institutional censorship authorized by the state and the Catholic Church« (27). Bachleitner's objective is »the reconstruction of the main lines of historical development of censorship institutions and procedures [...] followed by a delineation of the imposed prohibitions of printed works and interventions in plays, along with the motives for these proscriptions« (28). He pursues this goal in two complementary sections, the first detailing a history of censorship in Austria from 1751-1848 and the second providing a rich selection of case studies. In between these two we find a valuable »Look at the Crown Lands« (174). Here, Petr Píša, Michael Wögerbauer and Daniel Syrovy explore the idiosyncrasies of the censorship regime in the Kingdom of Bohemia and in Austria's Italian-speaking territories, respectively.

Bachleitner's history of Austrian censorship itself is divided into two major sections, the first of which considers the extent to which censorship between 1751 and 1791 could be understood as being »in the service of the enlightenment« (29). Bachleitner retraces »the fight for censorial dominance« between Jesuits and »the secular state faction« (39) from which the latter would eventually emerge victorious. His analysis also details how, gradually, »the office of the censor was professionalized« (47), leading, among other developments, to the end of official book burnings. Joseph II paired professionalization with centralization, and as of 1781 »bans could [...] only be declared in Vienna« (50). While Bachleitner concedes that the censorship of obscurantist and superstitious writings could to a certain degree be considered a contribution to the Enlightenment project, he ultimately concludes that the idea »of putative ›freedom of the press‹ under Joseph II frequently asserted in research [...] cannot be upheld« (60). This point is convincingly buttressed by the »Commented Statistics of Prohibition Activity between 1754 and 1791« (63-79) which conclude the chapter and which convey the far-reaching and tireless activities of the office of the censor.

The second historical chapter is dedicated to the years 1792-1848 and focuses on »Censorship as an Instrument of Repression« (80). At the turn of the century, Bachleitner observes a »transition phase between the instructionally oriented and

1848 (2010-2012). Both projects were funded by the Austrian Science Fund (Fonds zur Förderung der wissenschaftlichen Forschung).

2 Verdrängt, verpönt – vergessen? Eine Datenbank zur Erfassung der in Österreich zwischen 1750 und 1848 verbotenen Bücher, zensur.univie.ac.at/.

Enlightenment-focused censorship regime to the strictly prohibitive system instituted by Emperor Francis II in the post-revolutionary era« (80). This period witnessed the introduction of the regularly maintained, but rarely published, »lists of forbidden books« (83), as well as the practice of providing exceptions (*Scheden*) for reliable citizens, highlighting the role class played in these deliberations: »[I]t is clear that it was mostly members of higher societal strata, and occasionally middle-class individuals considered reliable, who received Scheden« (121). In other words, censorship became a tool to control the flow of socially and politically subversive ideas to the reading masses. At the same time, however, Bachleitner's study highlights the difficulty of prosecuting offences against the state's censorship laws. While, on the one hand, the law did not provide immediate access to private libraries, »the artifice and tricks employed by the booksellers,« on the other hand, led to a »difficulty of convicting booksellers of possession of or trade in prohibited books« (126). Nevertheless, the state continued its zealous crusade against heretic and liberal writings, documented once again in Bachleitner's excellent »Commented Statistics of Prohibition Activities« (136-173).

The subsequent chapters on the implementation of the Austrian censorship regime in Bohemia and Northern Italy explore the limits of imperial integration. First in the Kingdom of Bohemia and then in Veneto and Lombardy, Vienna sought »restriction of the regional autonomy regarding censorship on the one hand and professionalization of censorship, meaning its disentanglement from literary and intellectual life, on the other« (184). However, achieving these goals proved significantly more challenging further away from the imperial centre, due to the limited availability of qualified personnel and the lack of speedy communication channels. In Lombardy, for instance, »the transfer of censorial competence from religious to state institutions [...] was complicated in particular by the fact that clerics were often installed as censors in provincial towns (every town with a printer needed a censor)« (201). This »problematic interweaving of competencies, presumably also in connection with the slow mail service, repeatedly led to complaints regarding long processing times for censorship in the Italian provinces« (218).

An enlightening interlude on »The Censorship of Theater« in the Habsburg Empire discusses the establishment of »a theater censorship office independent of the book censorship authority« (223) in 1770 and the authority's »strategy of providing the populace with panem et circenses, tolerating public amusement as long as it avoided political issues« (229). This is followed by the second major section of *Censorship of Literature in Austria*: A remarkable collection of insightful case studies exploring the prohibition of popular journals and the writings of some of the era's most influential authors, from Gotthold Ephraim Lessing to Honoré de Balzac. In illuminating vignettes, Bachleitner details the lengths Austrian censors went to in order to keep famous texts on the market while ensuring that they would not incite political or social unrest. More often than not, this meant removing precisely those elements that were the foundation for the respective writer's popularity. From the historical novels of Walter Scott, for example, the censors purged the mediating glance at the politics and ideals of the warring parties: »Where Scott kept the plot alive and moving by way of conflicting ideas and principles, the expurgated Austrian edition supplanted the ebb and flow of unfolding events with the changelessness of the time-transcending ideals of monarchy and state religion« (318). In this manner, Bachleitner's vignettes provide a fascinating glimpse into the convictions of the censorship regime regarding art and politics.

Overall, *Censorship of Literature in Austria* is an achievement that deserves the title of *Lebenswerk* on the basis of both its thematic scope and its strong foundation in archival research spanning two decades. It is accessible for a general audience and will, at the same time, provide valuable insights to scholars and students alike. Researchers in the field will particularly appreciate the volume's remarkable appendix. In addition to an extensive bibliography, it offers an excellent selection of censorship records, regulations, guidelines and reports as well as three very useful indices for named persons, publishers and booksellers, and periodicals. Finally, Norbert Bachleitner is to be commended for enabling open access to this *magnum opus*. In a time when early career scholars still feel the pressure to place their publications into physical libraries or behind paywalls, it is empowering to see one of the leading figures in our field blaze a trail into the creative commons.

The University of British Columbia *Florian Gassner*

ERB, ANDREAS, *Die Deutschen Gesellschaften des 18. Jahrhunderts. Ein Gruppenbild*. Berlin / Boston: De Gruyter (2023) (= Hallesche Beiträge zur Europäischen Aufklärung, Bd. 69). xii + 687 S.

Die Deutschen Gesellschaften des achtzehnten Jahrhunderts werden meist wie selbstverständlich dem Kanon der Aufklärungsgesellschaften zugerechnet. Als solchen werden ihnen ausgesprochen moderne und demokratische Züge attestiert, die sie von ihrer ständischen Umwelt unterschieden. Indes hat Monika Neugebauer-Wölk bereits 1998 angemahnt, »[m]an sollte sich [...] in der Sozietätenforschung vor Sozialromantik hüten«.[1] So wichtig ist dieses Diktum für Andreas Erb, dass er es zweimal kurz hintereinander zitiert (529 Anm. 5; 536 Anm. 29). Statt die von ihm untersuchten Sozietäten aus der Sicht der bürgerlichen Moderne zu interpretieren, versteht er sie dezidiert als in der vormodernen Ständegesellschaft verwurzelte Gruppenbildungen. Vor diesem Hintergrund war, so Erbs Kernthese, die Beschäftigung mit der deutschen Sprache, die für die Deutschen Gesellschaften vordergründig konstitutiv war, »kein Selbstzweck, sondern Teil einer umfassenden Reform des Gelehrtenstandes« (122).

Diese These wird systematisch in sieben Kapiteln entwickelt, wobei bereits die Überschriften – ausnahmslos substantivierte Infinitive – auf den methodologischen Unterbau der Studie verweisen: Pierre Bourdieus Theorie »über die ›feinen Unterschiede‹ sowie seine ›Theorie der Praxis‹« (11). Damit greift Erb praxeologische Ansätze in der Frühneuzeitforschung auf, verbindet sie aber mit einem Methodenpluralismus, der hermeneutische Textarbeit und quantitative Strukturanalysen gleichermaßen umfasst. Mit ihrer Hilfe wird eine immense Datenbasis zu 38 Deutschen Gesellschaften, 2.821 Mitgliedern, 3.319 Mitgliedschaften und 4.753 Texten durchdrungen.

[1] Monika Neugebauer-Wölk, Literaturbericht: Absolutismus und Aufklärung. Teil III, in: Geschichte in Wissenschaft und Unterricht 49/11 (1998), S. 709-717, hier S. 712.

Den Rahmen bilden das erste und das letzte Hauptkapitel »Beginnen« (35-102) und »Enden« (512-526). Schlüssig werden die Ideen von Christian Thomasius, Johann Christoph Gottsched und Christian Wolff zur Förderung des Deutschen als Wissenschafts- und Literatursprache als Grundlage einer kohärenten, aber offenen Programmatik herausgearbeitet, die nicht so sehr »auf das Denken, sondern auf das Handeln der Mitglieder« (58) abzielte. Anschaulich wird das Hervorwachsen der Deutschen Gesellschaften aus der sprachreformerischen und universitär-gelehrten Sozietätsbewegung des siebzehnten und frühen achtzehnten Jahrhunderts sowie ihr Scheitern, Ende und Aufgehen in den Altertumsvereinen des neunzehnten Jahrhunderts dargestellt. Insgesamt konzentrierten sich die Deutschen Gesellschaften auf Universitäten und Gymnasien im protestantischen deutschen Sprachraum, während sie im katholischen Raum erst später und hier meist im Zusammenhang mit den Höfen, etwa in Wien und Mannheim, gegründet wurden. Hieran zeigt sich, »dass diese Sozietätsbewegung als genuin gelehrte Bewegung ins Leben trat und es weitgehend blieb« (102).

Die Orientierung am Gelehrtenstand lässt sich auch im Kapitel »Regeln« (103-161) nachvollziehen, in dem Erb die Satzungen der Gesellschaften mit ihrer konkreten Umsetzung konfrontiert. Als zentrales Motiv und Endziel der Sozietätsregeln postuliert er den »erneuerte[n] Gelehrten als ideales Mitglied« (122), den fernab gelehrter Pedanterie »[s]prachliche Reinheit, freundschaftliche Umgangsformen, Tugend, Weltgewandtheit« (137) auszeichneten und der für Staat und Gesellschaft nützlich war.

Inwieweit die Mitglieder diesem Ideal entsprachen, beleuchtet das folgende Kapitel »Beitreten« (162-293). Ausgehend von Bourdieus Kapitaltheorie werden die Motive für einen Eintritt bzw. die Aufnahme neuer Mitglieder diskutiert. Welches soziale, ökonomische, symbolische oder kulturelle Kapital erhofften sich die Akteure jeweils? Welche Personengruppen profitierten von einer Mitgliedschaft? Nach Erb waren es vor allem angehende protestantische Geistliche, Lehrer und Juristen, also Studenten, die für eine erfolgreiche Karriere über rhetorische Fähigkeiten verfügen mussten. Dennoch weist das soziale Spektrum der Mitglieder eine große Bandbreite auf: Nicht wenige Adlige beteiligten sich aktiv am Gesellschaftsleben, dazu etliche Katholiken und einige Frauen. Aber auch hier wird vor Sozialromantik gewarnt: »Als Vorkämpfer der Frauenemanzipation im heutigen Sinne sind die Deutschen Gesellschaften [...] schwerlich zu bezeichnen« (293).

Von den Mitgliedern geht es zum »Arbeiten« (294-391). Minutiös werden die finanziellen und materiellen Rahmenbedingungen, die meist eher mageren Etats und die zum Teil bis über 1.000 Bände umfassenden Bibliotheken thematisiert. Hiermit erweisen sich die Deutschen Gesellschaften wiederum als typisch für die gelehrte Sozietätsbewegung. Dem entsprach auch der meist wöchentliche Sitzungsturnus, in dem Texte vorgetragen und diskutiert wurden. Diese waren mehrheitlich in Prosa gehalten, umfassten aber auch viel Poesie, hauptsächlich Gelegenheitsgedichte. Übersetzungen aus dem Lateinischen, Französischen und anderen Sprachen dominierten die Textproduktion zwar nicht, waren aber durchgängig präsent. Sie dienten nicht zuletzt der Spracharbeit, wiewohl Erb das Vordringen der deutschen Wissenschaftssprache im achtzehnten Jahrhundert abwägend »sowohl als Ursache als auch als Folge« (347) für die Entwicklung der Deutschen Gesellschaften einschätzt. In einer Art Rückkopplungsschleife hätten sie einen Trend aufgegriffen und ihn durch ihre Beschäftigung mit deutscher Sprache und Literatur, oft verbunden mit Fragen der Religion, Ethik und Gemeinwohlorientierung, verstärkt. Dennoch spiegelten die Deutschen Gesellschaften kaum »Gottscheds Ideal einer Art Sprach- und Dichtungsakademie, sondern die Realität einer Übungsgesellschaft« (369) wider.

Unter dem Stichwort »Folgen« (392-436) werden Fäden aus dem ersten Kapitel wieder aufgegriffen. Ging es in »Beginnen« darum, aus der Sicht des heutigen Historikers die Ursprünge und Anfänge der Deutschen Gesellschaften zu rekonstruieren, liegt der Fokus nun darauf, wie sie sich selbst im Sinne einer »invention of tradition« (392) positionierten. Diskutiert wird, auf welche Weise Vorbilder wie die Fruchtbringende Gesellschaft, Leibniz' Sozietätsentwürfe oder das »Leitbild Leipzig« (400) – von Erb bewusst mit einem Fragezeichen versehen – evoziert, modifiziert und zurückgewiesen wurden. Dieser Diskurs entfaltete sich nicht zuletzt in einem intersozietären Netzwerk, das durch 387 Personen zusammengehalten wurde, die mehr als einer Deutschen Gesellschaft angehörten. Allerdings partizipierten hieran nicht alle Gesellschaften gleichermaßen. Zentral waren die großen Sozietäten in Jena, Göttingen, Helmstedt und Königsberg, während Leipzig nach dem Austritt Gottscheds 1738 eine relativ untergeordnete Rolle im Netzwerk spielte. Allerdings bleibt Erb nicht bei der Quantifizierung und Visualisierung der Mitgliederüberschneidungen stehen, sondern versucht, sie quellengestützt weiter zu qualifizieren. Auf diese Weise gelingt es ihm, enge Verbindungen und Kooperationen etwa zwischen den Gesellschaften in Göttingen, Helmstedt und Bremen oder Bern und Zürich zu rekonstruieren. Gewinnbringend wird hier Netzwerkanalyse mit hermeneutischer Quellenarbeit verbunden.

Um Netzwerke anderer Art geht es im Kapitel »Ehren« (437-511), nämlich um die Verflechtungen mit der ständischen, höfischen und gelehrten Umwelt. Sie bestimmten wesentlich das Ansehen der Deutschen Gesellschaften und damit letztlich ihren Erfolg oder Misserfolg. Über Privilegien und Patronagenetzwerke, durch Dichter- und Dichterinnenkrönungen sowie öffentliche Festsitzungen versuchten sie ihren Anspruch auf gesellschaftliche Relevanz zu untermauern. Dass es hierbei zu Konflikten mit den Obrigkeiten und insbesondere den Universitäten, in deren Schoß die meisten Deutschen Gesellschaften entstanden waren, kam, verwundert nicht. Nichtsdestotrotz war das Verhältnis von Sozietäten und Universitäten in der Regel wohl weniger von Konkurrenz als von Kooperation und Komplementarität geprägt. Je mehr sich aber das ästhetische Verständnis von Dichtung im Lauf des achtzehnten Jahrhundert wandelte, desto häufiger wurden die »literarischen Fingerübungen« (511) mit Spott überzogen. So waren sie etwa »auch in das Verdikt eingeschlossen, das Lessings 17. Literaturbrief 1759 über Gottsched fällte« (26).

Dieser Spott verstellte lange den Blick auf die Deutschen Gesellschaften, so dass man meinte, »vor einem gescheiterten Projekt zu stehen« (539). Demgegenüber kommt Erb zu einem ausgewogenen Urteil. Die Diskrepanz zwischen den hochgesteckten Ansprüchen und dem tatsächlich Geleisteten leugnet er nicht, kann aber eindrücklich zeigen, dass die Deutschen Gesellschaften eine Breitenwirkung entfalteten, die ihrem Ziel, den Gelehrtenstand im Medium deutscher Sprache und Literatur zu reformieren, entsprach. In diesem Sinne können sie den Aufklärungsgesellschaften zugerechnet werden, wiewohl ihre Geschichte zeigt, »dass viele Kriterien für die Einstufung einer Gesellschaft oder einer Sozietätsbewegung als aufgeklärte Gesellschaft einer Revision bedürfen« (537). Dem ist unbedingt zuzustimmen, und der

Autor öffnet viele Perspektiven für die weitere Forschung. Nicht nur stellt er mit den Tabellen und Diagrammen, die er aus einer Vielzahl von Quellen herausdestilliert hat, eine Vergleichsbasis für Arbeiten zu anderen Sozietätstypen zur Verfügung. Die Einzelbefunde sowie die handbuchartigen Artikel zu den verschiedenen Deutschen Gesellschaften im Anhang (541-604) bieten auch einen Anknüpfungspunkt für Detailstudien. In diesem Sinne wäre zu wünschen, dass neben dem Buch zeitnah auch die ihm zu Grunde liegenden Forschungsdaten frei nachnutzbar publiziert werden.

Alles in allem ist Andreas Erb in der Tat ein »möglichst dichtes Bild dieser Sozietätsbewegung« (13) gelungen, das sowohl in seiner Gesamtheit als auch im Detail überzeugt. Für die Aufklärungs- und Sozietätsforschung handelt es sich hier um ein wichtiges Referenzwerk für zukünftige Studien.

Herzog August Bibliothek Wolfenbüttel   *Maximilian Görmar*

GRUBNER, BERNADETTE / WITTEMANN, PETER (Hg.), *Aufklärung und Exzess. Epistemologie und Ästhetik des Übermäßigen im 18. Jahrhundert.* Berlin / Boston: de Gruyter (2022) (= Luxus und Moderne, Bd. 2). 292 S.

Die entscheidende Wendung, die Gotthold Ephraim Lessing in der Geschichte des Faust-Stoffs herbeiführte, bestand in seiner fundamentalen Umdeutung der *curiositas*, die er nicht als negativen Fürwitz begriff, sondern zur positiven Wissbegierde aufwertete. Nicht die (natur-)wissenschaftliche Neugier an sich ist das Problem wie in der *Historia von D. Johann Fausten* (1587), sondern ein mögliches ›Zuviel‹, das im Sinne der *Nikomachischen Ethik* des Aristoteles die Normativität des Maßes missachtet und damit das Gute und Richtige als Mitte zwischen den Extremen verfehlt. Die aristotelische *Mesotes*-Lehre situiert die Tugend zwischen den beiden einander entgegengesetzten Lastern des Übermaßes und des Mangels. Maßlosigkeit führt (nicht nur) in Lessings Werken zu schuldhaften Verfehlungen mit oftmals tragischem Ausgang. Die aufklärerische und aufgeklärte Ethik des Maßhaltens bildet auch den gedanklichen Ausgangspunkt des von Bernadette Grubner und Peter Wittemann herausgegebenen literaturwissenschaftlichen Tagungsbandes, der sich epistemologischen Auseinandersetzungen und ästhetischen Ausformungen des Übermäßigen und Exzessiven im achtzehnten Jahrhundert widmet. Der Band versammelt dreizehn Aufsätze, die vier thematischen, sich teilweise auch überschneidenden Schwerpunkten zugeordnet sind. Behandelt werden anthropologische Aspekte, insbesondere solche der Diätetik, die Produktivität des Exzesses, philosophische Perspektiven sowie das Übermäßige als »ein ästhetisches Faszinosum« (10), das sich in entsprechenden poetischen Ausprägungen und poetologischen Vorstellungen niederschlug.

Im ersten, der Anthropologie des ›ganzen Menschen‹ gewidmeten Abschnitt beleuchtet Carsten Zelle, wie die Interdependenz des aufklärerischen Selbstdenker- und diätetischen Selbstsorgediskurses noch im neunzehnten Jahrhundert auf die durch »Mäßigung, Dämpfung und Begrenzung« (26) geprägte Lebensordnung ausstrahlte, die Goethes in seinen *Wilhelm Meisters Wanderjahren* integrierte Erzählung *Der Mann von fünfzig Jahren* entwirft. Die bürgerliche Tugend des Maßhaltens propagierten moralische Wochenschriften des achtzehnten Jahrhunderts auch bei der Frage einer angemessenen Hundehaltung, mit der sich Raphael J. Müller auseinandersetzt. Während in galanten Gedichten um 1700 eine verzärtelnde bis erotisierende weibliche Liebe zum Hund noch »scherzhaft verspottet, nicht aber moralisch problematisiert« (58) wurde, warnten moralische Wochenschriften vor einer übermäßigen Hingabe ebenso wie vor Tierquälerei. Die satirisch-kritische Spiegelung ungezügelter emotionaler, zeitlicher und finanzieller Zuwendungen für Schoßhunde diente »als implizites Gegenmodell zu den exzessiven Praktiken des Adels« (44), die bürgerlichen Nützlichkeitsvorstellungen widersprachen. Gegen Grundprinzipien eines bürgerlichen Wertesystems verstieß auch die Trunksucht, die, wie Peter Wittemann verdeutlicht, im Laufe des achtzehnten Jahrhunderts nicht in erster Linie als Sünde, sondern als Krankheit angesehen wurde. Die verstärkte Hinwendung zur Anthropologie führte auch dazu, dass Kategorien wie Maß und Maßlosigkeit gegen Ende des achtzehnten Jahrhunderts biopolitisch akzentuiert wurden.

Beispiele für die Produktivität des Exzesses präsentieren die Aufsätze des zweiten Abschnitts. Selbst in der scherzhaften anakreontischen Lyrik finden sich, wie Martin Bäumel demonstriert, zeitbedingte Beispiele für Überschreitungen, etwa hervorgerufen durch kriegerische Gewalterfahrungen, denen »die Idee einer idyllischen Soziabilität« (132) überhaupt erst entsprang. Exzessive Sinnlichkeit konnte auch aus asketischer Praxis hervorgehen, wie Niklaus Largier anschaulich verdeutlicht. Als Beitrag zu einer radikalen Aufklärung versteht Alice Stašková Marquis de Sades Schrift *La Philosophie dans le boudoir ou Les instituteurs immoraux* (1795), die »Aufklärung und Exzess in ihrem wechselseitigen Verhältnis« (101) exponiert. Wenn »Exzesse nachträglich als heuristische Impulse zu einer Aufklärung über die wahre Ordnung fungieren« (113), werden sie selbst naturkonform und stellen bestehende Sittengesetze in Frage.

Philosophische Herausforderungen durch derartige Provokationen des Exzessiven behandeln die Beiträge des dritten Abschnitts. Dass Luxus die Sitten vermeintlich verfeinern, tatsächlich aber so verderben würde, dass sie jeden Bezug zur Natürlichkeit verlören, monierte Jean-Jacques Rousseau. Als Mittel sozialer Distinktion verstand er Luxus in erster Linie relational, wie Ruth Signer, an Pierre Bourdieus Habitus-Konzept anknüpfend, betont. Folgerichtig kritisierte Rousseau den aufklärerischen »Imperativ zur Maßhaltung« (184) selbst als maßlos, blendet dieser Anspruch doch die gesellschaftlichen Bedingungen von Luxus und seiner ungleichen Verteilung aus. Eine instruktive Vorgeschichte des Exzesses im achtzehnten Jahrhundert beleuchtet Johanna Schumm, indem sie den ausschweifenden spanisch-barocken Witz Baltasar Graciáns und seine ambivalente Rezeption mit »Descartes' Krönung der *raison*« (143) und »dem Maßhalten des französischen Klassizismus« (144) erhellend konfrontiert. Debatten dieser Art fügten sich in die grundsätzliche rationalistische Kritik an barockem Schwulst ein und profilierten rhetorische und poetische Leitprinzipien wie Klarheit und Deutlichkeit. Wenn Gottsched über das besondere Vermögen des Dichters zum Witz und dessen Nähe zur Fülle räsonierte, unterließ er es nicht, vor Gefahren des ›Zuviel‹ zu warnen. Sebastian Schönbeck zeigt, dass sich gegen stilistische Ausschweifungen (*excès*) und für das rhetorische und poetische *aptum*-Ideal etwa auch Georges-Louis Leclerc de Buffon in seiner *Histoire naturelle* aussprach. Als »Entgrenzung des Subjekts in der Gotteserfahrung« (203) beschreibt Bernadette Grubner das Genießen im Pantheismusstreit. Über allen Begriffen steht dieses Genießen deswegen, weil hier die Sprache »erlaubt zu *sagen*, was sich nicht *denken* lässt«: »Ex-zessiv« (214) im eigentlichen Sinn sei daher die Sprache selbst.

Die im vierten Abschnitt versammelten Aufsätze zur Poetik und Poetologie reflektieren das Übermaß beim Schreiben. Dem standen Stilideale wie *claritas* oder *perspicuitas*, mit denen die dichterische Sprache im achtzehnten Jahrhundert von allzu üppig ausgestaltetem barocken Zierrat befreit und gereinigt werden sollte, diametral entgegen. Gleichwohl wies Gottsched in seiner *Critischen Dichtkunst* »Verfahren der *amplificatio*« (222) nicht grundsätzlich zurück, sondern rang um das rechte Maß, wie Sebastian Meixner differenziert herausarbeitet. Der gute Geschmack sollte die Dichtung regulieren und »dabei den Überfluss begrenzen: das Zuviel an Details, das Zuviel an Wundern und das Zuviel an Unvernünftigem« (238). Auch die französische Klassik beschränkte sich keineswegs auf Regelhaftigkeit und Affektdämpfung. Roman Kuhn lotet vielmehr Positionen und insbesondere Verschiebungen zwischen Maß und Exzess aus und bestimmt dabei Luxus als eine auch dichtungstheoretische Kategorie bei Voltaire. Um nicht zum leeren Exzess zu verkommen, müssten Luxus und Dichtung indes auf die Einhaltung von Regeln verpflichtet und damit beschränkt werden. Luxus und Dichtung sind daher gleichermaßen »Überschuss in der Beschränkung« (265). Dynamiken des Überflusses prägen nicht zuletzt Shakespeares Dramen sowie deren deutsche Rezeption, der sich Claudia Olk widmet. Das »Exzessive, Verschwenderische und Überbordende« (276) der Werke Shakespeares wirkten freilich zuallererst verstörend und wurden dahingehend umgedeutet, dass ›Natur‹ als ästhetische Kategorie im letzten Drittel des achtzehnten Jahrhunderts auf deutschen Bühnen schauspieltechnisch neu definiert und wiederentdeckt wurde (284).

Resümierend betrachtet, loten die instruktiven Beiträge des Bandes die diskursiven Spannungen und dialektischen Verschränkungen des Oppositionsverhältnisses von Maß und Maßlosigkeit in Literatur und Philosophie des achtzehnten Jahrhunderts facetten- und perspektivenreich aus. Dass das Exzessive in aller Regel literarisch reizvoller als das Maßvolle war und ist und entsprechend plastisch ausgestaltet wurde, forderte den Normativitätsdiskurs der Aufklärung produktiv heraus. Auf die Kunstproduktion selbst bezogen, berühren die Aufsätze immer wieder auch Fragen einer Ethik der Ästhetik, die nicht nur, aber auch für das achtzehnte Jahrhundert eine weitergehende Betrachtung verdienen.

Albert-Ludwigs-Universität Freiburg *Peter Philipp Riedl*

SCHEIN, XENIA, *Die Öffentlichkeit im Privaten. Identität und Realität im bürgerlichen Drama von Autorinnen des achtzehnten und beginnenden neunzehnten Jahrhunderts*. Hannover: Wehrhahn (2023). 271 S.

Im späten achtzehnten Jahrhundert galt das Drama zunehmend als privilegierte Gattung, die nur von (vorwiegend männlichen) Genies produziert werden konnte. Dies führte dazu, dass sich die Literaturproduktion einiger Autorinnen auf andere Gattungen (Gedicht, Autobiografie, Briefroman) beschränkte, auch wenn sie als Schauspielerinnen oder Prinzipalinnen im Theater aktiv waren. Trotzdem kann man von einer kurzen »Konjunktur« (23) weiblicher Dramenproduktion zwischen 1770 und 1820 sprechen. Dieses von Anne Fleig aufgedeckte Aufblühen weiblicher Dramenproduktion steht im Fokus von Xenia Scheins Monografie, die aus ihrer 2022 in Saarbrücken eingereichten Dissertation hervorgegangen ist. Im Unterschied zu der früheren feministischen Literaturwissenschaft, in der oft von alternativen Genealogien weiblichen Schreibens oder gar von *écriture féminine* die Rede war, zielen Scheins Dramenanalysen auf die Aufdeckung von »Elementen des Realen« (230) in den Texten ab. Wie in der Einleitung angekündigt, betrachtet die Studie Werke von Frauen nicht isoliert, sondern im Rahmen eines literarischen Netzwerks, an dem auch Männer beteiligt waren. Nur so sei es möglich, die »Erfahrungshorizonte« schreibender Frauen in Texten zu beleuchten, die im Kontrast zu den gängigen Stereotypen und Diskursen der dramatischen Literatur stehen.

Analysiert werden Werke zwischen 1770 und 1820 von relativ prominenten Autorinnen, wie der Schauspielerin Friederike Sophie Hensel, der Dichterin Sophie Albrecht und Gellerts Briefkorrespondentin Christiane Karoline Schlegel, und von weniger bekannten Autorinnen, wie Viktorie von Rupp, Susanne von Bandemer, Johanna von Bültzingslöwen und Wilhelmine von Gersdorf. Leider bleiben Scheins Auswahlkriterien intransparent. So findet z. B. *Leichtsinn und gutes Herz oder die Folgen der Erziehung* (1786) von der zu Lebzeiten bekannten Schriftstellerin und Publizistin Marianne Ehrmann keine Erwähnung, und andere interessante Stücke, wie etwa Maria Antonia Teutschers *Fanny, oder die glückliche Wiedervereinigung* (1773), werden erst in einem der letzten Kapitel (»Ökonomie und Macht«) ausführlicher diskutiert.

Da sich die analysierten Dramen im Spektrum von »Mischgattung[en]« (71) der Empfindsamkeit (rührendes Lustspiel, bürgerliches Trauerspiel) bewegen, steht das emotionale Leben der bürgerlichen Familie, die mit verschiedenen inneren und äußeren Konflikten zu kämpfen hat, im Mittelpunkt. Schein demonstriert, dass die meisten Texte trotz ihrer Traditionsgebundenheit in vielen Punkten von den männlich bestimmten Genres und Figurentypen des achtzehnten Jahrhunderts abweichen. Durch Neukonfigurationen gängiger Muster, wie etwa das auch von Anne Fleig kommentierte »Tugend-Laster-Schema« (14) des bürgerlichen Trauerspiels, wird der »Erfahrungshorizont« (16) der Autorinnen zunehmend sichtbar. In fast allen analysierten Stücken lassen sich, so Schein, emanzipatorische Momente finden, auch wenn es sich nur um die Kritik an der Aussichtslosigkeit der weiblichen Hauptfiguren handelt.

In *Die Familie auf dem Lande* lässt Hensel z. B. die Aporien des bürgerlichen Trauerspiels von einer autoritären Mutter verkörpern, die im Nebentitel und von den anderen Figuren des Stückes als »zärtlich« (58) charakterisiert wird; dadurch werde der Machtmissbrauch »nicht einem Geschlecht zugeordnet, sondern einer Struktur« (247). Ähnlich unbequem ist die Darstellung der Familie in Viktoria von Rupps »rührendem Lustspiel« *Marianne, oder der Sieg der Tugend* (1777), in dem die neue Familienkonstellation im scheinbaren *Happy End* nur durch die Aufopferung der eigentlichen Liebesbeziehung ermöglicht wird. In manchen Fällen verstoßen die Stücke auch gegen gesellschaftliche Tabus, so etwa in Christiane von Schlegels *Düval und Charmille* (1778), in dem eine *menage à trois* dargestellt wird.

Trotz solcher offenkundigen Abweichungen von normativen Frauen- und Familienbildern stößt man in den analysierten Dramen kaum auf Figuren, die bewusst Widerstand gegen das System leisten. Zu den wenigen Ausnahmen gehört die Titelfigur in Sophie Albrechts *Theresgen* (1781), deren (eher passiver) »Widerstand« (125) gegen ihre ausweglose Situation in ihrem Freitod gipfelt. In Susanne von Bandemers *Sidney und Eduard* (1792) leistet die weibliche Protagonistin Widerstand gegen die

Ungerechtigkeit ihres autoritären Vaters und zeigt damit emanzipatorisches Potenzial, auch wenn ihre Subjektivität am Schluss des Stückes in die Opferbereitschaft für ihren Mann aufgeht. Darüber hinaus werden in Bandemers Stück auch Armut und weibliche Berufstätigkeit dargestellt, Themen also, die für das bürgerliche Drama des achtzehnten Jahrhunderts untypisch sind. Finanzielles Prekariat ist auch Thema in Johanna von Bültzingslöwens *Die Vergeltung* (1820), in der eine tugendhafte Frau von ihrem adeligen Mann verlassen wird und verzweifelt versucht, durch Handarbeiten die Familie über Wasser zu halten. Mit solchen Beispielen unterstützt Schein ihre These vom emanzipatorischen Potenzial der Dramen von Frauen um 1800. Als »Kontrapunkt« (182) diskutiert sie Wilhelmine von Gersdorffs *Die Zwillingsschwester* (1797), denn hier wird der weibliche Gehorsam gegenüber dem Onkel am Schluss des Stückes belohnt, wobei auch in diesem Fall Alternativen aufgezeigt werden, wie etwa die finanzielle Unabhängigkeit durch den Beruf der Erzieherin und die Scheidung, die als moralisch nachvollziehbare Reaktion auf einen Ehebruch dargestellt wird.

Die überzeugenden Einzelanalysen entfalten einen klaren Blick auf den sozial- und kulturhistorischen Hintergrund der Dramen, wobei die Fokussierung auf Themen und Topoi der bürgerlichen Dramen von Lessing und Schiller inhaltlich begründet sind. Zeitgenössische Dramentexte männlicher Autoren, die sich nicht an der Mitleidsästhetik, sondern eher am sozialen Realismus orientieren und den Missbrauch junger Frauen darstellen (J. M. R. Lenz' *Die Soldaten* und H. L. Wagners *Die Kindermörderin*) werden zwar erwähnt, aber nicht weiter mit Blick auf mögliche dramentheoretische und inhaltliche Resonanzen in Texten von Frauen untersucht.

In den Schlusskapiteln werden die Einzelanalysen durch die Erörterung gemeinsamer Topoi und Themen erweitert. Als gemeinsames Hauptthema erscheint dabei u. a. das Verhältnis von Ökonomie und Macht, das oft »recht pragmatisch« (200) behandelt wird; hierin sieht Schein einen Unterschied zum bürgerlichen Trauerspiel, in dem solche Fragen oft in moralischem Licht erscheinen. Auch die Rechtsprechung ist ein zentrales Thema, z. B. in Bandemers *Sidney und Eduard*, in dem eine der Hauptfiguren ein Londoner Friedensrichter ist. In solchen Dramen, die in einer Zeit geschrieben wurden, in der »die richterliche Unabhängigkeit in Deutschland noch kein Thema war« (211), wird der Ausgang eines Prozesses oft durch soziale, ökonomische, und politische Faktoren bestimmt. Auch bei der Darstellung von Wahnsinn wird eine Gender-Trennung sichtbar, wie etwa in Christine Schlegels *Düval und Charmille*, in dem der sogenannte Wahnsinn im Einklang mit damaligen Genderdiskursen »als Etikett für die Diskriminierung weiblichen Eigensinns« (226) dient. Im letzten Kapitel (»Brüche im System«) weist Schein erneut auf die Abweichung der Dramen von den Tugend- und Liebesidealen des bürgerlichen Trauerspiels hin und betont in Anlehnung an Virginia Woolfs *A Room of One's Own* das literaturwissenschaftliche »Potenzial, welches nur zur Entfaltung kommen kann, wenn vergessene Stücke wieder gelesen werden« (250-251). Auch wenn diese Stücke stereotype Figuren und Handlungen enthalten, entlarven sie »Brüche« (227) im bürgerlich-patriarchalischen Diskurs und Aporien der Privatsphäre als »Rückzugsraum« (244).

In fast jedem Kapitel werden Beispiele für »Bescheidenheitsgesten« (48) zitiert, mit denen sich Autorinnen für ihre schriftstellerische Tätigkeit entschuldigen und ihre intellektuellen Ambitionen in Abrede stellen. Solche Apologien waren der Preis für den Zutritt von Frauen zur Öffentlichkeit im achtzehnten Jahrhundert, der von

Wendy Arons als »impossible act« gekennzeichnet wurde.[1] Leider findet Arons' hervorragende Studie über weibliches Schreiben und den Authenzitätsdiskurs im achtzehnten Jahrhundert ebenso wenig Erwähnung wie andere internationale Beiträge zur Forschung. Wünschenswert wäre auch ein tieferer Blick in die Biografien der Autorinnen gewesen, die nur flüchtig am Anfang der Kapitel angesprochen werden. In der Diskussion von *Theresgen* fehlt zum Beispiel der Blick auf Albrechts Gesamtwerk und ihre literarische Selbstdarstellung, die Einfluss auf ihr Drama hatte.

Andererseits sind Auslassungen dieser Art in einer so vielseitigen Studie unumgänglich, nicht zuletzt wegen des immer noch lückenhaften Forschungsstandes. Insgesamt ist Scheins Buch ein Gewinn für die Forschung, denn die sorgfältigen Textinterpretationen geben einen guten Einblick sowohl in die historischen Entstehungsbedingungen der Dramen als auch in die komplexe Positionierung der Autorinnen in Diskursen von Geschlecht, Genre, Familie und Identität. Hervorzuheben ist auch die intensive Auseinandersetzung mit der feministischen Literaturwissenschaft zu Autorinnen des achtzehnten Jahrhunderts, wobei einmal mehr deutlich wird, wie marginalisert dieser Bereich noch immer ist. So stellt diese Monografie eine große Bereicherung dar, die in der transatlantischen Germanistik hoffentlich Anklang finden wird.

Georgetown University, Washington, D. C.   *Mary Helen Dupree*

SCHLIPPHACKE, HEIDI, *The Aesthetics of Kinship: Form and Family in the Long Eighteenth Century*. Lewisburg, PA: Bucknell University Press (2023) (New Studies in the Age of Goethe). 335 pp.

In the *Aesthetics of Kinship*, Heidi Schlipphacke offers an incisive rethinking of a widely naturalized construction of the bourgeois nuclear family and its representation in the long eighteenth century. With readings informed by an impressive range of theoretical and historical contexts, Schlipphacke challenges conventional literary practices that engage aesthetics, questions of form, social formations, and Marxist philosophy, by shifting the perspective away from presumed alignments between interiority and individual subjectivities. Schlipphacke draws from English, French, and German literature of the time, written by luminaries and the non-canonical alike, to redirect a critical gaze away from family-centric interiorities and toward relationalities – groupings, assemblages, and tableaux. In so doing, she opens aperçus into alternatives to the heteronormative model of the *Kleinfamilie*, a foundation for theories of the nation and an organizing principle of literary production. This book challenges ideological assumptions about the ways aesthetic value and the modern subject derive from the privileging of depths over surfaces.

Schlipphacke's earlier monograph, *Nostalgia after Nazism: History, Home, and Affect in German and Austrian Literature and Film* (Bucknell University Press, 2010), demonstrates sustained concerns about the interaction between cultural production

1 Vgl. Wendy Arons, The Impossible Act: Performance and Femininity in Eighteenth-Century Women's Writing, Palgrave Studies in Theatre and Performance History, New York 2006.

and socio-political realities; in the former work, these take the form of a longing for home, history, and a persistent need for the recovery of a »nation.« Her work on kinship, though similarly concerned with the political implications of gendered representations of power, revisits the aesthetics of non-normative sociability in the long eighteenth century. While acknowledging the nuclear family as foundational in Western political theory and »the ideal social trope for dialectical thought,« Schlipphacke looks beyond its dominance: »But the allure of recovering a literary picture of kinship that opens up paths for imagining alternative social constellations is similarly powerful, and that is the impetus for this book« (14). *The Aesthetics of Kinship* succeeds in forging a path toward reading forms of interrelation that have been present yet invisible, the view occluded by the portrait of a nuclear bourgeois family.

The elegantly written and expansively researched introduction lays the foundation for this ambitious project. Schlipphacke's approach is informed by careful readings of Marx and Hegel and the patrimony of critical and queer theory that destabilizes notions of gender, power, social class, and political empowerment. Her prose remains accessible as she situates the reader in a complex yet flowing argument about relationality. In particular, Schlipphacke does not limit alternative models to the *tableaux* and *tableaux vivants* that feature so prominently in canonical novels, such as Goethe's *Die Wahlverwandschaften*. Instead, she looks to various constellations in dramatic works that depict a grouping of figures within a kind of syntax of kinship. Examples would be the tableau at the close of Lessing's *Nathan der Weise*, or Goethe's *Stella*, or the moment Werther first glimpses Lotte in *Die Leiden des jungen Werthers*. Schlipphacke differentiates between non-imaginative and literary works in illuminating ways: »Kant, Hippel, and Hegel can write about the ideal case of the family in their theoretical and philosophical works, but the literary works of the period present a much more fraught and ultimately more interesting picture of the family via an intermedial aesthetics of kinship« (26).

The first chapter, »Middle Class / Bourgeois / Bürger: The Ideosyncrasies of German Dramatic Realism,« examines the divergence from French and English literature in German-language dramatic *tableaux* that frame not the nuclear family, »but instead heterogeneous social constellations« (29). »*Tableau / Tableau Vivant*: German-French Dramatic Encounters« then takes a closer look at Lessing's reception of Diderot. The third chapter extends the readings to works by Schiller and Goethe. Chapter 4, »Against Interiority,« focuses on letters and portraits as dramatic props in Gellert, Lessing, and Goethe. The integration of historical background on what makes a letter »German« in this epoch (89-95) is especially welcome. This chapter prefaces a sustained reading of »Material Kinship« in Lessing's *Nathan der Weise*. The context she creates around this canonical text of Enlightenment humanism adds yet another dimension to our understanding of its radical potential to enact inclusion. Schlipphacke moves into the tour-de-force, the fifth chapter's complex and fluid analysis of four novels and their »tableau of relations«: Gellert's *Das Leben der schwedischen Gräfin von G****; Sophie von La Roche's *Die Geschichte des Fräuleins von Sternheim*; Goethe's *Die Leiden des jungen Werthers*; and Dorothea Veit-Schlegel's *Florentin*. Schlipphacke carefully curates passages to the foreground so that despite the range, the argument advances persuasively toward a remarkable distilled conclusion: »The liberal use of the tableaux of heterogeneous relations lends a flatness to these works that highlights the experimental, transitory quality of imaginative social formations«

(196). With these six chapters locked down, the next and last turns to »Kinship and Aesthetic Depth: The Tableau Vivant in Goethe's *Wahlverwandtschaften*.« With Walter Benjamin as an interlocutor, Schlipphacke elaborates on the »*tableaux vivant* semiotics« so crucial to the scholarly archive of interpretations. Her reading, however, encompasses the three performances described in the novel, but also Ottilie's displayed corpse at its end. »These scenes,« she writes, »present temporal, material, and social dissonances, reminding us that aesthetic form does not simply reflect social shifts; instead, it complicates ideological smoothness« (230).

The concluding reflections usher the aesthetics of kinship into the present of the writing, concluded during the pandemic that isolated so many and shattered so much. Her book delimits the imagined frames around the portrait of the nuclear family, constructed in no small part by literature and the way we have read it. Instead, *Aesthetics of Kinship* offers us a »what-if« of reading retroactively. Throughout, kinship reimagined remains clear-eyed about the hegemonic forces of power, protected by private spaces, ownership, insulated by class, wealth, and education. It is difficult to project a tidy conservative/progressive model onto the *tableaux* of alternative spaces for non-familial community. *The Aesthetics of Kinship* provides us an opportunity to read backwards differently. Through this lens, imaginative literature becomes a written record of a more inclusive human interrelationality we have forgotten to recognize. Schlipphacke's book pays attention to tensions between political ideologies and materiality, along with representations of materiality in literature; this wide-angle lens additionally allows the »spaces between« seemingly random and otherwise unrelated figures within the frame to become legible as non-normative structures of affiliation and community.

University of Nebraska-Lincoln   *Patricia Anne Simpson*

SCHNEIDER, MARTIN, *Agonalität und Menschenliebe: Gefühlspolitik im Drama des 18. Jahrhunderts*. Paderborn: Brill Fink (2023). xxii + 501 S.

This fascinating study of the emotional politics (*Gefühlspolitik*) of eighteenth-century drama focuses on the intersection of the political and the sentimental in eighty-seven canonical and non-canonical plays, ranging from 1724 to 1804. It is a richly detailed, thorough study of a topic that has been under-researched up until now, as the author demonstrates. Schneider broadens his inquiry to include not only »eine Handvoll herausragender Dramen der Spätaufklärung, die die Forschung bis heute bestimmt« (xvi); instead, he examines a wealth of plays, juxtaposing his readings of classics such as Schiller's *Don Carlos* with readings of non-canonical texts that were, in their time, extraordinarily popular, such as Kotzebue's *Graf Benjowsky oder die Verschwörung auf Kamtschatka* (1795). He also emphasizes the need to study the entire eighteenth century. This broader perspective on Enlightenment theater provides readers with – just to give one example – thorough analyses of the interactions between politics, sentiment, and the public sphere in plays such as J.C. Gottsched's *Parisische Bluthochzeit* (1745) and Schiller's *Fiesko* (1783). In the preliminary methodological section, Schneider states the main thesis of the monograph, which represents the author's *Habilitationsschrift*: »Wie in den Dramentexten des 18. Jahrhunderts Agonalität und Antagonalität durch empfindsame Dispositionen eingehegt werden sollen, diese aber wiederum in das Spannungsfeld des Politischen hineingezogen werden, ist Thema dieser Arbeit« (47).

In part one, »Kontexte,« three chapters focus on Schneider's methodology. Drawing on ancient and modern thinkers from Aristotle to Arendt and Mouffe, Chapter one defines the concept of *Agonalität* and how it structures political communities. Significantly, Schneider emphasizes the non-linear development of eighteenth-century theater, whereby earlier subgenres persist alongside innovations like the sentimental comedy and the domestic tragedy. Chapters two and three delineate Schneider's concept of sentimental emotional politics, which he locates throughout the entire century and beyond the literary movement *Empfindsamkeit*, connecting sentimentalism with Enlightenment discourses on natural law. Drawing on the moral philosophy of Gellert, Smith, Shaftesbury, Hutcheson, Rousseau, and others, Schneider describes a »Matrix der Tugendempfindsamkeit« (59) that includes the elements »Balance von Vernunft und Gefühl, Aufrichtigkeit, Menschenliebe und Tatkraft« (62). Schneider reads sentimentalism as a political tactic which can be used to defuse conflict and to change society.

Part two, »Gattungen und Formen,« focuses on popular dramatic subgenres. Chapter four is dedicated to tragedy and analyzes the interactions between conflict (*Agonalität*) and sentiment (*Empfindsamkeit*). Schlegel's *Canut* stages sentimentalism as an effective ruling strategy to defuse conflict within the kingdom. Storm-and-Stress dramas like Goethe's *Götz von Berlichingen* and Klinger's *Die Zwillinge*, however, call the effectiveness of sentiment into question. The chapter then relativizes the teleological literary-historical narrative of sentimentalism's demise by examining less canonical texts. Chapter five discusses French and German dramaturgical writings, then considers the new subgenre *Schauspiel*. This chapter examines how the aforementioned »Matrix der Tugendempfindsamkeit« can intervene or prevent conflict rather than escalate it, as the Storm-and-Stress plays did. This chapter treats canonical plays such as Gellert's *Die zärtlichen Schwestern*, Lessing's *Nathan der Weise*, *Minna von Barnhelm*, and many popular non-canonical plays by Gemmingen-Hornberg, Großmann, Schröder, Engel, Brandes, and Iffland. The chapter ends by juxtaposing Schiller's *Don Carlos* with Kotzebue's *Graf Benjowsky*, whereby Schneider ascertains that the *Schauspiel* »eine optimistischere Perspektive entwirft« (434) when compared to the tragedy, while finding both subgenres inherently political.

Part three, »Fallstudien,« is perhaps the most interesting section. Chapter six offers readings of imprisonment functioning, among other things, as a site of introspection and sentimental improvement. Schneider examines Lillo's *The London Merchant*, Moore's *The Gamester*, Diderot's *Le Père de famille*, Goethe's *Götz*, *Egmont*, and *Tasso*, and Schiller's *Don Carlos* and *Maria Stuart*. Chapter seven concentrates on gender, specifically on »die Figur der weiblichen Diplomatin, deren Aufgabe es ist, agonale Konflikte zwischen Männern zu entschärfen« (435). This thesis is convincingly demonstrated in readings of Schlegel's *Der Triumph der guten Frauen* and Goethe's *Iphigenie auf Tauris*. This chapter also contains an interesting interpretation of Gellert's *Die zärtlichen Schwestern*, but the stated thesis applies less clearly here. The chapter ends with a discussion of literary depictions of female warriors and a reading of Kotzebue's *Die Spanier in Peru*. Chapter eight focuses on *Öffentlichkeit* and how political actors attempt to manipulate public opinion; special attention is paid here to Gottsched's *Parisische Bluthochzeit* and Schiller's *Fiesko*.

Schneider's commitment to combining readings of literary classics with popular non-canonical plays leads to a deeper, fuller understanding of the literary-historical context in which these plays existed. The volume is not without its weaknesses, however. At times, the argumentation does not seem to be as tightly linked to the central thesis as one would expect. The book also lacks an index, which, in a study of this wide a scope and wealth of detail, is unfortunate. Schneider offers many innovative readings on a wide variety of interesting texts, and information about the performance history, publication history, contemporary reception, and Schneider's own insightful analyses are often sprinkled throughout various chapters. The lack of an index will impede scholars from finding the specific references to the plays which they are most interested in studying. These are small flaws that detract from an otherwise valuable contribution to the scholarship of eighteenth-century drama and *Empfindsamkeit*.

Overall, this is a thorough, thoughtful, detailed, and innovative study that will provide food for thought for scholars of eighteenth-century drama and of sentimentalism. The conclusion is especially helpful, as it delineates clearly and specifically the study's contributions and lists various avenues for further research. Schneider hopes to inspire others to use *Agonalität* and/or *Gefühlspolitik* as lenses through which to view other dramas and periods. He also calls for greater scholarly attention to the popular literature of the eighteenth century, especially to authors like Iffland, Kotzebue, and others: »Die Reduzierung des Kanons auf die Werke weniger Autoren zeichnet ein verzerrtes Bild der Theaterlandschaft der Aufklärung« (438). Throughout the book, Schneider gives succinct summaries of relevant scholarship, and this, coupled with his extensive bibliography, will aid scholars undertaking further research in these areas. This study will be of great interest to scholars of eighteenth-century literature, intellectual history, theater history, and emotion studies.

Mississippi State University *Edward Potter*

SCHWARZ, OLGA KATHARINA, *Rationalistische Sinnlichkeit. Zur philosophischen Grundierung der Kunsttheorie. 1700 bis 1760. Leibniz – Wolff – Gottsched – Baumgarten*. Berlin: De Gruyter (2022) (= Quellen und Forschungen zur Literatur- und Kulturgeschichte, Bd. 102). 379 S.

Schwarz's *Rationalistische Sinnlichkeit* is an important contribution to a growing body of scholarly literature on the origins of aesthetics in eighteenth century Germany – a subject that was periodically forgotten and then rediscovered by different generations of scholars in the twentieth century. The book is an especially valuable contribution to this literature because Schwarz has a clear understanding of the philosophical context in which aesthetics emerged; appreciates Gottsched's contributions to its development in ways that few other scholars do; and is able to connect aesthetics to the theory of art in a compelling way. *Rationalistische Sinnlichkeit* is essential reading for anyone interested in the history of modern aesthetics and the theory of art.

In the first part of the book (»›Unser Verstand ist niemahls rein.‹ Sinnlichkeit und Verstand/Vernunft in der Erkenntnislehre«) Schwarz grapples with the psychological and epistemic foundations of the theory of art. She proceeds from an overview of the relationship between the mind and body in Leibniz, Wolff, Gottsched, and Baumgarten, in the first section, to a survey of the reception of Wolff's account of the cognitive faculties in the second section. The third section focuses, first, on the specific differences between sensible and intellectual cognition in Leibniz and Wolff and then, in the last two sections, on the innovative conceptions of sensibility proposed by Gottsched and Baumgarten. Schwarz contends that Wolff's treatment of the lower cognitive faculty – sensibility – is ambiguous, because it contains both physiological and cognitive elements (83-94). She also finds that Wolff grants sensibility an epistemic priority with respect to the higher cognitive faculties – understanding and reason –, which are dependent on sensibility in Wolff's empirical psychology. Her approach differs from other scholars by taking Gottsched seriously, instead of dismissing him as a dogmatic rationalist. Schwarz even suggests that the scholarly literature has overlooked Baumgarten's appropriation of Gottsched's conceptions of »sinnliche Vorstellung« and »sinnliche Erkenntnis« and, indeed, Gottsched's use of »sinnlich« as an adjective in the *Erste Gründe der gesamten Weltweisheit*, which appeared two years before Baumgarten's *Meditationes philosophicae de nonnullis ad poema pertinentibus* (131-132).

The second part of the book (»Die Erkenntnis muß demnach in ein Thun ausbrechen.‹ Die Kunst der sittlichen Erziehung«) explores the relationship between practical philosophy and the theory of art. Unlike Kant, who treats sensibility as a source of corrupt inclinations that are fundamentally opposed to the rational determination of the will, Schwarz argues that Wolff, Gottsched, and Baumgarten enlist sensibility in a program of rational moral education and edification where art, and especially poetry, come to play a special role. She starts with Leibniz's concept of happiness and the positive role that pleasure, understood as »die Empfindung einer Vollkommenheit« (155) plays in his moral philosophy. Wolff's moral philosophy is similar, because it connects perfection to desire and virtue – perfection is the object of desire, but virtuous desire is generated by a clear and distinct representation of perfection, which can be difficult to acquire. Schwarz carefully examines Wolff's attempts to define moral perfection and the kinds of desires that lead to virtue as well as the impediments to »richtiges Handeln« (173-174) with which human moral agents must contend. It turns out that poetry has a special role to play in overcoming these impediments and cultivating virtue for Wolff, Gottsched, and Baumgarten. Wolff saw literary fiction as a medium through which philosophical truth could be effectively communicated, particularly when it provides examples and illustrations of moral principles (195-201). Gottsched shared this view, though his poetics also focuses on the power of literature and drama to excite emotions in response to good and bad actions, shaping our desires as well as our skill in doing good (203-208). Baumgarten's aesthetics differs from Wolff's defense of literature and Gottsched's poetics, because it is not just a means of communicating the truths of moral philosophy. Aesthetics is »bereits ethisch im eigentlichen Sinn« (209), according to Schwarz, because the perfection of sensible cognition affects an agent's character and contributes to the ethical formation of the whole person.

In part three (»Schnittstellen. Die Kunsttheorie zu Beginn der Aufklärung«), Schwarz addresses the theory of art directly. In the first section, she argues that Wolff provides a »[p]hilosophisches Fundament einer Theorie der Künste (228). Though Wolff himself did not attempt to formulate an original theory of art, he insists that the arts fall within the domain of philosophy in the *Discursus praeliminaris de philosophia in genere* and formulates definitions of pleasure and beauty in his theoretical and practical philosophy that were elaborated by his followers. Schwarz sees Gottsched's *Critische Dichtkunst* as the most consistent attempt to apply Wolffian principles to art and contends, rightly, in my view, that it served as a »Probierstein« (267) for supporters and critics of Wolffian cognitivism and perfectionism. The controversy between Gottsched and the Swiss critics Bodmer and Breitinger about the role of the imagination is well-documented in the literature, but Schwarz argues that Baumgarten's aesthetics should also be seen as a response to Wolff's nascent theory of art and Gottsched's poetics. Instead of seeing Baumgarten's aesthetics as an anti-rationalist »Gegenentwurf« to Wolff and Gottsched, however, she suggests that Baumgarten is attempting to resolve the »Unstimmigkeiten of rationalist conceptions of art and beauty through »die Verlegung der Kunsttheorie in die Sinnlichkeit« (310).

Rationalistische Sinnlichkeit is clearly written, well-organized, and well-informed about the primary sources and the relevant secondary literature. Schwarz's arguments are rigorous and systematic throughout the book, making this study an especially valuable contribution to the scholarly literature on the history of aesthetics and the theory of art.

St. Mary's University, San Antonio, Texas   *J. Colin McQuillan*

SIEG, CHRISTIAN, *Die Scham der Aufklärung. Zur sozialethischen Produktivkraft einer Emotion in der literarischen Kultur des 18. Jahrhunderts.* Paderborn: Brill / Fink (2022) (= Laboratorium Aufklärung, Bd. 40). 225 S.

Die Scham ist eine wichtige Emotion, die immer mehr in den Fokus der spätaufklärerischen Texte rückt: »[Sie] ist ein so heftiger Affekt, wie irgend einer, und es ist zu verwundern, daß die Folgen desselben nicht zuweilen tödlich sind«.[1] So skizziert Moritz die Scham im zweiten Teil des *Anton Reiser*, als es um die Beschreibung einer Zurückweisung geht, die das kaum vorhandene Selbstwertgefühl des Protagonisten mit einer bloßen Absage zunichte macht. Moritz verdeutlicht, dass es sich um Affekte handelt, und klassifiziert die Scham somit als nicht kontrollierbare Empfindungen, wobei er als Erfahrungsseelenkundler seiner Zeit argumentiert. Hierauf geht auch die vorliegende Studie ein, in deren Einführung Christian Sieg erklärt: »[D]ie Scham [kam] mit der Selbsterkenntnis in die Welt« (vii). Selbsterkenntnis ist auch ein wichtiger Schlüsselbegriff im Werk von Karl Philipp Moritz, dessen *Anton Reiser* und das 1783 begründete *Magazin zur Erfahrungsseelenkunde* als Folie der Studie dienen. Als weiterer Untersuchungsgegenstand werden die Schriften von Christoph Martin Wieland analysiert, wobei der Fokus auf den satirischen Schriften liegt und der Wandel vom Verlachen zum literarischen Humor dargelegt wird, der zur Schamregulation dient.

In der Einleitung skizziert Sieg das bestehende Forschungsfeld konzise und verortet seinen Forschungsgegenstand in der Gemengelage des achtzehnten Jahrhun-

---

[1] Karl Philipp Moritz, Sämtliche Werke. Kritische und Kommentierte Ausgabe, Bd. 1 [2 Teilbände]: Anton Reiser, hg. von Christof Wingertzahn, Tübingen 2006, S. 146

derts. Hierbei entwickelt er mit kritischem Blick auf die bestehenden Grundlagen der Schamtheorie (vor allem von Elias und Benedict) eine eigene Definition von Scham, die er »aufgrund ihrer moralischen Qualität nicht nur als negative Emotion behandelt, sondern als Norm setzt« (xii). Ein weiterer Schwerpunkt ist der sich entwickelnde Emotionsdiskurs im achtzehnten Jahrhundert, wobei »diese Studie [...] eine kulturhistorische Konstellation zwischen 1750 und 1800 in den Blick [nimmt], in der Emotionen in ästhetischen und anthropologischen Diskursen sowie in literarischen Texten verstärkt problematisiert werden« (xvi). Auf dieser Basis wird auch die Textauswahl begründet: So will Sieg aus Wielands *Don Sylvio* eine Instruktion ableiten, »wie mit dem Schwärmer umzugehen« (xxii) sei, wobei eine Regulation durch Vermeidung als Ziel manifestiert wird. Als Gegenstück wird Karl Philipp Moritz als Erfahrungsseelenkundler herangezogen, der sowohl als Gattungsüberwinder im *Anton Reiser* als auch als selbstbeobachtender Vermittler im *Magazin zur Erfahrungsseelenkunde* zu therapeutischen Ansätzen hinführt, die als Lösung für alltägliche psychologische Phänomene im Diskurs entwickelt werden. Die Projekte beider Autoren haben gemein, dass die Scham als Hemmung einer individuellen Entwicklung zu verstehen ist, die es zu überwinden gilt.

Im ersten Kapitel wird zunächst skizziert, dass die Kultur im achtzehnten Jahrhundert eine Emotionalisierung erfuhr, die Sieg u. a. an Klopstocks *Messias* oder Lessings *Miss Sara Sampson* belegt (1). Hierdurch weist er auf die bedeutenden Tendenzen der Epoche hin, wie z. B. die Neuerungen im Drama durch Lessings Mitleidspoetik. Die Möglichkeit zur Identifikation mit Lessings Charakteren revolutionierte das Verständnis des Theaters und ebnete den Weg für die notwendige Möglichkeit zur Selbsterkenntnis, die für die Untersuchung noch von Bedeutung sein wird. Die Entwicklung der Satire wird sodann mit der sich etablierenden Schwärmerkritik in Zusammenhang gebracht, wobei der Satire die Funktion zugesprochen wird, eine neue Möglichkeit der Kommunikation zu begründen. So wird »in Wielands *Don Sylvio* [...] ein sozialethisch grundiertes Kommunikationsmodell [exemplifiziert], das den Schwärmer nicht mehr beschämt und ausgrenzt, sondern integriert« (94). Auf diese Weise werde ein Wechsel von der Darstellung zur Wahrnehmung möglich, der auch die Rezeption beeinflusse (vgl. 99-100).

Diese Erkenntnisse leiten zum zweiten Komplex der Arbeit über, der sich mit Karl Philipp Moritz einem der facettenreichsten Autoren des achtzehnten Jahrhunderts widmet. Moritz wird in diesem Fall als Erfahrungsseelenkundler *par excellence* dargestellt, der sich im *Anton Reiser* (1785-1790) und dem *Magazin zur Erfahrungsseelenkunde* (1783-1793) auf die Spuren der Selbsterkenntnis begibt. Hierin findet Sieg einen Schlüsselbegriff: *Anton Reiser* »schließt [...] an den poetologischen Diskurs über vermischte Empfindungen an und thematisiert die Funktion von Lektüre sowie Autorschaft für die Emotionsregulation« (105).

Sieg sieht das *Magazin* als weitere Entwicklungsstufe des *Reiser*, da dort Lösungen angeboten werden, die sich im Roman noch nicht finden lassen. Der These ist insofern zuzustimmen, als *Anton Reiser* Fragment geblieben ist, wohingegen sich Moritz im *Magazin* noch länger erfahrungsseelenkundlichen Phänomen widmen konnte. Auf die Selbsterkenntnis spielt auch schon der Titel des *Magazins* an: »Gnothi sauton« (»Erkenne dich selbst«). Somit wird ein wichtiger Schritt vollzogen, um Emotionen empfinden bzw. verstehen zu können.

Für die Selbsterkenntnis und Selbstbeobachtung fügt Sieg eine weitere Komponente, die im achtzehnten Jahrhundert eine nicht zu vernachlässigende Rolle spielt, in seine Theorie ein: die Religiosität. Hierfür werden pietistische Praktiken aufgedeckt, die sich im *Anton Reiser* finden lassen und prägend für Roman und Epoche sind. Dass Moritz diese Aspekte in seinen Roman einfließen lässt, verwundert kaum, war sein Vater doch bekennender Pietist und Anhänger der Madame Guyon, wie im ersten Teil ausführlich geschildert wird.[2] Hieraus resultiert ein weiterer wichtiger Punkt: »Anton Reiser ist keine Biografie, der Romanprotagonist Anton Reiser sehr wohl eine autobiografisch geprägte Figur, für dessen Gestaltung Moritz auf seine eigene Kindheit zurückgriff« (135). Es handelt sich, so eine logische Schlussfolgerung, schon im *Reiser* um eine Art des Selbstbildes und somit auch der Selbsterkenntnis, die sich ebenso mit der Scham auseinandersetzt und so einen Prozess beginnt, der im Magazin seine Fortführung findet und »das Tor zur Selbsterkenntnis aufstoßen will« (182).

Im Fazit führt Sieg seine brillanten Thesen pointiert zusammen und zeigt: »Der Geist der Schamvermeidung legitimiert humoristische Schreibweisen und generiert den therapeutischen Diskurs der Erfahrungsseelenkunde« (184).

Technische Universität Braunschweig   *Franziska Solana Higuera*

STANITZEK, GEORG (Hg.), *Semantik und Praktiken der Freundschaft im 18. Jahrhundert*. Hannover: Wehrhahn (2022) (Bochumer Quellen und Forschungen zum 18. Jahrhundert). 287 S.

Freundschaft gilt spätestens seit Jürgen Habermas' Studie *Strukturwandel der Öffentlichkeit* (1962) als Schlüsselbegriff der Aufklärung, als ein für die Entstehung einer kritischen bürgerlichen Öffentlichkeit zentrales Konzept, das zugleich den semantischen Kern der bürgerlichen Selbstbeschreibung im achtzehnten Jahrhundert bildet. Gemeint ist damit ein emphatischer Bund zwischen Gleichen, deren Vorstellungen von Tugend und Moral ein natürliches Band zwischen den Freunden knüpft. »Nun ist nach mehreren Jahrzehnten Forschungsgeschichte allerdings zu konstatieren«, so der Einwand, den der Herausgeber des hier angezeigten Bandes in seiner systematischen Einleitung formuliert, »dass Habermas' Öffentlichkeitskonzept in der literaturgeschichtlichen Forschung wenig empirischen Rückhalt gefunden hat« (8). Georg Stanitzek erklärt dies einerseits mit dem idealtypischen Charakter des Konzepts, das mehr auf der Soziologie Londons als auf der sehr viel heterogeneren des Heiligen Römischen Reiches beruht, und andererseits mit der Dominanz der durchaus ständisch geprägten Gelehrtenrepublik, die jene kritische Öffentlichkeit im deutschen Sprachraum dominierte. Der Freundschaftsdiskurs des achtzehnten Jahrhunderts konfiguriert sich hier also auf der Basis einer »Welt der Ungleichheit« (9), wodurch er seinerseits formalisiert wird. Vor dem Hintergrund der *Nikomachischen Ethik* mit ihrer Typologie der Tugend-, Lust- und Nutzfreundschaft (1156b-1157c) haben sich insbesondere im siebzehnten Jahrhundert Klugheitslehren etabliert, die pragmatisches Kalkül mit moralischen Erwägungen verbinden. Im Verlauf der Frühaufklärung, so Stanitzek, wurde das »Klugheitskalkül« zwar zunehmend aus der Rhetorik der Freundschaft eliminiert, gleichwohl entstand im Freundschaftsdiskurs

2 Vgl. Moritz, Anton Reiser, S. 40-41.

des achtzehnten Jahrhunderts der Netzwerkgedanke, der bisweilen durchaus mit utilitaristischen Erwägungen verbunden ist und die singuläre, hohe Tugendfreundschaft supplementiert.

In diesem unübersichtlichen diskursiven Feld sind die zwölf Studien des vorliegenden Bandes verortet, die sowohl Praktiken und Semantiken als auch Theorien und Poetiken der Freundschaft im achtzehnten Jahrhundert in den Blick nehmen. Julian Scherer untersucht »Feindschaft in Klugheitslehren der Frühen Neuzeit« und entdeckt den Feind als notwendiges Gegenstück zum Freund im Rahmen »privatpolitischer Erwägungen« (48) zu Klugheit und Lebensführung. Stephanie Bluhm verfolgt »Freundschaftssemantiken in poetologischer Lyrik der Frühaufklärung«. Ihre Beispiele sind Carl Christian Gärtners an Gellert gerichtetes Gedicht »Wider die Reimsucht« (1747) und Luise Adelgunde Gottscheds Versepistel »An dem Geburtstagsfeste ihres Gatten, den 2. Febr. 1737«, in der ihr Ehemann zugleich als Gatte und Freund apostrophiert wird. Trotz unterschiedlicher Kontexte gestalten sowohl der anti-gottschedianische *Bremer Beiträger* als auch die Frau des normativen Literaturklassizisten »in poetologischer Lyrik die aufklärerischen poetologischen Prinzipien, aber auch dichterische Bezugnahmen und Netzwerkbildungen«, die es erlauben, »die Forderung nach poetologischen Neuerungen als Austausch unter Gleichgesinnten positiv zu konnotieren« (66). Helmut Zedelmaier liest »Freundschaftliche Briefe« in der Perspektive der *longue durée*. Die historischen Amplituden seiner Beobachtungen reichen von der humanistischen Gelehrtenfreundschaft mit ihrem überkonfessionellen und transnationalen Selbstverständnis über die am Beispiel Gleims dargestellte Freundschaft der deutschen Aufklärung, die eher national und protestantisch kodiert ist. Ein Ausblick auf Freundschaft im digitalen Zeitalter relativiert das jeweilige (unhistorische) Staunen über Rituale und Praktiken der Freundschaft, deren Wandel sich in der *longue durée* als Kontinuität erweist.

In seinem Aufsatz »Freundschaft und Publikation: Praktiken literarischer Kooperation« zeigt der Bandherausgeber, wie sich in der Mitte des achtzehnten Jahrhunderts, ausgehend von den von Sulzer, Gleim und Lange 1746 herausgegebenen *Freundschaftlichen Briefen*, eine Gattung von Briefsammlungen etabliert, in denen sich eine »Spezialöffentlichkeit« manifestiert, eine »private Öffentlichkeit, für die sowohl die Publikation als auch der Einzugsbereich der in sie eigegangenen Privatbriefe [...] durchaus einsichtig sind« (86). Entgegen dem in der Forschung vorherrschenden Bild der Freundschaft als Kommunikationsraum einer gegen den Stände- und Maschinenstaat gerichteten Gegen-Öffentlichkeit arbeitet Stanitzek die in den Sammelpublikationen inszenierten Netzwerke als »exklusive[n] und in seiner Exklusivität spezifisch markierte[n] Zirkel« (90) heraus, dessen publizistische Praxis auf esoterischer Ebene das exoterisch vermittelte Selbstverständnis unterläuft. In eine ähnliche Richtung deuten die Beobachtungen von Tobias Heinrich: Für ihn ist das Freundschaftsnetzwerk Gleims der Ausgangspunkt, von dem aus das Ende von Freundschaften mit Kleist, Ramler, F. H. Jacobi und Heinse betrachtet wird. Die Perspektive auf das Ende von Freundschaften zeigt, wie delikat das Zusammenspiel von »Autorität, Abhängigkeit und Anerkennung« (114) und, so wäre hinzuzufügen, Empfindlichkeiten ist, dem die ihrem Selbstverständnis nach hierarchiefreie Freundschaft des Freundschaftsvirtuosen aus Halberstadt ihre Dynamik mitverdankt.

Carsten Zelle analysiert in seinem Beitrag »Diderots Erzählung *Die beiden Freunde von Borbonne*« die narrativ komplexe Inszenierung eines sich auf mehrere gesellschaftliche Ebenen erstreckenden Freundschaftsnetzwerks. Wie *Jacques le Fataliste* und *Le neveu de Rameau* erschien auch die erstmals 1770 in Grimms handschriftlicher *Correspondance littéraire* verbreitete Erzählung *Deux Amis* zuerst in deutscher Übersetzung. Diese stammte von Salomon Gessner, der Diderots Text 1772 in dem mit eigenen Zeichnungen versehenen Band *Moralische Erzæhlungen und Idyllen von Diderot und S. Gessner* herausgab. In dieser komplexen Erscheinungsform artikuliert der an sich schon selbstreflexive und anthropologisch skeptische Text, so Zelle, eine Dialektik, mit der die Erzählung das Vertrauen in die autonome, emphatische Freundschaft relativiert.

In einem der wichtigsten Aufsätze des Bandes lotet Andree Michaelis-König die Grenzen der Integration Moses Mendelssohns in der scheinbar so offenen Freundschaftskultur der Aufklärung aus. Hindernisse begegnen dem bekennenden Juden in der protestantischen Freundschaftskultur sehr schnell: So ist ihm der private Raum oftmals versperrt (die erste Begegnung mit Nicolai fand im ›Gelehrten Kaffeehaus‹ statt), und auch der Gleichheitsanspruch des Freundschaftskults der Aufklärung stand im offenen Widerspruch zu seiner prekären rechtlichen Stellung. Am Beispiel Gleims kann zudem gezeigt werden, wie oberflächlich dessen pathetische Freundschaftsbeschwörungen und wie wenig belastbar dessen persönliche Bande im Ernstfall – nämlich der begründeten Kritik an seinem dichterischen Schaffen – waren. Mendelssohn erschütterte dies nicht, weil er wohl dem rhetorischen Überschwang des Halberstädter Domherrn grundsätzlich misstraute. In einem Brief an den (wahren) Freund Lessing spricht er vom »Rauch«, den er bei der »lichtesten Flamme« der Gleim'schen Expektorationen »mit ziemlicher Gewißheit« voraussah:[1] »Skepsis angesichts einer allzu affektierten Freundschaftspraxis spricht sich hier aus, die nicht Kontinuität und gemeinsame Erkenntnis zum Ziel hatte, sondern sich in sich selbst erschöpfte« (153). Im Falle der Beziehung Mendelssohns zu Johann Caspar Lavater ist die Konstellation noch prekärer, weil sich die Lavater-Affäre, die 1769 mit der Aufforderung einsetzte, Mendelssohn solle die Wahrheit des Christentums widerlegen oder aber konvertieren,[2] »ursprünglich aus einer durchaus erfolgversprechenden Konstellation der Freundschaft heraus entwickelte« (155). Statt Gleichheit als Basis von Freundschaft vorauszusetzen, ging es Lavater, wie Michaelis-König zeigt, darum, Gleichheit erst durch Konversion zu erzwingen. Anders das Verhältnis Mendelssohns zu Lessing, mit dessen Darstellung der Aufsatz endet: Am Beispiel der Jahre nach 1770 wird demonstriert, wie symbiotisch Lessing seine grundsätzliche Kritik der Neologie im Vorfeld des Fragmentenstreits »aus der Verteidigungsrede des jüdischen Freundes heraus entwickelte« (160), die dieser als Antwort auf die Lavater-Zumutung formuliert hatte. Diese Idee eines »echten Freundschaftsdialogs« (160), so das skeptische Fazit des Aufsatzes, ist eben nicht repräsentativ für die überkonfessionellen Freundschaften Mendelssohns (und anderer Juden).[3]

1 JubA XII.1, S. 240.
2 Vgl. Cord-Friedrich Berghahn, Moses Mendelssohns »Jerusalem«. Ein Beitrag zur Geschichte der Menschenrechte und der pluralistischen Gesellschaft, 2. Aufl., Berlin/Boston 2011, S. 24-67.
3 Vgl. zur Freundschaft zwischen Lessing und Mendelssohn jetzt auch die Habilitationsschrift von Michaelis-König, in der die Freundschaft der beiden ausführlich dargestellt wird: Das Versprechen der Freundschaft. Politik und ästhetische Praxis

Hans Graubner wendet sich in seiner Studie »Freundschaft als Konkurrenz im Sturm und Drang« dem Verhältnis zwischen Herder, Hamann und dem jungen Goethe zu. Zunächst zeigt er, wie Hamann in der freundschaftlichen Korrespondenz mit Herder eine neuartige Schreibweise etabliert, die zwischen Eso- und Exoterik oszilliert; sie ist Teil seiner idiosynkratischen Schreibart, aber auch seines »theologisch begründete[n] kämpferische[n] Freundschaftsverständnis[ses]« (176) und färbt in beiderlei Hinsicht auf Herders Denken und Schreiben ab. Im Falle der Beziehung Herders zu Goethe, die sieben Jahre nach der Freundschaft mit Hamann einsetzt, ist der semantische Pfeil der Korrespondenz ein anderer. Im Austausch geht es sehr viel prononcierter um Fragen der Autonomie des Subjekts (vor allem Goethes) und der Individualität von Schreibweisen. Hamann lehnte, so Graubners Volte, ungeachtet vieler stilistischer Hamanniana im Schreiben Goethes diese Form der »säkulare[n] Selbstvervollkommnung« ab und deutete sie als Teil der »widergöttlichen Selbstüberhebung seines Zeitalters« (194).

Luisa Banki nimmt in dem von männlichen Freundschaften dominierten Band am Beispiel der Sophie von La Roche »Freundschaft, Tugendethik und die Möglichkeit weiblicher Autonomie« in den Blick. La Roche hat Freundschaft sowohl praktiziert als auch theoretisiert, und zwar nicht nur *en passant* im Erfolgsroman *Geschichte des Fräuleins von Sternheim*, sondern auch explizit in der Erzählung *Liebe, Mißverständnis und Freundschaft* (1783). Im Rahmen dieser Erzählung avanciert die Freundschaft nicht nur zur konfliktlösenden Instanz, sondern auch zum Weg in Richtung weiblicher Autonomie. Blank liest *Liebe, Mißverständnis und Freundschaft* als »Programmschrift […], in der La Roche die Beziehungsform der Freundschaft als Alternative zur auf die Ehe hin orientierten Liebe zwischen Frau und Mann präsentiert« (197). Auch bei der Beziehung zwischen Luise Mejer und Heinrich Christian Boie geht es um das Spannungsfeld zwischen Liebe und Freundschaft. Für Johanna Egger bildet Freundschaft den »Modus Operandi« (213) dieser mentalitätsgeschichtlich so bedeutsamen Beziehung. Im Laufe der Jahre avanciert die Freundschaft der Beamtentochter aus Hannover mit dem holsteinischen Landvogt nicht nur zu einem gegenseitigen Bildungsprojekt, sondern nimmt auch, wie Egger hervorhebt, eheähnliche Züge an, wobei im Unterschied zu Ehen der Zeit hier »das Moment der Gleichheit« dominiert, »insofern das Geschlecht für Freundschaft als solche eine untergeordnete Rolle spielt« (238).

In seinem Aufsatz »Arzt oder Freund?« fragt Christian Sieg nach der »Funktion der Freundschaftssemantik für das *Magazin zur Erfahrungsseelenkunde*«. In dieser von Karl Philipp Moritz zwischen 1783 und 1793 herausgegebenen ersten psychologischen Fachzeitschrift spielt Freundschaft gleich in mehrfacher Hinsicht eine Rolle. Zum einen liegt dies an der offenen Konzeption der Zeitschrift, die eben nicht nur von Ärzten gemacht wird und sich nicht nur an Gelehrte richtet, sondern deren Zielpublikum vielmehr »Menschenkenner und Menschenfreund« sind (Moritz zit. n. 243); zum anderen ist die publizistische Praxis des *Magazins* selbst dem »Ideal der Freundschaft« (247) verpflichtet. So schreibt Moritz über die Praxis der gesammelten Fallgeschichten: »Sollten nicht vielmehr zwei Freunde selber jeder in den andern wie in einen Spiegel blicken, um desto genauer mit sich selbst bekannt zu werden?«

jüdisch-nichtjüdischer Freundschaften in der deutschsprachigen Literaturgeschichte seit der Aufklärung, Heidelberg 2023, S. 147-225.

(zit. n. 248). Dieses freundschaftliche Band zwischen Beobachtern und Beobachteten macht, so Siegs Fazit, das *Magazin* zu einem Organ der Freundschaft zwischen Individuen, die mit ihrer (Kranken-)Geschichte bislang isoliert und ohne Verständnis oder Anerkennung leben mussten.

Den Schluss des Bandes bilden Gesa Frömmings Überlegungen »Zur Anonymität bei Theodor Gottlieb von Hippel«, die sie unter die Leitbegriffe »Öffentlichkeit / Freundschaft / Privatheit« (259) stellt. Im Zentrum des Aufsatzes steht Hippels kooperative Autorschaft, die wesentlich davon lebte, dass etwa die Anonymität des Autors von *Über die bürgerliche Verbesserung der Weiber* (1792) gewahrt blieb. Zugleich scheint Hippel – das zumindest legt der Nekrolog auf ihn, an dem einige seiner Freunde mitwirkten, nahe – elementare Regeln der Freundschaft insgeheim missachtet zu haben. Im Spannungsfeld von Hippels Ideal der (distanzierten) Freundschaft und seiner ambivalenten Praxis werden so elementare Fragen aufgeworfen, die sowohl politischer als auch ethischer Natur sind und erst dann diskutiert werden können, »wenn es einen Begriff literarischer und politischer Öffentlichkeit« gibt, der es erlaubt, Öffentlichkeit »auch als Überlieferungszusammenhang zu denken« (284).

Soweit ein Blick in diesen anregenden Band, der die Amplituden von realen Freundschaften und auch die von idealen Freundschaftskonzepten dokumentiert, mit denen das achtzehnte Jahrhundert seine Theoretiker und Historiker herausfordert. Dass der Herausgeber diesem wichtigen und thematisch weit gespannten Band nicht wenigstens ein Namensregister beigegeben hat, ist ausgesprochen bedauerlich.

Technische Universität Carolo-Wilhelmina zu Braunschweig   Cord-Friedrich Berghahn

WOLF, NORBERT CHRISTIAN, *Glanz und Elend der Aufklärung in Wien. Voraussetzungen – Institutionen – Texte.* Wien, Köln: Böhlau (2023) (= Literaturgeschichte in Studien und Quellen, Bd. 35). 452 S.

Es ist äußerst erfreulich, dass nach Franz Leander Fillafers historiografischer Untersuchung *Aufklärung habsburgisch. Staatsbildung, Wissenskultur und Geschichtspolitik in Zentraleuropa 1750-1850* (Göttingen: Wallstein 2020) nun auch eine neue literaturwissenschaftliche Studie zur josephinischen Aufklärung vorliegt. Norbert Christian Wolf, Professor für neuere deutsche Literatur an der Universität Wien, bedient sich hierfür einer literatursoziologischen Methodik. Ausgehend von Immanuel Kants kanonischer Definition von Aufklärung, bemüht er sich, mithilfe der von Pierre Bourdieu entwickelten soziologischen Feldtheorie die Herausbildung des Literatursystems in Wien darzustellen. In diesem System gestaltete sich das Verständnis von Aufklärung anders, wodurch es später zu pejorativen Einschätzungen einer kulturellen Rückständigkeit des süddeutsch-katholischen Raumes kam und die im weitesten Sinne als »österreichisch« zu bezeichnenden Literaten in den deutschen Literaturgeschichten vernachlässigt wurden.

Wolfs Monografie konzentriert sich auf die Phase der Alleinregierung Josephs II. (1780-1790), dessen Reformprogramm für die aufklärerischen Bestrebungen innerhalb der Habsburgermonarchie maßgebend war. Anders als vorhergehende literaturhistorische Analysen versteht Wolf die in Wien mit einiger Verspätung auftretenden Aufklärungsbemühungen nicht als »zögerliche[n] und diskontinuierliche[n] *Rezepti-*

*ons*prozess« (22), sondern als eigenständige, »von spezifischen Voraussetzungen« beeinflusste Entwicklung »kultureller Modernisierung« (23). Der zu diesem Zeitpunkt innerhalb des deutschsprachigen Raumes singuläre Großstadtcharakter Wiens rechtfertigt den Vergleich mit anderen europäischen Metropolen wie Paris oder London, und so dient Alain Vialas Untersuchung des Pariser Literaturbetriebs im siebzehnten Jahrhundert[4] als geeigneter Ausgangspunkt für eine eingehendere komparatistische Betrachtung. Diese ist verständlicherweise von zahlreichen Abweichungen geprägt, die Wolf im Kapitel zur Entstehung des Literatursystems in Wien (87-268) souverän skizziert, in dem er eine vorerst verzögerte, danach allerdings beschleunigte Aufklärungsdynamik konstatiert. Wolf setzt sich ausführlicher mit der Zensur und der 1781 von Joseph II. zugestandenen »erweiterten Preßfreiheit« (110) auseinander, die bereits der in Ungarn geborene australische Germanist Leslie Bodi 1977 als josephinisches »Tauwetter«[5] apostrophierte. Die Aufbruchsstimmung, die durch die josephinischen Reformen und die zwischenzeitliche Lockerung der Zensur ausgelöst wurde, stand hingegen im Kontrast zu den defizitären institutionellen Rahmenbedingungen, die die Herausbildung einer autonomen Schriftstellerei und die Legitimation der Autoren behinderten. Nicht nur das prekäre Verlags- und Buchhandelswesen, sondern auch der aus wirtschaftlichen Interessen staatlich geförderte Raubdruck ausländischer Werke tangierten das Sozialprestige der Wiener Literaten. Das Fehlen einer Akademie der Wissenschaften und Künste, das von Freimaurerorden wie der *Loge zur wahren Eintracht* nur bedingt kompensiert werden konnte, oder die aristokratische und später großbürgerliche Salonkultur, zu der Gelehrte anfangs keinen Zutritt hatten, verdeutlichen den ambivalenten Status der Autoren (215-268) und wohl auch die Tatsache, dass man in Österreich als Beamtendichter ökonomisch immer noch am besten abgesichert war. Hieraus resultierte ein von Wolf präzise beschriebener Markt, der durch »Broschürenflut« (109) und Tagesschriftstellerei die Richtung von großstädtischer Populärkultur und Boulevardjournalismus einschlug. Die daraus abzuleitende öffentliche Kontroverse zwischen Prekariat, Autonomie und Autorprestige diskutiert Wolf anhand von Aloys Blumauers Schrift *Beobachtungen über Österreichs Aufklärung und Litteratur* (1782), in der der zeitgenössischen Schreibsucht das Muster des »überständischen ›freien Schriftstellers‹ im Sinne des modernen subjektiven Autorenbegriffs« (255) entgegengehalten wird. Bezeichnend ist, dass auch Blumauers literarische Praxis seinen »eigenen diskursiven Vorgaben« nicht nachkam, was Wolf als Zeichen für den »Kampf um eine neue, legitime und tendenziell autonome Definition des Schriftstellerberufs in einem noch stark heteronom bestimmten literarischen Raum« (268) bewertet.

Als paradigmatische Dokumente des heteronomen literarischen Feldes der Wiener Aufklärung, die sich besonders durch Kirchenkritik, Antisubjektivismus und Staatsidolatrie auszeichnete, untersucht Wolf schließlich drei Werke, die zu den bekanntesten der österreichischen Aufklärungsliteratur zählen: Aloys Blumauers fragmentarisches komisches Versepos *Virgils Aeneis, travestirt* (1782-88), Johann Pezzls Roman

---

4 Alain Viala, Naissance de l'écrivain. Sociologie de la littérature à l'âge classique, Paris 1985.
5 Leslie Bodi, Tauwetter in Wien. Zur Prosa der österreichischen Aufklärung 1781-1795, Frankfurt a. M. 1977.

Faustin, oder das philosophische Jahrhundert (1783) sowie Emanuel Schikaneders und Wolfgang Amadeus Mozarts Singspiel *Die Zauberflöte* (UA 1791, Freihaustheater).

Blumauers satirisches Epos der *Travestierten Aeneis*, das einen enormen buchhändlerischen Erfolg erzielte, konstituiert sich aus einer Komik der Herabsetzung und aus der »Formel ›Aufklärung durch Lachen‹« (283). Hierbei markiert besonders seine Kirchenkritik und die Apotheose Josephs II. den historischen Kontext der josephinischen Aufklärung. Ähnliches gilt für den Roman *Faustin*, den der aus Bayern stammende Pezzl eigentlich vor seiner Übersiedlung nach Wien in Zürich veröffentlichte. Dennoch erscheint gerade dieser Text als exemplarischer Roman des Josephinismus, da er in seinem Leitmotiv – der Suche Faustins nach Aufklärung und Toleranz – die tagespolitischen Diskussionen um die josephinischen Reformen thematisiert und in Wien extensiv rezipiert wurde. Anders als in Voltaires Thesenroman *Candide ou l'optimisme* (1759), der Pezzl als Vorlage diente, wird die utopische Perspektive des Protagonisten durch seine Erfahrungen zwar relativiert, jedoch nicht gänzlich verworfen. Und so endet auch Pezzls Roman mit der Realutopie des Regierungsantritts Josephs II., die dem Autor wohl nicht zuletzt als Eintrittsbillett in das josephinische Wien dienen sollte, wo er bald die Bibliothek des Grafen Kaunitz betreute und später in den Beamtenstand eintrat.

Dass es sich mit der aufklärerischen Intention von Schikaneders und Mozarts *Zauberflöte* weitaus schwieriger verhält als bei den Texten Blumauers und Pezzls, erörtert Wolf in einer detaillierten Abrechnung mit der bisherigen Forschungsliteratur, die gerade dieses Werk zu einer »Ikone der Aufklärung« (333) stilisierte. An dem bis heute berühmten Singspiel, dessen Dramaturgie in vielerlei Hinsicht der Theaterpraxis der damaligen Vorstadtbühnen entspricht, zu deren Hauptgeschäft die Vermittlung von Aufklärung und Toleranz eben *nicht* zählte, gelingt es Wolf, die »Brüchigkeit, Ungleichzeitigkeit und Widersprüchlichkeit der Wiener Aufklärung« (341) darzustellen. Seine Textanalyse setzt sich einerseits mit der komödiantischen Figur, andererseits allerdings auch mit Misogynie, Xenophobie und Rassismus auseinander. Diese Gegenperspektiven auf ein europäisches Aufklärungsparadigma sowie Mozarts und Schikaneders Blick auf dessen totalitäre Aspekte verdeutlichen die Schattenseite des aufklärerischen Glanzes. Die *Zauberflöte* ist hierdurch weniger als Prototyp aufklärerischen Denkens zu verstehen, als dass in ihr die ambivalente und unvollendete Wiener Aufklärung zur Geltung kommt.

Wolfs Studie, die bereits jetzt als Standardwerk gelten darf, bietet einen imposanten Zugang zum literarischen Feld der Wiener Aufklärung, der wichtige Erkenntnisse für die zukünftige Forschung liefert. Einen Bereich, den es noch schärfer zu konturieren gilt, stellen die Repertoires der Hofbühnen dar, deren Möglichkeiten einer performativen Vermittlung von Aufklärung und bürgerlichen Verhaltensweisen in den Moralischen Wochenschriften und der Presse breit debattiert wurden. Dass es die aufklärerischen Stücke in Wien keineswegs leicht hatten, zeigt Wolf in einem Kapitel, in dem er einmal mehr die vielzitierte, von Eva König geschilderte und an das Improvisationstheater gemahnende Geste des Hofschauspielers Christian Gottlob Stephanie d. Ä. anführt, der bekanntlich als Odoardo in *Emilia Galotti* nach der Tötung seiner Tochter den Theaterdolch provokant abgeleckt haben soll. Dennoch können Wolfs Thesen zum ambivalenten Literatursystem und Autorverständnis durchaus auch auf die Versuche um die Etablierung eines deutschen Nationaltheaters in Wien übertragen werden, was darauf hoffen lässt, dass die Erforschung der österreichischen

Aufklärung durch die verdienstvollen Publikationen von Fillafer und Wolf in den nächsten Jahren intensiviert wird.

Universität Salzburg Matthias Mansky

WURST, KARIN A., *Imaginaries of Domesticity and Women's Work in Germany around 1800*. Rochester, New York: Camden House (2023) (= Women and Gender in German Studies, vol. 13). 236 pp.

In her thought provoking and informative book, Karin Wurst engages with the titular imaginaries of domesticity from several perspectives, alluded to by the image on the front cover – »Kinderzimmer« from the *Augsburger Klebealbum* (1783) – and the subtitle »Feeling at Home.« She argues that the structures and transformation of society around 1800 in the German states and its political trajectory were dependent upon the »high-value imaginary construct of domesticity,« which she defines as a »web of practices, emotions, and values« (3) managed by women, who were self-determining agents in constructing this cultural space through their enactment of theoretical principles advanced by philosophers and writers of the time.

The book is divided into four chapters framed by an introduction and conclusion which unravel aspects of women's emotional, social, cultural, and economical work in the domestic sphere related to Enlightenment ideals of the pursuit of happiness and perfectibility, which Wurst argues are embedded in prescriptive discourses surrounding the ideation of marriage, mothering, material culture, and home management at the turn of the century. In each chapter, she creates »Textual Encounters« (14) with central texts written by both men and women delineating different aspects of domesticity theoretically and practically. In the vast corpus of works addressed, the writings of Joachim Heinrich Campe (1746-1818) and Sophie La Roche (1731-1807) stand out amongst the primary sources.

Delving into the programmatic deployment of didactic texts on love, marriage, and gender difference around 1800, chapter one deals with the role that literature and women's literacy played in creating the domestic imaginaries of the *Liebesehe* based on emotional well-being. As well as autobiographical examples, Wurst compares texts about marriage by women authors Sophie La Roche (*Briefe an Lina*, 1785) and Karoline Wobeser (*Elisa oder das Weib wie es seyn sollte*, 1795) through the theoretical lens of »emotion work« (23) – extrapolating a term coined by Arlie Russell Hochschild (2018) that refers to the work of managing emotions. She argues that fiction played an important role in modelling emotive practices around 1800 and that emotional bonds in marriage and motherhood were integral to middle-class identity formation.

In chapter two, »Labour of Love: Mothering as a Dimension of Domesticity,« Wurst reviews changes in attitudes toward child-rearing around 1800, which focus on the importance of the mother-child bonding and the promotion of domestic space as a holistic environment for the early childhood education and socialization for the benefit of a civil society. Along with philosophical discourse, she integrates the medical knowledge of the time summarized in Johann Georg Krünitz's *Oekonomische Encyklopädie* (1779) related to conception, pregnancy, birthing, and breastfeeding, then turns to the creative work of women as pedagogues of domesticity through their organization of children's experiences, play spaces, material objects and activities that fostered memories and a feeling of home. Wurst includes and analyses contemporary iconographic depictions of family life in domestic spaces, including paintings, prints and images from the *Augsburger Klebealbum* as supporting evidence.

Advancing theories that »spaces, objects and practices mutually influence one another« (116), chapter three highlights the agency and cultural work of women in staging of domesticity through home design and decorating to create an atmosphere of »comfort and well-being« (145) enriched by leisure activities and extending into outdoor garden spaces. Wurst aims to illuminate women's invisible work behind the cultural performance of domesticity, which was informed by advice literature and illustrative popular print of the time. This involved the curation of objects, spaces, and experiences, bearing symbolic significance with respect to taste, class, and identity. Within the context of cultural and economic capital, Wurst's case studies focus on the differentiation between upper-class affluence and middle-class propriety as a determining factor in bourgeois self-fashioning.

Chapter four, entitled »With Heart, Head and Hand,« takes a closer look at the contribution of the *Hausfrau* to the economic success of the family and the ideation of »self-meaning« (162) through the mastery of household management skills, either taught at home or set forth in the household manuals that emerged as a new literary genre. Reading Sophie La Roche's epistolary novel *Briefe an Lina*, in which the aunt takes her niece on a literary tour of a well-run household as a herald of positive thinking, Wurst claims: »La Roche's text makes explicit that both the axis of time (women's workday) and that of space (various rooms in the house) are central and interwoven with the creation of women's identity and in the social and cultural imaginary of domesticity« (163). She argues that the varied facets of women's economic work, which demanded self-management, as well as fiscal astuteness, figured prominently in the construction of a middle-class identity.

In her conclusion, Wurst successfully weaves together the threads of women's multi-dimensional work in domestic spaces contributing to the feeling of home and the sense of belonging integral to the rise of bourgeois society in the German states around 1800.

University of British Columbia *Patricia Milewski*